LINCOLN LAW SCHOOL OF SAN JOSE
INTELLECTUAL PROPERTY SERIES

PATENT PROSECUTION WORKBOOK

Britten Sessions
*Associate Dean of Intellectual Property
Director, Intellectual Property Law Clinic
Lincoln Law School of San Jose*

PRETIUM PRESS
Mission Viejo, California

Pretium Press
23456 Madero, Suite 170
Mission Viejo, California 92691

Copyright © 2018 Pretium Press.

All rights reserved.

ISBN: 978-1983547003

No part of this publication may be reproduced, stored in a retrieval system, or transmitted in any form or by any means, electronic, mechanical, photocopying, recording or otherwise, without the prior permission of Pretium Press.

Any distribution or use of these materials in any endeavor is expressly prohibited without prior written consent.

Note to Readers

This publication is designed to provide accurate and authoritative information with regard to the subject matter covered. It is distributed with the understanding that the publisher is not engaged in rendering legal, accounting, or other professional service. If legal advice or other expert assistance is required, the services of a competent professional should be sought.

For David – my most recent professor of life's hands-on workshop

B.D.S.

TABLE OF CONTENTS

IP Clinic at Lincoln Law School i

Foreword ii

Chapter 1 Overview, strategies, Master Arguments, 102 Part I 1
   A.   Overview 1
   B.   Office Action Strategies Part I 1
      1.   Claim Listing 2
      2.   Objections/Rejections... 2
      3.   Strategy.. 2
   C.   Master Argument Template 3
   D.   Responding to 102 Rejections Part I 5
   E.   Reference Material for 102 Rejections 7
      1.   102(a)(1) & 102(b)(1): Conditions and Exceptions............................... 7
      2.   102(a)(1) & 102(b)(1): Examples 11
      3.   102(a)(2) & 102(b)(2): Conditions and Exceptions............................. 13
      4.   102(a)(2) & 102(b)(2): Examples 16
      5.   Pre-AIA v. Post-AIA Considerations.. 17

Chapter 2 Prosecution Flow, Claim Amendment Part I, 103 Part I 20
   A.   Prosecution Flow.. 20
   B.   Claim Amendments Part I 22
   C.   Reference Material for Claim Amendments 23
      1.   Independent Claims... 23
      2.   Dependent Claim Anatomy 35
      3.   Claim Drafting Methods.. 36
   D.   Responding to 103 Rejections Part I 39
   E.   Reference Material for 103 Rejections 42

Chapter 3 Examiners, Interviews, 102 Part II 45
   A.   Working with Patent Examiners 45
      1.   Game Points 45
   B.   Examiner Interviews.. 47
   C.   Responding to 102 Rejections Part II 52

Chapter 4 Claim Amendments Part II, 103 Part II 54
   A.   Claim Amendments Part II 54
   B.   Responding to 103 Rejections Part II 55

Chapter 5 Types of Rejections, Terminal Disclaimers, 101 59
   A.   Types of Rejections.. 59
      1.   Non-Final Office Action 59
      2.   Final Office Action 60
      3.   Further Actions 63
   B.   Terminal Disclaimers 63
   C.   Responding to 101 Rejections... 63
      1.   Double Patenting 64
      2.   Subject Matter Eligibility 66
      3.   Utility 69

Chapter 6 International, Spec/Drawing Amendments, 112 71
   A.   International Prosecution Considerations 71
   B.   Amendments to the Specification and Drawings 73
   C.   Responding to 112 Rejections... 74

    D. Reference Material for 112 Rejections 75
        1. Part (a) 76
        2. Part (b) 78
        3. Part (d) 80

Chapter 7 Restriction, Allowable Subject Matter, NOA, Appeals 81
    A. Restriction Practice 81
    B. Allowable Subject Matter 84
    C. Notice of Allowance 85
    D. Appealing an Action 86
    E. Reference Material for Appeals 87

Chapter 8 Continuation Practice, Post-Allowance 94
    A. Continuation Practice 94
    B. Post-Allowance Practices 96
        1. Amendments 96
        2. Corrections 97
        3. Inter Partes Review 99
        4. Post-Grant Review / Further AIA Practices 99

Chapter 9 Litigation Perspectives Part I 102
    A. Claim Construction 102
    B. Markman Hearing 103

Chapter 10 Litigation Perspective Part II 105
    A. Litigation Costs 105
        1. Attorney Costs 105
        2. Damages Costs 107
        3. Discovery Costs 109
        4. Time and Image Costs 110
        5. Litigation cost tips 110
    B. Forum Shopping 111

Exhibits 115
    35 U.S.C. 101 115
    35 U.S.C. 102 115
    35 U.S.C. 103 115
    35 U.S.C. 112 116
    Miscellaneous 116

IP CLINIC AT LINCOLN LAW SCHOOL

The IP Clinic at Lincoln Law School is dedicated to assisting both students and the public on intellectual property. To that end, the Clinic has released a manual of instruction on intellectual property which may assist in understanding about intellectual property. The manual is sold at printing cost and may be bought via Amazon.

In addition, the school frequently lectures in the Bay Area without charge, creates resources (such as this book) as a benefit for the public, and continually strives to provide high quality IP legal services (without cost) to as many as possible.

For more information, feel free to contact us at:

> 384 South Second St.
> San Jose, California 95113
>
> Office 408-977-7227
> Fax 408-977-7228
>
> ipclinic@lincolnlawsj.edu

FOREWORD

I love to ski. And skiing is very similar to learning how to engage in patent prosecution. I recall skiing as a boy in Southern California and being literally stuck on top of a mountain. The task of getting to the bottom seemed overwhelming. What made it especially a fathomable task was the fact that the mountain was one giant ice-cube, so normal skiing would not work in my case. I concluded that the best way to get from A to B was to simply slide my entire way down. So I sat down, and literally scooted my entire way down that hill. I learned that if we simply stop and allow ourselves to be overcome with the situation, we do not grow any closer to the end goal.

Engaging in patent prosecution can be a bit of a fathomable foe. There's procedural aspects to master, and substantive strategies to apply. But simply learning about it from a textbook does not help you get from A to B. As if often the case, there simply is not an easy way to convey knowledge. You learn often best by doing.

Such is the impetus for this book – to help you get moving. Each chapter corresponds with an in-class lecture. The lecture will analyze an office action (and response), and each class session will provide students the opportunity to work on an in-class assignment for immediate feedback. Further, each class session includes an additional assignment to further apply the concepts.

By the time you finish this book – and complete all of the assignments – you will be well on your way down the mountain of mastering patent prosecution. Good luck.

- Britten

CHAPTER 1
OVERVIEW, STRATEGIES, MASTER ARGUMENTS, 102 PART I

A. OVERVIEW

At a high level, the patent prosecution process follows the following procedure:

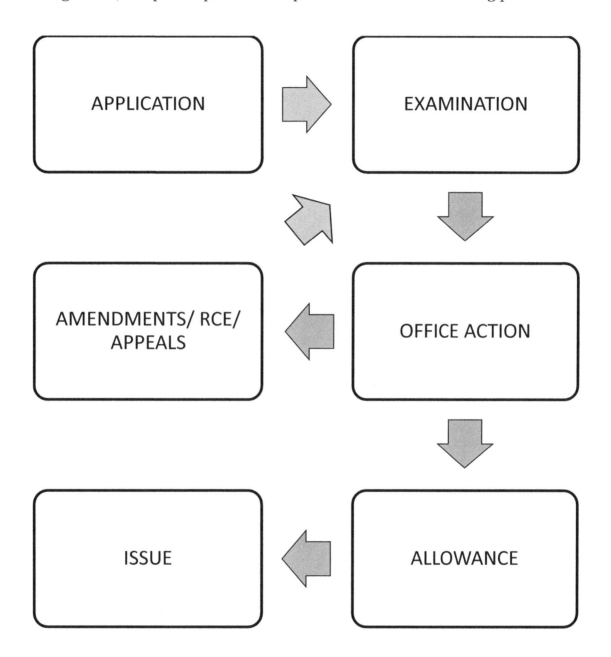

B. OFFICE ACTION STRATEGIES PART I

The following information should be included in a strategy document used to analyze the office action response.

- Claim Listing (per the most recent updates)
- Objections/Rejections
- Strategy on how to overcome each objection/rejection

Each of these sections will be briefly discussed.

1. CLAIM LISTING

This section is intended to be our starting point for analyzing the claims. Keep in mind that the metes and bounds of the protection are governed by the claims. As such, they become our reference book, our literal fenceposts, that we must reference and re-reference to determine whether the Examiner has satisfied the burden of showing applicable art.

There is a second utility of listing out the claims. As will be discussed below in the strategy section, you can underline/bold/highlight the word and phrases in the claimset that are not being specifically taught by the prior art presented in the objections/rejections.

2. OBJECTIONS/REJECTIONS

This section essentially becomes a synopsis of everything that the Examiner has put forth against the patent. It becomes the "todo" list of items that you need to specifically respond to and/or overcome.

When analyzing a rejection put forth, it is good to compare the reference or item cited by the Examiner against the explicit term or phrase of the claimset. It is important to be very precise here. Is the Examiner actually showing evidence that overcomes ALL of the language, or just some of the language?

In some instances, the Examiner may put forth prior art citations that do not meet all of the elements of the claims. In such instances, the next step is to look at the reference as a whole (beyond the citations put forth by the Examiner) to see if other parts of the reference teach the elements of the claims.

3. STRATEGY

KEY POINT
STRATEGY REVIEW

1. List the most recent status of the claims (and the claims themselves)

2. List the objection/rejections put forth by the Examiner

3. List the strategy on how to overcome each objection/rejection

KEY POINT
RESPONSE OPTIONS

A. Argue (set up for appeal)

B. Amend and argue both prior claim language and amended claim language

C. Amend and argue amended claim language

After analyzing each rejection, it is helpful to segment the claimset into two parts: those parts that are being taught by the prior art reference(s) and those parts which are NOT being taught by the prior art reference(s).

For those parts of the claims that are not being met, list the claim language and cite the excerpts (e.g. Col. 8, lines 1-10 and Paragraph [0044]) the Examiner relies upon. Present a brief excerpt of the citation and then provide a brief indication of how the cited art does not meet the claimed limitation.

If the art does teach the elements of the claims (or is sufficiently close that it is not worth arguing), it may make sense to make claim amendments. For claim amendments, we could either provide language directly from the Specification, or incorporate a dependent claim that you think has solid arguments. Provide a brief summary of why you think the cited art does not meet the incorporated limitation. Additionally, provide literal support (word for word support via underlining) for amendments from the Specification.

C. MASTER ARGUMENT TEMPLATE

Each patent practitioner will have their preference on arguing styling and format. This can easily be seen by comparing one file wrapper from a first practitioner to the file wrapper of another practitioner. Additionally, firms tend to have their own arguing styling guidelines as well. As you gain in experience in responding to office actions, know that there is flexibility to adapt the style and format to a bit of your own preference.

That being said, it is good to start with one set style and format. The format presented below is structured to minimize prosecution history estoppel, which is a legal doctrine whereby arguments made during prosecution may be used to further restrict and limit the claimset during subsequent litigation of the asset. As such, this particular format helps to minimize litigation issues and ensures arguments are kept very clean (i.e. do not limit the claim).

A few general guidelines to keep in mind:

1. When you argue the claim language, always quote the language (using quotation marks to show that the language is exactly the same to the claim language). Do not characterize the language. If you characterize (i.e. put the language in your own words), you increase the chance of prosecution history estoppel applying.

2. Keep the arguments to the point. There's no need to put in pages of prior art context if a single paragraph will suffice. Additionally, if there is a significant disjoint or misunderstanding, an examiner interview may be the better manner to bring such to the Examiner's attention. An additional benefit of calling the Examiner is that it minimizes what is put on file (again, it minimizes the impact of prosecution history estoppel).

3. Do not overly emphasize/bold/underline. If you want to make a point, underline just the key portion.

Here's the basic skeleton of our argument section that you should master:

With respect to Claim AAAA, the Examiner has relied on BBBB from the CCCC reference to make a prior art showing of applicant's claimed technique "XXXXXX" (see this or similar, but not necessarily identical language in the independent claims).

Applicant respectfully notes that the CCCC reference, as relied upon by the Examiner, discloses:

DDDD

See Paragraph [BBBB] – emphasis added.

However, disclosing that EEEE, as in the CCCC excerpt(s) relied upon, does not teach or suggest "XXXXXX" (emphasis added), as claimed by applicant.

This basic skeleton can apply to nearly any rejection response, including 102 and 103 responses which you will work on in this book. A few points on the notations:

- AAAA: you can argue all of the independent claims by simply stating "the independent claims". If not all of the independent claims have the same rejection, then you would need to then make specific arguments for each claim.

- BBBB: If the prior art is a publication, then you can cite the paragraph number. If it is a granted patent, then you would need to cite the column and line numbers.

- CCCC: For 102 rejections, you typically will only have one prior art source applied to your claim language. For 103 rejections, you typically will have more than one prior art source, and so would need to account for all prior art sources applied to the specific limitation.

KEY POINT SKELETON ARGUMENT TEMPLATE

1. An indication of which claim(s) you are responding to;

2. A recitation of the rejection(s) that are applied to the specific limitation in the indicated claim(s);

3. A disclosure of what the prior art teaches for that specific limitation; and

4. The argument of how the prior art does NOT teach a particular word, phrase, or entire limitation.

- DDDD: I recommend to simply copy and paste the excerpt from the prior art source directly (rather than copying the actual text and then pasting the actual text). This allows the Examiner to see the context of where you are pulling the excerpt from. You can add emphasize to such excerpt as appropriate to draw the Examiner's attention to a key teaching.

- EEEE: This is where you either can 1) succinctly characterize the prior art language (note that charactering the prior art is fine, just as long as we do not characterize the claim language); or 2) include a very brief section of the prior art as a quotation in your argument section. You can add emphasis as appropriate to this.

- XXXX: this is the exact language from the claim. No characterizing. If needed, add emphasis to the claim language to clearly show what is NOT being taught by the prior art language.

Let's take a quick step back. What does this template essentially come down to?

1. An indication of which claim(s) you are responding to;

2. A recitation of the rejection(s) that are applied to the specific limitation in the indicated claim(s);

3. A disclosure of what the prior art teaches for that specific limitation; and

4. The argument of how the prior art does NOT teach a particular word, phrase, or entire limitation.

Memorize this skeleton format. It comes down to four basic steps, but if applied correctly, can help you to put forward succinct, focused arguments that minimize litigation issues that may creep up later on.

D. RESPONDING TO 102 REJECTIONS PART I

In section E below, information on the legal analysis for analyzing 35 U.S.C. 102 is provided. The present section however is intended to give you some guidance on how to analyze section 102 rejections.

Strategies relating to 102 rejections are generally straight forward. In order for a 102 rejection to be valid, each and every part of the invention must be disclosed in one source. As such, in analyzing the rejection, the first thing to be done is to see if each and every claim element is actually found in the disclosed publication.

The M.P.E.P. provides some strategies you can use in your response:

> '[a] claim is anticipated only if each and every element as set forth in the claim is found, either expressly or inherently described, in a single prior art reference.' Verdegaal Bros. v. Union Oil Co. of California, 814 F.2d 628, 631, 2 USPQ2d 1051, 1053 (Fed. Cir. 1987).
> ...

'The identical invention must be shown in as complete detail as is contained in the ... claim.' Richardson v. Suzuki Motor Co., 868 F.2d 1226, 1236, 9 USPQ2d 1913, 1920 (Fed. Cir. 1989).[1]

Additionally, "[e]very element of the claimed invention must be literally present, arranged as in the claim."[2] Therefore, even if the prior art source has all of the elements of the claim, they must be arranged as is presented in the claim. This makes sense, however, for if our invention had the elements A, B, and C (e.g. think of a design of a chair, or the manner in which a computer program operates, or the manner in which a chemical molecule is combined together, etc.) and the prior art source discloses B, A, and C, in that order, it would make sense that such a prior art source would be potentially applicable (e.g. it has the same elements, etc.) but because the elements are not ordered in the same manner it does not disclose the claimed invention.

Lastly, 102 rejection are based on a single prior art source. Nonetheless, more than one source may arise with respect to inherency arguments. This comes up when a feature is an inherent characteristic of the thing taught in the primary reference. For example, prior art teaches A and B, but C would have been an inherent characteristic in combining A and B. Even though C was not taught in the prior art reference, because it is an inherent feature, other sources may be brought in. Consider this support:

> To serve as an anticipation when the reference is silent about the asserted inherent characteristic, such gap in the reference may be filled with recourse to extrinsic evidence. Such evidence must make clear that the missing descriptive matter is necessarily present in the thing described in the reference.[3]

KEY POINT NOVELTY TEST

Is each and every limitation of the claim taught by one (and only one) prior art source?

---

[1] M.P.E.P. § 2131.
[2] *Richardson v. Suzuki Motor Co., Ltd.*, 868 F.2d 1226, 1236 (Fed. Cir. 1989).
[3] *Continental Can Co. v. Monsanto Co.*, 948 F.2d 1264, 1268 (Fed. Cir. 1991).

> The use of extrinsic evidence is permissible to show that the missing descriptive material is necessarily present in the prior art reference description and that it would be so recognized by persons of ordinary skill.[4]

In analyzing whether inherency arguments are proper, recognize, as indicated above, that support exists for the Examiner to rely on another reference to clarify a fact in the prior art source. However, the supporting reference must in fact do this.[5] Therefore, determine whether the supporting reference actually discloses the fact that <u>inherently</u> is part of that disclosed in the prior art source.

As a quick overview, in order for a 102 rejection to be valid, ALL elements of the claims must be expressly taught by the <u>single</u> prior art reference. Remember that 102 is a test of novelty, and your invention must be novel. Therefore, when the Examiner puts forward a 102 rejection, in essence, the Examiner is indicating that all elements of your claim are being taught by the single prior art reference.

Usually, a 102 rejection can be expressly overcome by one of the following:

1. If the prior art reference does indeed teach all elements of the claims, then proceed forward with amending the claims to get around the prior art.

2. If the prior art reference does NOT teach all elements of the claims, then proceed forward with 1) putting forward arguments that rebut the rejection, and/or 2) putting forward additional amendments for the purposes of advancing prosecution.

E. REFERENCE MATERIAL FOR 102 REJECTIONS

During law school and when I studied for the patent bar, a lot of the class and study time was spent dissecting each part of section 102. Although we will analyze 102 here, recognize that much more (and many nuances) could be said further on the subject.

With the America Invents Act, some significant changes were brought about to section 102. As such, if you look online for arguments or strategies for section 102, make sure that you are looking at the updated requirements (implemented 03/2013). That being said, the new 102 does incorporate much of what was in the older 102, although numbering, formatting, and obviously some text is different as well.

The new changes to section 102 break the requirements into four parts: 1) novelty; 2) exceptions; 3) common ownership; and 4) prior art.

1. 102(A)(1) & 102(B)(1): CONDITIONS AND EXCEPTIONS

> (a) Novelty; Prior Art.— A person shall be entitled to a patent unless—

---

[4] *Id.* (citing In re Oelrich, 666 F.2d 578, 581 (CCPA 1981)).
[5] *See, e.g.,* In re Samour, 571 F.2d 559, 562 (CCPA 1978.

(1) the claimed invention was patented, described in a printed publication, or in public use, on sale, or otherwise available to the public before the effective filing date of the claimed invention;

(b) Exceptions.—
(1) Disclosures made 1 year or less before the effective filing date of the claimed invention.— A disclosure made 1 year or less before the effective filing date of a claimed invention shall not be prior art to the claimed invention under subsection (a)(1) if—
   (A) the disclosure was made by the inventor or joint inventor or by another who obtained the subject matter disclosed directly or indirectly from the inventor or a joint inventor; or
   (B) the subject matter disclosed had, before such disclosure, been publicly disclosed by the inventor or a joint inventor or another who obtained the subject matter disclosed directly or indirectly from the inventor or a joint inventor.

Prior Art 35 U.S.C. 102(a) (Basis for Rejection)		Exceptions 35 U.S.C. 102(b) (Not Basis for Rejection)
102(a)(1) Disclosure with Prior Public Availability Date	102(b)(1)	(A) Grace Period Disclosure by Inventor or Obtained from Inventor
		(B) Grace Period Intervening Disclosure by Third Party

It is helpful to remember that changes to section 102 were brought about to help it conform to more internationally recognized "first-to-file" patent systems. As such, the focus in the new section 102 is on defining prior art and exceptions to prior art. In short, if a prior art is found to which an exception does not apply, it may be applied to the invention disclosed.

First, 102(a) begins by indicating that a person shall be "entitled" to a patent. The burden therefore of showing that an invention does not meet the requirements is on the USPTO. Referencing our discussing above on Patent Examiners, their responsibility again is to determine whether the requirements are not met. If the requirements are met, then a person is entitled to a patent.

Next, 102(a)(1) mentions a "patented" or "printed publication" source. Such sources may include any preexisting publication anywhere in the world.

A "public use" is defined as that which is 1) accessible to the public and 2) commercially available.[6] Previously, section 102 included "secret" or "non public" sales. Now, however, section 102 does cover any secret or non public sale activity. Additionally, a secret or non public sale activity is one that assigns any obligation of confidentiality.[7] This makes sense because if the material has not been made public, the inventor could not know of it.

---

[6] "Prior Art Under AIA 35 U.S.C. 102(a)(1)" and "Exceptions to Prior Art Under AIA 35 U.S.C. 102(b)(1)," USPTO Slides (Mar. 15, 2013), available at http://www.uspto.gov/aia_implementation/.
[7] Id.

As if to make its point, the statute then provides "or otherwise available," which acts as a catch all for any other means of making the invention publicly available. The point here is simply to include any public material that is available in essentially any manner.

A "filing date" generally includes one of: 1) the filing date of the claimed invention; or 2) the filing date of an application the claimed invention depends on (e.g. claims priority to, etc.).

The exceptions which relate to 102(a)(1) are found in 102(b)(1) (as illustrated in Figure 18). Before analyzing the exceptions, three terms need to be briefly reviewed: disclosure, inventor, and one year or less.[8]

A disclosure "constitutes all documents and activities that were considered prior art."[9] Prior art includes any issued patent, published application, or any non-patent printed publication. Based on this understanding, a disclosure therefore is some evidence of the invention.

The term inventor is defined as "the individual who invented the device or, if it is a joint invention, the individuals who collectively invented or discovered the subject matter of the invention."[10] Additionally, the AIA has further indicated that "(g) The terms 'joint inventor' and 'coinventor' mean any one of the individuals who invented or discovered the subject matter of a joint invention."[11]

Lastly, the term "one year or less" refers to a new AIA concept of grace period, which refers to the amount of time in which an inventor must file an application after a disclosure in order for the disclosure not to count as prior art.[12]

With the above definitions in mind, let's briefly review the two exceptions. First, 102(b)(1)(A) relates to providing an exception for "disclosures of the inventor's own work (either by an inventor or a third party) that occur during the grace period."[13] As indicated by other attorneys, "[t]his [provision] simply continues the one year grace period practice established under the statutory bar provision of the Patent Act of 1952."[14] As such, this section relates to standard one year grace period associated with making a disclosure. In short, if a disclosure is made, an application must be filed by the inventor within a year in order for the disclosure not to be construed as prior art.

---

[8] *See, e.g., id.*
[9] *Id.*
[10] *Id.*
[11] 35 U.S.C. § 100(g).
[12] "Prior Art Under AIA 35 U.S.C. 102(a)(1)" and "Exceptions to Prior Art Under AIA 35 U.S.C. 102(b)(1)," USPTO Slides (Mar. 15, 2013), available at http://www.uspto.gov/aia_implementation/.
[13] *Id.*
[14] Arpita Bhattacharyya et al, "The Not-So-Amazing Grace Period Under the AIA," CIPA Journal (Sept. 2012), last accessed 04/24/2013), available at http://www.finnegan.com/resources/articles/articlesdetail.aspx?news=4acad2aa-4430-4d87-a197-3a202ac17c5b.

The next section, 102(b)(1)(B) relates to intervening disclosures. An intervening disclosure is simply a prior art disclosure before the filing date of the invention. This exception however permits the applicant to trace back to an earlier date if the inventor or inventor originated made a public disclosure before the intervening disclosure. Keep in mind that inventor or inventor originated public disclosure cannot be more than one year before the filing or the period would exceed the bounds of 102(b)(1) exception of a one year grace period. Although this exception can be quite useful in establishing priority, there are some potential warnings to be aware of. Consider the following:

> the USPTO's Proposed Rules for the "First-to-File" system, published in the July 26, 2012, issue of the Federal Register, has clarified that most disclosures by third parties will continue to be treated as prior art even when a third party disclosure is preceded by an inventor's own public disclosure. According to the USPTO's Proposed Rules, the § 102(b)(1)(B) exception can only be invoked if the subject matter in the third party disclosure is substantially identical to the subject matter previously disclosed by the inventor.
>
> ...
>
> Consider the following scenario: Inventor Alpha invents a widget, but rather than keeping the invention a secret and promptly filing a patent application, Inventor Alpha publishes an article disclosing elements A and B of his widget invention. After reading Inventor Alpha's article, Competitor Beta publishes his own article disclosing elements A, B, and C prior to the filing date of Inventor Alpha's patent application. Since Competitor Beta's article is not identical to Inventor Alpha's prior disclosure, Competitor Beta's article will become a prior art against Inventor Alpha's patent application. That is, the one-year grace period cannot be invoked to remove Competitor Beta's article as a prior art against Inventor Alpha's patent application.[15]

As such, although protection afforded by 102(b)(1)(B) does protect against intervening disclosure, recognize that it may be more narrowly construed than what the language initially conveys. Recognize additionally that this law is somewhat in flux as it was put into practice on March 16, 2013.

The question may have arisen as to how an inventor establishes the public disclosure to the USPTO. A Rule 130 declaration is used to show to the USPTO when a disclosure was made by the inventor. In fact, although each of the subsections relate to specific aspects of 120(b)(1) disclosures, in essence "the affidavit or declaration ... must provide a satisfactory showing that the inventor or a joint inventor is in fact the inventor of the subject matter of the disclosure."[16]

---

[15] *Id.*
[16] Proposed Rule 130(b); Courtenay C. Brinckerhoff, "Comments: USPTO First-Inventor-To File Roundtable," Sept. 6, 2012, available at http://www.uspto.gov/aia_implementation/120906-fittf-roundtable.pdf.

As far as guidelines, the Rule 130 Declaration should provide sufficient evidence that the disclosure was public (e.g. date, etc.), was made less than one year before the effective filing date of the invention, the content of the disclosure (e.g. is it the same as what was actually filed in the invention application, etc.), and who the disclosure was made by.[17] Note that if the authors of the disclosure are not the same as the listed inventors on the application that additional information may need to be supplied to show the discrepancy.

2. 102(A)(1) & 102(B)(1): EXAMPLES

In the foregoing section, we analyzed the requirements for novelty and the exceptions. I find that the best way to really understand such information is through examples. The following examples and explanations are taken from USPTO provided powerpoint slides.[18]

---

[17] *See, e.g.*, Courtenay C. Brinckerhoff, "Comments: USPTO First-Inventor-To File Roundtable," Sept. 6, 2012, available at http://www.uspto.gov/aia_implementation/120906-fittf-roundtable.pdf.

[18] *See, e.g.*, "Prior Art Under AIA 35 U.S.C. 102(a)(1)" and "Exceptions to Prior Art Under AIA 35 U.S.C. 102(b)(1)," USPTO Slides (Mar. 15, 2013), available at http://www.uspto.gov/aia_implementation/.

Example 1: Exception in 102(b)(1)(A)

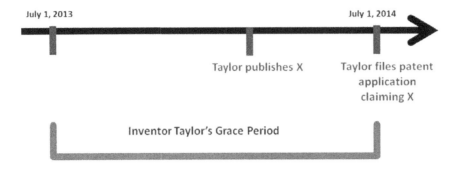

Taylor's publication is not available as prior art against Taylor's application because of the exception under 102(b)(1)(A) for a grace period disclosure by an inventor.

Example 2: Exception in 102(b)(1)(A)

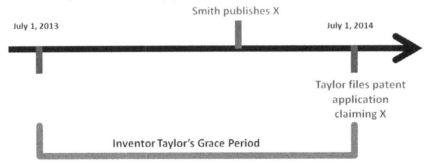

Smith's publication would be prior art to Taylor under 102(a)(1) if it does not fall within any exception in 102(b)(1). However, if Smith obtained subject matter X from Taylor, then it falls into the 102(b)(1)(A) exception as a grace period disclosure obtained from the inventor, and is not prior art to Taylor.

Example 3: Exception in 102(b)(1)(B)

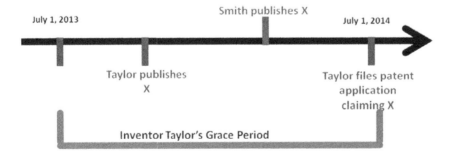

Smith's publication is not prior art because of the exception under 102(b)(1)(B) for a grace period intervening disclosure by a third party. Taylor's publication is not prior art because of the exception under 102(b)(1)(A) for a grace period disclosure by the inventor. If Taylor's disclosure had been before the grace period, it would be prior art against his own application. However, it would still render Smith inapplicable as prior art.

3. 102(A)(2) & 102(B)(2): CONDITIONS AND EXCEPTIONS

(a) Novelty; Prior Art.— A person shall be entitled to a patent unless—
...
(2) the claimed invention was described in a patent issued under section 151, or in an application for patent published or deemed published under section 122 (b), in which the patent or application, as the case may be, names another inventor and was effectively filed before the effective filing date of the claimed invention.

(b) Exceptions.—
...
(2) Disclosures appearing in applications and patents.— A disclosure shall not be prior art to a claimed invention under subsection (a)(2) if—
    (A) the subject matter disclosed was obtained directly or indirectly from the inventor or a joint inventor;
    (B) the subject matter disclosed had, before such subject matter was effectively filed under subsection (a)(2), been publicly disclosed by the inventor or a joint inventor or another who obtained the subject matter disclosed directly or indirectly from the inventor or a joint inventor; or
    (C) the subject matter disclosed and the claimed invention, not later than the effective filing date of the claimed invention, were owned by the same person or subject to an obligation of assignment to the same person.

Prior Art 35 U.S.C. 102(a) (Basis for Rejection)		Exceptions 35 U.S.C. 102(b) (Not Basis for Rejection)
102(a)(2) U.S. Patent, U.S. Patent Application, and PCT Application with Prior Filing Date	102(b)(2)	(A) Disclosure Obtained from Inventor
		(B) Intervening Disclosure by Third Party
		(C) Commonly Owned Disclosure

AIA Statutory Framework[19]

Section 102(a)(2) continues a theme that we discussed above with respect to 102(a)(1) in that it discusses further examples of prior art. In particular, the statute references "section 151" and "section 122 (b)."

---

[19] "Public Forum: First-Inventor-File Final Rules and Guidance," USPTO Public Forum Slides (Mar. 15, 2013), available at http://www.uspto.gov/aia_implementation/.

Section 151 of Title 35 refers simply to issued and published US patents.[20] Section 122(b) relates to a published US patent application, or a published patent application under the Patent Cooperation Treaty (PCT) that designates the United States.[21] In short, 122(b) refers to either a published application filed directly with the USTPO or through the PCT.

There are three exceptions that apply to these relatively straight forward rules. Before reviewing the exceptions, it is important to clarify two terms: PCT and effective filing date.[22]

We have previously discussed foreign filing considerations. A PCT application permits the applicant to obtain international patent protection by establishing an international effective filing date for their invention.[23] After a set time period, the application may enter the national stage in any country that was designated in the PCT application. If filing within the United States, the application must enter national phase by 30 months.[24] Additionally, although it may be obvious, an individual application must be filed in each country where protection is sought. To more fully get an overview of the process of a PCT application, a flowchart has been reproduced later in the next chapter (dealing with PCT foreign filing practices).

Additionally, a filing date is simply the date on which an application is filed. The effective filing date is a bit broader than simply a filing date, as it may include filing dates of a claim to priority. For example, an application may be filed 01/01/10 but may claim priority to a provisional, or to another application (e.g. think of a continuation, etc.) which may cause the effective filing date to be earlier, such as 01/01/09. With respect to a prior art source, the document must have an effective filing date before the effective filing date of the patent application under examination.

Further, in determining whether something is applicable as prior art (e.g. which relates to the effective filing date, etc.) under this section, 102(d) provides the following:

> (d) Patents and Published Applications Effective as Prior Art.— For purposes of determining whether a patent or application for patent is prior art to a claimed invention under subsection (a)(2), such patent or application shall be considered to have been effectively filed, with respect to any subject matter described in the patent or application—
> (1) if paragraph (2) does not apply, as of the actual filing date of the patent or the application for patent; or

---

[20] *See, e.g.,* 35 U.S.C. § 151.
[21] *See, e.g.,* 35 U.S.C. § 121(b); "Prior Art Under AIA 35 U.S.C. 102(a)(2)" and "Exceptions to Prior Art Under AIA 35 U.S.C. 102(b)(2)," USPTO Slides (Mar. 15, 2013), available at http://www.uspto.gov/aia_implementation/.
[22] *See, e.g.,* "Prior Art Under AIA 35 U.S.C. 102(a)(2)" and "Exceptions to Prior Art Under AIA 35 U.S.C. 102(b)(2)," USPTO Slides (Mar. 15, 2013), available at http://www.uspto.gov/aia_implementation/.
[23] *See, e.g., id.*
[24] *See, e.g.,* "Time Limits for Entering National/Regional Phase under PCT Chapters I and II," WIP PCT (Sept. 7, 2012), last accessed 04/24/2013, available at http://www.wipo.int/pct/en/texts/time_limits.html.

(2) if the patent or application for patent is entitled to claim a right of priority under section 119, 365 (a), or 365 (b), or to claim the benefit of an earlier filing date under section 120, 121, or 365 (c), based upon 1 or more prior filed applications for patent, as of the filing date of the earliest such application that describes the subject matter.

In discussing the applicable exceptions in this section, keep in mind that such exceptions only apply to potential prior art, including US Patents, US Patent applications which have been published, or PCT published applications, whose effective filing date predates the claimed invention's effective filing date.
Section 102(b)(2)(A) is where a disclosure made by someone who acquired the claimed invention's subject matter from its inventor(s) will not be considered prior art for the claimed invention.[25]

Section 102(b)(2)(B) relates to disclosures made by the inventor(s) prior to the subject matter's disclosure in documents.[26] Additionally, there is no requirement that this type of disclosure be the same as (or verbatim) to a disclosure of a US patent, a US published application, or a published PCT application.[27]

Lastly, section 102(b)(2)(C) relates to prior art which was filed before the effective filing date of the claimed invention, but which would not be considered prior art if the claimed invention and the disclosed subject matter are owned by (or under obligation to assign to) the same person.[28]

Again, recognize that all 102(b)(2) exceptions relate only to 102(a)(2) prior source documents, which may act as prior art from the date they are effective filed.[29] As such, a grace period is not relevant to 102(b)(2) prior art sources.

In addition to these exceptions, 102(c) relates to 102(b)(2)(C):

> (c) Common Ownership Under Joint Research Agreements.— Subject matter disclosed and a claimed invention shall be deemed to have been owned by the same person or subject to an obligation of assignment to the same person in applying the provisions of subsection (b)(2)(C) if—
> (1) the subject matter disclosed was developed and the claimed invention was made by, or on behalf of, 1 or more parties to a joint research agreement that was in effect on or before the effective filing date of the claimed invention;
> (2) the claimed invention was made as a result of activities undertaken within the scope of the joint research agreement; and
> (3) the application for patent for the claimed invention discloses or is amended to disclose the names of the parties to the joint research agreement.

---

[25] "Prior Art Under AIA 35 U.S.C. 102(a)(2)" and "Exceptions to Prior Art Under AIA 35 U.S.C. 102(b)(2)," USPTO Slides (Mar. 15, 2013), available at http://www.uspto.gov/aia_implementation/.
[26] *Id.*
[27] *Id.*
[28] *Id.*
[29] "Public Forum: First-Inventor-File Final Rules and Guidance," USPTO Public Forum Slides (Mar. 15, 2013), available at http://www.uspto.gov/aia_implementation/.

Section 102(c) focuses on common ownership under a joint research agreement. Additionally, 102(c) embodies the 2004 Cooperative Research and Technology Enhancement ("CREATE") Act:

> The enactment of section 102 (c) of title 35, United States Code, under paragraph (1) of this subsection is done with the same intent to promote joint research activities that was expressed, including in the legislative history, through the enactment of the Cooperative Research and Technology Enhancement Act of 2004.[30]

Under current law, common ownership or that which is subject to a joint research agreement has some implication to section 103(c) which, as we will discuss below, excludes prior art for obviousness purposes. However, section 102(c) expands the 103(c) exclusion to also exclude such prior art disclosures within a year of the application's filing date for novelty purposes as well.[31]

4.   102(A)(2) & 102(B)(2): EXAMPLES

The following examples should aid you in understanding the exceptions to 102(b)(2). As indicated above, the following examples and explanations are taken from USPTO provided powerpoint slides.[32]

---

[30] *See, e.g.,* "Notes" to 35 U.S.C. § 102.
[31] *See, e.g.,* "America Invents Act: New Section 102," Inventive Step Blog (Oct. 12, 2011), last accessed 04/24/2013, available at http://inventivestep.net/2011/10/12/america-invents-act-new-section-102/.
[32] *See, e.g.,* "Prior Art Under AIA 35 U.S.C. 102(a)(1)" and "Exceptions to Prior Art Under AIA 35 U.S.C. 102(b)(1)," USPTO Slides (Mar. 15, 2013), available at http://www.uspto.gov/aia_implementation/.

Example 1: Exception in 102(b)(2)(A)

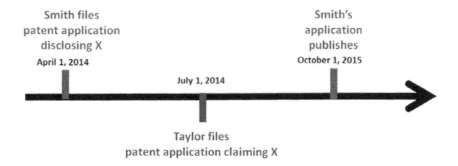

Smith's patent application publication is not prior art if Smith obtained X from Inventor Taylor because of the exception under 102(b)(2)(A) for a disclosure obtained from the inventor

Example 2: Exception in 102(b)(2)(B)

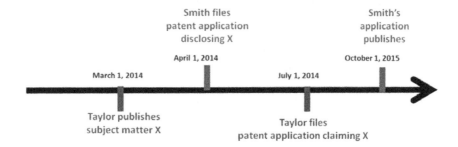

Smith's patent application publication is not prior art against Taylor's application because of the exception under 102(b)(2)(B) for an intervening disclosure by a third party.

Example 3: Exception in 102(b)(2)(C)

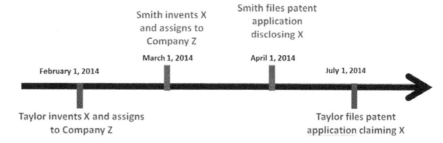

Smith's patent application publication is not prior art because of the exception under 102(b)(2)(C) for a commonly owned disclosure. There is no requirement that Smith's and Taylor's subject matter be the same in order for the common ownership exception to apply.

5. PRE-AIA V. POST-AIA CONSIDERATIONS

Most likely, those that are studying this book will deal most frequently with post-AIA procedures and rules described above. Nonetheless, it is worth mentioning that you will most likely need to apply both Pre-AIA and Post-AIA rules. For the Patent Bar Exam, you will need to know how to identify which set of rules to apply and apply them flawlessly and quickly.

Although many of the above considerations are specific to post-AIA, the pre-AIA 102 rules were a bit more complex. The greatest difference was that pre-AIA focused on a "first-to-invent" system whereas the post-AIA focused on a "first-to-file" which simplified the 102 rules a bit. If you receive an office action response dealing with Pre-AIA rules, I would recommend looking up the specific old Rule 102 section. Additionally, a plethora of sites online provide best strategies for dealing with each of the pre-AIA 102 rules.

Under pre-AIA rules, the focus was on who was the first to invent. Therefore, an applicant could "swear back" to a prior time of when the invention was actually invented. This "swearing back" process included providing some form of evidence to show the invention had been substantially created at a specific time. Additionally, the inventor was required to exercise "diligence" from the date the invention was conceived (called a date of conception) up until the time that the invention was actually reduced to practice. A quick example:

    01/01/2010: Inventor A conceives invention
    02/01/2010: Inventor B conceives invention
    03/01/2010: Inventor B reduces to practice
    04/01/2010: Inventor A reduces to practice
    05/01/2010: Inventor B files a patent application
    06/01/2010: Inventor A files a patent application

Who gets the resulting patent? Inventor A would be eligible for patent protection (e.g. by swearing back to 01/01/2010, etc.) if the inventor can prove that he/she was diligent from the initial time of the invention being conceived to actually reducing to practice the invention.

Based on this example, the pre-AIA rules focused heavily on ensuring that the actual inventor received the final patent. This is an important point, particularly because if an invention is filed now, we simply look at effective dates rather than having to delve into who actually invented the invention first. The scope of prior art therefore is broadened as a result of the AIA rules (e.g. inventor can no longer swear behind a reference, etc.). This is one of the reasons why a great rush of filing applications occurred just prior to the March 16, 2013 implementation of the AIA rules.

In comparing the two systems (Pre and Post AIA), some potential issues arise that you should be aware of. In the most simple of examples, if an application was filed on or after 3/16/13, then it would be under post-AIA rules. If the application was filed on or before 3/15/13, it would be under pre-AIA rules. However, if we start with priority documents, then this gets a little tricky. For example, let's say we file a provisional on 3/15/13. We later file an application claiming priority to the provisional on 3/16/13. The application however contains the same information as disclosed in the priority document. Based off of such, the application will be prosecuted under pre-AIA rules. Let's take the same example but now the specification is not the same between the application as filed and the priority document. In this instance, AIA may apply. If the claimed subject matter was fully supported in the priority document, then the application will be prosecuted under pre-AIA. If, however, the claimed subject was not disclosed in the priority document, then the application will be prosecuted under post-AIA rules.

Additionally, let's say you are prosecuting a patent under pre-AIA rules. An amendment to the claims is entered (consistent with the Specification), but unbeknownst to you, such support was not found in the priority document. This would automatically trigger the prosecution to switch from pre-AIA to post-AIA rules. Even if you go back and delete the entered in material (e.g. to conform it with priority document), it does not matter. Once an application has been switched to post-AIA, it cannot go back to pre-AIA.

The reality is that the post-AIA rules that we have reviewed in this book will become ultimately the focus of the US patent system. Nonetheless, the States are in a period of transition from one system to another. As such, be aware of these considerations.

Recognize also that for any application that you file now will be based on post-AIA rules. Nonetheless, as a patent practitioner you may be asked to work on applications that are still under pre-AIA rules. Make sure therefore that you navigate the transition waters correctly.

CHAPTER 2
PROSECUTION FLOW, CLAIM AMENDMENT PART I, 103 PART I

As a prelude to this chapter, it is worth mentioning that this chapter is geared substantially (and almost exclusively) towards patent prosecution within the United States. Chapter 6 will touch briefly on some international considerations. Within this context, therefore, when the term "foreign" is used, it means non-US jurisdictions.

A. PROSECUTION FLOW

Many do not realize that the prosecution process to obtain a patent may take many years. One of the reasons for this is, after an application is filed, it may take up to (or even longer) 18 months before a first substantive response is received. At that point, the ping-pong nature of prosecution begins, where the USPTO issues an office action, and then the applicant has up to 6 months (with extension fees) to respond. In response, the USPTO then takes another few months to respond. You can see how the time can quickly add up into years. The chart below shows many of the steps that can occur at each stage of prosecution.

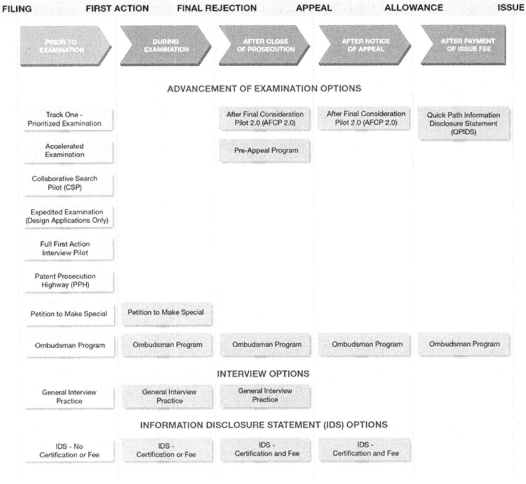

Patent Application Timeline[33]

---

[33] https://www.uspto.gov/patent/initiatives/uspto-patent-application-initiatives-timeline

Additionally, the following chart is a very global view timeline of the prosecution process. Such is not intended to be exhaustive of the entire process. Rather, it is simply to get you aligned to where you are in the entire process quickly.

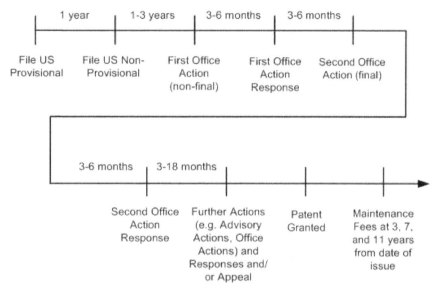

Stages of Patent Prosecution

Using this global timeline, let's briefly discuss the milestones in this process.

- Grace Periods: The calendar starts to tick whenever a public disclosure is made. Remember that once a public disclosure is given, you have one year to get an application on file (either provisional or non provisional). Recognize also that a disclosure may preclude protection in many (if not most) foreign jurisdictions. Do not rely on the grace period as a means to still file in foreign jurisdictions (i.e. you need to check the exact jurisdiction to ensure whether such grace period would even apply).

- Filing Dates: The non provisional application needs to be filed within one year of the disclosure or within one year of the provisional application. Additionally, a PCT application will need to be filed within one year of the provisional application.

- First Office Action: Normally, the USPTO goal is get this out within one year of the filing. However, recognize there is a backlog and so it may be much longer before it is received. Very few applications are ever granted before receiving a rejection in a first office action.

- First Office Action Response: Within three months of receiving the Office Action, a response must be filed. Recognize that although extensions are available, it will cost more money.

- Second Office Action: The patent examiner will review the response and may issue a second Office Action (e.g. non final, final, etc.). The process will continue until a patent is issued, the patent application is abandoned or if a final rejection of the application is issued.

- Granted: In an ideal world, an applicant receives a non-final office action, amends the claims, receives a final office action response, responds, and then the claims are granted. However, the count system (as later discussed in Chapter 3) may influence when a claim set is allowed.

- 18 Month Milestone: Eighteen months after filing a non-provisional or PCT patent application, the application is published.

- 30 Month Milestone: Within 30 months after filing the PCT application, the individual countries (if any) in which patent protection need to be designated.

- Maintenance Fees: Once the U.S. Patent has been issued, patent maintenance fees are due at 3, 7 and 11 years after issuance.

- Termination: The Patent expires 20 years from the non-provisional application filing date. At this point, the invention enters the public domain.

B. CLAIM AMENDMENTS PART I

Be aware that the MPEP has an entire section on amending claims, entitled "714 Amendments, Applicant's Action".[34] A good question to ask is whether it is necessary first to amend the claims. As a general rule, you don't typically amend the claims to simply amend the claims. It should reflect whatever strategy has been previously decided upon. With that in mind, here's some claim strategies to consider as you amend your claims:

- Does the prior art teach <u>each</u> and <u>every</u> aspect of the claimed language?

- How is your relationship with the Examiner? Can you work with the Examiner to help expedite prosecution by amending?

- How will the PTAB (Patent Trial and Appeal Board) view your action? Is this a subjective argument, or an objective argument (based on procedural error)?

KEY POINT CLAIM AMENDMENT

When amending, keep the following in mind:

- Does it distinguish the Prior Art?

- Does it advance prosecution?

- Do you have explicit support from the Specification for the claim amendments?

---

[34] MPEP Section 714

- Is the amendment already taught in another part of the prior art reference not yet relied on by the Examiner?

- Do you expect the additional limitation(s) to be easily rebutted by another prior art reference put forth by the Examiner?

We discussed briefly above ramifications of prosecution history estoppel. There's one ramification relating to claim amendments. In short, there is a presumption that if you amend, such is being added to get around the prior art. Such presumption may apply even if you simply incorporate a dependent claim (and argue it to get an allowance), or incorporate an already allowed dependent claim.[35] In view of such, when you amend, simply know that there is a presumption that you are making such amendments to get around the prior art.

Additionally, in some instances the prior art may be teaching all aspects of the claim. In such an instance, your options may include adding limitations from dependent claims into the rejected independent claim to more fully distinguish the claim from the prior art. Additionally, another option would be to cancel all of the previously presented claims and insert new claims that claim other aspects of the invention. If you pursue the second approach, know that the Examiner may respond with a restriction (if he feels that your new claim set has more than one invention), or a notice of non-compliant response (as the new claim may now require a new search which would occur after an RCE).

In addition to making amendments to the independent claim to get around the prior art and advance prosecution, you can do the same for dependent claims. Additionally, you might want to consider adding on 2-3 additional dependent claims that further distinguish the claim set from the prior art. Such dependent claims also may be good talking points if you have an examiner's interview – you could treat these dependent claims as "fall back" positions should the Examiner not be entirely convinced by your changes to the independent claim alone.

C. REFERENCE MATERIAL FOR CLAIM AMENDMENTS

An integral part – and perhaps the most important part – of a patent application is the claims. They define the scope of protection, the bounds of the fence, the everything of the invention. Due to their importance, we will review in detail below the elements of a claim and then focus on how to draft effective claims.

1. INDEPENDENT CLAIMS

To analyze how to properly draft claims, we will first dissect the structure of an independent claim, and then analyze each of the corresponding parts. The structure of a dependent claim will subsequently be examined as well. Following the discussion, we will apply the principles to several claim drafting examples.

---

[35] *See, e.g.,* John Chandler, "Both Ways of Amending Patent Claims Lead to Prosecution History Estoppel", Blog Post, 11/26/2013, available at http://www.chandlerip.com/?p=761.

We will start by reviewing a figure of a very basic invention and then write up a basic claim set. Although the following description will apply to physical construction (e.g. how the table is put together, etc.), recognize that similar type questions can be asked regardless of the invention subject matter. Without considering prior art, and only for purposes of claim drafting, here is our invention:

Possible questions to ask:

1. What are the elements to the invention?
2. How are the elements connected?
3. What is the function of the element?
4. Do the elements move?

Of course, it is good to also take a step back and always keep in mind the following:

1. What objective is the invention seeking to serve?
2. What is actually "new" about this invention?
3. What part or parts need the most protection?
4. How will the invention be marketed?
5. Who (or what type of business) may eventually infringe the invention? How much benefit/advantage/incremental value will the invention give to the infringement?
6. What features do you suspect will be the source of confusion or argument during litigation?

With these questions in mind, let's analyze the invention: it has a top flat square shaped surface with four accompanying legs. Nothing really novel there. Nonetheless, let's use these elements to construct a basic independent claim:

What is claimed is:

1. A table, which comprises:
   (a) a surface;
   (b) one or more support legs;
   (c) one or more attachments for attaching the one or more support legs to the surface, wherein the one or more support legs are mounted in a direction orthogonal to the surface and extend downwardly therefrom.

We are assuming at this stage that full support in the Specification exists. Additionally, notice that this broad claim set could have application to several different table modifications. For example:

Or, the table could have been:

The goal of claim drafting is that you want the language to be precise enough so it will protect the invention and get around prior art, but broad enough so it will encompass other related modifications of the invention as well.

Let's break down the claim set and discuss each of the parts.

What is claimed is:

1. [patent class and preamble] A table, [transition phrase] which comprises:
    (a) [claim body] a surface;
    (b) [claim body] one or more support legs;
    (c) [claim body] one or more attachments for attaching the one or more support legs to the surface, wherein the one or more support legs are mounted in a direction orthogonal to the surface and extend downwardly therefrom.

Keep in mind that this is just one such way to claim the invention. So if your claim set does not look exact, that is just fine.

The patent claim is one complete sentence. Although it is often broken up into separate parts, recognize that it is still one complete sentence and abides by regular grammar principles. Additionally, an introductory phrase precedes the actual claim, such as "I claim" or "What is claimed is:." There is only one introductory phrase for the entire claim set and is placed before the first claim. As far as numbering the claims, they are ordered in ascending consecutive numbers. Although some attorneys start with the broadest claim (e.g. claim 1, etc.) and narrow the claims as they ascend, this is not a rule.

PATENT CLASS AND PREAMBLE

The preamble is the introductory part of the patent claim and indicates the class (e.g. process, machine, manufacture, composition of matter, etc.) as well as any functional language (e.g. indicating the purpose or function of the invention, etc.).

A process class may be synonymous with a method claim, which involves a series of steps for making something. The focus in this type of claim class is on the "steps" and not necessarily the physical elements associated with the invention. Normally, in terms of infringement, an infringer would have to be responsible for each and every step of the method/process. However, the law on this particular point is in transition.[36] Recognize that the more steps you have, the harder it may be to find direct infringement. Additionally, also know that a method or process usually must be tied to a machine or transformation to be valid.[37] I say "usually" because although the *Bilski* decision reaffirmed that the machine or transformation test is relevant to determining validity, it is not the only test that may be applied.

A machine class is precisely as it sounds – an apparatus, a device, a system, a widget. The Federal Court has stated that:

> The Supreme Court has defined the term "machine" as "a concrete thing, consisting of parts, or of certain devices and combination of devices." Burr v. Duryee, 68 U.S. (1 Wall.) 531, 570 (1863). This "includes every mechanical device or combination of mechanical powers and devices to perform some function and produce a certain effect or result." Corning v. Burden, 56 U.S. 252, 267 (1854).[38]

A manufacture class typically refers to an article of manufacture, and describes a manufactured product. This class differs from a machine in that an article of manufacture generally has no moving parts.

---

[36] This law is in flux as the Federal Circuit has indicated that an infringer may not need to practice each and every step in order to be found liable. Consider, for example, induced infringement or joint infringement. *See, e.g., Akamai Tech. v. Limelight Networks* (Fed. Cir. 2012).

[37] For case law on this particular point, see *In re Bilski*, 545 F.3d 943 (Fed. Cir. 2008); *Gottschalk v. Benson* 409 U.S. 63 (1972); *Parker v. Flook*, 437 U.S. 584 (1978); *Diamond v. Diehr* 450 U.S. 175 (1981).

[38] *In re Nuitjen*, 500 F.3d 1346 (Fed. Cir. 2007).

The Supreme Court has defined "manufacture" (in its verb form) as "the production of articles for use from raw or prepared materials by giving to these materials new forms, qualities, properties, or combinations, whether by hand-labor or by machinery." Diamond v. Chakrabarty, 447 U.S. 303, 308 (1980) (quoting American Fruit Growers, Inc. v. Brogdex Co., 283 U.S. 1, 11 (1931). The term is used in the statute in its noun form, Bayer AG v. Housey Pharms., Inc., 340 F.3d 1367, 1373 (Fed. Cir. 2003), and therefore refers to "articles" resulting from the process of manufacture. The same dictionary the Supreme Court relied on for its definition of "manufacture" in turn defines "article" as "a particular substance or commodity: as, an article of merchandise; an article of clothing; salt is a necessary article." 1 Century Dictionary 326 (William Dwight Whitney ed., 1895). These definitions address "articles" of "manufacture" as being tangible articles or commodities.[39]

The last class is a composition of matter, which the Supreme Court has defined as "all compositions of two or more substances and all composite articles, whether they be the results of chemical union, or of mechanical mixture, or whether they be gases, fluids, powders or solids."[40] This definition is somewhat problematic as a "composite article" may also be considered articles of manufacture, such as plywood.[41] Generally, composition of matter covers a chemical compound or molecule.

As a quick overview:

Class	General Rule
Process	It includes a method. It focuses on the steps of the method or process.
Machine	An apparatus, device, system, or widget.
Manufacture	An article (generally non moving parts) produced by a process of manufacture.
Composition of Matter	It covers chemical compounds or molecules.

To emphasize a patent claim must start with a clear indication of the class to which the invention belongs. Further, as indicated above, the preamble may include functional language associated with the patent class. Some examples of functional language include: "A device for pouring concrete...;" "A compound X for use as a medicament for treating gout..." Where an invention is generally known (e.g. a table, etc.), a preamble may not need as much functional language to lay the framework for the invention. However, where the general invention is completely novel, more functional language may be necessary to provide a proper context for the invention.

---

[39] *In re Nuitjen*, 500 F.3d 1346 (Fed. Cir. 2007).
[40] *Diamond v. Chakrabarty*, 447 U.S. 303, 308 (1980).
[41] *See, e.g.,* http://en.wikipedia.org/wiki/Composition_of_matter.

CHAPTER 2

Regardless, a general rule is that it is better to minimize the amount of language in the preamble. This is because any language used therein *may* be construed as a limitation at a later time. The courts again are not quite clear on this.[42] However, to avoid potentially incorporating further limitations into your claim based on preamble language, it is best to try and minimize the preamble to only that which is necessary.[43]

OTHER TYPES OF CLAIM TYPES

In addition to the clear-cut classes defined above, it is important to note that there are other types of claim classes:

Type	Definition
Beauregard	A claim directed to a computer program embodied on a computer readable medium.[44]
Markush	A claim which recites alternatives in a format such as "selected from the group consisting of A, B and C."[45]
Jepson	A claim focusing on an improvement of a prior invention and which includes the language "wherein the improvement comprises."[46]
Means-Plus-Function (or "means for")	A claim where an element may be "expressed as a means or step for performing a specified function without the recital of structure, material, or acts in support thereof, and such claim shall be construed to cover the corresponding structure, material, or acts described in the specification and equivalents thereof."[47]
Product-by-Process	A claim which is a hybrid between method and manufacture classes. The focus of this claim is on the structure and not the steps.[48]

Type	Example
Beauregard	"A <u>non-transitory computer-readable storage medium having instructions</u> stored thereon that, when executed by one or more processors, cause the one or more processors to perform operations to recover one or more virtual machines from an image level backup, the operations comprising:"[49]

---

[42] *See, e.g., American Medical Systems, Inc. v. Biolitec, Inc.* (Fed. Cir. 2010).
[43] *See, e.g.,* Jason Rantanen "Preambles as Limitations," Patently-O (09/13/10), last accessed 04/13/13, available at http://www.patentlyo.com/patent/2010/09/construction-of-preamble.html.
[44] *See, e.g., In re Beauregard*, 53 F.3d 1583 (Fed. Cir. 1995) ("The Commissioner now states "that computer programs embodied in a tangible medium, such as floppy diskettes, are patentable subject matter under 35 U.S.C. § 101 and must be examined under 35 U.S.C. §§ 102 and 103.'").
[45] M.P.E.P. § 803.02.
[46] *See, e.g.,* 37 C.F.R. §1.75.
[47] 35 U.S.C. § 112(f).
[48] *See, e.g.,* M.P.E.P. § 2113.
[49] U.S.P.N. 8332689.

Markush	"wherein at the second side of the milking box or boxes at least one <u>is placed selected from the group consisting of at least one feeder trough, a separation zone or zones, or outdoors</u>."[50]
Jepson	"a hand grip mounted on said hub to support said reel during the winding thereof; <u>wherein the improvement comprises</u>,"[51]
Means-Plus-Function (or "means for")	"a second engagement means, detachably engagable with said first engagement means, comprising a hitch member having an enlarged head portion, connected to a <u>means for</u> raising and lowering said hitch member above and substantially level with or below said stage surface,"[52]
Product-by-Process	"A <u>system for producing</u> a three-dimensional object from a fluid medium capable of solidification when subjected to prescribed synergistic stimulation, said system comprising:"[53]

There are some considerations to keep in mind with regard to the special types of claims listed above. For example, for Beauregard claims, it is generally accepted that tying a software invention to a physical aspect (e.g. computer readable medium, etc.) is patentable. However, this area is constantly in flux and the courts have given conflicting interpretations of what language is sufficient to be deemed patentable.[54]

With respect to Markush claims, the grouping must be a closed set. A closed set is simply one where all of the possibilities are listed. "Consisting of" is considered a closed set. Contrast this with an open set, which is defined as a set which may include one or all of the elements listed as well as others not listed. "Comprising of" (or which comprises) is considered an open set.[55]

In terms of infringement, open v. closed sets of possibilities are important. For example, if the claim set requires "a frame consisting of a metal bracket and a wooden post," then in order to infringe, the frame must only have those two parts. If the claim set indicated "a frame comprising a metal bracket and a wooden post," then a potential infringement must have at least those two parts but may have other additional parts also.

---

[50] U.S.P.A.N. 2013/0036974.
[51] U.S.P.N. 8360352.
[52] U.S.P.N. 5255452.
[53] U.S.P.N. 4575330.
[54] *See, e.g.,* "Post-Bilski BPAI Approves of Beauregard Claims," Patently-O (11/13/08), last accessed 04/13/13, available at http://www.patentlyo.com/patent/2008/11/post-bilski-bpa.html; "If the software method is not patentable, then neither is the "computer readable medium," Patently-O (08/16/11), last accessed 04/13/13, available at http://www.patentlyo.com/patent/2011/08/if-the-software-method-is-not-patentable-then-neither-is-the-computer-readable-medium.html.
[55] *See, e.g.,* "Transitional Phrases in Patent Claims: Comprising vs. Consisting Of," PatentLens, last accessed 04/13/13, available at http://www.patentlens.net/daisy/patentlens/2618.html.

With respect to Jepson claims, you are essentially admitting upfront that a prior invention serves as prior art. The invention seeking patent protection is therefore some improvement of an invention that is already protected. From a licensing point of view, in order to practice an invention embodied in one or more Jepson claims, it may be necessary to get a license from the patent owner of the original invention. For example, let's say the original invention was a table, and the Jepson Claim was an improvement of the table where now the legs have wheels attached. In order to create the improved product, it is necessary to first create the original product and then add on the improvement. Accordingly, in some situations, the Jepson claim may really only make sense when the applicant is also the patent owner of the prior invention.

The Jepson claim, although not as readily used in the United States, is very similar to the "two-part form" requirement for claims prosecuted before the EPO. For instance, per the two-part form requirement:

> (1) The claims shall define the matter for which protection is sought in terms of the technical features of the invention. Wherever appropriate, claims shall contain:
> (a) a statement indicating the designation of the subject-matter of the invention and those technical features which are necessary for the definition of the claimed subject-matter but which, in combination, form part of the prior art;
> (b) a characterising portion, beginning with the expression "characterised in that" or "characterised by" and specifying the technical features for which, in combination with the features stated under sub-paragraph (a), protection is sought.[56]

The means-plus-function claim has grown out of favor over the years. One of the benefits is that rather than reciting each and every combination of an element, the "means for" allows such an element to be determined as defined by the Specification. For example, our original claim could have been:

> A table, which comprises:
> (a) a surface;
> (b) one or more support legs;
> (c) <u>means for</u> attaching the one or more support legs to the surface, wherein the one or more support legs are mounted in a direction orthogonal to the surface and extend downwardly therefrom.

The Specification may have included the following language: "The surface may be attached to the support legs through the use of any attachment fixture, such as an L-brace, a threaded insert, a dovetail joint, etc." If this patent was litigated later on, the "means for" would most likely be limited by the examples given. As such, if "means for" is used, one must be very careful that clear support is given in the Specification.

---

[56] The European Patent Convention, Rule 43(1).

Because "means for" can be a bit ambiguous without looking at the Specification, patent attorneys typically shy away from using this type of claim. Although "means for" language may help to broaden a claim set, it introduces a level of ambiguity to the claim, which may require a court of law to later interpret what "means for" actually signifies. The goal, however, is to introduce as little ambiguity into the claims as possible. For this reason, I do not recommend "means for" claims.[57]

Lastly, with respect to product-by-process claims, these claims focus on the product and not necessarily the process. For example,

> "[E]ven though product-by-process claims are limited by and defined by the process, determination of patentability is based on the product itself. The patentability of a product does not depend on its method of production. If the product in the product-by-process claim is the same as or obvious from a product of the prior art, the claim is unpatentable even though the prior product was made by a different process." In re Thorpe, 777 F.2d 695, 698, 227 USPQ 964, 966 (Fed. Cir. 1985).[58]

From an infringement point of view, a product-by-process claim is less strong. For example, if our product-by-process claim was directed to using steps A, B, and C, but an infringing product was produced using steps A, B, and D, then it would not be infringing. The focus here should have been on the product itself (more broad) then simply a specific process of making the product.

Additionally, during prosecution, the applicant may have a higher level of burden of proving the unobviousness of the product-by-process invention (as compared to a more typical style claim set):

> "The Patent Office bears a lesser burden of proof in making out a case of prima facie obviousness for product-by-process claims because of their peculiar nature" than when a product is claimed in the conventional fashion. In re Fessmann, 489 F.2d 742, 744, 180 USPQ 324, 326 (CCPA 1974). Once the examiner provides a rationale tending to show that the claimed product appears to be the same or similar to that of the prior art, although produced by a different process, the burden shifts to applicant to come forward with evidence establishing an unobvious difference between the claimed product and the prior art product. In re Marosi, 710 F.2d 798, 802, 218 USPQ 289, 292 (Fed. Cir. 1983)."[59]

The more direct and simple the structure, the stronger the claim will be. It will require less interpretation, less guess-work, and will provide an unambiguous framework for the protection sought, which is precisely our goal. So although it is good to be aware of the above types of special claim cases, the more direct and clear you can be, the better.[60]

---

[57] See also Dennis Crouch, "Means Plus Function Claiming," Patently-O (01/14/13), last accessed 04/13/13, available at http://www.patentlyo.com/patent/2013/01/means-plus-function-claiming.html (finding that the number of patent applications with "means for" in the claimset has dramatically decreased over the prior ten years).
[58] M.P.E.P. § 2113.
[59] M.P.E.P. § 2113.
[60] Although some special claim types are less popular, there are some, such as the Beauregard that are quite essential for software claim drafting.

TRANSITION PHRASE

A transition phrase follows the preamble and links the preamble to the body of the claim. The USPTO has indicated that "[t]he transitional phrases "comprising", "consisting essentially of" and "consisting of" define the scope of a claim with respect to what unrecited additional components or steps, if any, are excluded from the scope of the claim."[61]

Additionally, the "[t]he transitional term "comprising", which is synonymous with "including," "containing," or "characterized by," is inclusive or open-ended and does not exclude additional, unrecited elements or method steps." Conversely, the phrases "consisting of" or "consisting essentially of" are exclusive or closed-ended.[62]

BODY OF THE CLAIM

The body of the claim follows the preamble and transition, sets forth the elements of the invention, and describes, as appropriate, each of the elements. With respect to the exemplary table claim discussed above, the body of the claim stated the elements of the invention (e.g. legs, surface, attachment) and provided some details with regard to the attachments and how they would be used to mount the legs to the surface, namely, in an orthogonal, downward direction.

From an infringement point of view, the body of the claim should contain the so called "meat" of the claim. The preamble and class should be no more than a bare-bones introduction, with the transition phrase leading to the body. But the body of the claim contains the actual limitations that define the scope of desired patent protection. It is here in the body that we define the metes and bounds of the claimed invention – the "fence" or "map" – and ultimately add value and substance to the claim.

Simply put, the limitations in the body helps keep everything in one place. Although this is the recommended practice, words or phrases may somehow creep into the preamble, adding ambiguity to the claim set (e.g. is the preamble now a limitation?).

What is claimed is:

1. Patent Class / Preamble + Transition Phrase:
    a. Body Element 1
    b. Body Element 2.

---

[61] M.P.E.P. § 2111.03.
[62] *Id.*

On a final note, some practitioners put a purpose or "whereby" or "such that" clause into the claim structure. Generally, the purpose of such a clause is to give the limitation some context (e.g. to aid in understanding the purpose of the limitation, etc.). For example, "machining the workpiece, <u>whereby chips are removed from the workpiece</u>, with at least one machining tool coming into direct contact with the lubricant and being lubricated by the lubricant, and the lubricant transforming from a solid to a liquid state during machining of the workpiece by the machining tool."[63] The whereby clause here is meant to give some explanation as to the purpose for "machining the workpiece." However, the courts will not give great weight to such a clause.[64]

Because a "whereby" clause is not afforded much, if any, weight, I would recommend not including them. On one hand, you may argue that a whereby clause may help to frame the claim set. On the other hand, adding a "whereby" clause adds additional language that may also add an additional element of ambiguity. The requirements for a claim and for a specification do not require that they be written in a typical lay person's terms. Nonetheless, the claims will be interpreted by a lay person jury member. The claims should be capable of being understood by a lay person regardless of whether a whereby clause is included. Again, the claims define the boundaries of patent protection. Thus, they should be drafted in a clear and concise manner without additional unnecessary phrases.

It is critical to note that although a "whereby" clause is not afforded much weight, a similarly sounding "wherein" clause is given legal weight. A wherein clause is meant to restrict or limit the claim in some manner.[65] For example, let's dissect a claim from USPN 7,698,711:

> 1. A multi-tasking method in a pocket-sized mobile communication device including an MP3 playing capability

The patent class here is process or method. The preamble here introduces a mobile communication device including an MP3 playing capability. Although the term "including" is an open phrase, this may be construed, in some cases, as limiting.

Next, we have:

> the multi-tasking method comprising:

This is the transition phrase linking the preamble to the body. Again note that "comprising" is an open transition phrase.

In addition, we have:

> generating a music background play object, wherein the music background play object includes an application module including at least one applet;"

---

[63] U.S.P.N. 6890131 (emphasis added).
[64] *See, e.g.,* M.P.E.P. § 2111.04.
[65] *See e.g.,* Griffin v. Bertina, 283 F.3d 1029, 1034 (Fed. Cir. 2002) (finding that a "wherein" clause limited a process claim where the clause gave "meaning and purpose to the manipulative steps"); M.P.E.P. § 2111.04.

Here, we have our first invention element dealing with a "generating" step. Notice that the generated object is being limited by a wherein clause which specifies what the object includes – an application module. The claim does contain other body elements, but for simplicity we will stop there.

In the body of the claim, each element may be indicated by a sub-number or letter (e.g. a, b, c, 1, 2, 3, etc.). However, this is not a requirement. Additionally, it is helpful to break up each of the elements by separating them onto separate lines. In this manner, the claim can easily be organized and visually grouped.

Elements are commonly introduced by using the article "a" or "an." When the element is referred to later on in the claim set, the article "the" is used to refer back to the original article. Having correct articles in the correct location is referred to as having proper antecedent basis. If a claim element does not have a proper antecedent basis, the claim may be subject to an indefiniteness rejection.[66] It is easy to avoid such a rejection, however, by simply reviewing the claim set before it is sent to the USPTO. I would add also that many patent software programs include an "antecedent" analysis to aid in the reviewing/editing process.

2. DEPENDENT CLAIM ANATOMY

Often, the more novel aspects of an invention are initially found in the dependent claims. Such claims incorporate each and every element enumerated in their respective parent claims – i.e. the claims they depend from – and then add in additional elements or limitations.[67]

From a strategy point of view, it may not be wise to put too many limitations in the independent claim to start with as this may unnecessarily limit the claim. For example, although very rare, the first claim set you submit to the USPTO may be allowed. Such may be an indication that perhaps the independent claim was overly limiting on the first time around.

Based on this reasoning, practitioners may not find the line or the best balance between desired and eligible patent protection until after the examiner performs a search of the prior art and the first office action is received. You can think of this as a border dispute. The competition may be located miles away. If your independent claim is too narrow starting out, the competition may still remain far away, leaving miles of unclaimed eligible patent protection between you. What you want, however, is to know precisely where the border is located. A broad independent claim may allow you more flexibility in defining the layout of the land and to establish where the existing borders are already located.[68]

---

[66] *See, e.g.,* 35 U.S.C. § 112 (second paragraph).
[67] *See, e.g.,* 37 C.F.R. § 1.75; M.P.E.P. § 608.01(i).
[68] Some practitioners prefer starting out with very broad independent claims. However, if the claims are too broad (not specific enough), you may end up spending more time and more of your client's money to narrow down the claims sufficiently. So, as in all things, a balance is necessary. Try to avoid writing overly broad claims, but put in enough details that it represents a good "starting point" to determine the layout of the land.

If the initial independent claims represent the base layout of our invention, the dependent claims may represent the more specific nuances or embodiments of our invention. Think of this in terms of how we wrote our specification. The "broad embodiment" may represent the starting point for our independent claim. Each of the more specific embodiments may represent the details which we can use to narrow the scope of the claim.

Let's go back to our table example, but now filter in (assuming proper Specification support, etc.) two dependent claims.

What is claimed is:

1. A table, which comprises:
    (a) a surface;
    (b) one or more support legs;
    (c) one or more attachments for attaching the one or more support legs to the surface, wherein the one or more support legs are mounted in a direction orthogonal to the surface and extend downwardly therefrom.

2. The table of claim 1, wherein the surface is in a rectangular shape.

3. The table of claim 1, wherein the one or more support legs include four support legs.

In the first dependent claim (claim 2), the dependent claim limits the surface of the table. In the second dependent claim (claim 3), the support legs are limited with regard to the number of legs. The point of these dependent claims is to put in limitations that will distinguish the invention from other prior art sources.

3. CLAIM DRAFTING METHODS

CENTRAL V. PERIPHERAL CLAIMING

Professor Fromer of Fordham Law School has taught one method for claim drafting, including labeling a claim as "central" or "peripheral" and "exemplar" or "characteristic". She explained that:

CHAPTER 2 37

To claim the set of things protected by an intellectual property right, one might be required to delineate to the public the set's bounds so that a third party could determine whether any particular embodiment is a set member thus protected by the right. This sort of claiming is known as peripheral claiming.[] Alternatively, one might publicly describe only some members of the set, which are clearly protected under the right, and use them to determine whether other items are similar enough to the enumerated members to fall also within the same right. This sort of claiming is known as central claiming, in that the rightsholder describes the central, or prototypical, set members, but the right tends to cover a broader, similar set of items.[] Central and peripheral claiming might be seen as two points on a spectrum of how many members of the set must be described by the claim, with peripheral claims describing more members than central ones[69]

To illustrate how these types of claiming may be applied, take a look at the following Figure on the next page. Notice that the central focuses on a very particular implementation, whereas the peripheral encompasses more than one form of the invention. Additionally, in writing out the claims, the central again gives a very specific implementation of the invention (e.g. an instrument made out of sterling silver), whereas the peripheral is very broad and general (e.g. an implement).

---

[69] Jeanne C. Fromer, "Claiming Intellectual Property," The University of Chicago Law Review, Vol. 76 (2009), available at
http://lawreview.uchicago.edu/sites/lawreview.uchicago.edu/files/uploads/76.2/76_2_Fromer.pdf.

	Central Claiming	Peripheral Claiming
Claiming by Exemplar []	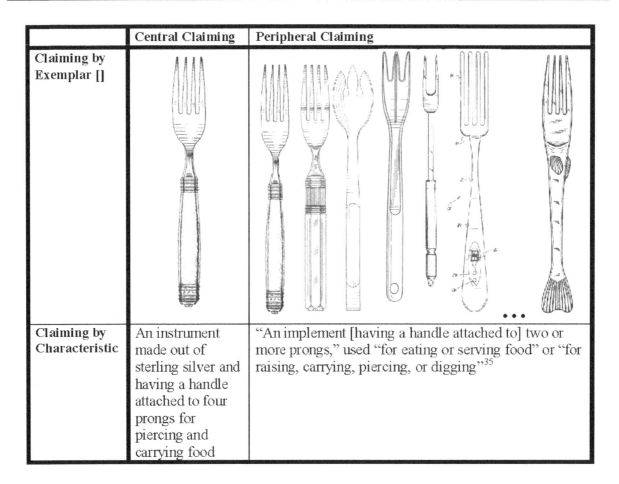	
Claiming by Characteristic	An instrument made out of sterling silver and having a handle attached to four prongs for piercing and carrying food	"An implement [having a handle attached to] two or more prongs," used "for eating or serving food" or "for raising, carrying, piercing, or digging"[35]

Additionally, Professor Fromer indicates that:

> There are thus two relevant dimensions on which claiming can vary: first, peripheral or central, and second, by exemplar or characteristic. To illustrate the four types of claims that can occur in this two-dimensional system, consider the claiming of the fork in Table 1. Pursuant to a system of peripheral claiming by exemplar, one would claim the set of forks by cataloging each possible fork in the set. In a system of central claiming by exemplar, by contrast, the set of forks might be claimed by enumerating at least one prototypical set member—here, one with four tines and some ornamental design on the handle. In either form of claiming by exemplar, the claim can be communicated using the actual work, drawings, writings, or other modes.[] The set of forks in a system of peripheral claiming by characteristic would be claimed by describing the characteristics that each member of the set must possess, namely: that it have a handle, that the handle be attached to two or more tines, and that the tines be used for holding and lifting food or other items in agriculture. Compare a system of central claiming by characteristic, in which the set of works is claimed by outlining the characteristics of a prototypical subset of forks in the set—here, that they be made out of silver, that the fork have a handle, that the handle be attached to four tines, and that the tines be used for holding and lifting food.

The method of ascertaining the extent of the set of protected embodiments, for evaluating validity or infringement, depends on the type of claiming. For peripheral claiming by exemplar, one can determine whether a particular embodiment is protected by observing whether the embodiment matches any claimed exemplar. Does the fork in question match a fork in the pictured set? For peripheral claiming by characteristic, one must decide whether the embodiment possesses the claimed features. Central claiming by exemplar requires divination of the essential features of each claimed exemplar, followed by a determination whether the embodiment is sufficiently similar in those features to a claimed exemplar. And with central claiming by characteristic, one must decide whether the embodiment is sufficiently similar in its features to those claimed.[][70]

I like these examples a lot. I think they are clear and to the point and help to illustrate the different ways in which a claim may be drafted.

Although all of this instruction may be great, the big question remains however, how do I construct a claim? As indicated in the prior subsection, look at the general class of the invention. This will help you get a sense of how the invention could be defined. I would then evaluate the purpose of the claim. Is it to protect a specific feature which needs to be clearly indicated, or is it to potentially be used for defensive or offensive work. Obviously, the strategy associated with patent application (e.g. core technology, market protection, defensive, offensive, etc.) come into play in deciding how the claim should be drafted.

D. RESPONDING TO 103 REJECTIONS PART I

> **KEY POINT**
> **OBVIOUS TEST**
>
> Is each and every limitation of the claim taught by more than one prior art sources in combination?
>
> ** NOTE: There are many other potential test and/or issues which may arise to obviousness, but this test is the most frequently used and argued.

---

[70] *Id.*

For 103 rejections, the focus is on whether in view of multiple (generally) prior art sources the claimed invention would be rendered obvious. As such, whereas for 102 rejections each and every limitation must be taught by a single art reference, a 103 rejection mandates that each and every limitation be taught in combination by multiple prior art references.

The short guidance therefore is how does a 102 rejection differ from a 103? Fundamentally, the analysis and process is the same – you look to see if the relied upon excerpt actually teaches the claim. The key difference is simply that rather than looking at one reference as in 102, in 103, you are looking at a combination of multiple references.

As far as how to strategize in responding to a 103 rejection (given that there's a host of potential issues that may creep up), it is good to first start with a basic framework. In prior editions of the M.P.E.P., the following teaching-suggestion-motivation ("TSM") test was given:

> "[t]o establish a prima facie case of obviousness, three basic criteria must be met. First, there must be some suggestion or motivation, either in the references themselves or in the knowledge generally available to one of ordinary skill in the art, to modify reference or to combine reference teachings. Second, there must be a reasonable expectation of success. Finally, the prior art reference (or references when combined) must teach or suggest all the claim limitations. The teaching or suggestion to make the claimed combination and the reasonable expectation of success must both be found in the prior art, and not based on applicant's disclosure.[71]

I would note upfront that the TSM test is no longer the standard test for obviousness.[72] Nonetheless, this standard TSM test is great because it breaks down the analysis into three distinct and separate inquiries that can be addressed by the practitioner. For this reason, many practitioners have continued to use this same test as it used to be applied.

To give you a slightly more full perspective, if we do not apply the TSM test, then we go back to the *Graham* case and apply what was indicated there. Unfortunately, although the *Graham* case is beneficial to stepping through the obviousness process, it does not set forth a clear test.[73] As such, although the TSM may not be standard test, it is at least *some* test that can be used to analyze the obviousness of the invention.

---

[71] M.P.E.P. § 2142-3 (8th ed.).
[72] *See, e.g., KSR Int'l Co. v. Teleflex, Inc.*, 550 U.S. 398 (2007) (rejecting the rigid TSM as the standard test).
[73] *See, e.g.,* "Responding to Post-KSR Obviousness Rejections before the USPTO—What Now?," Miller Matthais & Hull White Paper, last accessed 04/27/2013, available at http://www.millermatthiashull.com/inbrief/1/KSRWhitePaper.pdf.

In analyzing the first requirement, provide arguments that show that the art of record neither teaches nor suggest all of the limitations of the claim. Additionally, provide arguments that show that the Examiner has insufficiently shown the motivation to combine the listed prior art sources. Generally, arguments relating to this subsection are not typically given unless there the two art sources really are not synonymous. For example, prior art source A may deal with car alarms and source B deals with baby monitoring systems, and they are being combined to teach the claimed invention. Although there may be some overlap (e.g. both deal with some level of monitoring, etc.), the problems and issues faced in each of those subject areas may not necessarily be harmonious to teaching the claimed invention. In our above example, a problem/issue solved in the car alarm system (e.g. prevent break-ins, etc.) may be very different than a baby monitoring system (e.g. alert parent of baby activity, etc.). So look in the listed prior art sources to see if it actually makes sense to combine them.

Some general questions you can use in your analysis are:

1. Are the prior art sources in the same field (e.g. scientific expertise)?
2. What problem was each of the sources trying to solve?
3. Did the prior art source limit the possibility of doing a disclosed embodiment in a different manner (i.e. did the prior source give no indication to do it in a different manner, such as is disclosed in the second reference)?

The second Graham requirement deals with whether one reading the prior art sources would have a reasonable expectation of success in modifying/combining the references as proposed by the Examiner.

> Obviousness does not require absolute predictability, however, at least some degree of predictability is required. Evidence showing there was no reasonable expectation of success may support a conclusion of nonobviousness. In re Rinehart, 531 F.2d 1048, 189 USPQ 143 (CCPA 1976).[74]

Additionally, "[w]hether an art is predictable or whether the proposed modification or combination of the prior art has a reasonable expectation of success is determined at the time the invention was made."[75]

The third Graham requirement deals with whether the prior art sources teach all of the claimed limitations. This is usually the most straight forward of the three requirements. The M.P.E.P. explains:

> 'All words in a claim must be considered in judging the patentability of that claim against the prior art.' In re Wilson, 424 F.2d 1382, 1385, 165 USPQ 494, 496 (CCPA 1970). If an independent claim is nonobvious under 35 U.S.C. 103, then any claim depending therefrom is nonobvious. In re Fine, 837 F.2d 1071, 5 USPQ2d 1596 (Fed. Cir. 1988).[76]

---

[74] M.P.E.P. § 2143.02(II).
[75] M.P.E.P. § 2143.02(III).
[76] M.P.E.P. § 2143.03.

For example, prior art sources A and B may have been provided to teach elements X1-5. However, in analyzing your claim set, neither source A or source B provide element X4. As such, you can make arguments that simply show that neither prior art source teaches the claimed element.

A general outline may be something like:

> Examiner has rejected claim X (under 35 U.S.C. § 103(a)) for being unpatentable over REF[1], and further in view of REF[2].
>
> With respect to claim X, the following excerpts were relied on by the Examiner to make a prior art showing of applicant's claimed "[claim element]."
>
> [Provide prior art excepts that supposedly teach the element.]
>
> However, [excepts (as indicated above)] do not teach claim element X4.

Such an outline may not only be used with respect to the just the third requirement of the TSM test but potentially many of your other requirements (e.g. 102 test analysis, etc.) as well. Hopefully it gives you a general idea of how to structure your argument.

Usually, a 103 rejection can be expressly overcome by one of the following:

1. If the prior art reference does indeed teach all elements of the claims, then proceed forward with amending the claims to get around the prior art.

2. If the prior art reference does NOT teach all elements of the claims, then proceed forward with 1) putting forward arguments that rebut the rejection, and/or 2) putting forward additional amendments for the purposes of advancing prosecution.

E. REFERENCE MATERIAL FOR 103 REJECTIONS

Section 103 focuses on the obviousness of the invention. In showing this element, the Examiner is permitted to pull many references together to teach the claimed invention. Specifically, the M.P.E.P. provides:

> An invention that would have been obvious to a person of ordinary skill at the time of the invention is not patentable. See 35 U.S.C. 103(a). As reiterated by the Supreme Court in KSR, the framework for the objective analysis for determining obviousness under 35 U.S.C. 103 is stated in Graham v. John Deere Co., 383 U.S. 1, 148 USPQ 459 (1966). Obviousness is a question of law based on underlying factual inquiries. The factual inquiries enunciated by the Court are as follows:
>
> (A) Determining the scope and content of the prior art; and
> (B) Ascertaining the differences between the claimed invention and the prior art; and
> (C) Resolving the level of ordinary skill in the pertinent art.[77]

---
[77] M.P.E.P. § 2141(II).

The whole focus of 103 is whether the invention as a whole is simply obvious. If our invention was a chair in the cockpit of plane, would the prior art sources of a regular chair and a chair in a car be sufficient to show a cockpit chair? We won't resolve that question here. The point is simply that obviousness takes the invention and compares it to the known prior art, and then asks quite succinctly, "is it obvious." In summation, "[t]he proper analysis is whether the claimed invention would have been obvious to one of ordinary skill in the art after consideration of all the facts."[78]

In making this rather seemingly global determination, the M.P.E.P. indicated that "[f]actors other than the disclosures of the cited prior art may provide a basis for concluding that it would have been obvious to one of ordinary skill in the art to bridge the gap."[79] Further, one or more rationales may be used for obviousness, including:

> (A) Combining prior art elements according to known methods to yield predictable results;
> (B) Simple substitution of one known element for another to obtain predictable results;
> (C) Use of known technique to improve similar devices (methods, or products) in the same way;
> (D) Applying a known technique to a known device (method, or product) ready for improvement to yield predictable results;
> (E) "Obvious to try" – choosing from a finite number of identified, predictable solutions, with a reasonable expectation of success;
> (F) Known work in one field of endeavor may prompt variations of it for use in either the same field or a different one based on design incentives or other market forces if the variations are predictable to one of ordinary skill in the art;
> (G) Some teaching, suggestion, or motivation in the prior art that would have led one of ordinary skill to modify the prior art reference or to combine prior art reference teachings to arrive at the claimed invention.[80]

Additionally, it is helpful to remember who has the burden at this stage of prosecution:

> Once Office personnel have established the Graham factual findings and concluded that the claimed invention would have been obvious, the burden then shifts to the applicant to (A) show that the Office erred in these findings or (B) provide other evidence to show that the claimed subject matter would have been nonobvious. 37 CFR 1.111(b) requires applicant to distinctly and specifically point out the supposed errors in the Office's action and reply to every ground of objection and rejection in the Office action. The reply must present arguments pointing out the specific distinction believed to render the claims patentable over any applied references.

---

[78] M.P.E.P. § 2141(III).
[79] *Id.*
[80] M.P.E.P. § 2141(III).

> If an applicant disagrees with any factual findings by the Office, an effective traverse of a rejection based wholly or partially on such findings must include a reasoned statement explaining why the applicant believes the Office has erred substantively as to the factual findings. A mere statement or argument that the Office has not established a prima facie case of obviousness or that the Office's reliance on common knowledge is unsupported by documentary evidence will not be considered substantively adequate to rebut the rejection or an effective traverse of the rejection under 37 CFR 1.111(b). Office personnel addressing this situation may repeat the rejection made in the prior Office action and make the next Office action final. See M.P.E.P. § 706.07(a).[81]

If you are like me, the first I read through these requirements, I thought, "so the USPTO basically combines prior art sources and says 'looks obvious to me' and then the applicant can respond with 'nope, doesn't look obvious to me.'" One of the inherent features of obviousness is that there is some degree of subjectivity. What I see as obvious may not be what you see as obvious. For this precise reason, when dealing with 103 rejections, an objective point of view is used. This mythical objective viewpoint is known as "a person having ordinary skill in the art to which said subject matter pertains."[82] Commonly, a person having ordinary skill in the art is shortened to the acronym "POSITA" or "PHOSITA."

> The person of ordinary skill in the art is a hypothetical person who is presumed to have known the relevant art at the time of the invention. Factors that may be considered in determining the level of ordinary skill in the art may include: (1) "type of problems encountered in the art;" (2) "prior art solutions to those problems;" (3) "rapidity with which innovations are made;" (4) "sophistication of the technology; and" (5) "educational level of active workers in the field." In re GPAC, 57 F.3d 1573, 1579, 35 USPQ2d 1116, 1121 (Fed. Cir. 1995). " In a given case, every factor may not be present, and one or more factors may predominate." Id.. See also Custom Accessories, Inc. v. Jeffrey-Allan Industries, Inc., 807 F.2d 955, 962, 1 USPQ2d 1196, 1201 (Fed. Cir. 1986); Environmental Designs, Ltd. V. Union Oil Co., 713 F.2d 693, 696, 218 USPQ 865, 868 (Fed. Cir. 1983).[83]

So the arguments are not based on your perception or my perception of what is obvious but rather are based on the perception of a PHOSITA.

---

[81] M.P.E.P. § 2141(IV).
[82] 35 U.S.C. § 103(a).
[83] M.P.E.P. § 2141(II)(C).

CHAPTER 3
EXAMINERS, INTERVIEWS, 102 PART II

A. WORKING WITH PATENT EXAMINERS

I sometimes get the feeling from patent practitioners that they view themselves as the "good guy" trying to get an allowance for their client from the Examiner, the "bad guy." I would advise upfront that taking this approach has several disadvantages. For example, it is important to recognize – from the start – that both you and the Examiner are really on the same team. As a patent practitioner, you have the responsibility to draft claims relating to a new and novel invention. The Examiner has the responsibility of ensuring that such drafted claims are indeed new and novel.

Consider the patent prosecution process for a minute. If the Examiner did not provide some resistance to the process, the claims would be potentially ineffective. If the Examiner received the claim, failed to do a thorough search, and essentially said "look's good to me," how would this affect the actual patentability and future validity of our claims? For instance, if our claimed invention is litigated, it would be most likely tossed back into reexamination and may be heavily narrowed beyond the original scope of the claim. Therefore, in order to withstand the demands of litigation, the claims must be properly vetted and scrutinized. The value and strength of any patent depends on it.

Now put yourself into the Examiner's shoes. You are required to see whether this invention is indeed "novel" or "nonobvious" in view of all that has been created in the public domain. This is a pretty daunting task. What if you put in the wrong search terms, or failed to include all relevant search terms? And, on top of that, remember that you do not have days to spend on this but rather hours. Accordingly, you have to be extremely effective and efficient with your time, and somehow, determine whether the claims are indeed novel.

Having this background should help you as you correspond with the patent office. The more you can clearly indicate where the prior art is deficient (e.g. with respect to your claims, etc.), the easier you are making it on the Examiner. I know of some patent attorneys who schedule a telephonic meeting with the Examiner and prepare slides to be reviewed in real time by both parties. The patent attorney prepares a brief overview of the prior art cited by the Examiner and shows how the invention is different from the prior art.

Remember, the easier you can make the Examiner's job, the more effective the prosecution process will be. Some practitioners wish that the Examiner would simply indicate what is novel in the invention. However, that is not the responsibility of the Examiner. The Examiner analyzes the claims that you present and indicates whether they are new in view of the prior art. It is your job therefore to assess what is novel in your invention in view of the prior art.

1. GAME POINTS

There is obviously strategy associated with not narrowing the claims beyond what is required in the prior art. There are also strategies associated with interacting with the Examiner. Sometimes it simply doesn't make sense why the Examiner refuses to grant the allowance. But then you file a RCE and suddenly an allowance is given.

The Examiner is motivated by a workflow point system, with points allocated for different actions. Understanding how this system works may allow you to gain the strategic 'upper hand' – i.e. to maximize the Examiner's points and thereby potentially increase your chance of moving the application along.

The following chart is from a USPTO power point which provides point allocation for actions prior to 2010. Be aware that the point system changes from time to time, including some change implementing in 2010.

With the current system, 1.25 points are awarded when a first office action is sent out to the applicant, 0.25 points when a final office action is sent out, and 0.5 points when the action is disposed (e.g. allowed or abandoned, etc.). The combined points add to 2 total points per "balance disposal" ("BD").

As far as the strategy, consider the following examples:

> If an examiner issues a first action allowance, the examiner will be credited for 2.00 counts all at once. If the examiner allows a case in response to a reply to a first action, the examiner will be credited 0.75 counts. If a Request for Continued Examination (RCE) is filed by the Applicant after the final Office Action is issued, the examiner is credited for 0.50 counts for a disposal, may be further credited at the rate of 1.75 counts per BD, and then at the rate of 1.50 counts per BD when second and subsequent RCEs are filed thereafter.
>
> When you receive a courtesy telephone call from an examiner who, after waiting six months from when an Office Action was issued, is checking to see whether a response was filed or the case was abandoned, your confirmation of abandonment or the filing of an RCE will probably put a smile on the examiner's face, since he or she will be credited with half a count, (i.e., several hours worth of work). In addition, supervisors may actually redocket potentially abandoned applications from the dockets of examiners who left the USPTO to other examiners as "compensation" for performing tasks that they would typically not receive counts for, or for

KEY POINT
EXAMINER POINTS

The USPTO has set up an incentive program to reward examiners based on point allocation. In sum, examiners get points based on:

- First Office Action
- Final Office Action
- Disposal Action

Additionally, examiners receive points if a RCE is filed.

A few notes:

- Point allocation decreases as the number of actions increase
- No points are given for some pilot programs or for examiner interviews

applications that are very complex.[84]

If we took a myopic view and had an unlimited purse, we could simply focus on maximizing the Examiner's counts, which may aid pushing the application along to a grant. However, in all reality, you will most likely be under a budget and other constraints. Nonetheless, if at times you simply cannot understand why the Examiner is not allowing your claim set, consider the count system. Filing an RCE may help push it to grant, and increase the Examiner's points at the same time.

Revisions to Count System

Current Count System Original Case (Non-RCE)			1st RCE			2nd & Subsequent RCEs			Current Counts	
FAOM	Final	All/Abn	FAOM	Final	All/Abn	FAOM	Final	All/Abn		
1.00									2	Original
1.00	1.00									
1.00			1.00						2	1st RCE
1.00	1.00		1.00	1.00						
1.00			1.00			1.00			2	2nd & Subsequent RCEs
1.00	1.00		1.00	1.00		1.00	1.00			

Proposed Count System Original Case (Non-RCE)			1st RCE			2nd & Subsequent RCEs			Proposed Counts	
FAOM	Final	All/Abn	FAOM	Final	All/Abn	FAOM	Final	All/Abn		
1.25	0.25	0.5							2.00	Original
1.25	0.25	0.5	1.00	0.25	0.5				1.75	1st RCE
1.25	0.25	0.5	1.00	0.25	0.5	0.75	0.25	0.5	1.50	2nd & Subsequent RCEs

B. EXAMINER INTERVIEWS

Examiner interviews may occur at several times during the prosecution process. As the name implies, it is simply a conversation with the examiner which usually occurs by telephone.

Examiner interviews can be extremely effective. You can discuss prior art concerns, clarify misunderstandings, and resolve issues immediately. And, another benefit is that all of this conversation occurs essentially "off the record" which is great for promissory estoppel concerns because arguments cannot be used against you to narrow the meaning of a term or limitation.

Such interviews are additionally underutilized. I've talked to many practitioners over the years who have indicated that despite its effectiveness, many practitioners either do not conduct examiner interviews, or if they do so, they fail to conduct an effective interview. The point of this section is therefore how to conduct an effective examiner interview.

The M.P.E.P. gives the basis for the examiner interviews. Specifically, it provides:

---

[84] "The USPTO Count System," IP Frontline (Jan. 5, 2012), last accessed 04/20/2013, available at http://www.ipfrontline.com/depts/article.aspx?id=26194&deptid=2.

(1) Interviews with examiners concerning applications and other matters pending before the Office must be conducted on Office premises and within Office hours, as the respective examiners may designate. Interviews will not be permitted at any other time or place without the authority of the Director.

(2) An interview for the discussion of the patentability of a pending application will not occur before the first Office action, unless the application is a continuing or substitute application or the examiner determines that such an interview would advance prosecution of the application.

(3) The examiner may require that an interview be scheduled in advance.[85]

It is helpful to remember that an interview is not a right, it is a privilege. And as such, it must be requested of the examiner. At times, the Examiner may even request an interview with the applicant to discuss some matters. Normally, however, an interview is scheduled beforehand by the practitioner.

As far as techniques are concerned, I've broken them up into three sections: before the interview, during the interview, and after the interview.

<u>Before the Interview</u>

As with an inventor disclosure, preparation for the interview is key. Although not required (and even at times not requested by the Examiner), a good practice is to submit an agenda for the interview. The point of the agenda is to focus the discussion on the most needed topics. This is helpful for the applicant because it helps to clarify the items of misunderstanding. Additionally, this is helpful for the Examiner as they can then be prepared to discuss such topics.

KEY POINT INTERVIEWS

Keep the following in mind in relation to interviews with examiners:

- Be respectful of their time. Remember they do not get points for meeting with you.

- Have a strategy on moving the case forward.

- Submit an agenda BEFORE the interview

- Submit a summary immediately AFTER the interview, including the agenda as an appendix.

- Attitude counts. Stand in the examiner's shoes. Try to understand his/her position.

---

[85] 37 C.F.R. § 1.333(a); *see also* M.P.E.P. § 713.

This is additionally helpful because it indicates who should be present at the interview. For example, if the items to be discussed are solely legal or procedural issues, then the attorney or agent may only need to be present. On the other hand, if the topics to be discussed relate to the technology and complex technical issues, then it may be appropriate to have the inventor along with you. This may be particularly useful when the interview occurs before the first office action and a purpose of the interview is to educate the Examiner on the invention.

Be aware though that having an inventor along with you may also be a downside. For example, anything that they say may be used against them – and they may not even realize that they are saying potentially limiting things. So if the inventor does come along with you, prep the inventor so that he/she only speaks about very specific matters.[86] In such cases, therefore, it may be appropriate to prep the inventor on what items can be discussed.

The Interview Request Form (PTOL-413A) may be used not only to request an interview but also to provide the agenda for the meeting (see next page). Additionally, however, a separate agenda may be submitted to the Examiner. Keep in mind that such an agenda may be added to the file wrapper at the Examiner's discretion (and possibly cause prosecution history estoppel issues). In view of this, keep your agenda to the point, with the issues clearly indicated, and avoid making any further statements.

As an alternative, many Examiners are open to receiving calls to set up an Examiner interview. If you send the Examiner anything (such as an agenda with claim amendments), make sure that you grant approval using the "AUTHORIZATION FOR INTERNET COMMUNICATIONS IN A PATENT APPLICATION OR REQUEST TO WITHDRAW AUTHORIZATION FOR INTERNET COMMUNICATIONS" form.[87]

---

[86] *See, e.g.,* Sheetal S. Patel, "How to Prepare for, Conduct and Conclude Examiner Interviews," Found Persuasive Blog, last accessed 05/01/2013, available at
http://www.foundpersuasive.com/examiner_interview_article.aspx.
[87] USPTO form PTO/SB/439 (11-15), available at
https://www.uspto.gov/sites/default/files/documents/sb0439.pdf *l*

Doc Code: M865 or FAI.REQ.INTV

PTOL-413A (10-09)
Approved for use through 07/31/2012. OMB 0651-0031
U.S. Patent and Trademark Office: U.S. DEPARTMENT OF COMMERCE

Applicant Initiated Interview Request Form

Application No.: _____ First Named Applicant: _____
Examiner: _____ Art Unit: _____ Status of Application: _____

Tentative Participants:
(1) _____ (2) _____

(3) _____ (4) _____

Proposed Date of Interview: _____ Proposed Time: _____ (AM/PM)

Type of Interview Requested:
(1) [ ] Telephonic (2) [ ] Personal (3) [ ] Video Conference

Exhibit To Be Shown or Demonstrated: [ ] YES [ ] NO
If yes, provide brief description: _____

Issues To Be Discussed

Issues (Rej., Obj., etc)	Claims/ Fig. #s	Prior Art	Discussed	Agreed	Not Agreed
(1) _____	_____	_____	[ ]	[ ]	[ ]
(2) _____	_____	_____	[ ]	[ ]	[ ]
(3) _____	_____	_____	[ ]	[ ]	[ ]
(4) _____	_____	_____	[ ]	[ ]	[ ]

[ ] Continuation Sheet Attached
[ ] Proposed Amendment or Arguments Attached
Brief Description of Arguments to be Presented:
_____
_____
_____

An interview was conducted on the above-identified application on _____.
NOTE: This form should be completed by applicant and submitted to the examiner in advance of the interview (see MPEP § 713.01).
This application will not be delayed from issue because of applicant's failure to submit a written record of this interview. Therefore, applicant is advised to file a statement of the substance of this interview (37 CFR 1.133(b)) as soon as possible.

_____   _____
Applicant/Applicant's Representative Signature   Examiner/SPE Signature

_____
Typed/Printed Name of Applicant or Representative

_____
Registration Number, if applicable

This collection of information is required by 37 CFR 1.133. The information is required to obtain or retain a benefit by the public which is to file (and by the USPTO to process) an application. Confidentiality is governed by 35 U.S.C. 122 and 37 CFR 1.11 and 1.14. This collection is estimated to take 21 minutes to complete, including gathering, preparing, and submitting the completed application form to the USPTO. Time will vary depending upon the individual case. Any comments on the amount of time you require to complete this form and/or suggestions for reducing this burden, should be sent to the Chief Information Officer, U.S. Patent and Trademark Office, U.S. Department of Commerce, P.O. Box 1450, Alexandria, VA 22313-1450. DO NOT SEND FEES OR COMPLETED FORMS TO THIS ADDRESS. SEND TO: Commissioner for Patents, P.O. Box 1450, Alexandria, VA 22313-1450.
If you need assistance in completing the form, call 1-800-PTO-9199 and select option 2.

Applicant Initiated Interview Request Form[88]

<u>During the Interview</u>

As you start the interview, stick to the agenda. One good way to open the interview is to discuss what the invention is. This many times can then lead into a discussion of how the prior art (or whatever the issues are that you identified) is different from the invention.

Although talking about the broad overview of the invention may be helpful, keep in mind that what you should really focus on is the invention *as claimed*. As such, your remarks should give a quick global view of the invention but then dive into the specific limitations of the invention and how such limitations are not being taught by the prior art.

I've heard often that one of the things that Examiners do not like to hear is "what needs to be added in order to get the claim allowed." In essence, you are asking the Examiner to do your job for you. So an alternative would be to come prepared with one or two limitations that you can propose to the Examiner to help push the claim to allowance. In some instances, the Examiner may propose some additional language that may push the claim to allowance.

Additionally, it is good to focus on what you both agree on rather than simply those things that you disagree over. As such, it may be beneficial during your interview to use the phrase, "Do you agree that..." as it may help for you both to discover where you are on the same page and where the source of the disagreement really lies.[89]

Towards the end of the interview, it may be good to summarize what you agree on and the things that were accomplished. In some instances, no agreement may be reached. Nonetheless, even if an agreement was not immediately reached, it may have helped to clarify your position and the Examiner's position.

After the Interview

An interview summary paper is filed after the interview to record what was discussed. Normally, an applicant interview summary and an Examiner interview summary are both submitted following the interview.

With the Examiner interview summary, the practitioner should review it before it goes on record. The point of this is to ensure that nothing is in writing which may be construed as limiting (in view of prosecution history estoppel).

With the applicant interview summary, the practitioner may file the interview summary as a separate document, or it may be filed as part of the response to an office action. Although no formal requirements exist for the document, usually it includes the following items:

- Date of the interview
- Names of those who attended
- Interview in person or by telephone or by video conference

---

[88] Form PTOL-413A, USPTO, available at http://www.uspto.gov/web/forms/PTOL413A.pdf.
[89] *See, e.g.,* "Best Practices for Conducting Examiner Interviews," Nutter Legal Update (Nov. 15, 2012), last accessed 05/01/2013, available at http://www.nutter.com/Best-Practices-for-Conducting-Examiner-Interviews-11-15-2012/.

- Was an agreement reached?
- Was an allowable subject matter identified?

Although other items may be included, remember that anything that is stated is going on record. So keep things brief and to the point.

Conclusion

Examiner interview can be very time effective. Correspondence with the Patent Office can be long and drawn out. A live interview allows you to potentially cover much ground rather than simply arguing back and forth in writing. If you come prepared to discuss and work with the Examiner, you may find that they can be very efficient and cost effective prosecution strategy.

C. RESPONDING TO 102 REJECTIONS PART II

It is recommended while reviewing this section that the student also review the Master Argument Document used with the IP Clinic for further examples and templates that can be implemented for this type of rejection.

Typically, 102 rejections are fairly cut and dry type responses. Either the reference does teach or it doesn't teach the claim. That being said, there are a few peripheral subjects to be aware of. Although there are other subjects which may appear for 102 novelty, the ones below are the more frequent side-issues to pop up.

Inherency

102 novelty requires that each limitation be shown in a single reference. If not all limitations are shown, the Examiner may rely on an inherency argument that such feature is "inherently" part of the prior art. In response, you can provide arguments on how not every feature of the claimed invention is being met by the prior art reference.

No Reasoning

The Examiner has the burden of putting forth, in complete detail, how each and every claim element is shown by the cited art. Often, the Examiner may apply globally the entire reference to the claim or the limitations without specifically pointing out in detail how each feature is being met by the prior art.

Not Prior Art

The prior art must qualify as prior art to be valid. A good habit to get into is to double check to verify if the prior art is indeed prior art. It sounds almost too banal for this to even be mentioned. That being said, I've seen instances where the prior art supplied was filed _after_ the priority date of the application, in which case, the prior art is in fact not prior art and cannot be relied upon by the Examiner. Other potential topics that may arise include:

- Whether the prior art is a publication of applicant's own invention. Remember that there are some potential exceptions which might apply if the prior art originates from the same inventor.

- Whether the prior art is not publicly available. If it was not publicly available, it may not qualify as prior art.

Misconstruction of a Claim Element

Misunderstandings, like many other parts of life, arise also in the prosecution context. The Examiner simply may not have correctly interpreted the claim language. If such is the case, a phone call (or Examiner's Interview) may assist in their understanding. Sometimes, the claim language may be amended to more clearly show how the claim or limitation is to be interpreted.

Misconstruction of the Asserted Reference

Misunderstanding may also apply to the prior art reference. The Examiner may feel a certain art reference teaches a particular subject matter. In all reality, however, it may not. You can right the wrong by, again, bringing it to the Examiner's attention. That being said, be tactful in stating that the prior art was incorrectly interpreted. Such could be construed as a type of "slap in the face" to the Examiner – and you want to avoid causing offense. I'd also note that these types of issues often are the basis for appeals – where the Examiner maintains a prior art reference does teach X, and the applicant asserts it does not teach X.

CHAPTER 4
CLAIM AMENDMENTS PART II, 103 PART II

A. CLAIM AMENDMENTS PART II

Claim Amendments Part I focused on some of the substantive type considerations. The present section focuses on the some of the mechanics of claim amendments.

Claim Status

Each claim should include (in parenthesis) an indication of the status of the claim. Such status should be one of: (Original), (Currently amended), (Canceled), (Withdrawn), (Previously presented), (New), and (Not entered).[90]

Claim Markings

The text of any added material is shown by underlining the added text (example). Deleted text is shown via strike-through (example) if the deleted text is more than 5 characters. If less than 5 characters, deleted text is shown via double brackets before and after the characters ([[examp]]).

Claim markings should only be shown for those claims having the status of "currently amended" or "withdrawn".

Claim Numbering

Claim numbers are not reused during prosecution, even if a claim is canceled and a subsequent new claim is added. The canceled claim simply includes a status identifier of "Canceled". The new claim would be appended to the end of the claim set and receive the next consecutive number (the next number after the formerly last claim in the claim set).

Note that once a claim set issues, the USPTO will renumber all of the claims (into a consecutive claim numbering) of all claims that have been allowed.

Claim Grouping

Typically (although not a strict requirement), a dependent claim should be located (in the claim set) within a first order of the parent claim. In lay man's terms, what this means is that no other independent claim should be located between the parent independent claim and the dependent claim. Quick example – if dependent Claim 14 relies upon independent Claim 1, then no other independent Claim should exist between Claims 1 and 14.

Realistically, this often does not work, particularly when amendments are added on during prosecution. For example, in response to prior art A, you might add on new dependent claims 21-24 stemming from Claim 1, despite the fact that independent Claims 1, 19, and 20 already exist.

---

[90] For more information, look at 37 CFR 1.121(c)

Simply recognize that the USPTO has indicated this as the model to follow.[91]

Antecedent Basis

Whenever you introduce a term for the first time, it should be preceded immediately by "a" or "an." After introducing the term, it is later referenced in dependent claims (or in other parts of the independent claim set) by including a "the" immediately before the term. For example, if you had the term "a first oscillator" in the claim set, any time "first oscillator" is referenced thereafter, it would be "the first oscillator."

Recognize that much can be said about antecedent basis. As with any rule almost, there are a few exceptions. For example, an indefinite article (such as "a" or "an") should not be included if the first reference to an element is plural or is a substance. For example, "chopping 6 celery sticks; and adding THE 6 celery sticks to the stuffing" or "adding butane to a first canister; and water vapor to THE butane."

Word Choice

When claiming a grouping of items, keep in mind the following:

- Consisting of /composed of: these phrases indicate that no more and no less of the following elements. In practical terms, if you indicate "a seat consisting of two layers of foam", the limitation will be construed as ONLY having two layers of foam. This is known as closed transition term.

- Comprising: this word indicates that the following elements may be included but does not exclude others. In practical terms, if you indicate "a seat comprising two layers of foam", the limitation will construed as having two layers of foam, but anything more than two layers may also be applicable. This is known as an open transition term.

As a side note, recognize that "comprising" is generally the preferred word to use (especially when compared to use of "consisting of."

B. RESPONDING TO 103 REJECTIONS PART II

It is recommended while reviewing this section that the student also review the Master Argument Document used with the IP Clinic for further examples and templates that can be implemented for this type of rejection.

There are many arguments that potentially may apply to 103 obviousness. Each of the following are very particular arguments which may be applicable to the office action rejection. Note that most if not all of these arguments will not come up in every office action. They are included here so that you are aware of some of the issues which may be raised.

---

[91] MPEP 608.01(n)

Before analyzing such arguments, it is good to take a step back and recognize that there is often a great team of individuals you work with when responding to a rejection. First, you have the client/inventor who is often a great resource. Call the client to discuss the rejection. Often, such individual may be aware of a nuance between the prior art and the claimed invention. Second, as you get experience in formulating strategies, consider touching base with someone who does have more experience. Last, a good reference point when creating a strategy is to look at the 103 rejection neutrally and dispassionately and to ask yourself how the Patent and Trademark Appeal Board would analyze such arguments. Usually, after studying the rejection and conducting such an analysis, it is clear what arguments can be made (or potentially what course of action, such as amending, abandoning) should be taken.

Unfit for Intended Purpose

This section may be used to argue an improper rationale for combining references.

Combining references A and B renders reference A unfit for its intended purpose. This is based on the case *In re Gordon* (733 F.2d 900, 221 USPQ 1125 (Fed. Cir. 1984)) where a blood filter assembly was claimed. The prior art disclosed was applied in an upwards-down configuration to meet the limitations in the claim. On appeal, the Court confirmed that to turn the prior art reference upside down would render the invention inoperable for its intended purpose. In other words, the apparatus would no longer function as intended.

No Reason to Combine

This section may be used to argue an improper rationale for combining references.

Generally, references A and B are taken from the same general technological background. For example, the invention may relate to electrical circuits, and reference A relates to circuit design and reference B relates to electronic conductivity. Sometimes, however, there may be no motivation to actually combine the two references. For example, as an exaggerated example, a first reference may relate to swimming pool technology, and the second reference may relate to biomedical assay work. In all likelihood, the two likely do not relate to the same technology. Such nuances are likely not as easily seen between references within the same art group. However, if one reference is solving a problem using aspect A, and the second reference is solving the same problem using aspect B, that would be another scenario where it likely doesn't make sense to combine them (as one took one direction and the other took a different direction). The main question to ask for this section is whether the combination of the references make sense. If not, then there is likely not a reason to combine the references.

Teaching Away

This section may be used to argue inapplicability of the reference(s) to the claim.

When references are combined, the combination is intended to teach all the elements of the claim. Sometimes, a reference may in fact teach away from (rather than supporting) the claim. A recent case, *Meiresonne v. Google, Inc.* (Fed. Cir. Mar. 7, 2017), indicated that "A reference teaches away "when a person of ordinary skill, upon reading the reference, would be discouraged from following the path set out in the reference, or would be led in a direction divergent from the path that was taken" in the claim. Galderma Labs., L.P. v. Tolmar, Inc., 737 F.3d 731, 738 (Fed. Cir. 2013)." As such, courts are often looking to whether the references discourage a person of ordinary skill in the art from making the combination of such art.

Impermissible Hindsight

This section may be used to argue an improper rationale for combining references. Note that impermissible hindsight may be used as the basis for other arguments. It surfaces generally in relation to the motivation to combine the references (i.e. the Examiner is relying on impermissible hindsight to combine references).

The Examiner is not allowed to use information gleaned from the applicant's application as a basis for obviousness. All of the facts (and rationale) for obviousness must be found in the prior art.

Insufficient Rationale

This section may be used to argue that the prima facie case of obviousness has not been met.

The Applicant is not required to "guess" on the position taken by the USPTO. If an appropriate rationale is not provided in the substantive action, then the Examiner has not satisfied their burden. If such is the case, you can request another office action be sent with proper rationale.

Official Notice

The standard for asserting Official Notice are very strict. As such, this section may be used to argue that such standard has not been met.

Official Notice is simply where the Examiner relies on a general "obvious" basis for rejecting a limitation, without providing a proper basis. In a legal sense, a court may take official notice on <u>very</u> objective (completely undisputed) facts, such as whether a full moon was present on a particular night, or economic conditions during a specific time period.

If an Examiner improperly provides an official notice, this is an objective basis for arguing (rather than subjective). If they rely on official notice for a fact which may <u>not</u> be completely undisputed, then that is something that should be responded to in a response.

Consider applying the following example template:

In addition, with respect to Claim XXXXXX, the Examiner has simply dismissed the same under Official Notice. Specifically, the Examiner has stated that it would have been obvious for one of ordinary skill in the art at the time the invention was made to "XXXXXX." Applicant respectfully disagrees. In particular, applicant respectfully asserts that XXXXXX.

Therefore, applicant has adequately traversed the Examiner's assertion of obviousness, and thus formally requests a specific showing of the subject matter in ALL of the claims in any future action. Note excerpts from MPEP below.

> "It is never appropriate to rely solely on common knowledge in the art without evidentiary support in the record as the principal evidence upon which a rejection was based." See MPEP 2144.03(E), as well as *Zurko*, 258 F.3d at 1386, 59 USPQ2d at 1697; *Ahlert*, 424 F.2d at 1092, 165 USPQ 421.

> "If the applicant traverses such an [Official Notice] assertion the examiner should cite a reference in support of his or her position." See MPEP 2144.03.

Secondary Considerations

This section may be used to argue against obviousness.

In reference to the Graham case, secondary considerations may be argued as evidence of non obviousness. In particular, such secondary considerations may include commercial success, long felt but unresolved needs, the failure of others, and unexpected results.

As a reminder, the Graham factors include:

(A) Determining the scope and content of the prior art;
(B) Ascertaining the differences between the claimed invention and the prior art; and
(C) Resolving the level of ordinary skill in the pertinent art.

See Graham v. John Deere Co., 383 U.S. 1, 148 USPQ 459 (1966).

Conclusion

There are many other narrow arguments that may apply. When in doubt, my recommendation is to google the MPEP for guidance on the requirements and burden the USPTO may satisfy. In particular, MPEP 2143 and 2145 contain explanations on the burden that must be satisfied, as well as possible arguments that the applicant may put forth.

CHAPTER 5
TYPES OF REJECTIONS, TERMINAL DISCLAIMERS, 101

A. TYPES OF REJECTIONS

1. NON-FINAL OFFICE ACTION

Typically, the first office action received is a non-final office action. In responding to such an action, the M.P.E.P. indicates that:

> (b) In order to be entitled to reconsideration or further examination, the applicant or patent owner must reply to the Office action. The reply by the applicant or patent owner must be reduced to a writing which distinctly and specifically points out the supposed errors in the examiner's action and must reply to every ground of objection and rejection in the prior Office action. The reply must present arguments pointing out the specific distinctions believed to render the claims, including any newly presented claims, patentable over any applied references. If the reply is with respect to an application, a request may be made that objections or requirements as to form not necessary to further consideration of the claims be held in abeyance until allowable subject matter is indicated. The applicant's or patent owner's reply must appear throughout to be a bona fide attempt to advance the application or the reexamination proceeding to final action. A general allegation that the claims define a patentable invention without specifically pointing out how the language of the claims patentably distinguishes them from the references does not comply with the requirements of this section.
>
> (c) In amending in reply to a rejection of claims in an application or patent under reexamination, the applicant or patent owner must clearly point out the patentable novelty which he or she thinks the claims present in view of the state of the art disclosed by the references cited or the objections made. The applicant or patent owner must also show how the amendments avoid such references or objections.[92]

So in responding to the non-final office action response, you must fully respond to the Examiner's arguments. Rather than responding to each claim individually, typically all of your independent claims will be grouped and rejected together. You can respond by arguing the appropriate claim limitation but indicating something like:

> "Claim XX requires [quote the "similar" language of the corresponding claim]. Accordingly, the rejection inherits the deficiencies of the rejection of claim 1 for reasons similar to those set forth above regarding the rejection of claim 1."

Or, you may simply include the language "see this or similar but not necessarily identical claim language in each of the independent claims." The second example may create some level of prosecution history estoppel as arguments made for one claim are applied and inherited to other claim sets as well.

---

[92] M.P.E.P. § 714.02; 37 C.F.R. § 1.111.

Additionally, it is not necessary to argue each and every dependent claim. Typically, a few dependent claims will be argued. But at the end of the arguments, stock language can be inserted similar to:

> Claims X1-X2 have been objected to as being dependent upon a rejected base claim. Such objection is deemed avoided by virtue of the arguments set forth herein.

In this manner, because the dependent claims stem from the independent claim, the arguments for the independent claims would inherently also apply to the dependent claims as well. Indeed, for obviousness rejections, there is case law that provides authority for this proposition. In particular, if an independent claim is nonobvious under 35 U.S.C. § 103, then any claim depending therefrom is nonobvious. *See In re Fine*, 837 F.2d 1071 (Fed. Cir. 1988).

2. FINAL OFFICE ACTION

In a perfect world, the Examiner will read your non-final office action response, be persuaded by your arguments and possible amendments, and grant the patent. Alas, 'tis not often the case. Usually, the Examiner may change slightly the arguments. But usually, if the Examiner is not persuaded by your arguments, a final office action will issue.

The M.P.E.P. gives some guidance on the reason for the final office action:

> Before final rejection is in order a clear issue should be developed between the examiner and applicant. To bring the prosecution to as speedy conclusion as possible and at the same time to deal justly by both the applicant and the public, the invention as disclosed and claimed should be thoroughly searched in the first action and the references fully applied; and in reply to this action the applicant should amend with a view to avoiding all the grounds of rejection and objection. Switching from one subject matter to another in the claims presented by applicant in successive amendments, or from one set of references to another by the examiner in rejecting in successive actions claims of substantially the same subject matter, will alike tend to defeat attaining the goal of reaching a clearly defined issue for an early termination, i.e., either an allowance of the application or a final rejection.[93]

Based on the direction from the M.P.E.P. , if the Examiner believes the practitioner is incorrect (i.e. the references do teach the claimed limitation, etc.), then a final office action may be issued.

You may be wondering what happens if the Examiner is persuaded by the arguments. In that case, there is a possibility that the claims may be allowed. Most likely, however, the Examiner will find a different prior art source and re-issue a non-final office action. The M.P.E.P. indicates when an improper finality:

> Under present practice, second or any subsequent actions on the merits shall be final, except where the examiner introduces a new ground of rejection that is neither necessitated by applicant's amendment of the claims, nor based on information submitted in an information disclosure statement filed during the period set forth in 37 CFR 1.97(c) with the fee set forth in 37 CFR 1.17(p).[94]

Additionally, as indicated in the paragraph, if the amendments made to the claims in your response caused the Examiner to issue a new grounds of rejection, then finality (e.g. issuing a final office action response) may be proper. The M.P.E.P. indicates that in such a case, the Examiner may provide the following paragraph.

> Applicant's amendment necessitated the new ground(s) of rejection presented in this Office action. Accordingly, THIS ACTION IS MADE FINAL. See M.P.E.P. § 706.07(a). Applicant is reminded of the extension of time policy as set forth in 37 CFR 1.136(a).[95]

In essence, therefore, if new grounds of rejection have been introduced (by the applicant), then a final office action may be proper.[96] A new grounds of rejection may include a new type of rejection (e.g. 102 rather than 103, etc.), a new prior art reference, or new facts or rationale for rejecting.[97]

---

[93] M.P.E.P. § 706.07.
[94] M.P.E.P. § 706.07(a).
[95] M.P.E.P. § 706.07(a) ¶7.40.
[96] For further arguments, *see, e.g.,* "Compact Prosecution and Cost Control: New Grounds of Rejection," Crawford Maunu Firm Publication, last accessed 04/30/2013, available at http://www.ip-firm.com/pdfs/1.pdf.
[97] *See, e.g.,* "Now What? Strategies for Responding to Final Office Actions," McDonnell Boehnen Hulbert & Berghoff LLP Firm Publication (3/19/2012), last accessed 04/30/2013, available for download at http://www.jdsupra.com/legalnews/now-what-strategies-for-responding-to-f-60871/.

An example is worth a thousand words. How do you respond to the Examiner to indicate that the finality is not proper? Consider the following template:

> The Office Action stated on page [PAGE NUMBER] that "Applicant's amendment necessitated the new ground(s) of rejection presented in this Office action. Accordingly, THIS ACTION IS MADE FINAL. See M.P.E.P. § 706.07(a)." [Note that this is boilerplate language used by the USPTO] However, Applicants did not submit any amendments in the previous Response. Rather, Applicants submitted arguments traversing the rejection of [CLAIMS] under [ART-BASED GROUNDS]. As such, the finality of the outstanding Office Action is improper.
>
> Applicants note that the section of the M.P.E.P. cited by the Office Action states that "second or any subsequent actions on the merits shall be final, except where the examiner introduces a new ground of rejection that is neither necessitated by applicant's amendment of the claims, nor based on information submitted in an information disclosure statement filed during the period set forth in 37 CFR 1.97(c) with the fee set forth in 37 CFR 1.17(p)" (M.P.E.P. § 706.07(a), emphasis added). In this case, newly cited document [NAME] was not submitted in an IDS. Further, per the above, no amendments were made to the claims. Thus, the rejection of claims [NUMBERS] under [GROUNDS] in the outstanding Office Action constitutes new grounds of rejection that were not necessitated by Applicants.
>
> Accordingly, it is respectfully submitted that the finality of the outstanding Office Action is improper and respectfully requested that the finality be withdrawn.[98]

If the final office action is indeed proper, then we go to the next step of what we can argue. Any amendment that occurs in the final office action response cannot necessitate a new search. Therefore, no new material can be added to the claims (i.e. cannot take support from the Specification and put it in the claim, etc.). However, amendments to the independent claim made may include previously reviewed dependent claims.

In the office action response, if a dependent claim has been allowed, then it is usually a straight forward matter of incorporating such a claim into the independent claims, assuming of course that such a course of action is consistent with your client's objectives.

If no dependent claim has been allowed, then the most likely option is essentially to persuasively argue that the prior art sources are not teaching the claimed limitation. On one hand, if your arguments are sound and solid, stick to them. The Examiner may have simply made a mistake. Even if after the final office action, if the Examiner still does not agree, you can then appeal the matter to have it reviewed.

---

[98] "Office Action Improperly Made Final," Found Persuasive Blog, last accessed 04/30/2013, available at http://www.foundpersuasive.com/improper_finality.aspx. Consider reviewing other templates also available on this site. It is a great resource.

On the other hand, if your arguments are not completely solid (or even if they are), another alternative is simply to put the claims in a better position for allowance. This may include distinguishing the prior art sources from the claims, or incorporating subject matter from the dependent claims into the independent claims.

3. FURTHER ACTIONS

Usually, after you file a final office action response, one of three things may occur: 1) nothing; 2) USPTO sends out an advisory action; or4 3) a notice of allowance. In the case where nothing occurs, make sure that you proactively take action to keep the patent application from going abandoned. Sometimes a practitioner will wait for an advisory action. Unfortunately, however, you may miss the statutory deadline while waiting. So be proactive.

The USPTO may issue an "advisory action" which usually is a brief reason as to why the Examiner does not agree with your reasoning in your final office action. An advisory action is not mandatory, so you may very well not receive one. If you try to reply to an advisory action, the only benefit would be to essentially put something on record in the file wrapper, as there is no statutory requirement to review any response to an advisory action. Note that in order to be eligible to receive an advisory action, a response to the final office action must be filed within two months.

B. TERMINAL DISCLAIMERS

A terminal disclaimer is a statement by the owner of a patent in which the owner gives up certain legal rights to a patent (or one to be granted). It typically surfaces when an owner has a first granted patent and then pursues additional claim coverage, which may overlap in some manner with the first granted patent. Based on the overlap, the Examiner may require a terminal disclaimer, or may indicate the additional claim coverage is allowed contingent upon a terminal disclaimer being filed against the first granted patent.

A terminal disclaimer will cause a later filled application to terminate at an earlier date. For example, if Patent A was filed first and granted and Patent B was filed later and granted with a terminal disclaimer, Patent B will expire at the same time as Patent A. Requiring a terminal disclaimer in appropriate circumstances coincides with the principle behind double patenting rejections, namely the prevention of allowing a patent to extend beyond the permitted 20 years.

In order to file a terminal disclaimer, the patents must be commonly owned, or subject to a joint research agreement. Additionally, the commonly owned must remain in effect for the life of the patent. In other words, going back to our prior example, Patent B would have to be commonly owned with Patent A (and potentially vice versa) to remain in effect. That may have a direct effect on licensing activities post-grant, for Patent A would always need to be sold along with Patent B (and vice versa). As such, a terminal disclaimer creates a literal binding between the linked assets.

C. RESPONDING TO 101 REJECTIONS

Section 101 deals with three types of potential rejections: double patenting, subject matter eligibility, and utility.

1. DOUBLE PATENTING

There are two flavors of double patenting: statutory and non-statutory obviousness. Statutory double patenting deals with preventing the same invention from being patented twice. Specifically, the M.P.E.P. indicates with reference to 35 U.S.C. 121 that "[i]f two or more independent and distinct inventions are claimed in one application, the Director may require the application to be restricted to one of the inventions."[99]

Additionally, the M.P.E.P. has indicated that:

> In determining whether a statutory basis for a double patenting rejection exists, the question to be asked is: Is the same invention being claimed twice? 35 U.S.C. 101 prevents two patents from issuing on the same invention. "Same invention" means identical subject matter...
>
> A reliable test for double patenting under 35 U.S.C. 101 is whether a claim in the application could be literally infringed without literally infringing a corresponding claim in the patent. In re Vogel, 422 F.2d 438, 164 USPQ 619 (CCPA 1970). Is there an embodiment of the invention that falls within the scope of one claim, but not the other? If there is such an embodiment, then identical subject matter is not defined by both claims and statutory double patenting would not exist. For example, the invention defined by a claim reciting a compound having a "halogen" substituent is not identical to or substantively the same as a claim reciting the same compound except having a "chlorine" substituent in place of the halogen because "halogen" is broader than "chlorine." On the other hand, claims may be differently worded and still define the same invention. Thus, a claim reciting a widget having a length of "36 inches" defines the same invention as a claim reciting the same widget having a length of "3 feet."[100]

In essence, this means that "if a claim in the first patent is identical to a claim of the second patent, no practice would infringe one claim without infringing the other," and "the second patent to issue is invalid."[101]

To overcome a proper rejection of this type, there is really only one course of action. You will need to amend the claims to show that a different invention is being claimed.

With respect to a non-statutory obviousness rejection, this requirement came about to prevent "the unjustified or improper timewise extension of the right to exclude granted by a patent."[102] Where a statutory rejection focused on whether the claimed inventions were identical, a non-statutory obviousness rejection focuses on whether the claimed inventions are patentably distinct.[103] Additionally,

---

[99] M.P.E.P. § 804.
[100] M.P.E.P. § 804(II)(A).
[101] Arnold Silverman, "Double Patenting—One Patent per Invention," JOM 48(6) (1996), p. 67.
[102] M.P.E.P. § 04(II)(B).
[103] See, e.g., David McEwing, "Double Patenting," Law Blog, last accessed 04/23/2013, available at http://www.houstoninternetlaw.com/patents/double-patenting.html.

[i]n determining whether a nonstatutory basis exists for a double patenting rejection, the first question to be asked is - does any claim in the application define an invention that is merely an obvious variation of an invention claimed in the patent? If the answer is yes, then an "obviousness-type" nonstatutory double patenting rejection may be appropriate. Obviousness-type double patenting requires rejection of an application claim when the claimed subject matter is not patentably distinct from the subject matter claimed in a commonly owned patent , or a non-commonly owned patent but subject to a joint research agreement as set forth in 35 U.S.C. 103(c)(2) and (3), when the issuance of a second patent would provide unjustified extension of the term of the right to exclude granted by a patent.

Interestingly, a non-statutory obviousness rejection is akin to a rejection based on the non-obviousness requirement of 35 U.S.C. § 103, except that "the patent principally underlying the double patenting rejection is not considered prior art."[104] Based on the similarities, nonetheless, the M.P.E.P. instructs that a factual inquiry, as will be discussed below with respect to a 103 rejection, includes:

> (A) Determine the scope and content of a patent claim relative to a claim in the application at issue;
> (B) Determine the differences between the scope and content of the patent claim as determined in (A) and the claim in the application at issue;
> (C) Determine the level of ordinary skill in the pertinent art; and
> (D) Evaluate any objective indicia of nonobviousness.[105]

KEY POINT
101 CONTEXT

Section 101 is a highly charged area of law, likely due to, at a minimum:

- lack of uniformity among courts (in deciding 101 actions)

- the *Alice* decision which reaffirmed the eligibility of software patents but which also introduced ambiguity as to which software inventions are patent eligible

- greater attention by the public at large who feel that the cause of patent trolling is insufficient patent eligibility requirements

Contrary to establishing a rejection under 35 U.S.C. § 103, a nonstatutory obviousness-type double patenting rejection involves analysis of merely the claims of the application and reference. In other words, a nonstatutory obviousness-type double patenting determination is solely based on whether the invention defined in a claim of an application would have been an obvious variation of the invention defined in the claim of the reference.

---

[104] M.P.E.P. § 04(II)(B)(1).
[105] *Id.*

In most situations, the likely recourse to such a rejection is simply to file a terminal disclaimer.[106] In some instances, another recourse would be to argue that one claim set is not obvious in view of another (i.e. do not file a terminal disclaimer). However, I would most likely only choose this route if a terminal disclaimer could not be filed, or if the rejection is blatantly incorrect.[107]

2. SUBJECT MATTER ELIGIBILITY

Patent eligibility is defined as:

> Whoever invents or discovers any new and useful process, machine, manufacture, or composition of matter, or any new and useful improvement thereof, may obtain a patent therefor, subject to the conditions and requirements of this title.[108]

The invention therefore must fall into one of four categories: process, machine, manufacture, or composition of matter and improvements thereof. Rather than construing explicitly what each of these terms mean, the Courts have rather defined at times what is not eligible, such as laws of nature (e.g. naturally occurring correlations, etc.), natural phenomena (e.g. wind, etc.), or abstract ideas (e.g. mental processes, etc.).[109]

In short, inventions that do not fall within one of the four eligible categories are not patent eligible. Further, even if an invention falls into one of the four eligible categories, the invention must not relate to one of the judicial exemptions indicated by the Courts.[110]

In making the determination of eligibility, the broadest interpretation of the claim is applied.[111] One of the most problematic issues with the four statutory categories deals with software patenting. *In re Nuijten* (on appeal) taught that although computer signals may be new and novel, they do not nonetheless fall into one of the four statutory categories, and are therefore not patent eligible.[112]

---

[106] *See, e.g.,* 37 C.F.R. § 1.321.
[107] *See, e.g.,* "Creative, but losing, arguments against obviousness-type double patenting," All Things Pro (Mar. 29, 2013), last accessed 04/23/2013, available at
http://allthingspros.blogspot.com/2013/03/board-appeal-double-patenting-losing.html (finding that arguments over obviousness-type double patenting generally are not effective).
[108] 35 U.S.C. § 101.
[109] *See, e.g.,* "Evaluating Subject Matter Eligibility Under 35 U.S.C. § 101: August 2012 Update," Slideshow Presentation, Office of Patent Legal Administration, USPTO, available at
http://www.uspto.gov/patents/law/exam/101_training_aug2012.pdf.
[110] *Id.*
[111] *Id.*
[112] *See, e.g.,* "In re Nuijten: Are Tangibility and Permanence Required For Patentability?," SheppardMullin Blog (Oct. 7, 2008), last accessed 04/23/2013, available at
http://www.intellectualpropertylawblog.com/archives/153544-print.html.

Computer readable media (that which is stores the software) has therefore been found to include signals *per se* unless defined otherwise in the application specification.[113] The USPTO has indicated that if the claims were amended to include "non-transitory" in the claim language that it would exclude the signal embodiment.[114] It should be noted that "non-transitory" is not the only way to get around a signal *per se* rejection. Nonetheless, it is one of the most frequently used amendments.

With respect to living organisms, they have always been patent ineligible. Nonetheless, "nonnaturally occurring, nonhuman multicellular living organisms, including animals"[115] are patent eligible. Additionally, engineered organisms are another example. With respect to a biological invention, an argument would need to be shown how the invention is not naturally occurring.

With respect to software inventions, recent years have caused an immense amount of scrutiny, ambiguity, and frustration on how to properly respond to subject-matter eligible rejections. The Supreme Court in the *Alice* decision reaffirmed that software generally was eligible for patent protection, but did not provide explicit guidance on what types of software inventions were valid.[116]

In view of such ambiguity, courts across the country have struggled on the proper tests to be applied in determining whether a software invention is valid. The USPTO has provided some guidance (in particular for the Examiners who likewise have also struggled as well). For example, in the USPTO's memorandum "Formulating a Subject Matter Eligibility Rejection and Evaluating the Applicant's Response to a Subject Matter Eligibility Rejection" ("Formulating Memo"), the USPTO has indicated that:

> "After determining what the applicant invented and establishing the broadest reasonable interpretation of the claimed invention, the eligibility of each claim should be evaluated as a whole using the two-step analysis detailed in the Interim Eligibility Guidance.
>
> When making the rejection, the Office action must provide an explanation as to why each claim is unpatentable, which must be sufficiently clear and specific to provide applicant sufficient notice of the reasons for ineligibility and enable the applicant to effectively respond."

Further, with respect to the first step of *Alice*, the USPTO's Interim Eligibility Guidance Sheet indicates that the rejection should:

> "identify the judicial exception by referring to what is recited (i.e., set forth or described) in the claim and explain why it is considered an exception;

---

[113] *See, e.g.,* "Evaluating Subject Matter Eligibility Under 35 U.S.C. § 101: August 2012 Update," Slideshow Presentation, Office of Patent Legal Administration, USPTO, available at http://www.uspto.gov/patents/law/exam/101_training_aug2012.pdf.
[114] *See, e.g.,* "Subject Matter Eligibility of Computer Readable Media," USPTO (Jan 27, 2010), available at http://www.uspto.gov/patents/law/notices/101_crm_20100127.pdf.
[115] M.P.E.P. § 2105.
[116] Alice Corp. v. CLS Bank International, 573 U.S. __, 134 S. Ct. 2347 (2014)

identify any additional elements (specifically point to claim features/limitations/steps) recited in the claim beyond the identified judicial exception; and

With respect to the second step of *Alice*, the Interim Eligibility Guidance Sheet indicates that the rejection should:

explain the reason(s) that the additional elements taken individually, and also taken as a combination, do not result in the claim as a whole amounting to significantly more than the judicial exception" (emphasis added).

In view of such, in responding to a 101 rejection, it is helpful to first analyze Step 1 of Alice:

Step 1 of *Alice*

The Examiner has indicated in relation to Claim XXXX that "XXXXXX." Specifically, the Examiner has relied on support from the XXXX court case to support the position that XXXX.

However, merely concluding that a "XXXXXX" is a "XXXXXX" fails to provide a reasoned rationale as to how such is a concept that the courts have identified as being an abstract idea.

You can then proceed to analyze Step 2 of Alice:

Step 2 of *Alice*

In the rejection, the Examiner has focuses on the first word of every limitation (e.g. XXXXXX, XXXXXX, etc.), which fails to specifically point out claim limitations (in their entirety) and how such claim limitations relate to a judicial exception.

The Examiner is reminded that in the USPTO "July 2015 Update: Subject Matter Eligibility" memo, the USPTO has taught that "courts have held computer-implemented processes to be significantly more than an abstract idea (and thus eligible), where generic computer components are able in combination to perform functions that are not merely generic", including, for example, "digital image processing...GUI for relocating obscured textual information...and ...rubber manufacturing." Further, "[t]he importance of considering the additional elements in combination was emphasized in examiner training" including, for example, "digital image processing...global positioning system...transmission of stock quote data...and ...rubber manufacturing[] illustrate how generic computer components that individually perform merely generic computer functions (e.g., a CPU that performs mathematical calculations or a clock that produces time data) are able in combination to perform functions that are not generic computer functions and that amount to significantly more."

Further, the USPTO has indicated in the "Recent Subject Matter Eligibility Decision Memorandum" (November 2, 2016) that "an "improvement in computer-related technology" is not limited to improvements in the operation of a computer or a computer network per se, but may also be claimed as a set of "rules" (basically mathematical relationships) that improve computer-related technology by allowing computer performance of a function not previously performable by a computer."

Further, concluding that the "dependent claims...stand rejected...based on the same rationale" fails to provide sufficient details as to how such a limitation relates to a judicial exception.

Here, applicant respectfully notes that the Claims amount to more than just a mere "generic computer to perform generic computer functions" as indicated by the Examiner. For example, the independent claims include, at a minimum, elements which are more than a mere generic recitation of computer components:

> XXXXXX

(emphasis added), all of which convey a method which is much more than merely a generic recitation of computer components.

As such, the claim language is much more than a generic recitation of components. Further, the specificity and complexity of the claims, individually and collectively, rise to a level above a mere "generic computer to perform generic computer functions." Therefore, since applicant's claim language is clearly not an abstract idea, and alternately includes unique functionality that constitutes more than an abstract idea, such language is statutory subject matter.

3. UTILITY

A separate 101 rejection may deal with the requirement that the invention be "useful."[117] In order to overcome such a rejection, the applicant must show that the invention has a utility which is specific, substantial, and credible:

> (i) A claimed invention must have a specific and substantial utility. This requirement excludes "throw-away," "insubstantial," or "nonspecific" utilities, such as the use of a complex invention as landfill, as a way of satisfying the utility requirement of 35 U.S.C. 101.
> (ii) Credibility is assessed from the perspective of one of ordinary skill in the art in view of the disclosure and any other evidence of record (e.g., test data, affidavits or declarations from experts in the art, patents or printed publications) that is probative of the applicant's assertions. An applicant need only provide one credible assertion of specific and substantial utility for each claimed invention to satisfy the utility requirement.[118]

---

[117] *See, e.g.,* 35 U.S.C. § 101.
[118] M.P.E.P. § 2107(II)(B)(1).

Additionally, "[a] 'specific utility' is specific to the subject matter claimed and can 'provide a well-defined and particular benefit to the public.' In re Fisher, 421 F.3d 1365, 1371, 76 USPQ2d 1225, 1230 (Fed. Cir. 2005)," whereas general utility "would be applicable to the broad class of the invention."[119] Further, "'to satisfy the 'substantial' utility requirement, an asserted use must show that the claimed invention has a significant and presently available benefit to the public.' Fisher, 421 F.3d at 1371, 76 USPQ2d at 1230."[120]

---

[119] M.P.E.P. § 2107.01(I)(A).
[120] M.P.E.P. § 2107.01(I)(B).

CHAPTER 6
INTERNATIONAL, SPEC/DRAWING AMENDMENTS, 112

A. INTERNATIONAL PROSECUTION CONSIDERATIONS

There is much that could be said on filing internationally. M.P.E.P. section 1800 alone is devoted to the PCT and its procedures. The point of this section therefore is not to give an exhaustive analysis of international procedures. Rather, the focus here is on some strategies that should be considered while filing and prosecuting patent applications.

First, recognize that there is not an international patent. The rights and privileges afforded by a patent are governed by national jurisdictions. Therefore, if you want rights in a country, you will need to get specific protection within the country. Additionally, each country tends to have its own laws and its own notions regarding intellectual property.

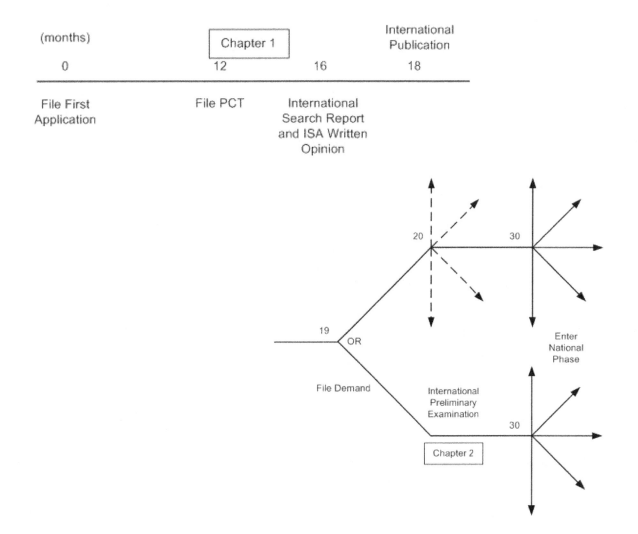

PCT System[121]

Second, the costs associated with filing internationally can be immense. Some of the reasons for this include translation costs, separate filing and maintenance costs, as well as the need to potentially engage foreign prosecuting firms. That being said, foreign jurisdictions are seeking to come up with alternative methods to reduce overall costs.[122]

Third, consider the timing of an international application. The following timing possibilities are just some of the ways a PCT application may be used:

- Option 1:
  o File a non-provisional patent application originally in the United Sates
  o File a PCT application within one year of the date of the original filing
  o Use the PCT as the vehicle to pursue protection in foreign countries
- Option 2:
  o File a provisional patent application originally in the United States
  o File a PCT application within one year of the date of the original filing
  o Use the PCT as the vehicle to pursue protection in the United States and in foreign countries
- Option 3:
  o File a provisional patent application originally in the United States
  o File a non-provisional application and a PCT application within one year of the date of the original filing
  o Use the PCT as the vehicle to pursue protection in foreign countries, and the non-provisional application to pursue protection within the United States

KEY POINT INTERNATIONAL

When considering whether to go international, keep the following in mind:

- Cost – they can quickly add up, particularly if any translation is needed
- Timing – at a minimum, a PCT application needs to be filed within one year of a filing (non provisional or provisional)
- Market – will the invention be implemented in a product sold overseas?
- Competition – where is the competition located?
- Recourse – if infringement occurs, what are the effects? What type of court, jury, damages, timing of such recourse?

---

[121] Based off of Figure 1842_1 in M.P.E.P. § 1842.
[122] Consider, e.g., the European Unitary Patent which would be valid in all European states. *See, e.g.*, "European Patent Office welcomes historic agreement on unitary patent," EPO News (Dec 11, 2012), last accessed 05/01/2013, available at http://www.epo.org/news-issues/news/2012/20121211.html.

CHAPTER 6

Of course, there are many other timing strategies that potentially could be implemented (e.g. file initially in a foreign country and use PCT to pursue protection in the US). However, these three options represent the most common timing strategies that are often implemented.

All of the foregoing considerations are important when you are evaluating whether to go internationally. However, a few strategy considerations should also be kept in mind. For example, choose your foreign markets carefully. What protection will be granted in the foreign jurisdiction? Where is the main competition located? Where do you expect your product to expand to?

Although timing alternatives are available, remember that a public disclosure of the invention may preclude patent protection in absolute novelty jurisdictions. That being said, most first-to-file systems employ a grace period similar to that which we have discussed in the United States. Nonetheless, you need to be very careful of public disclosure if you intend to file internationally.

Additionally, filing a PCT application may be strategically wise to test the market, as it does not have to enter the national phase for up to 30 months. So in the short run it may save money as you don't have to pay costs initially. It would also allow the applicant to determine after a set time whether to pursue national phase entry based on market conditions after a set time has passed.

Further, consider the amount of time and energy that may be required to enforce the patent rights. Although you may get lots of patents in many jurisdictions, is your client financially prepared to defend and assert patent protection in each of those jurisdictions? It may make more sense to get a few patents in a few key jurisdictions and not deplete the financial reserves so that the client can then be in a position to assert patent protection.

Although much more could be said on the subject, hopefully the above gave you a taste of international considerations. Know that international considerations are not just a legal theoretical exercise. In today's growing international market, a business needs to be aware of, and respond to, international IP options.

B. AMENDMENTS TO THE SPECIFICATION AND DRAWINGS

Generally, amendments to the Specification and/or drawings arise based on:

1. Applicant wanting typically to amend the Specification to correct for grammatical, punctuation, or other non-substantive errors; or

2. The Examiner requesting a change.

With respect to the Applicant taking action, most of the actions are non substantive, and therefore, generally without issue. However, one of the greatest issues that comes up to amending the Specification is with respect to correcting a claim to priority. Recognize that there are strict guidelines that must be satisfied in order to correct a claim to priority. Additionally, whereas a focus was made in the past to correct the claim to priority in the Specification, oftentimes, such change may occur now-a-days simply in a supplemental ADS filed to correct the claim to priority.

With respect to the Examiner requesting a change, such information would likely be contained within an office action rejection. For example, such issues may include:

1. A change to the title. The most frequent objection here is that the title is too generic. The Examiner may request that the title be changed to reflect more accurately the subject matter of the claims.

2. A correction to a figure item number (e.g. not being represented in the Specification) or some other deficiency.

3. A correction to the Figure. For example, the Examiner may indicate that the figure is not clear enough, or fail to show a specific detail that is described in the Specification and essential to an understanding of the invention.

To remedy a change to the Specification, include a section similar to the following example:

Amendments to the Specification:

Please amend the paragraph on lines X-X on page X, as follows:

Be sure to be <u>precise</u> in specifying the exact lines to be edited. Additionally, use the same mark-up techniques (e.g. underline, strike through) you would use otherwise in claims whenever you edit the Specification.

To remedy a change to the Figures, include a section in the response similar to the following example:

Amendments to the Drawings:

The Examiner has objected to the drawings. Such objection is deemed avoided by virtue of the replacement sheets submitted herewith.

Within the drawings themselves, if you edit a drawing and re-submit it, be sure to label the top of the drawing "REPLACEMENT SHEET".

C. RESPONDING TO 112 REJECTIONS

Typically, a 112 rejection relates to one of two

**KEY POINT
112 RESPONSE**

Some key take aways for 112:

- If the rejection is based on lack of support, show the support in the specification (including the drawings if needed). If support is not found, then amend your claims as appropriate.

- If the rejection is based on lack of clarity, consider amending the claim to clarify the particular term or phrase. If you feel such term/phrase is clear, provide factual reasoning as to how one skilled in the art would interpret such term/phrase. Be aware that such arguments would likely affect the claims if granted under prosecution history estoppel.

rationales:

1. failing to comply with the written description requirement; and/or

2. failing to particularly point out and distinctly claim the subject matter of the invention

With respect to the written description requirement, verify whether there is explicit support for the term or phrase within the Specification. If so, then you can respond by walking the Examiner through the specific excerpts from the Specification that show explicit support for such term or phrase. Keep in mind that the Specification includes also the Figures – and such term or phrase may have explicit support within the Figures (which may be especially useful if support is lacking within the written text).

With respect to distinctly claiming the subject matter of the invention, this usually arises if a specific term or phrase may cause confusion or ambiguity. As such, one option is simply to amend the claim to more specifically describe the term or phrase. If you feel the term or phrase is sufficiently clear, then you could apply the test of 112 of whether "those skilled in the art would understand what is claimed when the claim is read in light of the specification." *Orthokinetics, Inc. v. Safety Travel Chairs, Inc.*, 806 F.2d 1565, 1576, 1 USPQ2d 1081, 1088 (Fed. Cir. 1986). As such, you can put forth arguments on how one skilled in the art would read such term or phrase. Keep in mind that in such arguments are fact-dependent, meaning that in your rebuttal you would need to show facts showing the understanding of those skilled in the art.

As set forth in the following section, there are many more details and nuances that may arise within the context of 112 rejections, but the foregoing two rationales are the two you will most likely come across the most.

D. REFERENCE MATERIAL FOR 112 REJECTIONS

Section 112 deals generally with requirements of the Specification. Specifically, it provides:

> (a) In General.— The specification shall contain a written description of the invention, and of the manner and process of making and using it, in such full, clear, concise, and exact terms as to enable any person skilled in the art to which it pertains, or with which it is most nearly connected, to make and use the same, and shall set forth the best mode contemplated by the inventor or joint inventor of carrying out the invention.
>
> (b) Conclusion.— The specification shall conclude with one or more claims particularly pointing out and distinctly claiming the subject matter which the inventor or a joint inventor regards as the invention.
>
> (c) Form.— A claim may be written in independent or, if the nature of the case admits, in dependent or multiple dependent form.

(d) Reference in Dependent Forms.— Subject to subsection (e), a claim in dependent form shall contain a reference to a claim previously set forth and then specify a further limitation of the subject matter claimed. A claim in dependent form shall be construed to incorporate by reference all the limitations of the claim to which it refers.

(e) Reference in Multiple Dependent Form.— A claim in multiple dependent form shall contain a reference, in the alternative only, to more than one claim previously set forth and then specify a further limitation of the subject matter claimed. A multiple dependent claim shall not serve as a basis for any other multiple dependent claim. A multiple dependent claim shall be construed to incorporate by reference all the limitations of the particular claim in relation to which it is being considered.

(f) Element in Claim for a Combination.— An element in a claim for a combination may be expressed as a means or step for performing a specified function without the recital of structure, material, or acts in support thereof, and such claim shall be construed to cover the corresponding structure, material, or acts described in the specification and equivalents thereof.[123]

Usually, a 112 rejection relates to one of paragraphs 1-4. As such, each of these paragraphs will be analyzed separately.

1. PART (A)

The first subpart of section 112 deals with three aspects: written description, enablement, and best mode. To satisfy the written description, the Specification must clearly show the invention that is claimed. Keep in mind that no new matter can be added to the Specification after it is filed. As such, the written description must be sufficient on its own without any additional matter added to satisfy this requirement.

To argue this issue, the test to apply is one of possession: "a patent specification must describe the claimed invention in sufficient detail that one skilled in the art can reasonably conclude that the inventor had possession of the claimed invention."[124] Additionally, during prosecution, a claim may be amended and trigger a 112 paragraph 1 rejection. Usually, the issue is whether there was "adequate support" for the amendments in the Specification, or whether "new matter" was added by the Amendment.[125] In the case of adequate support, direct the Examiner to the specific provisions in the Specification where support is shown. Additionally, with respect to the "new matter" rejection, show support in the Specification where such matter is indicated. If the "new matter" is indeed new material, then it would need to be taken out as it would be in violation of 35 U.S.C. § 132.

---

[123] 35 U.S.C. § 112.
[124] M.P.E.P. § 2163(I).
[125] *Id.*

One additional thing to note is that the determination of whether a written description is sufficient is made on a case-by-case basis.[126] Additionally, there is a presumption that the description as filed is adequate until the Examiner presents evidence to the contrary.[127]

The test for enablement has been explained as such:

> Any analysis of whether a particular claim is supported by the disclosure in an application requires a determination of whether that disclosure, when filed, contained sufficient information regarding the subject matter of the claims as to enable one skilled in the pertinent art to make and use the claimed invention. The standard for determining whether the specification meets the enablement requirement was cast in the Supreme Court decision of Mineral Separation v. Hyde, 242 U.S. 261, 270 (1916) which postured the question: is the experimentation needed to practice the invention undue or unreasonable? That standard is still the one to be applied. In re Wands, 858 F.2d 731, 737, 8 USPQ2d 1400, 1404 (Fed. Cir. 1988).[128]

Additionally, "[t]he test of enablement is not whether any experimentation is necessary, but whether, if experimentation is necessary, it is undue. In re Angstadt, 537 F.2d 498, 504, 190 USPQ 214, 219 (CCPA 1976)."[129]

Determining whether experimentation is undue is a balancing test. The M.P.E.P. offered some factors for the Examiner to consider when making this determination:

> (A) The breadth of the claims;
> (B) The nature of the invention;
> (C) The state of the prior art;
> (D) The level of one of ordinary skill;
> (E) The level of predictability in the art;
> (F) The amount of direction provided by the inventor;
> (G) The existence of working examples; and
> (H) The quantity of experimentation needed to make or use the invention based on the content of the disclosure.[130]

Indeed, any enablement rejection requires the examiner to consider <u>all</u> of these factors. Failure to do so renders the rejection improper. To argue enablement, consider this strategy:

---

[126] *See e.g.,* In re Wertheim, 541 F.2d 257, 262 (CCPA 1976).
[127] *See, e.g.,* In re Marzocchi, 439 F.2d 220, 224 (CCPA 1971).
[128] M.P.E.P. § 2164.01.
[129] *Id.*
[130] M.P.E.P. § 2164.01(a).

Once the examiner has weighed all the evidence and established a reasonable basis to question the enablement provided for the claimed invention, the burden falls on applicant to present persuasive arguments, supported by suitable proofs where necessary, that one skilled in the art would be able to make and use the claimed invention using the application as a guide. In re Brandstadter, 484 F.2d 1395, 1406-07, 179 USPQ 286, 294 (CCPA 1973). The evidence provided by applicant need not be conclusive but merely convincing to one skilled in the art.[131]

Lastly, the best mode requirement requires the applicant to disclose the best way of carrying out the invention:

> The best mode requirement creates a statutory bargained-for-exchange by which a patentee obtains the right to exclude others from practicing the claimed invention for a certain time period, and the public receives knowledge of the preferred embodiments for practicing the claimed invention." Eli Lilly & Co. v. Barr Laboratories Inc., 251 F.3d 955, 963, 58 USPQ2d 1865, 1874 (Fed. Cir. 2001).

> The best mode requirement is a safeguard against the desire on the part of some people to obtain patent protection without making a full disclosure as required by the statute. The requirement does not permit inventors to disclose only what they know to be their second-best embodiment, while retaining the best for themselves. In re Nelson, 280 F.2d 172, 126 USPQ 242 (CCPA 1960).[132]

An inquiry into the best mode requirement is a two prong analysis:

> First, it must be determined whether, at the time the application was filed, the inventor possessed a best mode for practicing the invention. This is a subjective inquiry which focuses on the inventor's state of mind at the time of filing. Second, if the inventor did possess a best mode, it must be determined whether the written description disclosed the best mode such that a person skilled in the art could practice it. This is an objective inquiry, focusing on the scope of the claimed invention and the level of skill in the art. Eli Lilly & Co. v. Barr Laboratories Inc., 251 F.3d 955, 963, 58 USPQ2d 1865, 1874 (Fed. Cir. 2001).[133]

As with other parts of the paragraph, there is a presumption that the best mode is satisfied unless evidence is presented to the contrary.[134] Keep in mind that in order to satisfy the first prong of the best-mode requirement test, there must be some evidence showing the inventor had either purposefully concealed, or what was disclosed was so poor it effectively results in concealment.[135]

2. PART (B)

---

[131] M.P.E.P. § 2164.05.
[132] M.P.E.P. § 2165.
[133] *Id.*
[134] M.P.E.P. § 2165.03.
[135] *See, e.g.,* M.P.E.P. § 2165.04.

The point of the second subpart is to ensure that the boundaries of the patent are sufficiently clear. The reason for this is that if an invention was not clear, it would essentially not aid in fostering innovation and progress. Only when the metes and bounds of the claims are clearly disclosed can the public then be in a position to benefit from the disclosure and aid in fostering innovation.[136]

This paragraph sets forth two requirements to be met:

> (A) the claims must set forth the subject matter that applicants regard as their invention; and
>
> (B) the claims must particularly point out and distinctly define the metes and bounds of the subject matter that will be protected by the patent grant.[137]

The first requirement is subjective in nature as it is based on something the applicant views. The second requirement is objective in that it assesses whether the claims are definite (e.g. clear in scope, etc.).[138]

One of the clear teachings from this paragraph is that applicants are their own lexicographers. They can define claims in any manner as long as such meaning is clearly defined in the Specification.

The test for definiteness is as follows:

> The essential inquiry pertaining to this requirement is whether the claims set out and circumscribe a particular subject matter with a reasonable degree of clarity and particularity. Definiteness of claim language must be analyzed, not in a vacuum, but in light of:
>
> (A) The content of the particular application disclosure;
>
> (B) The teachings of the prior art; and
>
> (C) The claim interpretation that would be given by one possessing the ordinary level of skill in the pertinent art at the time the invention was made.[139]

Additionally, "[s]ome latitude in the manner of expression and the aptness of terms should be permitted even though the claim language is not as precise as the examiner might desire."[140]

In responding to a rejection under this paragraph, the M.P.E.P. gives some guidance:

---

[136] *See, e.g.,* M.P.E.P. § 2173.
[137] M.P.E.P. § 2171.
[138] *See id.*
[139] M.P.E.P. § 2173.02.
[140] *Id.*

the examiner should provide enough information in the Office action to permit applicant to make a meaningful response, as the indefiniteness rejection requires the applicant to explain or provide evidence as to why the claim language is not indefinite or amend the claim. For example, the examiner should point out the specific term or phrase that is indefinite, explain in detail why such term or phrase renders the metes and bounds of the claim scope unclear and, whenever practicable, indicate how the indefiniteness issues may be resolved to overcome the rejection.

As indicated, this rejection can be overcome by following the test as outlined above, as well as indicating why the term is not indefinite. Additionally, it may be appropriate to compare the definition in the Specification with a dictionary or other reliable source.[141]

As a last matter, recognize that in analyzing 112 second paragraph, such an analysis may invoke an analysis of the sixth paragraph as well (e.g. determine whether there is proper support for "means" or "function," etc.).[142]

3. PART (D)

The fourth subpart requires correct dependency. This is usually a straight forward matter to deal with:

> Where a claim in dependent form is not considered to be a proper dependent claim under 37 CFR 1.75(c), the examiner should object to such claim under 37 CFR 1.75(c) and require cancellation of such improper dependent claim or rewriting of such improper dependent claim in independent form. See Ex parte Porter, 25 USPQ2d 1144, 1147 (Bd. of Pat. App. & Inter. 1992) (A claim determined to be an improper dependent claim should be treated as a formal matter, in that the claim should be objected to and applicant should be required to cancel the claim (or replace the improper dependent claim with an independent claim) rather than treated by a rejection of the claim under 35 U.S.C. 112, fourth paragraph.). The applicant may thereupon amend the claims to place them in proper dependent form, or may redraft them as independent claims, upon payment of any necessary additional fee.[143]

More likely than not, such a rejection is easily overcome by amending the claims as appropriate. In like manner, paragraphs 3 and 5 are somewhat related to paragraph 4 in that it relates to the form (e.g. independent v dependent, etc.) and structure (e.g. base of stemming, dependency, etc.) of the claims.

---

[141] *See, e.g.,* 2173.05(a)(III).
[142] *See, e.g.,* 2173.01(II).
[143] M.P.E.P. § 608.01(n)(II).

CHAPTER 7
RESTRICTION, ALLOWABLE SUBJECT MATTER, NOA, APPEALS

A. RESTRICTION PRACTICE

Technically, a restriction requirement is not a formal rejection. It is the process of selecting the proper invention to be analyzed by the Examiner. Nonetheless, because restrictions occur at the beginning of the prosecution process, I have placed it here first under the rejection section.

Restriction is a codified requirement. It is found in 37 C.F.R. §1.142:

> (a) If two or more independent and distinct inventions are claimed in a single application, the examiner in an Office action will require the applicant in the reply to that action to elect an invention to which the claims will be restricted, this official action being called a requirement for restriction (also known as a requirement for division). Such requirement will normally be made before any action on the merits; however, it may be made at any time before final action.
>
> (b) Claims to the invention or inventions not elected, if not canceled, are nevertheless withdrawn from further consideration by the examiner by the election, subject however to reinstatement in the event the requirement for restriction is withdrawn or overruled.[144]

Additionally, the M.P.E.P. defines a restriction as:

> the practice of requiring an applicant to elect a single claimed invention (e.g., a combination or subcombination invention, a product or process invention, a species within a genus) for examination when two or more independent inventions and/or two or more distinct inventions are claimed in an application.[145]

The requirements of restriction provide two factors to be considered:

> (A) the reasons (as distinguished from the mere statement of conclusion) why each invention as claimed is either independent or distinct from the other(s); and
>
> (B) the reasons why there would be a serious burden on the examiner if restriction is not required, i.e., the reasons for insisting upon restriction therebetween as set forth in the following sections.[146]

With respect to the first factor, the term "independent" simply means no dependence.[147] Again, the M.P.E.P. clarifies that:

---

[144] 37 C.F.R. § 1.142.
[145] M.P.E.P. § 802.02.
[146] M.P.E.P. § 808.
[147] *See, e.g.,* M.P.E.P. § 802.01.

> [t]he term "independent" (i.e., unrelated) means that there is no disclosed relationship between the two or more inventions claimed, that is, they are unconnected in design, operation, and effect. For example, a process and an apparatus incapable of being used in practicing the process are independent inventions.[148]

With respect to "distinct," the test to be applied depends on the relationship between the different "inventions" identified by the Examiner. For example, "if the inventions are in different statutory categories, e.g., a process and an apparatus, then a one-way showing of distinctness is generally sufficient."[149] On the other hand, "if the inventions are related as combination/subcombination or as related products or processes, then a two-way showing of distinctness is required."[150]

To satisfy a two-way showing, three requirements must be met:

> (A) the inventions as claimed do not overlap in scope, i.e. are mutually exclusive;
>
> (B) the inventions as claimed are not obvious variants; and
>
> (C) the inventions as claimed are either not capable of use together or can have a materially different design, mode of operation, function, or effect.[151]

With respect to the second factor identified with restriction, "[i]f the search and examination of all the claims in an application can be made without serious burden, the examiner must examine them on the merits, even though they include claims to independent or distinct inventions."[152]

Assuming the Examiner has properly issued a restriction requirement (i.e. the Examiner has shown two-way distinctness and reasons for insisting on restriction)[153], the applicant may respond by "suggest[ing] an example of a different utility or an alternative process, apparatus, product, etc., to explain why the inventions are distinct."[154]

Additionally, if you decide to restrict your invention, you simply choose what invention you want to be evaluated. In fact, you must first elect an invention regardless of whether you intend to argue the merits of the restriction.

After you select an invention, you then choose whether you elect "with" or "without" traverse (i.e. argue the restriction). There are some potential benefits of either approach. If you elect with traverse, there is a chance you might win. Additionally, you preserve the "right to petition."

---

[148] M.P.E.P. § 802.01(I).
[149] "Crafting a Suggested Requirement for Restriction (SRR) Under Final Rule 142(c)," McCracken & Frank (Nov. 2007), last accessed 05/11/13, available at http://www.mccrackenfrank.com/srr.pdf.
[150] Id.
[151] M.P.E.P. § 806.05.
[152] M.P.E.P. § 803.
[153] See, e.g., M.P.E.P. § 808.02 (burden associated with the Examiner).
[154] Crafting a Suggested Requirement for Restriction (SRR) Under Final Rule 142(c)," McCracken & Frank (Nov. 2007), last accessed 05/11/13, available at http://www.mccrackenfrank.com/srr.pdf.

However, a petition is not the same as the ability to appeal a decision. With a petition, an Art Group leader reviews the matter to verify whether the restriction was necessary, most likely consulting the Supervisory Patent Examiner ("SPE") (the SPE usually manages many other Examiners). The SPE in turn discusses the matter with the Examiner who issued the restriction requirement. Although there is some chance the Examiner and SPE will determine that such a restriction was not proper, more often than not the original requirement will remain. In arguing, however, you have increased the fees and bills for your client, unless of course your arguments are found persuasive which may save fees as the client would not need to file another application.

In view of the foregoing, I'd recommend saving your restriction arguments for when the Examiner really does make a mistake (e.g. an invention should not have been split up, etc.). Rather than arguing at every opportunity, choose your battles wisely.[155]

If you choose to elect with traverse, consider the following requirements that the Examiner must satisfy for a restriction requirement:

> [T]he examiner, in order to establish reasons for insisting upon restriction, must explain why there would be a serious burden on the examiner if restriction is not required. Thus the examiner must show by appropriate explanation one of the following:
>
> (A) Separate classification thereof: This shows that each invention has attained recognition in the art as a separate subject for inventive effort, and also a separate field of search. Patents need not be cited to show separate classification.
>
> (B) A separate status in the art when they are classifiable together: Even though they are classified together, each invention can be shown to have formed a separate subject for inventive effort when the examiner can show a recognition of separate inventive effort by inventors. Separate status in the art may be shown by citing patents which are evidence of such separate status, and also of a separate field of search.
>
> (C) A different field of search: Where it is necessary to search for one of the inventions in a manner that is not likely to result in finding art pertinent to the other invention(s) (e.g., searching different classes/subclasses or electronic resources, or employing different search queries[)], a different field of search is shown, even though the two are classified together. The indicated different field of search must in fact be pertinent to the type of subject matter covered by the claims. Patents need not be cited to show different fields of search.[156]

---

[155] *See, e.g.,* Roger Bell, "Restriction Requirements," Blog (Oct. 21, 2007), last accessed 04/21/13, available at http://robertplattbell.blogspot.com/2007/10/restriction-requirements.html.
[156] M.P.E.P. § 808.02.

It should be noted that if you non-elected inventions are not lost. A divisional application can be submitted for each invention set, and must be submitted before the parent application issues as a patent. Moreover, these applications are shielded from double patenting rejections under 35 U.S.C. § 121, which we will discuss in further detail later.

B.   ALLOWABLE SUBJECT MATTER

Hooray! Once you have allowable subject matter, there is a path forward generally for the matter to be allowed and subsequently issued. When analyzing allowable subject matter, consider the following concepts:

1. Does the allowable subject matter overly restrict the invention as claimed?

2. What is the relationship with the Examiner? If you take action to amend or reject the allowed subject matter, does that have any influence on your ability to engage in further communication with the Examiner?

3. Can such allowable subject matter be leveraged in other pending applications? Sometimes, an Examiner may have several applications all from the same inventor and which relate to the same invention. In some instances, it may make sense to leverage the allowable subject matter from a first application and apply it to another application (to facilitate in moving such application along). This assumes claim diversity between the claim sets, as one would obviously not want to end up with simply two claim sets of nearly identical claims.

4. Do you have strong arguments for the claims as presently presented? If so, it may make sense to potentially still pursue such claims (and not take the allowance). As an alternative, to maintain a good relationship with the Examiner, another option would be to accept the allowable subject matter, but pursue the claims (as presently presented) via a continuation application to continue the prosecution process.

If you do accept such allowable subject matter, consider using the following template:

> Allowable Subject Matter
>
> The Examiner is thanked for the allowable subject matter of Claims XXXXXX-XXXXXX and XXXXXX. The Examiner has noted that such claims would be allowable if rewritten in independent form including all of the limitations of the base claim and any intervening claims. Applicant respectfully asserts that such allowable claims have been amended to include the subject matter of the base claim and any intervening claims. Further, any rejected claims have either been made to depend from an allowable independent claim, or canceled. Allowance of all pending claims is respectfully requested.

C. NOTICE OF ALLOWANCE

When analyzing a notice of allowance, you want to verify a few items:

1. Statement of Reasons for Allowance

This is where the Examiner indicates the basis for the allowance. The key thing to analyze here is whether the Examiner has characterized, in any manner, the claim language. If so, you will need to submit comments to rebut such characterization.

Keep in mind that often such comments refer to all of the independent claims as grouped together. However, often an apparatus claim will have slightly different terms than a method or computer program claim. As such, make sure that whatever the Examiner is pointing to as the basis for the allowance is indeed explicitly found in each of the independent claims as indicated.

Additionally, even if you do not need to rebut a characterization or error, it may still be good to submit comments on the statement of reasons for allowance and put on record something like the following:

> Although Applicant agrees with the Examiner's conclusion that these claims are allowable, Applicant notes that the claims may be allowable for reasons other than those identified by the Examiner and does not concede that the Examiner's characterizations of the terms of the claims and the prior art are correct. Each of the claims stands on its own merits and is patentable because of the combination it recites and not because of the presence or absence of any one particular element.
>
> The Examiner's Statement was not prepared by Applicant and only contains the Examiner's possible positions in one or more reasons for allowability. Thus, any interpretation with respect to the Examiner's Statement of Reasons for Allowance should not be imputed to the Applicant.

2. Examiner's Amendment

The Examiner may request an Examiner's Amendment (by calling up the representative) to put the claims in a state for allowance. If an Examiner's Amendment is present, verify that the proposed amendments are consistent with what you discussed with the Examiner.

3. Continuation Strategy

The following chapter will discuss continuation strategies in more detail. Suffice it to say, you need to keep a continuation strategy in mind, as one would need to be implemented preferably at the same time as payment of the issue fee (although realistically it could be implemented at any point <u>before</u> the issuance of the matter).

4. Indicated Claims

Verify that the claims indicated as being allowed coincide with the current state of the last draft of the claims that were sent to the Examiner. This is simply a double-check step to ensure (before the claims become final, literally) that the claims are correctly identified. It is also a good idea to verify that there are no further grammatical or typo mistakes within the claims. If any correction is needed, you could file a Rule 312 Amendment (i.e. Amendment after Notice of Allowance) and indicate that such amendment is being submitted solely to correct typographical type issues (i.e. non substantive).

D. APPEALING AN ACTION

Many years ago, appealing a decision was considered a very cost-effective way to receive a favorable decision to advance prosecution, assuming the arguments were well made with solid support. In more recent years, uncertainty (e.g. with 101) has shifted the balance a bit such that there is less certainty of receiving a favorable decision. In view of such, some clients have advocated for use of other strategies (e.g. file a continuation with a new claim set, file a continuation and amend the title/background/summary to increase chance of different art unit placement, etc.) which some feel are better use of funds.

In short, simply realize upfront that there's a time and place for appeals, but the world is changing such that they are not as popular today as they once were.

Here's some considerations to go into deciding whether to appeal a decision:

1. Are the arguments based on an objective deficiency (e.g. based on the examiner not following procedural requirements) or subjective argument? The more objective the basis, the greater the likelihood the appeals decision will be in your favor.

2. What is the end-game goal? To get to the granted patent as quickly as possible? To capture the most broad claim? It may make sense to pursue an appeal if the patent is the golden nugget of the inventor. It may make sense if more immediate timing results are not needed (appeals can take many months, if not 1+ years, to go through the entire process).

3. Does it touch on 101? If the patent subject matter's patent eligibility is suspect, recognize that there is a likelihood (for software related patents) that it will be found patent ineligible.

4. What is the strength of the prior art? Obviously, if you do not have a strong position against the prior art as presented, appeals is not an option. But if you feel that the prior art really is not teaching the claimed invention, and efforts to work with the examiner have failed, then appeals may make sense.

5. Effects on your relationship with the examiner – in an appeal, you are requesting, in essence, that the defect in the Examiner's reasoning be recognized, with a decision in your favor. Some examiners may feel that an appeal is a bit of a "slap in the face." In short, some may choose to take offense and not be as likely to work with you, e.g., in examiner interviews.

6. Effects on prosecution history estoppel – an appeal brief should include the same type of argument considerations we discussed above relating to responding to office actions. Do not characterize the claim language. That being said, by far, most appeal briefs do include some – or quite a bit – of characterization of the claims (to get to the 'gist' of what the claims are trying to get at). Be aware that such arguments, although they may be favorable to get an appeals decision in your favor, may be detrimental with respect to prosecution history estoppel.

When writing an appeal brief, the reference material below will provide guidance on how to actually construct the brief and what information should go into which section. With respect to the actual argument section, however, keep your arguments focused. Point out the deficiencies in the prior art, and when comparing such to the actual claim language, use the skeleton argument section (referenced above in Chapter 1) as a basis for your arguments in the appeal brief.

E. REFERENCE MATERIAL FOR APPEALS

One option at the final office action stage is to proceed forward with appealing the matter. In order to appeal, the M.P.E.P. indicates:

> (a) PATENT APPLICANT.— An applicant for a patent, any of whose claims has been twice rejected, may appeal from the decision of the primary examiner to the Board of Patent Appeals and Interferences, having once paid the fee for such appeal.[157]

When a final office action issues, if the finality is proper, the claims at that stage have been twice rejected, once in the non-final, and second in the final. As such, the claims may be ripe to be appealed. Keep in mind that a final office action is not necessarily required in order for the claims to be ready to be appealed. All that is required is that a claim has been twice rejected.

---

[157] M.P.E.P. § 1204, *citing* 37 C.F.R. § 134.

When you decide to appeal, you first file a notice of appeal. One of the reasons for this is that it stops the abandonment clock from ticking since you last received the final office action response.[158] The final office action requires a response by the applicant by a certain time period (for a final office action, it is usually a shortened statutory time period of three months). A notice of appeal can be filed which halts the time so that the application does not go abandoned within the window described below.

Within two months from filing a notice of appeal, either an appeal brief or a withdrawal from appeal and RCE needs to be filed with the USPTO to avoid abandonment.[159] However, this time period can be extended for up to an additional five months.[160]

As far as what needs to go into the appeal brief, the rules are quite clear, as shown below. Many times, however, a notice of non-compliance will be issued because one or more rules were not followed. So make sure that you follow each and every rule.

> (i) Real party in interest. A statement identifying by name the real party in interest at the time the appeal brief is filed, except that such statement is not required if the named inventor or inventors are themselves the real party in interest. If an appeal brief does not contain a statement of the real party in interest, the Office may assume that the named inventor or inventors are the real party in interest.

> (ii) Related appeals and interferences. A statement identifying by application, patent, appeal or interference number all other prior and pending appeals, interferences or judicial proceedings (collectively, ``related cases'') which satisfy all of the following conditions: Involve an application or patent owned by the appellant or assignee, are known to appellant, the appellant's legal representative, or assignee, and may be related to, directly affect or be directly affected by or have a bearing on the Board's decision in the pending appeal, except that such statement is not required if there are no such related cases. If an appeal brief does not contain a statement of related cases, the Office may assume that there are no such related cases.

---

[158] *See, e.g.* 37 C.F.R. § 1.134 ("An Office action will notify the applicant of any non-statutory or shortened statutory time period set for reply to an Office action. Unless the applicant is notified in writing that a reply is required in less than six months, a maximum period of six months is allowed").
[159] *See, e.g.,* 37 C.F.R. § 41.37.
[160] *See, e.g.,* 37 C.F.R. § 1.136.

(iii) Summary of claimed subject matter. A concise explanation of the subject matter defined in each of the rejected independent claims, which shall refer to the specification in the Record by page and line number or by paragraph number, and to the drawing, if any, by reference characters. For each rejected independent claim, and for each dependent claim argued separately under the provisions of paragraph (c)(1)(iv) of this section, if the claim contains a means plus function or step plus function recitation as permitted by 35 U.S.C. 112, sixth paragraph, then the concise explanation must identify the structure, material, or acts described in the specification in the Record as corresponding to each claimed function with reference to the specification in the Record by page and line number or by paragraph number, and to the drawing, if any, by reference characters. Reference to the patent application publication does not satisfy the requirements of this paragraph.

(iv) Argument. The arguments of appellant with respect to each ground of rejection, and the basis therefor, with citations of the statutes, regulations, authorities, and parts of the Record relied on. The arguments shall explain why the examiner erred as to each ground of rejection contested by appellant. Except as provided for in §§ 41.41, 41.47 and 41.52, any arguments or authorities not included in the appeal brief will be refused consideration by the Board for purposes of the present appeal. Each ground of rejection contested by appellant must be argued under a separate heading, and each heading shall reasonably identify the ground of rejection being contested (e.g., by claim number, statutory basis, and applied reference, if any). For each ground of rejection applying to two or more claims, the claims may be argued separately (claims are considered by appellant as separately patentable), as a group (all claims subject to the ground of rejection stand or fall together), or as a subgroup (a subset of the claims subject to the ground of rejection stand or fall together). When multiple claims subject to the same ground of rejection are argued as a group or subgroup by appellant, the Board may select a single claim from the group or subgroup and may decide the appeal as to the ground of rejection with respect to the group or subgroup on the basis of the selected claim alone. Notwithstanding any other provision of this paragraph, the failure of appellant to separately argue claims which appellant has grouped together shall constitute a waiver of any argument that the Board must consider the patentability of any grouped claim separately. Under each heading identifying the ground of rejection being contested, any claim(s) argued separately or as a subgroup shall be argued under a separate subheading that identifies the claim(s) by number. A statement which merely points out what a claim recites will not be considered an argument for separate patentability of the claim.

(v) Claims appendix. An appendix containing a copy of the claims involved in the appeal.

Typically, an appeal brief will include the foregoing items and be organized as such, each section being on a separate page:

I   REAL PARTY IN INTEREST

II	RELATED APPEALS AND INTERFERENCES
III	SUMMARY OF CLAIMED SUBJECT MATTER
IV	ARGUMENT
V	CLAIMS APPENDIX

It is important to note that any substantive issue to be considered on appeal must be raised in the Appeal Brief. There is no "hiding the ball" for your reply, as the Patent Trials and Appeals Board (also known as the "PTAB" or "Board") will simply ignore those portions of the Reply Brief. As such, be diligent, thorough, and concise in your Appeal Brief. You will have an opportunity to elaborate and respond in your Reply.

One of the big issues that comes up while writing an appeal brief is how to group the claims together. As indicated in the foregoing rules, the Board may choose one representative claim from the grouping to evaluate. As such, if you have claims that have separate issues, it is wise to separate the grouping so that each issue is independently evaluated. This consideration must be balanced against brief length, which if excessive, will cause the Board to glaze over or ignore some or all of your best arguments. Indicate, where it is possible, the patentable differences in each claim group. This would help to avoid the Board treating the claims as "standing and falling" together. The MPEP gives some helpful examples:

> For example, if Claims 1 to 5 stand rejected under 35 U.S.C. 102(b) as being anticipated by U.S. Patent No. Y and appellant is only going to argue the limitations of independent claim 1, and thereby group dependent claims 2 to 5 to stand or fall with independent claim 1, then one possible heading as required by this subsection could be "Rejection under 35 U.S.C. 102(b) over U.S. Patent No. Y" and the optional subheading would be "Claims 1 to 5." Another example is where claims 1 to 3 stand rejected under 35 U.S.C. 102(b) as being anticipated by U.S. Patent No. Z and appellant wishes to argue separately the patentability of each claim, a possible heading as required by this subsection could be "Rejection under 35 U.S.C. 102 (b) over U.S. Patent No. Z," and the optional subheadings would be "Claim 1," "Claim 2" and "Claim 3." Under each subheading the appellant would present the argument for patentability of that claim. The best practice is to use a subheading for each claim for which separate consideration by the Board is desired.[161]

After you submit your appeal brief, the Examiner has one chance to respond which is known as the Examiner's answer.

> (a)
> (1) The primary examiner may, within such time as may be directed by the Director, furnish a written answer to the appeal brief including such explanation of the invention claimed and of the references relied upon and grounds of rejection as may be necessary, supplying a copy to appellant. If the primary examiner determines that the appeal does not comply with the provisions of §§ 41.31 and 41.37 or does not relate to an appealable action, the primary examiner shall make such determination of record.
> (2) An examiner's answer may include a new ground of rejection.

---
[161] M.P.E.P. § 1205.02.

> (b) If an examiner's answer contains a rejection designated as a new ground of rejection, appellant must within two months from the date of the examiner's answer exercise one of the following two options to avoid sua sponte dismissal of the appeal as to the claims subject to the new ground of rejection:
>
>> (1) Reopen prosecution. Request that prosecution be reopened before the primary examiner by filing a reply under § 1.111 of this title with or without amendment or submission of affidavits (§§ 1.130, 1.131 or 1.132 of this title) or other evidence. Any amendment or submission of affidavits or other evidence must be relevant to the new ground of rejection. A request that complies with this paragraph will be entered and the application or the patent under ex parte reexamination will be reconsidered by the examiner under the provisions of § 1.112 of this title. Any request that prosecution be reopened under this paragraph will be treated as a request to withdraw the appeal.
>>
>> (2) Maintain appeal. Request that the appeal be maintained by filing a reply brief as set forth in § 41.41. Such a reply brief must address each new ground of rejection as set forth in § 41.37(c)(1)(vii) and should follow the other requirements of a brief as set forth in § 41.37(c). A reply brief may not be accompanied by any amendment, affidavit (§§ 1.130, 1.131 or 1.132 of this title) or other evidence. If a reply brief filed pursuant to this section is accompanied by any amendment, affidavit or other evidence, it shall be treated as a request that prosecution be reopened before the primary examiner under paragraph (b)(1) of this section.[162]

If the applicant desires to maintain the appeal, then a reply brief may be filed in response to the Examiner's Answer. It is strongly advised that you file a Reply Brief, even if the Examiner's Answer is truly inadequate. The timing here is important to remember, as action must be taken within two months (of the Examiner's answer) or the appeal is dismissed. The reply brief is essentially the last word of the argument before it is seen by the appeal board. So the arguments should be very refined, to the point, and focused. As far as what should be included in the reply brief, consider the following:

> (1) A reply brief shall not include any new or non-admitted amendment, or any new or non-admitted affidavit or other Evidence. See § 1.116 of this title for amendments, affidavits or other evidence filed after final action but before or on the same date of filing an appeal and § 41.33 for amendments, affidavits or other Evidence filed after the date of filing the appeal.
>
> (2) Any argument raised in the reply brief which was not raised in the appeal brief, or is not responsive to an argument raised in the examiner's answer, including any designated new ground of rejection, will not be considered by the Board for purposes of the present appeal, unless good cause is shown.[163]

---

[162] 37 C.F.R. § 41.39.
[163] 37 C.F.R. § 41.41.

After the reply brief is submitted, a supplemental reply may be issued by the Examiner. Usually, however, that does not occur unless the reply brief raised a new issue or the Examiner is directed (e.g. by the Board) to reply to the reply brief. In most cases, after the reply brief has been filed, it is then reviewed by the appeal board. Additionally, new appeal rules went into effect on 01/23/12 which abolished the supplemental reply.

Recognize there is a bit of a backlog with the appeals process. So even if you file your appeal today, it may be a year or two down the line before you hear back on a final decision.[164] When your case does come up to be reviewed, consider also having an oral hearing.[165]

A final decision may be in a variety of flavors:

> (1) The Board, in its decision, may affirm or reverse the decision of the examiner in whole or in part on the grounds and on the claims specified by the examiner. The affirmance of the rejection of a claim on any of the grounds specified constitutes a general affirmance of the decision of the examiner on that claim, except as to any ground specifically reversed. The Board may also remand an application to the examiner.[166]

Usually, once the decision issues, the applicant then reopens prosecution and continues the process, based on the input given by the Appeals Board.

We have covered a lot in this section on appeals. To help you get an idea of the entire appeals process, I would recommend looking up USPAN 11/465,498 on Public PAIR. Rather than reprinting all of the actions here, take a look in particular at the following items in the file wrapper:

1. Notice of Appeal
2. Appeal Brief
3. Non-final rejection (prosecution reopened by examiner)
4. Applicant's response to the non-final rejection
5. Final rejection
6. Appeal Brief
7. Notice of defective appeal brief
8. Appeal Brief
9. Examiner's answer
10. Decision by the Board

This action is a bit old, and you may have noticed that some of the structure/organization was not what we had discussed (the rules have changed since this was written). Nonetheless, I selected this application simply because it gives a good overview of the entire process and things that may occur during appeals.

---

[164] *See, e.g.,* "Ex Parte Patent Appeal Results," Patently-O Blog (Sept. 19, 2012), last accessed 05/01/2013, available at http://www.patentlyo.com/patent/2012/09/ex-parte-patent-appeal-results.html.
[165] *See, e.g.,* William F. Smith, "An Overview of Petitions, Appeals and Interferences in the USPTO," AIPLA Patent Boot Camp 2008, last accessed 05/01/2013, available at
http://www.aipla.org/learningcenter/library/papers/bootcamps/08patentbootcamp/Documents/Smith-paper.pdf.
[166] 37 C.F.R. § 41.50; *see also* M.P.E.P. § 1213.

CHAPTER 8
CONTINUATION PRACTICE, POST-ALLOWANCE

A. CONTINUATION PRACTICE

Continuation procedures are vital in the prosecution process. They are what permit us to keep the application alive, and subject to continued examination by the Patent Office.

There are three main continuation practices: continuations, continuation-in-part (CIP), a divisional, and a request for continued examination. Back in the day, CPA (continued prosecution application) used to be another option, but that is only used for design patent applications now.

I have summarized many of the continuation procedures below in a series of succinct tables.

Practice	Application Process
Continuation	Starts a new application from the beginning (restarts the prosecution process).
Divisional	Starts a new application from the beginning (restarts the prosecution process).
CIP	Starts a new application from the beginning (restarts the prosecution process).
RCE	Continues forward with prosecution based on the last action taken in the application.

Practice	When it is normally used
Continuation	To advance prosecution and obtain an allowance on a set of the allowable subject matter. To pursue protection on an additional claim set.
Divisional	Normally filed in response to a restriction requirement by the Examiner. Goal is to protect separately patentable subject matter.
CIP	Claim additional patentable subject matter not disclosed in the priority document.
RCE	Continue prosecution after it has been closed (e.g. after final office action and allowance has not been given, etc.).

As indicated, a continuation, divisional, and CIP are all treated as a new application. As such, they must meet all the requirements of an original patent application, and must correctly claim priority to the appropriate document(s).

A continuation application is not as widely used as it used to be. Here is a good example though of when it would be effective to be used:

One situation commonly giving rise to consideration of a continuation is this. Say that claims 1-5 have been finally rejected, claims 6-10 have been allowed, and the Examiner has refused to enter amendments or evidence needed to advance prosecution of claims 1-5. The client wants a patent to issue as soon as possible, as well as obtaining the best possible coverage ultimately.

Claims 1-5 could be prosecuted after the final rejection by filing an RCE; an RCE, if effective, will re-open prosecution of the entire application and no patent will issue until prosecution is completed again. But the client wants some patent to issue as soon as possible. That leaves the other tool for re-opening prosecution after it is closed: a continuation application.

You can get your client a patent on claims 6-10 promptly by canceling claims 1-5, after which the Examiner will mail a Notice of Allowance of claims 6-10. Once the issue fee is paid, claims 6-10 will issue in a patent. Meanwhile, a continuation application can be filed containing claims 1-5. This continuation should contain the same disclosure as its parent, with formal matters such as the priority claim, docket number, etc., updated.[167]

A divisional is exactly as it sounds. We have the original patent pie application and we divide the patentable subject matter pie up into one or more applications. A continuation in part is really designed where we want to claim part of the benefit of an earlier filed application, but want to disclose additional information.

Lastly, a RCE is very common strategy and simply allows the applicant to continue the prosecution process with the application. No new matter is added, and a new application does not need to be filed. The process simply continues wherever it was last left off. One downside of filing an RCE is that it reopens the prosecution process and so may delay getting claims to allowance. As such, as indicated in the continuation example, it may make sense in some instances to file a continuation to claim allowed subject matter and then file a RCE to prosecute the remaining items.

One other option for continuation practice is in fact to abandon the application. This is hard subject however. To talk about abandoning a patent application is somewhat akin to having to break up a long term relationship. You've invested time, money, and energy at this point. Can abandoning really be an option?

The answer is simply that yes it is an option. And that all may depend on the strategy associated with the client. For example, let's say that we filed a patent designed to penetrate the market. Unfortunately, however, while the application was being prosecuted, your competitor released a similar product with a granted patent that would predate your product. Although you could proceed forward and try to "hedge" in the patent of your competitor, it may also make sense simply to say that the market's saturation may exceed the value of getting the patent.

---

[167] George Wheeler, "CONTINUATION AND RCE PRACTICE," AIPLA Patent Prosecution Boot Camp 2008, last accessed 05/01/2013, available at
http://www.aipla.org/learningcenter/library/papers/bootcamps/08patentbootcamp/Documents/Wheeler-paper.pdf.

Abandoning a patent application is very much an economic cost/benefit analysis. On one hand, spending an additional $10k may help get the patent to grant, but then you have to consider at the expense of what. For example, that same $10k could be invested towards a separate patent that may be targeted for a market niche not yet exploited.

In other words, the same amount of money may be better spent – and reward with greater value and protection – than an otherwise less desirable route. The reality is that sometimes we simply do not know the market conditions until we are in the midst of the prosecution process. Based off of such an analysis, however, abandoning an application may be in the client's best interest because that may free up some financial resources, which may then be used on some other avenues of protection.

As such, abandoning does not mean giving up. It simply means to strategically assess the value of the patent even while it is being examined.

B. POST-ALLOWANCE PRACTICES

So you have battled long and hard through the prosecution process and finally, against all odds, the patent has been granted. Hooray. Unfortunately, however, the work is not done. The following items are some common practices that arise after the patent has been granted.

1. AMENDMENTS

It seems too often that a change to the Specification, the drawings, or even to the claims needs to be done after the patent has been allowed. It is interesting because there is a myriad of practices relating to the exact time of when an amendment is entered (e.g. after notice of allowance but before issuance, after payment of issue fee, etc.). Look through M.P.E.P. section 714 for exact instructions regarding how to amend given your timing.

Regardless, recognize that as time advances after the claims have been allowed the harder it is to change what is in there. Even after a notice of allowance is given, the applicant is still required to show:

> (A) why the amendment is needed;
> (B) why the proposed amended or new claims require no additional search or examination;

KEY POINT CORRECTIONS

A patent may be corrected by:
- A reissue application

- A certificate of correction

- A disclaimer

- A reexamination application

(C) why the claims are patentable; and
(D) why they were not presented earlier.[168]

Usually, such amendments usually relate to correcting a formal matter in the patent application. If your proposed amendment requires greater analysis, recognize that the Examiner may need to get approval from a Supervisory Patent Examiner (SPE) in order to enter the amendment.

2. CORRECTIONS

A patent may be corrected in four ways:

(A) by reissue,
(B) by the issuance of a certificate of correction which becomes a part of the patent,
(C) by disclaimer, and
(D) by reexamination.[169]

With respect to a reissue, there must be a legitimate reason why the patent needs to be reissued. In fact, the error must be "deemed wholly or partly inoperative or invalid, by reason of a defective specification or drawing, or by reason of the patentee claiming more or less than he had a right to claim in the patent."[170] Mistakes such as spelling, grammar, typing, or other like characteristics would not be sufficient therefore as the basis for a reissue (although they may certainly be corrected during the reissue process).

> A reissue application is filed to correct an error in the patent which was made without any deceptive intention, where, as a result of the error, the patent is deemed wholly or partly inoperative or invalid. An error in the patent arises out of an error in conduct which was made in the preparation and/or prosecution of the application which became the patent.
> ...
> The most common bases for filing a reissue application are:
>
> (A) the claims are too narrow or too broad;
> (B) the disclosure contains inaccuracies;
> (C) applicant failed to or incorrectly claimed foreign priority; and
> (D) applicant failed to make reference to or incorrectly made reference to prior copending applications.[171]

Lastly, if the reissue is filed two years after the grant of the original patent, the scope of the claims cannot be enlarged.[172]

---

[168] M.P.E.P. § 714.16.
[169] M.P.E.P. § 1400.01.
[170] M.P.E.P. § 1402.
[171] *Id.*
[172] *See, e.g.,* M.P.E.P. § 1403.

A certificate of correction is used to correct minor mistakes in the patent. The Patent Office may submit a certificate of correction when the mistake was incurred through the fault of the Patent Office.[173] Additionally, the applicant may also submit a certificate of correction where the mistake was made in good faith (e.g. not intentional, etc.).[174]

With respect to a disclaimer, the M.P.E.P. indicates:

> Whenever, without any deceptive intention, a claim of a patent is invalid the remaining claims shall not thereby be rendered invalid. A patentee, whether of the whole or any sectional interest therein, may, on payment of the fee required by law, make disclaimer of any complete claim, stating therein the extent of his interest in such patent. Such disclaimer shall be in writing, and recorded in the Patent and Trademark Office; and it shall thereafter be considered as part of the original patent to the extent of the interest possessed by the disclaimant and by those claiming under him.[175]

Lastly, a reexamination may be filed relating to the patent. Unlike with a reissue, a reexamination may never broaden the claims but may only restrict or narrow the claims additionally. In order to be eligible for reexamination, "the Office must determine whether 'a substantial new question of patentability' affecting any claim of the patent has been raised."[176]

Reexaminations come in two flavors: ex parte and inter partes. Ex parte is where the involvement of the proceedings is only between the patentee and the USPTO. It may be initiated however by a third party, but after the proceedings begin, the third party does not play a role in the process. In some cases, the patentee may not take any action in response to the proceedings taking place. If, however, the patentee does take action (e.g. file a response to the proceedings, etc.), the third party may in such an instance file a reply. That is the extent of the participation of the third party however.

Inter partes reexamination allows the third party to actively participate in the reexamination process. For example, the third party can file a submission to the USPTO each time the patentee responds to an office action.[177] Additionally, the third party may appeal the decision.[178]

Although a third party may have greater participation in an inter partes reexamination, that may not necessarily be the best decision. For example, with an inter partes reexamination, the identity of the third party is known. In an ex parte reexamination, the third party may remain anonymous. Additionally, due to the higher level of involvement, greater fees may be accumulated.

---

[173] *See, e.g.,* M.P.E.P. § 1480.
[174] *See, e.g.,* M.P.E.P. § 1481.
[175] M.P.E.P. § 1490.
[176] M.P.E.P. § 2216.
[177] *See, e.g.,* "Patent Reexamination," Firm Document Maier and Maier, last accessed 05/01/2013, available at http://www.maierandmaier.com/documents/Patent-Reexamination-FAQs.pdf.
[178] 35 U.S.C. § 315.

Although it may be obvious why a third party may want to have a patent be reexamined (many such reexamines occur during a patent litigation case), it may be less obvious why someone other than a third party (e.g. a patent owner) may wish to put a patent into reexamination proceedings. Keep in mind however, that a patent in reexamination can be amended. So if the claims are so broad they are of no value, amending the claims and narrowing the scope of the claims in reexam may produce a higher value patent.

Reexamination may be also a more attractive alternative than a reissue. For example, a reissue will cause all of the claims to be reevaluated. In contrast, the reexamination may be limited to a specific claim. Additionally, the potential prior art sources in a reexamination is more narrow and is limited to patents and printed publications under 35 U.S.C. §§ 102 and 103.

3. INTER PARTES REVIEW

In the prior section, we discussed inter partes reexamination. A post grant procedure known as inter partes review was introduced by the AIA. The inter partes review is intended to replace the inter partes reexamination.

Like the inter partes reexamination, the inter partes review can be requested by a third party. Additionally, the third party can be actively involved throughout the process, and the applicable prior art is consistent with the inter partes reexamination.

There are some differences however.

> One major different between inter partes review and pre-AIA inter partes reexamination is the standard used for granting such review. The Director will grant an inter partes review if there is a reasonable likelihood that the third party will prevail with respect to at least one of the patent claims challenged. Under the pre-AIA inter partes reexamination proceeding, the third party had to establish a substantial new question of patentability for the petition to be granted.
>
> An inter partes review may not be instituted if the third party filed a civil action challenging the validity of a claim of the patent before the petition for inter partes review, or the petition is filed more than one year after the petitioner, real party in interest, or privy is served with a complaint alleging infringement of the patent.[179]

The inter partes review went into effect on September 16, 2012, and applies to any patents issued before, on, or after that date.

4. POST-GRANT REVIEW / FURTHER AIA PRACTICES

Another new AIA post allowance practice is post grant review. This is somewhat similar to the European practice of oppositions. Post-grant review and inter-partes review were intended in combination to replace the prior inter partes reexamination.

---

[179] "Inter Partes Review," America Invents Act Rulemaking, last accessed 05/01/2013, available at http://www.aiarulemaking.com/rulemaking-topics/group-2/inter-partes-review.php.

Any third party may request a post-grant review. Additionally, the basis for the review is broader, as 101, 102, 103, and even some 112 issues may be the basis for review.[180] Additionally, unlike an inter partes review, a post grant review may consider evidence beyond patents and publications, such as expert testimony.

As far as the procedure of the post grant review, it resembles a mini trial:

> If the Office does institute a post-grant review, the patent owner will have an opportunity to present evidence detailing why each claim is valid, propose a substitute for any challenged claim, or cancel any challenged claim. Both parties will also have the opportunity to conduct discovery. If the two parties come to a settlement regarding patentability, the Office will terminate the post-grant review upon a joint request, unless it has already decided the merits of the proceeding before the request to terminate was filed.
>
> The decision by the Director whether to institute a post-grant review is final and nonappealable. Also, the petitioner, real party in interest, or privy, after the final written decision by the Patent Trial and Appeal Board, is prohibited from filing a civil action under 28 U.S.C. § 1338 (or in a proceeding before the International Trade Commission) or requesting a proceeding before the Office on any ground that the petitioner raised or reasonably could have raised during the post-grant review. Either party is allowed to appeal the decision of the Patent Trial and Appeal Board.[181]

Lastly, a post-grant review must be submitted within nine months after the grant of a patent. However, even after the nine months have ended, the patent may still be submitted to an inter partes review.

Although we have discussed some AIA aspects such as inter partes review and post grant review, recognize that there are many other new rules that may apply to your prosecution strategies. For sake of brevity, I will simply list them and bring them to your attention:

1. Preissuance submissions: third parties may submit relevant documents during the pendency of a patent application.[182]
2. Supplemental proceedings: at the request of the patent owner, any relevant information not considered, inadequately considered, or incorrectly considered during the examination of a patent may be presented to the Patent Office.[183]
3. Derivation proceedings: occurs when a dispute arises between two applicants as to who is the true inventor. The proceeding is intended to ensure that the

---

[180] *See, e.g.,* 35 U.S.C. § 282(b).
[181] "Post-Grant Review," America Invents Act Rulemaking, last accessed 05/01/2013, available at http://www.aiarulemaking.com/rulemaking-topics/group-2/post-grant-review.php.
[182] "Preissuance Submissions by Third Parties," America Invents Act Rulemaking, last accessed 05/01/2013, available at http://www.aiarulemaking.com/rulemaking-topics/group-2/third-party-submission-prior-art-patent-application.php.
[183] "Supplemental Examination," America Invents Act Rulemaking, last accessed 05/01/2013, available at http://www.aiarulemaking.com/rulemaking-topics/group-2/supplemental-examination.php.

person receiving the patent is the true inventor and did not derive it from another.[184]

---

[184] "Derivation Proceeding," America Invents Act Rulemaking, last accessed 05/01/2013, available at http://www.aiarulemaking.com/rulemaking-topics/group-3/derivation-proceedings.php.

CHAPTER 9
LITIGATION PERSPECTIVES PART I

A. CLAIM CONSTRUCTION

It is helpful to remember how the claim will be construed. Normally, as a patent infringement case advances, a Markman hearing will be held. At such a hearing, a judge will hear evidence (e.g. intrinsic and extrinsic, etc.) to determine the definition or meaning associated with key words or phrases from the claim.

Intrinsic evidence includes information relating directly (or within the branch of) the patent. For example, the claims, specification, and prosecution history should all be reviewed (and usually in that order). The closer the source of meaning (e.g. where it is defined, etc.) is to the claims, the stronger the weight of the meaning. In practical terms, if the term is not clear from the claims, then we look to the specification, and if it is not clearly described there, then we look to the prosecution history to see if the term was limited or used in some manner.

Extrinsic evidence is everything else outside of the umbrella of the patent, and may include a dictionary, treaty, or encyclopedia. Normally, extrinsic evidence is given less weight simply because it is not connected to the patent itself. The logical reason for this is that the claim language and the specification as written by the applicant should serve as the primary reference for proper claim interpretation. The moment extrinsic words or definitions are applied to the patent, we are, in essence, adding more to the patent than what was originally there (and which may conflict with the actual intended scope of the patent). Patents are intended to stand on their own. For these reasons, extrinsic evidence is given relatively little weight in trying to understand an ambiguous term in the claim.

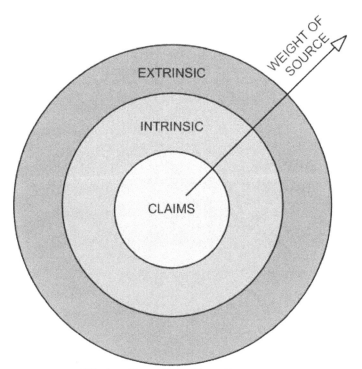

Claim Construction Sources

This Figure shows the weight given to sources. As indicated above, the further you are from the claims, the less weight the source will be given during claim construction. As such, you want to make sure that the most important information is found closest to the claims to avoid any ambiguity.

Keep in mind that no two people think alike. In fact, keep in mind that no two judges think alike.[185] As such, there are two main lessons we should learn from claim construction:

1. Keep your terms clear and unambiguous.
2. Define your terms clearly in your Specification.

By following these two rules, claim interpretation should remain less problematic, and the Specification (an intrinsic evidence source) should be the ultimate source of all terms and phrases.

B. MARKMAN HEARING

A Markman hearing is arguably one of the most important phases of patent litigation. The hearing is where the claims are constructed and construed. In essence, the judge will hear arguments as to how a term or phrase should be conclude, and then the judge will give an order regarding the definitions that will apply at trial.[186] Contrast this, however, with the responsibility of the jury which decides questions or issues of facts.

In short, if you receive a definition that is unfavorable to your position, it may be fatal to your case.

As far as timing, a Markman hearing may occur nearly at any time: early during the discovery process, after discovery, or even after trial (e.g. the ITC, etc.). However, as the Markman may be one of the most important phases, it should be conducted after enough time to conduct some discovery (e.g. grow your case, etc.) but may be beneficial to conduct the hearing earlier on in the process to keep costs down.

> The more patent-experienced jurisdictions have recognized the importance of construing the claims after meaningful discovery, but meaningfully before trial. This process is typically favored among litigants because it resolves the critical issue of claim construction within the context of the accused products, but well before the considerable costs of a trial are incurred. Hence this process often leads to an earlier and more meaningful settlement. Unfortunately, ... the International Trade Commission ("ITC"), does not follow this process. Instead, the ITC judges typically construe the claims after the trial at the same time they issue their determination on the merits. This process is particularly burdensome to respondents at the ITC.

---

[185] *See, e.g.*, Dennis Crouch, "Stent Patent Cannot Heal Divided Claim Construction: Four Judges = Four Different Claim Constructions," Patently-O (08/12/13), last accessed 04/13/13, available at http://www.patentlyo.com/patent/2013/04/stent-patent-cannot-heal-divided-claim-construction.html?cid=6a00d8341c588553ef017c388f39e6970b.
[186] *See, e.g., Markman v. Westview Instruments, Inc.*, 517 U.S. 370 (1996).

Because claim construction is so vitally important to resolving disputes in patent cases, Markman hearings cannot be taken lightly. Indeed, though a Markman hearing may occur well before the trial, the parties should have fully developed their positions on the merits by this time to ensure that their claim construction positions are consistent with the evidence in the case. Both parties in a patent litigation must typically navigate tens of thousands of documents related to accused products and numerous pieces of prior art. At a Markman hearing, good litigators will be fully steeped in this evidence and the issues of their cases and prepared to address any issues the judge may have.[187]

As far as information and evidence which may be presented, there are generally two classes of materials: intrinsic and extrinsic. Intrinsic includes the actual patent specification, claims, figures, etc. as well as documents found in the prosecution history (in the file wrapper). Extrinsic evidence is, as the name suggests, extrinsic to the body of information associated with the patent, and may include dictionaries, encyclopedias, etc. In some jurisdictions, the inventor may be called as witness to testify at the Markman hearing. Additionally, it is helpful to note that intrinsic sources are generally considered more reliable than extrinsic sources, and therefore are given potentially greater weight.

In other words, the words, phrases, and arguments used during the prosecution stages will primarily determine how the term is construed at trial.

Markman hearings are actually very interesting to watch. It usually involves a scientific session where the parties will present the scientific matter which will be analyzed in the claims. I've heard some great experts give very thorough expositions on the details of the subject matter, but fail to convey that in lay-man's terms that may be easily understood by non-scientific people (e.g. the judge) in the audience. This is actually a very important point. The manner in which the scientific information is presented can mean all the difference in a Markman hearing. Remember as we have discussed earlier, the true test of mastery of a subject is being able to distill the intricacies and details of a complex matter into simple and easily-digestible pieces.

---

[187] Vincent P. Kovalick, "Markman Hearings and Their Critical Role in U.S. Patent Litigation," China IP News (Oct. 2009), last accessed 05/07/2013, available at
http://www.finnegan.com/resources/articles/articlesdetail.aspx?news=9a8bf39b-c419-4329-9f6a-08ac0a647c7c.

CHAPTER 10
LITIGATION PERSPECTIVE PART II

A. LITIGATION COSTS

I have yet to hear a patent attorney indicate to a client that litigation is a cheap and sure way to resolve any dispute. It truly is not. It is neither cheap, nor is it predictable. With that basic understanding, therefore, let's dig a bit more into the details.

1. ATTORNEY COSTS

Patent litigation can be extremely complex. It requires a thorough understanding of the technology, an ability to organize mass amounts (and I mean literally tens of thousands of pages) of documentation, and the ability of a team of attorneys and practitioners to distill the information usually to 1-4 attorneys who will present the case at trial.

From a logical point of view, the more complex the case, the more time it takes to digest, and the more costs go up. The more people that need to be involved, the more costs go up. And distilling tens of thousands of pages worth of documentation takes time, and time means more money. It doesn't help either that litigation attorneys are generally not cheap with their high hourly rates. Add that up all together and you have bankruptcy. Just kidding. But for a small company, or a startup, it very well could mean bankruptcy.

The following Figure gives some idea of the average costs associated with a patent litigation suit. Notice that although the years may change, the price stays relatively in the same range.

MEDIAN LITIGATION COSTS FOR PATENT INFRINGEMENT				
	2005	2007	2009	2011
Less than $1M at risk				
End of Discovery	$350K	$350K	$350K	$350K
All Costs	$650K	$650K	$650K	$650K
$1M – $25M at risk				
End of Discovery	$1.25M	$1.25M	$1.5M	$1.5M
All Costs	$2.0M	$2.5M	$2.5M	$2.5M
More than $25M at risk				
End of Discovery	$3.0M	$3.0M	$3.0M	$3.0M
All Costs	$4.5M	$5.0M	$5.5M	$5.0M

Patent Lawsuit Legal Costs[188]

These costs only relate to legal fees associated with those that are representing the case for the client. This does not take into account additional fees or damages associated with the suit, particularly if you lose the battle. However, these legal costs may also include expert testimony which may range anywhere from a few thousand to a few million.

No matter which way you look at it, the legal costs alone are expensive.[189]

In relation to the Apple v. Samsung case, what does this all mean?

> Court documents show that some Morrison Foerster partners and of counsel billed a median rate of $582 an hour for work on portions of the case, while some Quinn Emanuel partners billed on average $821 per hour. Spokeswomen for both law firms did not immediately respond to requests for comment.
>
> "This is big, high-stakes litigation," said Donald R. Dunner, a patent law expert and senior partner at Finnegan, Henderson, Farabow, Garrett & Dunner, LLP. "They've got the best lawyers they could find, and they charge fees that are commensurate with their talent."
>
> Mr. Dunner estimated that each side could have spent $10 to $20 million on the case.
>
> Others said the cost could be much more. "My estimate for this trial is a half a billion total," said intellectual property lawyer Mark A. Lemley, a professor at Stanford Law School and founding partner of the law firm Durie Tangri LLP.
>
> Included in the total: about $4 million apiece for expert witnesses, according to one estimate by Brian Love, an associate law professor at Santa Clara University School of Law.[190]

Expert testimony may have cost a few million dollars alone. And the total legal fees could have been easily $10M. Quite a high bill.

---

[188] The figure is based on the numbers disclosed in "Typical Costs of Litigation," Report of the Economic Survey 2011, American Intellectual Property Law Association, available for download at http://www.aipla.org/learningcenter/library/books/econsurvey/2011/Pages/Table-of-Contents.aspx; *see also* Jim Kerstetter, "How much is that patent lawsuit going to cost you?," CNET Bootstrap (Apr. 5, 2012), available at http://news.cnet.com/8301-32973_3-57409792-296/how-much-is-that-patent-lawsuit-going-to-cost-you/.

[189] If you want to make millions, I'd recommend not spending your time writing a textbook. I heard that if you recoup the costs spent writing the book, you are doing well. Of course, this really didn't sink in for me until I was down to the end of this book.

[190] Jennifer Smith, "Check, Please: Experts Say Apple, Samsung Face Sky-High Legal Fees," The Wall Street Journal (Aug. 24, 2012), last accessed 05/06/2013, available at http://blogs.wsj.com/law/2012/08/24/check-please-experts-say-apple-samsung-face-sky-high-legal-fees/.

CHAPTER 10

Let's put this in perspective however. As we will discuss in the next subsection, the amount at stake may justify spending tens of millions of dollars on legal related fees. If you knew that $1B as at stake, in all reality, what is another few million if it improves your chances of winning?

Although high stake litigation, such as the *Apple v. Samsung* case, may fetch top dollars, the majority of the patent litigation cases do not necessarily incur as high legal fees, nor do the damages amount to the same level. Nonetheless, because of the Apple v. Samsung case, is there now an expectation by both attorneys and clients of the costs associated with litigation? The clients may now expect a higher damage recovery with the expectation perhaps that if they pay enough for legal related costs, in the end it will pay off. Such may not be the case. Nonetheless, it is worth at least recognizing how this case may influence the perception and views of other businesses considering filing a patent infringement case.

2. DAMAGES COSTS

So how can much can you recover if you are successful? Or, on the flip side, how much can you be found liable for with respect to damages?

In the Apple v. Samsung case, it was a good day for Apple, to the tune of $1.05 billion.[191] However, the damages figure was later reduced to a measly $599 million.[192] No matter how you view it, Apple won a sizable amount.

This really is where many of the subjective factors start to come into play. With respect to legal costs, although they were high, they were somewhat predictable. With respect to expected damages, the nature of litigation in general is so dynamic that it makes it extremely hard – if not impossible – to predict.

The law provides a basis for how damages should be determined:

> Upon finding for the claimant the court shall award the claimant damages adequate to compensate for the infringement, but in no event less than a reasonable royalty for the use made of the invention by the infringer, together with interest and costs as fixed by the court.
>
> When the damages are not found by a jury, the court shall assess them. In either event the court may increase the damages up to three times the amount found or assessed. Increased damages under this paragraph shall not apply to provisional rights under section 154 (d).
>
> The court may receive expert testimony as an aid to the determination of damages or of what royalty would be reasonable under the circumstances.[193]

---

[191] Josh Lowensohn, "Jury awards Apple more than $1B, finds Samsung infringed," CNET (Aug 24, 2012), last accessed 05/06/2013, available at http://news.cnet.com/8301-13579_3-57500159-37/jury-awards-apple-more-than-$1b-finds-samsung-infringed/.
[192] Christian Zibreg, "Judge slashes $450M from $1B Apple v. Samsung verdict," iDownloadBlog (Mar. 1, 2013), last accessed 05/06/2013, available at
http://www.idownloadblog.com/2013/03/01/apple-v-samsung-450m-usd-stricken/.
[193] 35 U.S.C. § 284.

In a nutshell, the role of damages is to compensate the damaged party for the infringement. From a contract perspective, damages helps to make right the wrong and to return the wronged party in a position had the infringement not occurred. Interesting enough, the statute does provide a threshold floor for damages – "no less than a reasonable royalty."

Additionally, the Supreme Court has reasoned that:

> Congress sought to ensure that the patent owner would in fact receive full compensation for "any damages" he suffered as a result of the infringement. Congress expressly provided in § 284 that the court "shall award the claimant damages adequate to compensate for the infringement.[194]

The focus therefore is on the damages incurred and not necessarily on the profits received by the infringing party. Further, where lost profits or a reasonable royalty alone would not adequately compensate for the infringement, the court may look to a combination of the two.[195]

In determining lost profits, consider the following test, known as the *Panduit* factors:

> To obtain as damages the profits on sales he would have made absent the infringement, i.e., the sales made by the infringer, a patent owner must prove: (1) demand for the patented product, (2) absence of acceptable noninfringing substitutes, (3) his manufacturing and marketing capability to exploit the demand, and (4) the amount of profit he would have made.[196]

We will not discuss further the factors (and others) considered to determine lost profits and/or reasonable royalties. Know simply at this point that tests are applied to determine the appropriate amount of damages to be applied.

Consider also that if it is determined that the party willfully infringed, then according to section 284, it may be permissible to increase the damages by up to three times. Think of that in terms of the Apple v. Samsung case. If it was found that Samsung willfully infringed Apple's patents, the total damages could have been $3 billion.[197] Wow.

Moral of the story is do not infringe. And if you do, make sure it is not willful because then that may triply hurt your client.

---

[194] *General Motors Corp. v. Devex Corp.*, 461 U.S. 648, 654—55 (1983).
[195] *See, e.g.,* Michael A. Morin, "Processing Grain: Lost Profits Damages and Some Practical Considerations for the Patent Litigator," IP Litigator (July/August 2005), last accessed 05/06/2013, available at http://www.finnegan.com/resources/articles/articlesdetail.aspx?news=c29ba550-8c55-4b4f-a9a5-b2c72b1749c4.
[196] *Panduit Corp. v. Stalin Bros. Fibre Works, Inc.*, 575 F.2d 1152, 1156 (6th Cir. 1978).
[197] Based on the original damages amount.

Lastly, although the foregoing has a statutory basis and a Supreme Court reasoning, I want you to recognize that damages is very fluid. It is really up to the jury to decide how much a party has been damaged (using reports provided by the parties), and how much should be allocated to right the wrong. Later in this chapter, I have provided part of the jury instruction in the *Apple v. Samsung* case. As you read it, I think you will be surprised by how much of a responsibility is placed on the juror to decide whether the patent is valid, and if it is, whether infringement occurred. And if infringement did occur, the juror then decides the damages that should be applied.

In conclusion, damages can hurt business. Avoid them. They cost a lot.

3. DISCOVERY COSTS

The discovery process in the United States is a bit different than in other parts of the world. When I lived in Germany, a number of European patent attorneys indicated to me that for them, discovery was price capped process to discover the most essential items needed to prove infringement. Contrast this, however, with the United States where we have the mantra "We will not leave any stone unturned." And we don't either. We analyze every stone, every remnant of a stone, and anything which may appear to be like a stone.

Although our discovery process is extremely (and I mean very extremely) thorough, it comes with a cost. In fact, many of the costs associated with the litigation may stem, at least in part, from this discovery process.

> Discovery, in general, and e-discovery in particular, is widely blamed for most of the excess costs of litigation. As Federal Circuit Chief Judge Randall Rader explained in a 2011 speech, "I saw one analysis that concluded that .0074% of the documents produced actually made their way onto the trial exhibit list – less than one document in ten thousand. And for all the thousands of appeals I've evaluated, email appears even more rarely as relevant evidence."
>
> Consequently, Judge Rader endorsed a model order drafted by the Federal Circuit Advisory Council, containing measures intended to help rein in the costs of discovery, such as excluding e-mail and metadata from FRCP Rule 34 and 45 requests, absent good cause; imposing presumptive limits of five custodians and five search terms for e-mail requests; and shifting costs for disproportionate e-discovery requests. Courts in Texas, Illinois, California, Colorado, Delaware and other jurisdictions have adopted that model order or variations of it and prudent counsel will urge their court to do the same.
>
> Even without a court order, one can reduce discovery costs by tailoring requests precisely (and narrowly) to avoid creating discovery disputes or receiving overly voluminous responses, much of which will be of limited relevance and usefulness, but all of which will require costly hosting, processing and reviewing the documents.[198]

---

[198] Chris Neumeyer, "Managing Costs of Patent Litigation," IPWatchdog (Feb. 5, 2013), last accessed 05/06/2013, available at http://www.ipwatchdog.com/2013/02/05/managing-costs-of-patent-litigation/id=34808/.

With respect in particular to patent infringement, you can rest assured that for every thirty minutes you take to write part of an embodiment, the litigation teams will take weeks, or months even, dissecting every nuance of the language you used. They will find nuances and meaning in your language that perhaps you were never aware of.

4. TIME AND IMAGE COSTS

Patent litigation is not a quick process. So if your company needs money fast, litigation realistically may not be possible. For example, using a distribution of cases from 1995 to 2011, the average (70% of cases) time to trial occurs within three years.[199]

Those three years may feel like an eternity for your client who has to pay out legal costs for that entire time period. The conclusion here is simply that if your client wants to take the litigation route, it will take time, and sometimes a lot of time. So be prepared.

Additionally, beyond the monetary cost considerations, there are also non-monetary costs associated with litigation. For example, what image does the company wish to portray? Do they want to be known as an entity that aggressively litigates its patent portfolio? Do they want to be known as a company that goes after everyone and anything?

Although we may laugh inwardly at such considerations, keep in mind that a company's image plays an indirect role in the valuation of the company. For example, if the company has a good image, the public may more quickly invest in it. Likewise, if the company has a poor image (or has lost in a litigation suit), the public may not as quickly invest in such a company (and may even withdraw investing from).

As we just discussed, litigation can take time. And time in litigation can be taxing as you have to devote resources to this project. On the flip side, however, the company may get a lot of free (well perhaps indirectly) PR, due to the coverage of the trial by the media. Consider the *Apple v. Samsung* case. While that was going on, it was hard not to hear something about Apple or Samsung on any media source. There may be therefore *some* benefit of litigation, although you are indirectly paying a lot for it.

In summation, litigation takes time. And, it can play a role in influencing non-monetary considerations, such as a company's image.

5. LITIGATION COST TIPS

The costs of litigation can be very high. Nonetheless, there are some additional costs that should be considered.

---

[199] "2012 Patent Litigation Study," PWC (2012), last accessed 05/06/2013, available at http://www.pwc.com/en_US/us/forensic-services/publications/assets/2012-patent-litigation-study.pdf.

First, the company should clarify why it is pursuing litigation. This should coincide with the business strategy of the company, such as to dominate the market, to take out a competitor, to give a public image, to impress the investors, etc. The list really can go on and on. On one hand, there are some things that are worth fighting for. To wrong an injustice? Yes, of course this could be a valid reason. Matter of principle? Well, morals are good, but if it bankrupts your company, it is not doing your company much good. The point here is simply the client needs to really analyze why it is pursuing litigation. If it is a valid reason, the cost/benefit analysis points to litigation, and the client has money to weather the litigation storm, then proceed ahead. Otherwise, out of court resolutions may be much more cost-effective. [200]

Second, is the client prepared to lose? Of course we all want to win. Who doesn't? The reality however is that most sides fight in litigation legitimately believing they will win. Or, put differently, they believe their case is better than the opposing side. Every side will usually put forth some good points.[201] However, at the end of the day, if the case proceeds to trial, there will be a loser. And there is a 50% chance it will be your client. Are they prepared for this? Again, if they cannot deal with the financial loss, the public image loss, or other factors, alternative resolutions may be more practical.

Third, I have mentioned several times already that alternative resolutions may be possible. However, this is assuming that the client is in the driver's seat, the one that is driving the litigation. If you are responding to litigation, then that is a completely different battle. In such a case, the client needs to defend. Notwithstanding, even if you are roped into litigation as a defendant, the defendant can still be in the "driver's seat" by proactively asserting some form of resolution. Time, energy, and money can be saved by coming to a resolution earlier on in the litigation process. And, I've heard judges even up to the last day of arguments and testimony ask the parties if they would like to resolve the dispute before it is submitted to the jury. The courts therefore push for resolution no matter at whatever stage the parties or the litigation process is at.

B. FORUM SHOPPING

For you law students, this was subject you probably thought ended in civil procedure. Well, I hate to burst your bubble, but it is back again in all its grandeur, except now it's fun.

Forum shopping is protected by statute:

> Any civil action for patent infringement may be brought in the judicial district where the defendant resides, or where the defendant has committed acts of infringement and has a regular and established place of business.[202]

---

[200] *See, e.g.,* Jeremy Phillips, "KEEP IT CHEAP: TEN TIPS FOR MINIMIZING IP DISPUTE SETTLEMENT COSTS," WIPO Magazine (2010), available at http://www.wipo.int/export/sites/www/wipo_magazine/en/pdf/2010/wipo_pub_121_2010_01.pdf.
[201] I can remember one case that I sat on where the defense was horrible. No opening statement. No objections. No good points. Not only did I almost fall asleep, I'm pretty sure counsel did too.
[202] 28 U.S.C. § 1400(b).

Essentially, the proper forum is any forum where the defendant's product is used or sold.[203]

Usually, there are three considerations that parties consider when selecting the right forum: (1) likelihood of winning; (2) likelihood of getting to trial; and (3) speed of getting to trial.[204] For patent owner plaintiffs, they generally want a high likelihood of winning, a high likelihood of getting to trial, and fast speed. For defendants, they generally want the exact opposite: low likelihood of the plaintiff winning, low likelihood of going to trial, and slow speed.

In Professor Lemley's 2010 study, he concluded that

> the Eastern District of Texas, while it has a higher than average plaintiff win rate, is not in the top five districts. And the districts that are in the top five (the Northern District of Texas, the Middle District of Florida, the District of Nevada, the District of Delaware, and the District of Oregon) are not normally thought of as plaintiff patent jurisdictions of choice. Indeed, accused infringers often choose the District of Delaware, filing declaratory judgment actions there. Conversely, patent plaintiffs often file suit in districts like the District of New Jersey that have a surprisingly low win rate

I have provided below an excerpt from Professor Lemley's chart indicating the results. Note that Professor Lemley's anlaysis takes into consideration much more than simply the number of filings per district.

---

[203] *See, e.g.,* Mark A. Lemley, "Where to File Your Patent Case," Aipla Quarterly Journal (Oct. 27, 2010), last accessed 05/07/2013, available at http://papers.ssrn.com/sol3/papers.cfm?abstract_id=1597919.
[204] *Id.*

District	Claimant Win	Claim Defendant Win	Procedural	Indeterminate	Likely Settlement	Consent Judgment	TOTAL
Central District of California	125	219	193	11	1401	340	2289
Northern District of California	56	159	131	0	1007	71	1424
Northern District of Illinois	47	97	119	3	874	93	1233
Eastern District of Texas	52	77	150	0	703	42	1024
Southern District of New York	51	87	87	1	676	116	1018
District of Delaware	62	75	137	0	682	61	1017
District of New Jersey	29	109	201	0	588	60	987
District of Minnesota	25	54	28	0	450	43	600
District of Massachusetts	43	69	41	1	392	38	584

Forum Summary Statistics[205]

Based off of his analysis, Professor Lemley concluded that the best plaintiff friendly districts are:

> Middle District of Florida, District of Delaware, Eastern District of Virginia, and the Western District of Wisconsin. The best districts for accused infringers include Eastern District of Wisconsin, the Southern District of Ohio, or the District of Columbia because patent cases in those districts move slowly and more-frequently end with summary judgment in favor of the accused infringer.[206]

Although some of the more current 'hot' forums may have changed since Professor Lemley conducted his analysis, I believe the same considerations still apply to litigation parties.

Additionally, although not the only factor to consider, the top patent filing districts for the year 2012 were: (1) East Texas (1,260 cases filed); (2) Delaware (almost 1,000 cases filed); (3) Central District of California (541 cases filed); (4) Northern District of California (258 cases filed); and (5) Northern District of Illinois (237 cases filed).[207]

---

[205] *Id.*
[206] "Patent Litigation Forum Shopping," Patently-O (May 4, 2010), last accessed 05/07/2013, available at http://www.patentlyo.com/patent/2010/05/patent-litigation-forum-shopping.html.
[207] Joe Mullin, "Why East Texas courts are back on "top" for patent lawsuits," Ars Technica (Jan. 16, 2013), last accessed 05/07/2013, available at http://arstechnica.com/tech-policy/2013/01/east-texas-courts-are-back-on-top-for-patent-lawsuits/.

Again, like disclaimers in my book, the list is not intended to be exhaustive. It is simply to get you acclimated to the idea that forum shopping for patent cases does occur. Be therefore aware of the forum you are dealing with, as it may directly influence the outcome of the case (e.g. plaintiff friendly, slow litigation pace, etc.).

35 U.S.C. 101

USPAN	Type of Action	Issue	Action Page	Response Page
14/503,210	NFOA	101 Statutory	118	130
14/547,079	NFOA	101 Non Statutory	177	181
14/887,211	NFOA	101 Non Statutory	377	383
15/253,721	FOA	101 Double Patenting	449	466

35 U.S.C. 102

USPAN	Type of Action	Issue	Action Page	Response Page
14/503,210	NFOA	102	118	130
14/742,430	NFOA	102	229	237
14/806,548	NFOA	102	266	289
14/815,871	NFOA	102	304	318
14/823,993	NFOA	102	329	344
15/145,757	NFOA	102 multiple rejections	395	410
15/201,283	NFOA	102 allowable subject matter	432	440
15/289,039	NFOA	102	481	497

35 U.S.C. 103

USPAN	Type of Action	Issue	Action Page	Response Page
14/503,210	NFOA	103	118	130
14/547,077	FOA	103 multiple combination	144	161
14/582,178	NFOA	103 single basis	193	199
14/731,282	NFOA	103 single basis	209	218
14/796,998	NFOA	103 multiple combination	247	257
14/806,548	NFOA	103 multiple combination	266	289
14/815,871	NFOA	103	304	318
14/823,993	NFOA	103 multiple combination	329	344
14/859,501	NFOA	103 multiple combination	360	369
15/145,757	NFOA	103 multiple combination	395	410
15/253,721	FOA	103 multiple combination	449	466
15/289,039	NFOA	103	481	497
15/354,935	NFOA	103 single basis	511	527

35 U.S.C. 112

USPAN	Type of Action	Issue	Action Page	Response Page
14/742,430	NFOA	112(b)	229	237
14/796,998	NFOA	112(b)	247	257
14/806,548	NFOA	112(a)	266	289
15/145,757	NFOA	112(d)	395	410
15/253,721	FOA	112(a) and 112(b)	449	466
15/289,039	NFOA	112(f)	481	497
15/354,935	NFOA	112(f)	511	527

MISCELLANEOUS

USPAN	Type of Action	Issue/Subject Matter	Action Page	Response Page
14/742,430	NFOA	Objection to Drawings	229	237
14/796,998	NFOA	Claim Objection	247	257
14/815,871	NFOA	Claim Objection	304	318
15/201,283	NFOA	Allowable Subject Matter	432	440
14/718,083		Examiner Agenda		542
14/718,083		Examiner Interview Summary		550
14/718,083	NOA		560	
14/742,430	NOA		567	
14/547,074		Comments on Statement of Reasons for Allowance		578

LINCOLN LAW SCHOOL OF SAN JOSE
INTELLECTUAL PROPERTY SERIES

EXHIBIT: OFFICE ACTION

UNITED STATES PATENT AND TRADEMARK OFFICE

UNITED STATES DEPARTMENT OF COMMERCE
United States Patent and Trademark Office
Address: COMMISSIONER FOR PATENTS
P.O. Box 1450
Alexandria, Virginia 22313-1450
www.uspto.gov

APPLICATION NO.	FILING DATE	FIRST NAMED INVENTOR	ATTORNEY DOCKET NO.	CONFIRMATION NO.
14/503,210	09/30/2014	Adam Feder	DUELP001/DL020	8161

28875   7590   01/12/2016
Zilka-Kotab, PC
1155 N. 1st St.
Suite 105
SAN JOSE, CA 95112

EXAMINER
WU, JINGGE

ART UNIT	PAPER NUMBER
2665	

NOTIFICATION DATE	DELIVERY MODE
01/12/2016	ELECTRONIC

Please find below and/or attached an Office communication concerning this application or proceeding.

The time period for reply, if any, is set in the attached communication.

Notice of the Office communication was sent electronically on above-indicated "Notification Date" to the following e-mail address(es):

zk-uspto@zilkakotab.com
chrisc@zilkakotab.com

PTOL-90A (Rev. 04/07)

EXHIBITS 119

Office Action Summary	Application No. 14/503,210	Applicant(s) FEDER ET AL.
	Examiner JINGGE WU	Art Unit 2665	AIA (First Inventor to File) Status Yes

-- The MAILING DATE of this communication appears on the cover sheet with the correspondence address --

Period for Reply

A SHORTENED STATUTORY PERIOD FOR REPLY IS SET TO EXPIRE 3 MONTHS FROM THE MAILING DATE OF THIS COMMUNICATION.
- Extensions of time may be available under the provisions of 37 CFR 1.136(a). In no event, however, may a reply be timely filed after SIX (6) MONTHS from the mailing date of this communication.
- If NO period for reply is specified above, the maximum statutory period will apply and will expire SIX (6) MONTHS from the mailing date of this communication.
- Failure to reply within the set or extended period for reply will, by statute, cause the application to become ABANDONED (35 U.S.C. § 133).
- Any reply received by the Office later than three months after the mailing date of this communication, even if timely filed, may reduce any earned patent term adjustment. See 37 CFR 1.704(b).

Status

1) ☒ Responsive to communication(s) filed on _9/30/2014_.
☐ A declaration(s)/affidavit(s) under **37 CFR 1.130(b)** was/were filed on _____.
2a) ☐ This action is **FINAL**. 2b) ☒ This action is non-final.
3) ☐ An election was made by the applicant in response to a restriction requirement set forth during the interview on _____; the restriction requirement and election have been incorporated into this action.
4) ☐ Since this application is in condition for allowance except for formal matters, prosecution as to the merits is closed in accordance with the practice under *Ex parte Quayle*, 1935 C.D. 11, 453 O.G. 213.

Disposition of Claims*

5) ☒ Claim(s) _21-40_ is/are pending in the application.
5a) Of the above claim(s) _____ is/are withdrawn from consideration.
6) ☐ Claim(s) _____ is/are allowed.
7) ☒ Claim(s) _21-40_ is/are rejected.
8) ☐ Claim(s) _____ is/are objected to.
9) ☐ Claim(s) _____ are subject to restriction and/or election requirement.

* If any claims have been determined allowable, you may be eligible to benefit from the **Patent Prosecution Highway** program at a participating intellectual property office for the corresponding application. For more information, please see http://www.uspto.gov/patents/init_events/pph/index.jsp or send an inquiry to PPHfeedback@uspto.gov.

Application Papers

10) ☐ The specification is objected to by the Examiner.
11) ☐ The drawing(s) filed on _____ is/are: a) ☐ accepted or b) ☐ objected to by the Examiner.
Applicant may not request that any objection to the drawing(s) be held in abeyance. See 37 CFR 1.85(a).
Replacement drawing sheet(s) including the correction is required if the drawing(s) is objected to. See 37 CFR 1.121(d).

Priority under 35 U.S.C. § 119

12) ☐ Acknowledgment is made of a claim for foreign priority under 35 U.S.C. § 119(a)-(d) or (f).
Certified copies:
a) ☐ All b) ☐ Some** c) ☐ None of the:
1. ☐ Certified copies of the priority documents have been received.
2. ☐ Certified copies of the priority documents have been received in Application No. _____.
3. ☐ Copies of the certified copies of the priority documents have been received in this National Stage application from the International Bureau (PCT Rule 17.2(a)).

** See the attached detailed Office action for a list of the certified copies not received.

Attachment(s)

1) ☒ Notice of References Cited (PTO-892)
2) ☐ Information Disclosure Statement(s) (PTO/SB/08a and/or PTO/SB/08b) Paper No(s)/Mail Date _____.
3) ☐ Interview Summary (PTO-413) Paper No(s)/Mail Date _____.
4) ☐ Other: _____.

U.S. Patent and Trademark Office
PTOL-326 (Rev. 11-13) Office Action Summary Part of Paper No./Mail Date 20160104

Application/Control Number: 14/503,210 Page 2
Art Unit: 2665

The present application, filed on or after March 16, 2013, is being examined under the first inventor to file provisions of the AIA.

DETAILED ACTION

Election/Restrictions

1. Applicant timely elected without traversed the restriction (election) requirement in the reply filed on Dec. 16 2015. Accordingly, claims 21-40 are now presented for prosecution.

Double Patenting

2. The nonstatutory double patenting rejection is based on a judicially created doctrine grounded in public policy (a policy reflected in the statute) so as to prevent the unjustified or improper timewise extension of the "right to exclude" granted by a patent and to prevent possible harassment by multiple assignees. See *In re Goodman*, 11 F.3d 1046, 29 USPQ2d 2010 (Fed. Cir. 1993); *In re Longi*, 759 F.2d 887, 225 USPQ 645 (Fed. Cir. 1985); *In re Van Ornum*, 686 F.2d 937, 214 USPQ 761 (CCPA 1982); *In re Vogel*, 422 F.2d 438, 164 USPQ 619 (CCPA 1970);and, *In re Thorington*, 418 F.2d 528, 163 USPQ 644 (CCPA 1969).

A timely filed terminal disclaimer in compliance with 37 CFR 1.321(c) may be used to overcome an actual or provisional rejection based on a nonstatutory double patenting ground provided the conflicting application or patent is shown to be commonly owned with this application. See 37 CFR 1.130(b).

Application/Control Number: 14/503,210 Page 3
Art Unit: 2665

Effective January 1, 1994, a registered attorney or agent of record may sign a terminal disclaimer. A terminal disclaimer signed by the assignee must fully comply with 37 CFR 3.73(b).

3. Claims 21-35, 39-40 are provisionally rejected on the ground of nonstatutory obviousness-type double patenting as being unpatentable over claims 1-20 of copending Application No. 14/503224. Although the conflicting claims are not identical, they are not patentably distinct from each other because the claimed subject matter of claims 21-35 and 39-40 of the instant invention is the similar version or exact wording of above mentioned claims 1-20 of copending Application No. 14/503224 such as DIO, synthetic image, behavior metadata, ambient image and flash image etc.

This is a provisional obviousness-type double patenting rejection because the conflicting claims have not in fact been patented.

Claim Rejections - 35 USC § 101

4. 35 U.S.C. 101 reads as follows:

> Whoever invents or discovers any new and useful process, machine, manufacture, or composition of matter, or any new and useful improvement thereof, may obtain a patent therefor, subject to the conditions and requirements of this title.

5. Claims 21, 39, 40 are rejected under 35 U.S.C. 101 because the claimed invention is directed to non-statutory subject matter.

Under *Alice v. CLS Bank*, 573 U.S. ___ (2014), a claim is nonstatutory if it is directed to a judicial exception, such as an abstract idea, and does not include "significantly more" such that the claim is not directed solely to the judicial exception itself. In the present case, claims 1, 39 and 40 are directed to the abstract idea of

Application/Control Number: 14/503,210 Page 4
Art Unit: 2665

identifying data/images/metadata, gathering/creating a package of data/image, and transmitting the data in general, which is similar to concepts that have been identified as abstract by the courts. There are no limitations to provide "significantly more" to render the claims not abstract. Accordingly, the claim pre-empts a judicial exception and is therefore nonstatutory.

Claim Rejections – 35 USC 102

6. The following is a quotation of the appropriate paragraphs of 35 U.S.C. 102 that form the basis for the rejections under this section made in this Office action:

> A person shall be entitled to a patent unless –
>
> (a)(1) the claimed invention was patented, described in a printed publication, or in public use, on sale or otherwise available to the public before the effective filing date of the claimed invention.
>
> (a)(2) the claimed invention was described in a patent issued under section 151, or in an application for patent published or deemed published under section 122(b), in which the patent or application, as the case may be, names another inventor and was effectively filed before the effective filing date of the claimed invention.

7. Claims 21, 22, 25-26, 29, 35, 38-40 are rejected under 35 U.S.C. 102(a)(2) as being anticipated by et al. (US 2015/0063694 A1, hereafter Shroff).

As to claim 21, Shroff discloses that a computer program product embodied on a non-transitory computer readable medium, comprising:

code for identifying a first image and a second image ([0039]-[0041], [0059], claims 1-3);

Application/Control Number: 14/503,210 Page 5
Art Unit: 2665

code for identifying metadata (characteristics or equalization ratio r') associated with each of the two or more images ([0007]-[0010], [0031]-[0032], [0047])

code for creating a package of the two or more images and the metadata ([0010], [0034]-[0049]); and

code for transmitting the package to a destination ([0059]-[0060]).

As to claims 22 and 25, Shroff further discloses that the computer program product of Claim 1, wherein the computer program product is operable such that first image is an ambient image and the second image is a flash image ([0039]).

As to claim 26, Shroff further discloses that the computer program product of Claim 21, wherein the computer program product is operable such that the metadata includes image metadata (see the rejection of claim 1).

As to claim 29, Shroff further discloses that the computer program product of Claim 21, and further comprising code for processing at least one of the two or more images to produce at least one processed image ([0034]-[0049]).

As to claim 35, Shroff further discloses that the computer program product of Claim 21, wherein the computer program product is operable for making the package accessible over a network ([0059]-[0060]).

Application/Control Number: 14/503,210 Page 6
Art Unit: 2665

As to claim 38, Shroff further discloses that the computer program product of Claim 21, wherein the transmitting occurs based on at least one of availability of the package, bandwidth availability, data allocation, and user connection ([0059]-[0060]).

As to claims 39 and 40, the claim is corresponding method and apparatus claims to claim 21, the discussions are addressed with respect to claim 21.

Claim Rejections - 35 USC § 103

8. The following is a quotation of 35 U.S.C. 103 which forms the basis for all obviousness rejections set forth in this Office action:

> A patent for a claimed invention may not be obtained, notwithstanding that the claimed invention is not identically disclosed as set forth in section 102 of this title, if the differences between the claimed invention and the prior art are such that the claimed invention as a whole would have been obvious before the effective filing date of the claimed invention to a person having ordinary skill in the art to which the claimed invention pertains. Patentability shall not be negated by the manner in which the invention was made.

The factual inquiries set forth in *Graham v. John Deere Co.*, 383 U.S. 1, 148 USPQ 459 (1966), that are applied for establishing a background for determining obviousness under pre-AIA 35 U.S.C. 103(a) are summarized as follows:

1). Determining the scope and contents of the prior art.

2). Ascertaining the differences between the prior art and the claims at issue.

3). Resolving the level of ordinary skill in the pertinent art.

4). Considering objective evidence present in the application indicating obviousness or nonobviousness.

In the event the determination of the status of the application as subject to AIA 35 U.S.C. 102 and 103 (or as subject to pre-AIA 35 U.S.C. 102 and 103) is incorrect, any

Application/Control Number: 14/503,210	Page 7
Art Unit: 2665

correction of the statutory basis for the rejection will not be considered a new ground of rejection if the prior art relied upon, and the rationale supporting the rejection, would be the same under either status.

9. Claims 23-24, 27-28, 30-34 are rejected under 35 U.S.C. 103(a) as being unpatentable over Shroff in view of Lee et al. (US 2007/0101251 A1, hereafter Lee)

As to claims 23-24, 30-34, Shroff mentions object with dynamic images combined in that at least one image is processed image([0010], [0053]-[0060]) and the synthetic image as a package.

Lee, in an analogous environment, discloses that the computer program product is operable such that the two or more images and the metadata are stored in a dynamic image object as a package ([0011]-[0024], [0061]-[0076]).

The knowledge that utilizing dynamic image object (DIO) stored image objects to generate an output image (composite image) is a desirable way to subject that would have been within the skill in the art, as evidenced by Lee. Therefore, it would have been obvious to one having ordinary skill in the art at the effective filing date of the invention to combine the well-known elements of Lee with the well-known technique in image processing of Shroff because the combination is nothing more than a "predictable use of prior art elements according to their established functions." *KSR*, 550 U.S., at 417.

Application/Control Number: 14/503,210 Page 8
Art Unit: 2665

As to claims 27-28   Lee further discloses that the computer program product of Claim 21, wherein the computer program product is operable such that the metadata includes view and generation behavior metadata ([0049]-[0072]).

10. Claims 36-37 are rejected under 35 U.S.C. 103(a) as being unpatentable over the combination of Shroff and Lee, further in view of Kazui et al. (US 2004/0059783 A1, hereafter Kazui).

As to claim 36, the combination of Shroff and Lee does not mention URL, which is well known.

Kazui, in an analogous environment, further discloses that creating the package includes creating local URLs associated with at least one of the two or more images and the metadata (Fig. 5, [108]-[0110], [0134]-[0135], [0214]).

The knowledge that utilizing URL with image object (DIO) is a desirable way to subject that would have been within the skill in the art, as evidenced by Kazui. Therefore, it would have been obvious to one having ordinary skill in the art at the effective filing date of the invention to combine the well-known elements of Kazui with the well-known technique in image processing of the combination of Shroff and Lee because the combination is nothing more than a "predictable use of prior art elements according to their established functions." *Id.*, at 417.

As to claim 37, the combination of Shroff, Lee and Kazui discloses that the computer program product of Claim 21, wherein creating the package includes creating URLs, but not cloud information, which is well known in the art.

Application/Control Number: 14/503,210 Page 9
Art Unit: 2665

However, Examiner takes Official Notice that utilizing URL with cloud information such as cloud server is well known in the art.

The knowledge that utilizing URL with cloud information is a desirable way to subject that would have been within the skill in the art, as evidenced by Official Notice. Therefore, it would have been obvious to one having ordinary skill in the art at the effective filing date of the invention to combine the well-known elements of Official Notice with the well-known technique in image processing of the combination of Shroff and Lee because the combination is nothing more than a "predictable use of prior art elements according to their established functions." *Id.*, at 417.

Examiner Notes

11. Examiner cites particular figures, paragraphs, columns and line numbers in the references as applied to the claims for the convenience of the applicant. Although the specified citations are representative of the teachings in the art and are applied to the specific limitations within the individual claim, other passages and figures may apply as well. It is respectfully requested that, in preparing responses, the applicant fully consider the references in entirety as potentially teaching all or part of the claimed invention, as well as the context of the passage as taught by the prior art or disclosed by the examiner.

Application/Control Number: 14/503,210　　　　　　　　　　　　　　　　　　　　Page 10
Art Unit: 2665

Contact Information

Any inquiry concerning this communication or earlier communications should be directed to Jingge Wu whose telephone number is (571)-272-7429. He can normally be reached Monday through Thursday from 8:00 am to 4:30 pm. The examiner can be also reached on second alternate Fridays.

If attempts to reach the Examiner by telephone are unsuccessful, the Examiner's supervisor, Bhavesh Mehta, can be reached at (571) 272-7453.

/Jingge Wu/

Primary Examiner, Art Unit 2665

TC 2600

LINCOLN LAW SCHOOL OF SAN JOSE
INTELLECTUAL PROPERTY SERIES

EXHIBIT: OFFICE ACTION RESPONSE

IN THE UNITED STATES PATENT AND TRADEMARK OFFICE

In re Application of:	Confirmation No.: 8161
Adam Feder	Examiner: Jingge WU
Application No.: 14/503,210	Art Unit: 2665
File Date: 2014-09-30	Docket No.: DUELP001
Title: SYSTEMS, METHODS, AND COMPUTER PROGRAM PRODUCTS FOR DIGITAL PHOTOGRAPHY	Date: May 12, 2016

AMENDMENT A

Commissioner for Patents
P.O. Box 1450
Alexandria VA 22313-1450

Examiner:

In response to the communication mailed 01-12-2016 (hereafter "Non Final Office Action" or "NFOA"), please consider the following amendments believed to place the claims in condition for allowance.

Application No.: 14/503,210
Date: May 12, 2016
Response to Office Action

Amendments to the Claims:

The listing of amended claims follows:

1. – 20. (Canceled)

21. (Currently amended) A~~ comp~~n apparatus ~~uter program product embodied on a non-transitory computer readable medium~~, comprising:

  circuitry for:

   causing an image sensor to capture two or more images;

   ~~code for~~ identifying the two or more images;

   ~~code for~~ identifying metadata associated with each of the two or more images, wherein the metadata includes at least two of a resolution, a color scheme, a compression type, a camera model type, a camera processor type, a lens make or model, user behavior, and user connections, further wherein the metadata includes one or more functions used to generate a display image, an additional image, or a combination of the display image and the additional image;

   storing the two or more images and the metadata in a data object associated with a dynamic image object, wherein the dynamic image object includes the two or more images and the metadata;

   ~~code for~~ creating a package ~~of the two or more images and the metadata~~ including the dynamic image object, wherein creating the package includes at least one of:

Application No.: 14/503,210
Date: May 12, 2016
Response to Office Action

<u>creating local URLs associated with at least one of the two or more</u>

<u>images and the metadata; and</u>

<u>creating URLs associated with cloud-based information</u>; [[and]]

~~code for~~ transmitting the package to a destination<u>; and</u>

<u>allowing the package to be rendered based on the dynamic image object.</u>

22. (Currently amended) The ~~computer program product~~<u>apparatus</u> of Claim 21, wherein the <u>apparatus</u>~~computer program product~~ is operable such that <u>the</u> two or more images include at least one of an ambient image and a flash image.

23. (Canceled)

24. (Canceled)

25. (Currently amended) The <u>apparatus</u>~~computer program product~~ of Claim 21, wherein the <u>apparatus</u>~~computer program product is~~ operable such that <u>the</u> two or more images include at least one ambient image and one flash image.

26. (Currently amended) The <u>apparatus</u>~~computer program product~~ of Claim 21, wherein the <u>apparatus</u>~~computer program product~~ is operable such that the metadata includes image metadata.

Application No.: 14/503,210
Date: May 12, 2016
Response to Office Action

27. (Currently amended) The apparatus~~computer program product~~ of Claim 21, wherein the apparatus~~computer program product~~ is operable such that the metadata includes view behavior metadata.

28. (Currently amended) The apparatus~~computer program product~~ of Claim 21, wherein the apparatus~~computer program product~~ is operable such that the metadata includes generation behavior metadata.

29. (Currently amended) The apparatus~~computer program product~~ of Claim 21, the circuitry further~~and further comprising code~~ for processing at least one of the two or more images to produce at least one processed image.

30. (Currently amended) The apparatus~~computer program product~~ of Claim 29, wherein the apparatus~~computer program product~~ is operable such that the at least one processed image is stored in an object.

31. (Currently amended) The apparatus~~computer program product~~ of Claim 30, wherein the apparatus~~computer program product~~ is operable such that the object includes [[a]]the dynamic image object.

Application No.: 14/503,210
Date: May 12, 2016
Response to Office Action

32. (Currently amended) The apparatus ~~computer program product~~ of Claim 30, wherein the apparatus ~~computer program product~~ is operable such that the object is stored in the package.

33. (Currently amended) The apparatus ~~computer program product~~ of Claim 29, the circuitry further ~~and further comprising code~~ for generating a synthetic image based on the two or more images and the processed image.

34. (Currently amended) The apparatus ~~computer program product~~ of Claim 33, wherein the apparatus ~~computer program product~~ is operable such that the synthetic image is stored in the package.

35. (Currently amended) The apparatus ~~computer program product~~ of Claim 21, wherein the apparatus ~~computer program product~~ is operable for making the package accessible over a network.

36. (Currently amended) The apparatus ~~computer program product~~ of Claim 21, wherein creating the package includes creating the local URLs associated with at least one of the two or more images and the metadata.

37. (Canceled)

Application No.: 14/503,210
Date: May 12, 2016
Response to Office Action

38. (Canceled)

39. (Currently Amended) An ~~apparatus~~ computer program product embodied on a non-transitory computer readable medium, comprising:

~~at least one processor for:~~

code for causing an image sensor to capture two or more images;

code for identifying the two or more images;

code for identifying metadata associated with each of the two or more images, wherein the metadata includes at least two of a resolution, a color scheme, a compression type, a camera model type, a camera processor type, a lens make or model, user behavior, and user connections, further wherein the metadata includes one or more functions used to generate a display image, an additional image, or a combination of the display image and the additional image;

code for storing the two or more images and the metadata in a data object associated with a dynamic image object, wherein the dynamic image object includes the two or more images and the metadata;

code for creating a package ~~of the two or more images and the metadata~~ including the dynamic image object, wherein creating the package includes at least one of:

creating local URLs associated with at least one of the two or more

images and the metadata; and

creating URLs associated with cloud-based information; [[and]]

code for transmitting the package to a destination; and

Application No.: 14/503,210
Date: May 12, 2016
Response to Office Action

<u>code for allowing the package to be rendered based on the dynamic image object.</u>

40. (Currently Amended) A method, comprising:

<u>causing an image sensor to capture two or more images;</u>

identifying <u>the</u> two or more images;

identifying metadata associated with each of the two or more images<u>, wherein the metadata includes at least two of a resolution, a color scheme, a compression type, a camera model type, a camera processor type, a lens make or model, user behavior, and user connections, further wherein the metadata includes one or more functions used to generate a display image, an additional image, or a combination of the display image and the additional image</u>;

<u>storing the two or more images and the metadata in a data object associated with a dynamic image object, wherein the dynamic image object includes the two or more images and the metadata;</u>

creating a package ~~of the two or more images and the metadata~~<u>including the dynamic image object, wherein creating the package includes at least one of:</u>

<u>creating local URLs associated with at least one of the two or more images and the metadata; and</u>

<u>creating URLs associated with cloud-based information;</u> [[and]]

transmitting the package to a destination<u>; and</u>

<u>allowing the package to be rendered based on the dynamic image object.</u>

7

Application No.: 14/503,210
Date: May 12, 2016
Response to Office Action

Remarks:

Claims 21-35, and 39-40 have been provisionally rejected on the ground of nonstatutory obviousness type double patenting as being unpatentable over claims 1-20 of copending Application No. 14/503,224. Because this is a provisional rejection, Applicant respectfully submits that filing a Terminal Disclaimer is not presently necessary, and that a Terminal Disclaimer may be filed if necessary, at the appropriate time, e.g., if and when the obviousness type double patenting rejection is the only remaining rejection in this and/or the copending application. See MPEP § 804(I)(B)(I).

The Examiner has rejected Claims 21, 39, and 40 under 35 U.S.C. 101 as being directed to non-statutory subject matter. Applicant respectfully asserts that such rejection is avoided in view of the amendments made hereinabove to Claims 21, 39, and 40.

The Examiner has rejected Claims 21-22, 25-26, 29, 35, and 38-40 under 35 U.S.C. 102(a)(2) as being anticipated by Shroff et al (U.S. Publication No. 2015/0063694). Additionally, the Examiner has rejected Claims 23-24, 27-28, 30-34 under 35 U.S.C. 103(a) as being unpatentable over Shroff in view of Lee et al. (U.S. Publication No. 2007/0101251). Applicant respectfully disagrees with such rejections, especially in view of the amendments made hereinabove to each of the independent claims.

Specifically, applicant has amended the independent claims as follows:

<u>circuitry for:</u>

<u>causing an image sensor to capture two or more images;</u>

~~code for~~ <u>identifying the</u> two or more images;

~~code for~~ identifying metadata associated with each of the two or more images<u>,</u>

<u>wherein the metadata includes at least two of a resolution, a color scheme, a</u>

<u>compression type, a camera model type, a camera processor type, a lens make or</u>

<u>model, user behavior, and user connections, further wherein the metadata includes one</u>

<u>or more functions used to generate a display image, an additional image, or a</u>

<u>combination of the display image and the additional image;</u>

Application No.: 14/503,210
Date: May 12, 2016
Response to Office Action

> storing the two or more images and the metadata in a data object associated with a dynamic image object, wherein the dynamic image object includes the two or more images and the metadata;
>
> ~~code for~~ creating a package ~~of the two or more images and the metadata~~ including the dynamic image object, wherein creating the package includes at least one of:
>
> creating local URLs associated with at least one of the two or more images and the metadata; and
>
> creating URLs associated with cloud-based information; [[and]]
>
> ~~code for~~ transmitting the package to a destination; and
>
> allowing the package to be rendered based on the dynamic image object. (as amended, see this or similar, but not necessarily identical language in the independent claims).

Applicant respectfully notes that the Shroff reference, as relied upon by the Examiner, discloses that "[t]echniques are described for combining two or more images that are taken with varying brightness degrees to generate a composite image" (See Abstract – emphasis added) and that "[c]ertain embodiments present an apparatus for generating a composite image by combining a first image of a scene with a second image of the scene" (See Paragraph [0010] – emphasis added). Additionally, Shroff discloses that "when flash does not reach parts of the scene, the composite image is generated by similar procedures that are used in generation of high dynamic range (HDR) images" such as "when ambient image is too dark, the weight masks may be generated such that the composite image takes its color and brightness values from the flash image." (See Paragraph [0049] – emphasis added).

However, disclosing that a composite image may be generated, which may rely on weight masks, as in Shroff, fails to disclose:

Application No.: 14/503,210
Date: May 12, 2016
Response to Office Action

>> circuitry for:
>>
>>> causing an image sensor to capture two or more images;
>>>
>>> identifying the two or more images;
>>>
>>> identifying metadata associated with each of the two or more images, <u>wherein the metadata includes at least two of</u> a <u>resolution</u>, a <u>color scheme</u>, a <u>compression type</u>, a <u>camera model type</u>, a <u>camera processor type</u>, a <u>lens make or model</u>, <u>user behavior</u>, and <u>user connections</u>, further wherein <u>the metadata includes one or more functions used to generate a display image, an additional image, or a combination of the display image and the additional image</u>;
>>>
>>> <u>storing the two or more images and the metadata in a data object associated with a dynamic image object, wherein the dynamic image object includes the two or more images and the metadata</u>;
>>>
>>> creating a **package** including <u>the dynamic image object</u>, wherein creating the package includes at least one of:
>>>
>>>> <u>creating local URLs</u> associated with at least one of the two or more images and the metadata; and
>>>>
>>>> <u>creating URLs associated with cloud-based information</u>;
>>>
>>> transmitting the package to a destination; and
>>>
>>> allowing the package to be rendered <u>based on the dynamic image object</u>.

(emphasis added), as claimed by applicant.

The Examiner is reminded that a claim is anticipated only if each and every element as set forth in the claim is found, either expressly or inherently described in a single prior art reference.

Application No.: 14/503,210
Date: May 12, 2016
Response to Office Action

Verdegaal Bros. v. Union Oil Co. Of California, 814 F.2d 628, 631, 2 USPQ2d 1051, 1053 (Fed. Cir. 1987). Moreover, the identical invention must be shown in as complete detail as contained in the claim. Richardson v. Suzuki Motor Co.868 F.2d 1226, 1236, 9USPQ2d 1913, 1920 (Fed. Cir. 1989). The elements must be arranged as required by the claim.

This criterion has simply not been met by the above reference excerpt(s), as noted above.

With respect to the subject matter of former Claims 23-24 (now at least substantially incorporated into each of the independent claims), the Examiner has relied on Paragraphs [0010] and [0053]-[0060] from the Shroff reference, in addition to Paragraphs [0011]-[0024] and [0061]-[0076] from the Lee reference to make a prior art showing of applicant's claimed technique wherein "storing the two or more images and the metadata in a data object associated with a dynamic image object, wherein the dynamic image object includes the two or more images and the metadata" (see this or similar, but not necessarily identical language in the independent claims, as amended).

Applicant respectfully notes that the Shroff reference, as relied upon by the Examiner, discloses that "a composite image [may be generated] by combining a first image of a scene with a second image of the scene." See Paragraph [0011] – emphasis added.

Applicant respectfully notes that the Lee reference, as relied upon by the Examiner, discloses that "the term 'template' is used to refer to a frame in which content, such as pictures and dynamic image objects, is arranged" where "[t]he template is used for an image unit group, which is a unit for the structure of the dynamic image object" and "the template may include a background image 210, a layout 220 wherein content may be arranged, a sticker 230 for decorating the background image 210, and a caption 240, noting that alternatives are equally available." See Paragraph [0048] – emphasis added. Additionally, "the system 100 may also include a storage module 170 to store the dynamic image object in which content are arranged and a display module 180 to display the dynamic image object in which the content are arranged." See Paragraph [0063] – emphasis added).

However, disclosing that a composite image may be generated, as in Shroff, in addition to teaching that a template is a unit for a dynamic image object, where a template may include a background image, layout, sticker, and a caption, in addition to disclosing that content may be arranged, as in Lee, simply fails to teach or suggest "storing the two or more images and the metadata in a data object associated with a dynamic image object, wherein the dynamic image object includes the two or more images and the metadata" (emphasis added), as claimed by applicant.

Application No.: 14/503,210
Date: May 12, 2016
Response to Office Action

To establish a prima facie case of obviousness, three basic criteria must be met. First, there must be some suggestion or motivation, either in the references themselves or in the knowledge generally available to one of ordinary skill in the art, to modify the reference or to combine reference teachings. Second, there must be a reasonable expectation of success. Finally, the prior art reference (or references when combined) must teach or suggest all the claim limitations. The teaching or suggestion to make the claimed combination and the reasonable expectation of success must both be found in the prior art and not based on applicant's disclosure. *In re Vaeck*, 947 F.2d 488, 20 USPQ2d 1438 (Fed.Cir.1991).

Applicant respectfully asserts that at least the third element of the prima facie case of obviousness has not been met, since the prior art excerpts, as relied upon by the Examiner, fail to teach or suggest all of the claim limitations, as noted above.

Further, with respect to Claim 37 (now at least substantially incorporated into each of the independent claims), the Examiner has relied on Official Notice to make a prior art showing of applicant's claimed technique "creating the package includes creating URLs associated with cloud-based information." Specifically, the Examiner has stated that "Examiner takes Official Notice that utilizing URL with cloud information such as cloud server is well known in the art."

However, the Claim does not require merely "utilizing URL with cloud information," as suggested by the Examiner, but requires "<u>creating the package</u> includes <u>creating URLs</u> associated with <u>cloud-based information</u>" (emphasis added), as claimed by applicant. As noted in the MPEP, "[i]f the applicant traverses such an [Official Notice] assertion the examiner should cite a reference in support of his or her position." See MPEP 2144.03.

Therefore, applicant has adequately traversed the Examiner's assertion of Official Notice (specifically, with regard to Claim 37), and again thus formally requests a specific showing of the subject matter in ALL of the claims in any future action.

Again, applicant respectfully asserts that at least the third element of the prima facie case of obviousness has not been met, since the excerpts from the prior art references, as relied upon by the Examiner, fail to teach or suggest all of the claim limitations, as noted above.

It is believed that all of the pending issues have been addressed. However, the absence of a reply to a specific rejection, issue, or comment does not signify agreement with or concession of that rejection, issue, or comment. In addition, because the arguments made above may not be exhaustive, there may be reasons for patentability of any or all pending claims (or other claims) that have not been expressed. Still yet, nothing in this reply should be construed as intention to

Application No.: 14/503,210
Date: May 12, 2016
Response to Office Action

concede any issue with regard to any claim, except as specifically stated in this reply. Finally, it should be noted that no claims are intended to be construed under 35 U.S.C. 112, paragraph 6.

Applicant hereby requests an extension of time to respond and encloses the appropriate fee. Applicant does not believe that any additional fees are due. However, in the event that any other fees are due, the Director is hereby authorized to charge any required fees due (other than issue fees), and to credit any overpayment made, in connection with the filing of this paper to Deposit Account No. 50-1351 (Order No. DUELP001).

Respectfully submitted,

Zilka-Kotab, PC.

/Britten Sessions/

Britten Sessions
Reg. No. 68278
1155 N. 1st Street, Suite 105
San Jose, CA 95112-4925
408-971-2573

LINCOLN LAW SCHOOL OF SAN JOSE
INTELLECTUAL PROPERTY SERIES

EXHIBIT: OFFICE ACTION

UNITED STATES PATENT AND TRADEMARK OFFICE

UNITED STATES DEPARTMENT OF COMMERCE
United States Patent and Trademark Office
Address: COMMISSIONER FOR PATENTS
P.O. Box 1450
Alexandria, Virginia 22313-1450
www.uspto.gov

APPLICATION NO.	FILING DATE	FIRST NAMED INVENTOR	ATTORNEY DOCKET NO.	CONFIRMATION NO.
14/547,077	11/18/2014	William Rivard	DUELP015/DL024	2978

135841   7590   05/12/2017
Zilka-Kotab, PC - DUEL
1155 N. 1st St.
Suite 105
SAN JOSE, CA 95112

EXAMINER
TRAN, TAN H

ART UNIT	PAPER NUMBER
2141	

NOTIFICATION DATE	DELIVERY MODE
05/12/2017	ELECTRONIC

Please find below and/or attached an Office communication concerning this application or proceeding.

The time period for reply, if any, is set in the attached communication.

Notice of the Office communication was sent electronically on above-indicated "Notification Date" to the following e-mail address(es):

zk-uspto@zilkakotab.com
eofficeaction@appcoll.com

PTOL-90A (Rev. 04/07)

EXHIBITS 145

Office Action Summary	Application No. 14/547,077	Applicant(s) RIVARD ET AL.
	Examiner TAN TRAN	Art Unit 2141 / AIA (First Inventor to File) Status: Yes

-- The MAILING DATE of this communication appears on the cover sheet with the correspondence address --

Period for Reply

A SHORTENED STATUTORY PERIOD FOR REPLY IS SET TO EXPIRE **3** MONTHS FROM THE MAILING DATE OF THIS COMMUNICATION.
- Extensions of time may be available under the provisions of 37 CFR 1.136(a). In no event, however, may a reply be timely filed after SIX (6) MONTHS from the mailing date of this communication.
- If NO period for reply is specified above, the maximum statutory period will apply and will expire SIX (6) MONTHS from the mailing date of this communication.
- Failure to reply within the set or extended period for reply will, by statute, cause the application to become ABANDONED (35 U.S.C. § 133).
- Any reply received by the Office later than three months after the mailing date of this communication, even if timely filed, may reduce any earned patent term adjustment. See 37 CFR 1.704(b).

Status

1) ☒ Responsive to communication(s) filed on *4/10/2017*.
☐ A declaration(s)/affidavit(s) under **37 CFR 1.130(b)** was/were filed on _____.
2a) ☒ This action is **FINAL**.   2b) ☐ This action is non-final.
3) ☐ An election was made by the applicant in response to a restriction requirement set forth during the interview on _____; the restriction requirement and election have been incorporated into this action.
4) ☐ Since this application is in condition for allowance except for formal matters, prosecution as to the merits is closed in accordance with the practice under *Ex parte Quayle*, 1935 C.D. 11, 453 O.G. 213.

Disposition of Claims*

5) ☒ Claim(s) *1-4 and 6-23* is/are pending in the application.
5a) Of the above claim(s) _____ is/are withdrawn from consideration.
6) ☐ Claim(s) _____ is/are allowed.
7) ☒ Claim(s) *1-4 and 6-23* is/are rejected.
8) ☐ Claim(s) _____ is/are objected to.
9) ☐ Claim(s) _____ are subject to restriction and/or election requirement.

* If any claims have been determined allowable, you may be eligible to benefit from the **Patent Prosecution Highway** program at a participating intellectual property office for the corresponding application. For more information, please see http://www.uspto.gov/patents/init_events/pph/index.jsp or send an inquiry to PPHfeedback@uspto.gov.

Application Papers

10) ☐ The specification is objected to by the Examiner.
11) ☐ The drawing(s) filed on _____ is/are: a) ☐ accepted or b) ☐ objected to by the Examiner.
Applicant may not request that any objection to the drawing(s) be held in abeyance. See 37 CFR 1.85(a).
Replacement drawing sheet(s) including the correction is required if the drawing(s) is objected to. See 37 CFR 1.121(d).

Priority under 35 U.S.C. § 119

12) ☐ Acknowledgment is made of a claim for foreign priority under 35 U.S.C. § 119(a)-(d) or (f).
Certified copies:
a) ☐ All   b) ☐ Some**   c) ☐ None of the:
1. ☐ Certified copies of the priority documents have been received.
2. ☐ Certified copies of the priority documents have been received in Application No. _____.
3. ☐ Copies of the certified copies of the priority documents have been received in this National Stage application from the International Bureau (PCT Rule 17.2(a)).
** See the attached detailed Office action for a list of the certified copies not received.

Attachment(s)

1) ☒ Notice of References Cited (PTO-892)
2) ☒ Information Disclosure Statement(s) (PTO/SB/08a and/or PTO/SB/08b) Paper No(s)/Mail Date *4/10/2017*.
3) ☐ Interview Summary (PTO-413) Paper No(s)/Mail Date. _____.
4) ☐ Other: _____.

U.S. Patent and Trademark Office
PTOL-326 (Rev. 11-13)   Office Action Summary   Part of Paper No./Mail Date 20170505

Application/Control Number: 14/547,077 Page 2
Art Unit: 2141

1. The present application, filed on or after March 16, 2013, is being examined under the first inventor to file provisions of the AIA.

DETAILED ACTION

2. This Office Action is sent in response to Applicant's Communication received on 04/10/2017 for application number 14/547,077.

Response to Amendments

3. The Amendment filed 04/10/2017 has been entered. Claims 1, 6, 14, and 18-20 have been amended. Claim 5 has been canceled. Claims 21-23 have been added. Claims 1-4 and 6-23 remain pending in the application.

4. Applicant's amendments to the claim 11 has been fully considered and is persuasive. The objection to this claim is respectfully withdrawn.

5. Applicant's amendment to the claim 18 has been fully considered and is persuasive. The amendment provided to overcome the 112(b) rejection issued in the last office action is sufficient. The 35 U.S.C § 112(b) rejection of claim 18 is respectfully withdrawn.

Response to Arguments

6. **Argument 1**, Applicant argues that teaching that a "tool is activated" in one part of the screen, after which such tool feature is used to manipulate "the displayed image," as in the UBILLOS excerpt(s) relied upon, does not teach or suggest "code for, while continually receiving the first user input, receiving a second user input in connection with one or more portions of displayed content in a second region of the graphical user interface" (emphasis added), as claimed by applicant, especially "while continually receiving the first user input," where in context, the "first user input in a first region of a graphical user interface, wherein the first region displays one or more tools" (emphasis added), as claimed by applicant.

Application/Control Number: 14/547,077 Page 3
Art Unit: 2141

7. **Responding to Argument 1**, the argument is moot since this is a newly presented limitation, thus changes the scope of the claim. However, a newly found reference, Hicks, is applied.

Claim Rejections – 35 USC § 103

8. The following is a quotation of 35 U.S.C. 103 which forms the basis for all obviousness rejections set forth in this Office action:

> A patent for a claimed invention may not be obtained, notwithstanding that the claimed invention is not identically disclosed as set forth in section 102 of this title, if the differences between the claimed invention and the prior art are such that the claimed invention as a whole would have been obvious before the effective filing date of the claimed invention to a person having ordinary skill in the art to which the claimed invention pertains. Patentability shall not be negated by the manner in which the invention was made.

9. **Claims 1-4, 6-10, 12-13, 16-21 are rejected under 35 U.S.C. 103 as being unpatentable over Ubillos et al. (U.S. Patent Application Pub. No. US 20130235071 A1) in view of Hicks et al. (U.S. Patent Application Pub. No. US 20140306899 A1).**

Claim 1: Ubillos teaches a computer program product embodied on a non-transitory computer readable medium, comprising:

code for receiving a first user input in a first region of a graphical user interface *(i.e. fig. 12, the user then selects the icon 421 displayed in the tool selection pane 420. In response, the image editing application at stage 1203 activates the cropping and straightening tool; para. [0178])*, wherein the first region displays one or more tools *(i.e. fig. 12, the tool options display at the bottom of the image editing application; para. [0178])*;

code for, while receiving the first user input *(i.e. fig. 12, he image editing application highlights the icon 421 to indicate that the cropping and straightening tool is activated; para. [0178])*, receiving a second user input in connection with one or more portions of displayed content in a second region of the graphical user interface *(i.e. fig. 12, the user touches the image with two fingers 1235 and 1240 and rotates the two fingers clockwise; para. [0180])*; and

Application/Control Number: 14/547,077 Page 4
Art Unit: 2141

code for computing one or more operations in connection with the one or more portions of the displayed content, based on the first user input and the second user input *(i.e. fig. 12, the user has rotated the fingers 1235 and 1240 clockwise past the predefined threshold degrees. The cropping and straightening tool rotates the displayed image 445 accordingly; para. [0180]).*

Ubillos does not explicitly teach while continually receiving the first user input, receiving a second user input in connection with one or more portions of displayed content in a second region of the graphical user interface.

However, Hicks teaches while continually receiving the first user input, receiving a second user input in connection with one or more portions of displayed content in a second region of the graphical user interface *(i.e. fig. 3, the shift key is being held down (by the user's other hand) while making a swipe gesture from the multidirectional swipe key to cause the text to be highlighted and/or selected in combination with the cursor movement shown (from the initial cursor position in FIG. 3 a). As previously described, the highlight activation action may include various actions such as selecting the shift key/function before performing multidirectional swipe key gestures for cursor movement; para. [0049]).*

Therefore, it would have been obvious to one of ordinary skill in the art before the effective filling date of the claimed invention to modify the invention of Ubillos to include the feature of Hicks. One would have been motivated to make this modification because it provides the capability to utilize multi-gesture inputs as taught by Hicks *(para. [0049]).*

Claim 2: Ubillos and Hicks teach the computer program product of Claim 1. Ubillos further teaches wherein the computer program product is operable such that the first region is predefined with set boundaries *(i.e. fig. 12, the tool options display at the bottom of the image editing application; para. [0178]).*

Claim 3: Ubillos and Hicks teach the computer program product of Claim 1. Ubillos further teaches wherein the computer program product is operable such that the second region of the graphical

Application/Control Number: 14/547,077
Art Unit: 2141

Page 5

user interface corresponds with an image *(i.e. fig. 12, the image editing application displays the image 445, represented by the thumbnail 440, in the image display area 410 in response to the selection of the thumbnail 440; para. [0177])*.

Claim 4: Ubillos and Hicks teach the computer program product of Claim 1. Ubillos further teaches wherein the computer program product is operable such that the second region of the graphical user interface corresponds with text *(i.e. the source files 4640 stores the media content (e.g. text, audio, image, and video content); para. [0431])*.

Claim 6: Ubillos and Hicks teach the computer program product of Claim 1. Ubillos further teaches wherein the computer program product is operable such that additional tools are capable of being displayed in the first region through at least one of a region depth or layer, screens associated with the region, or window frames of the region *(i.e. fig. 20, a set of selectable UI items 2025 that represent these on-image brush tools in the tool display area; para. [0229])*.

Claim 7: Ubillos and Hicks teach the computer program product of Claim 1. Ubillos further teaches wherein the computer program product is operable such that the second user input is capable of including one or more points *(i.e. fig. 20, the user rubs the water and a tip of the oar left and right multiple times using a finger 2070. The blemish removal tool identifies the area that has been rubbed by the user and applies blemish removal operation to the area; para. [0235])*.

Claim 8: Ubillos and Hicks teach the computer program product of Claim 7. Ubillos further teaches wherein the computer program product is operable such that the one or more points include at least one of a range of data, an average of data, or a specific location on the graphical user interface *(i.e. fig. 20, the user rubs the water and a tip of the oar left and right multiple times using a finger 2070. The blemish removal tool identifies the area that has been rubbed by the user and applies blemish removal operation to the area; para. [0235])*.

Application/Control Number: 14/547,077 Page 6
Art Unit: 2141

Claim 9: Ubillos and Hicks teach the computer program product of Claim 8. Ubillos further teaches wherein the computer program product is operable such that the one or more points include the range of data, and the computer program product is further operable such that the range of data includes a range of pixels on an image *(i.e. the pixel that is considered to have been touched is the average pixel coordinate of the set of pixels that were touched by the user's finger; para. [0346]).*

Claim 10: Ubillos and Hicks teach the computer program product of Claim 9. Ubillos further teaches wherein the computer program product is operable such that computing the one or more operations includes using the range of pixels on the image, the range including an average of pixels *(i.e. the pixel that is considered to have been touched is the average pixel coordinate of the set of pixels that were touched by the user's finger; para. [0346]).*

Claim 12: Ubillos and Hicks teach the computer program product of Claim 1. Ubillos further teaches wherein the computer program product is operable such that the second user input is capable of including two or more points, each of the points being associated with a specific one or more operations *(i.e. fig. 12, the user has rotated the fingers 1235 and 1240 clockwise past the predefined threshold degrees. The cropping and straightening tool rotates the displayed image 445 accordingly; para. [0180]).*

Claim 13: Ubillos and Hicks teach the computer program product of Claim 1. Ubillos further teaches wherein the computer program product is operable such that receiving the second user input includes receiving multiple points in connection with the one or more portions of the displayed content *(i.e. fig. 12, the user has rotated the fingers 1235 and 1240 clockwise past the predefined threshold degrees. The cropping and straightening tool rotates the displayed image 445 accordingly; para. [0180]).*

Application/Control Number: 14/547,077 Page 7
Art Unit: 2141

Claim 16: Ubillos and Hicks teach the computer program product of Claim 1. Ubillos further teaches further comprising code for automatically detecting an edge in the second region *(i.e. fig. 27, **The smart edge detection tool analyzes the pixels in the portion of the image 2720 that is initially touched by the finger 2730 and sets the criteria for other pixels in other portions of the image to satisfy in order for the lightening tool to apply the lightening effect to those pixels; para. [0288]**)*.

Claim 17: Ubillos and Hicks teach the computer program product of Claim 16. Ubillos further teaches wherein the computer program product is operable such that the second user input is capable of including a contributing area for use in selecting a region based on one or more points of interest *(i.e. fig. 27, **because the portion of the image that is initially touched is in the sea shown in the image 2720, the lightening tool in this example applies the lightening effect on only those pixels that have a color similar to the sea's color; para. [0288]**)* and the automatically detected edge *(i.e. fig. 27, **The smart edge detection tool analyzes the pixels in the portion of the image 2720 that is initially touched by the finger 2730 and sets the criteria for other pixels in other portions of the image to satisfy in order for the lightening tool to apply the lightening effect to those pixels; para. [0288]**)*.

Claim 18: Ubillos and Hicks teach the computer program product of Claim 1. Ubillos further teaches wherein the computer program product is operable such that, in connection with the second user input, the computer program product is operable for automatically detecting an edge in the second region *(i.e. fig. 27, **The smart edge detection tool analyzes the pixels in the portion of the image 2720 that is initially touched by the finger 2730 and sets the criteria for other pixels in other portions of the image to satisfy in order for the lightening tool to apply the lightening effect to those pixels; para. [0288]**)*, selecting an area of the second region, processing the selected area based on the automatically detected edge, creating at least one ordered list for pixels selected, and displaying a resulting selected area; the computing one or more operations includes processing the at least one vector to display the resulting image based on the one or more operations *(i.e. fig. 27, **because the portion of the image that is initially touched is in the sea shown in the image 2720, the lightening tool in this example**

Application/Control Number: 14/547,077 Page 8
Art Unit: 2141

applies the lightening effect on only those pixels that have a color similar to the sea's color; para. [0288]).

Claim 19: Ubillos teaches an apparatus, comprising:

Circuitry for *(i.e. application specific integrated circuits; para. [0473])*:

receiving a first user input in a first region of a graphical user interface *(i.e. fig. 12, the user then selects the icon 421 displayed in the tool selection pane 420. In response, the image editing application at stage 1203 activates the cropping and straightening tool; para. [0178])*, wherein the first region displays one or more tools *(i.e. fig. 12, the tool options display at the bottom of the image editing application; para. [0178])*;

while receiving the first user input *(i.e. fig. 12, he image editing application highlights the icon 421 to indicate that the cropping and straightening tool is activated; para. [0178])*, receiving a second user input in connection with one or more portions of displayed content in a second region of the graphical user interface *(i.e. fig. 12, the user touches the image with two fingers 1235 and 1240 and rotates the two fingers clockwise; para. [0180])*; and

computing one or more operations in connection with the one or more portions of the displayed content, based on the first user input and the second user input *(i.e. fig. 12, the user has rotated the fingers 1235 and 1240 clockwise past the predefined threshold degrees. The cropping and straightening tool rotates the displayed image 445 accordingly; para. [0180])*.

Ubillos does not explicitly teach while continually receiving the first user input, receiving a second user input in connection with one or more portions of displayed content in a second region of the graphical user interface.

However, Hicks teaches while continually receiving the first user input, receiving a second user input in connection with one or more portions of displayed content in a second region of the graphical user interface *(i.e. fig. 3, the shift key is being held down (by the user's other hand) while making a swipe gesture from the multidirectional swipe key to cause the text to be highlighted and/or selected in combination with the cursor movement shown (from the initial cursor position in FIG.*

Application/Control Number: 14/547,077 Page 9
Art Unit: 2141

3 a). As previously described, the highlight activation action may include various actions such as selecting the shift key/function before performing multidirectional swipe key gestures for cursor movement; para. [0049]).

Therefore, it would have been obvious to one of ordinary skill in the art before the effective filling date of the claimed invention to modify the invention of Ubillos to include the feature of Hicks. One would have been motivated to make this modification because it provides the capability to utilize multi-gesture inputs as taught by Hicks *(para. [0049])*.

Claim 20: Ubillos teaches a method, comprising:

receiving a first user input in a first region of a graphical user interface *(i.e. fig. 12, the user then selects the icon 421 displayed in the tool selection pane 420. In response, the image editing application at stage 1203 activates the cropping and straightening tool; para. [0178])*, wherein the first region displays one or more tools *(i.e. fig. 12, the tool options display at the bottom of the image editing application; para. [0178])*;

while receiving the first user input *(i.e. fig. 12, he image editing application highlights the icon 421 to indicate that the cropping and straightening tool is activated; para. [0178])*, receiving a second user input in connection with one or more portions of displayed content in a second region of the graphical user interface *(i.e. fig. 12, the user touches the image with two fingers 1235 and 1240 and rotates the two fingers clockwise; para. [0180])*; and

computing one or more operations in connection with the one or more portions of the displayed content, based on the first user input and the user second input *(i.e. fig. 12, the user has rotated the fingers 1235 and 1240 clockwise past the predefined threshold degrees. The cropping and straightening tool rotates the displayed image 445 accordingly; para. [0180])*.

Ubillos does not explicitly teach while continually receiving the first user input, receiving a second user input in connection with one or more portions of displayed content in a second region of the graphical user interface.

Application/Control Number: 14/547,077 Page 10
Art Unit: 2141

However, Hicks teaches while continually receiving the first user input, receiving a second user input in connection with one or more portions of displayed content in a second region of the graphical user interface *(i.e. fig. 3, the shift key is being held down (by the user's other hand) while making a swipe gesture from the multidirectional swipe key to cause the text to be highlighted and/or selected in combination with the cursor movement shown (from the initial cursor position in FIG. 3 a). As previously described, the highlight activation action may include various actions such as selecting the shift key/function before performing multidirectional swipe key gestures for cursor movement; para. [0049])*.

Therefore, it would have been obvious to one of ordinary skill in the art before the effective filing date of the claimed invention to modify the invention of Ubillos to include the feature of Hicks. One would have been motivated to make this modification because it provides the capability to utilize multi-gesture inputs as taught by Hicks **(para. [0049])**.

Claim 21: Ubillos and Hicks teach the computer program product of Claim 1. Ubillos does not explicitly teach the first user input is continually received even after the second user input has completed being received and the one or more operations are computed after the first user input has completed being received.

However, Hicks further teaches the first user input is continually received even after the second user input has completed being received and the one or more operations are computed after the first user input has completed being received *(i.e. fig. 3, the user may hold down the copy key, move the cursor and select text using the multidirectional swipe key, and release the copy key to copy the selected text; para. [0049])*.

Therefore, it would have been obvious to one of ordinary skill in the art before the effective filing date of the claimed invention to modify the invention of Ubillos to include the feature of Hicks. One would have been motivated to make this modification because it provides the capability to utilize multi-gesture inputs as taught by Hicks **(para. [0049])**.

Application/Control Number: 14/547,077 Page 11
Art Unit: 2141

10. **Claim 11 is rejected under 35 U.S.C. 103 as being unpatentable over Ubillos et al. (U.S. Patent Application Pub. No. US 20130235071 A1) in view of Hicks et al. (U.S. Patent Application Pub. No. US 20140306899 A1) and further in view of Nepomniachtchi et al. (U.S. Patent Application Pub. No. US 20130287265 A1).**

Claim 11: Ubillos and Hicks teach the computer program product of Claim 9. Ubillos further teaches wherein the computer program product is operable such that computing the one or more operations includes using the range of pixels on the image *(i.e. the pixel that is considered to have been touched is the average pixel coordinate of the set of pixels that were touched by the user's finger; para. [0346])*.

Ubillos and Hicks do not explicitly teach the range including histogram data.

However, Nepomniachtchi teaches the range including histogram data *(i.e. the grayscale image has pixel in a range from 0-255, and the histogram is built by iterating through each value in this range and counting the number of pixels in the grayscale image having this value; para. [0302])*.

Therefore, it would have been obvious to one of ordinary skill in the art before the effective filling date of the claimed invention to modify the combination of Ubillos and Hicks to include the feature of Nepomniachtchi. One would have been motivated to make this modification because it provides the capability to visualize the range of data in histogram format as taught by Nepomniachtchi *(para. [0302])*.

11. **Claim 14 is rejected under 35 U.S.C. 103 as being unpatentable over Ubillos et al. (U.S. Patent Application Pub. No. US 20130235071 A1) in view of Hicks et al. (U.S. Patent Application Pub. No. US 20140306899 A1) and further in view of Icho et al. (U.S. Patent Application Pub. No. US 20100010986 A1).**

Claim 14: Ubillos and Hicks teach the computer program product of Claim 7. Ubillos further teaches wherein the computer program product is operable such that the one or more points include a

Application/Control Number: 14/547,077 Page 12
Art Unit: 2141

range of data *(i.e. the pixel that is considered to have been touched is the average pixel coordinate of the set of pixels that were touched by the user's finger; para. [0346])*.

Ubillos and Hicks do not explicitly teach the data is based on one or more union regions.

However, Icho teaches the range of data is based on one or more union regions *(i.e. fig. 6, union of set A and set B; para. [0164])*.

Therefore, it would have been obvious to one of ordinary skill in the art before the effective filling date of the claimed invention to modify the combination of Ubillos and Hicks to include the feature of Icho. One would have been motivated to make this modification because it provides contents beneficial for users and stimulating interest in users from various viewpoints as taught by Icho *(abs)*.

12.   **Claim 15 is rejected under 35 U.S.C. 103 as being unpatentable over Ubillos et al. (U.S. Patent Application Pub. No. US 20130235071 A1) in view of Hicks et al. (U.S. Patent Application Pub. No. US 20140306899 A1) and further in view of Iwema et al. (U.S. Patent Application Pub. No. US 20040021701 A1).**

Claim 15: Ubillos and Hicks teach the computer program product of Claim 1. Ubillos and Hicks do not explicitly teach a union function between two or more points displayed in the region.

However, Iwema teaches a union function between two or more points displayed in the region *(i.e. fig. 11, The union select enables a user to selection additional graphical objects for different selection paths, e.g. paths having a start and end or a tap on a graphical object; para. [0069])*.

Therefore, it would have been obvious to one of ordinary skill in the art before the effective filling date of the claimed invention to modify the combination of Ubillos and Hicks to include the feature of Iwema. One would have been motivated to make this modification because it provides a selection tool that will allow a user to conveniently select one or more graphical objects in their entirety, without requiring an inconvenient amount of precision from the user and provide a significant degree of freedom for selection as taught by Iwema *(para. [0011])*.

Application/Control Number: 14/547,077　　　　　　　　　　　　　　　　　　　　　　　　Page 13
Art Unit: 2141

13.　**Claims 22 and 23 are rejected under 35 U.S.C. 103 as being unpatentable over Ubillos et al. (U.S. Patent Application Pub. No. US 20130235071 A1) in view of Hicks et al. (U.S. Patent Application Pub. No. US 20140306899 A1) and further in view of Laute et al. (U.S. Patent Application Pub. No. US 20160196042A1).**

Claim 22: Ubillos and Hicks teach the computer program product of Claim 1. Ubillos and Hicks do not explicitly teach after the second user input has been received but while the first user input is still being received, a third user input is received via a sensor in connection with one or more portions of displayed content in a third region of the graphical user interface.

However, Laute teaches after the second user input has been received *(i.e. fig. 6, the user uses a second finger 220 to create a second user input contact point 240 in the first element 620; para. [0045])* but while the first user input is still being received *(i.e. fig. 6, the first user input contact point 230; para. [0044])*, a third user input *(i.e. fig. 6, input contact point 240 to an area of the second element 630; para. [0045])* is received via a sensor in connection with one or more portions of displayed content in a third region of the graphical user interface *(i.e. fig. 6, the user interface on the touchscreen; para. [0043-0045])*.

Therefore, it would have been obvious to one of ordinary skill in the art before the effective filing date of the claimed invention to modify the combination of Ubillos and Hicks to include the feature of Laute. One would have been motivated to make this modification because it provides a more user intuitive method of providing user input as taught by Laute *(para. [0005])*.

Claim 23: Ubillos, Hicks, and Laute teach the computer program product of Claim 1. Ubillos and Hicks do not explicitly teach the one or more operations are computed based on the first user input, the second user input, and the third user input.

However, Laute further teaches the one or more operations are computed based on the first user input, the second user input, and the third user input *(i.e. fig. 6, operations are based on first, second, and third user inputs; para. [0043-0045])*.

Application/Control Number: 14/547,077
Art Unit: 2141

Therefore, it would have been obvious to one of ordinary skill in the art before the effective filling date of the claimed invention to modify the combination of Ubillos and Hicks to include the feature of Laute. One would have been motivated to make this modification because it provides a more user intuitive method of providing user input as taught by Laute *(para. [0005])*.

Conclusion

Applicant's amendment necessitated the new ground(s) of rejection presented in this Office action. Accordingly, **THIS ACTION IS MADE FINAL**. See MPEP § 706.07(a). Applicant is reminded of the extension of time policy as set forth in 37 CFR 1.136(a).

A shortened statutory period for reply to this final action is set to expire THREE MONTHS from the mailing date of this action. In the event a first reply is filed within TWO MONTHS of the mailing date of this final action and the advisory action is not mailed until after the end of the THREE-MONTH shortened statutory period, then the shortened statutory period will expire on the date the advisory action is mailed, and any extension fee pursuant to 37 CFR 1.136(a) will be calculated from the mailing date of the advisory action. In no event, however, will the statutory period for reply expire later than SIX MONTHS from the date of this final action.

Any inquiry concerning this communication or earlier communications from the examiner should be directed to TAN TRAN whose telephone number is (303)297-4266. The examiner can normally be reached on Monday - Thursday -7:30 am - 6:00 pm.

If attempts to reach the examiner by telephone are unsuccessful, the examiner's supervisor, Amy Ng can be reached on 571-270-1698. The fax phone number for the organization where this application or proceeding is assigned is 571-273-8300.

Application/Control Number: 14/547,077 Page 15
Art Unit: 2141

Information regarding the status of an application may be obtained from the Patent Application Information Retrieval (PAIR) system. Status information for published applications may be obtained from either Private PAIR or Public PAIR. Status information for unpublished applications is available through Private PAIR only. For more information about the PAIR system, see http://pair-direct.uspto.gov. Should you have questions on access to the Private PAIR system, contact the Electronic Business Center (EBC) at 866-217-9197 (toll-free). If you would like assistance from a USPTO Customer Service Representative or access to the automated information system, call 800-786-9199 (IN USA OR CANADA) or 571-272-1000.

/TAN TRAN/
Examiner, Art Unit 2141

/AMY NG/
Supervisory Patent Examiner, Art Unit 2141

LINCOLN LAW SCHOOL OF SAN JOSE
INTELLECTUAL PROPERTY SERIES

EXHIBIT: OFFICE ACTION RESPONSE

EXHIBITS 161

IN THE UNITED STATES PATENT AND TRADEMARK OFFICE

In re Application of:	Confirmation No.: 2978
William Rivard	Examiner: Tran, Tan H
Application No.: 14/547,077	Art Unit: 2141
File Date: 11/18/2014	Docket No.: DUELP015/DL024
Title: SYSTEM AND METHOD FOR COMPUTING OPERATIONS BASED ON A FIRST AND SECOND USER INPUT	Date: September 12, 2017

AMENDMENT B (37 CFR 1.112) WITH RCE (37 CFR 1.114)

Commissioner for Patents
P.O. Box 1450
Alexandria VA 22313-1450

Examiner:

In response to the communication mailed 2017-05-12 (hereafter "Final Office Action" or "FOA"), please consider the following amendments believed to place the claims in condition for allowance, as follows:

— **Amendments to the Claims** are reflected in the listing of the claims that begins on page 2 of this paper.
— **Remarks/Arguments** begin on page 7 of this paper.

Applicant : Duelight Llc
Application No. : 14/547,077

Attorney's Docket No.: DUELP015/DL024
Page : 2 of 14

Amendments to the Claims:

This listing of claims replaces all prior versions and listings of claims in the application:

1. (Currently amended) A computer program product embodied on a non-transitory computer readable medium, comprising:
 code for presenting a first presentation of a graphical user interface;
 code for receiving a first [[user]]touch input in a first region of [[a]]the graphical user interface, wherein the first region displays one or more tools, and the first touch input is continuously received without interruption during a first time interval;
 code for, while continually receiving the first user inputmaintaining the presenting of the first presentation, receiving a second [[user]]touch input that is a selection of in connection with one or more portions of a first imagedisplayed content in a second region of the graphical user interface, wherein the second touch input is received during a second time interval;
 code for detecting a respective edge associated with each of the one or more portions of the first image based on the second touch input;
 code for refining the selection based on the detected edge associated with each of the one or more portions of the first image; and
 code for computing performing one or more operations in connection withto a portion of the one or more portions of the displayed first image that corresponds to the refined selectioncontent, based on the one or more tools displayed in the first region associated with the first [[user]]touch input and the second user input;
 wherein the second time interval occurs during a portion of the first time interval.

2. (Original) The computer program product of Claim 1, wherein the computer program product is operable such that the first region is predefined with set boundaries.

3. (Original) The computer program product of Claim 1, wherein the computer program product is operable such that the second region of the graphical user interface corresponds with an image.

4. (Cancelled)

5. (Cancelled)

6. (Previously presented) The computer program product of Claim 1, wherein the computer program product is operable such that additional tools are capable of being displayed

Applicant : Duelight Llc
Application No. : 14/547,077

Attorney's Docket No.: DUELP015/DL024

in the first region through at least one of a region depth or layer, screens associated with the region, or window frames of the region.

7. (Currently amended) The computer program product of Claim 1, wherein the computer program product is operable such that the second [[user]]touch input is capable of including one or more points.

8. (Original) The computer program product of Claim 7, wherein the computer program product is operable such that the one or more points include at least one of a range of data, an average of data, or a specific location on the graphical user interface.

9. (Original) The computer program product of Claim 8, wherein the computer program product is operable such that the one or more points include the range of data, and the computer program product is further operable such that the range of data includes a range of pixels on an image.

10. (Original) The computer program product of Claim 9, wherein the computer program product is operable such that computing the one or more operations includes using the range of pixels on the image, the range including an average of pixels.

11. (Currently Amended) The computer program product of Claim 9, wherein the computer program product is operable such that computing performing the one or more operations includes using the range of pixels on the image, the range including histogram data.

12. (Currently amended) The computer program product of Claim 1, wherein the computer program product is operable such that the second [[user]]touch input is capable of including two or more points, each of the points being associated with a specific one or more operations.

13. (Currently amended) The computer program product of Claim 1, wherein the computer program product is operable such that receiving the second [[user]]touch input includes receiving multiple points in connection with the one or more portions of the first image displayed content.

14. (Previously presented) The computer program product of Claim 7, wherein the computer program product is operable such that the one or more points include a range of data, and the computer program product is further operable such that the range of data is based on one or more union regions.

Applicant : Duelight Llc
Application No. : 14/547,077

Attorney's Docket No.: DUELP015/DL024
Page : 4 of 14

15. (Currently amended) The computer program product of Claim 1, wherein the computer program product is operable such that the second [[user]]touch input is capable of including a union function between two or more points displayed in the second region.

16. (Cancelled)

17. (Currently amended) The computer program product of Claim [[16]]1, wherein the computer program product is operable such that the second [[user]]touch input is capable of including a contributing area for use in selecting a region based on one or more points of interest and the ~~automatically~~ detected respective edge.

18. (Currently amended) The computer program product of Claim 1, wherein the computer program product is operable such that, in connection with the second [[user]]touch input, the computer program product is operable for ~~automatically detecting an edge in the second region,~~ selecting an area of the second region, processing the selected area based on the ~~automatically~~ detected respective edge, creating at least one ordered list for pixels selected, and displaying a resulting selected area; the ~~computing~~ performing one or more operations includes processing the at least one vector to display a resulting image based on the one or more operations.

19. (Currently amended) An apparatus, comprising:
circuitry for:
presenting a first presentation of a graphical user interface;
receiving a first [[user]]touch input in a first region of [[a]]the graphical user interface, wherein the first region displays one or more tools, and the first touch input is continuously received without interruption during a first time interval;
while ~~continually receiving the first user input~~ maintaining the presenting of the first presentation, receiving a second [[user]]touch input that is a selection of ~~in connection with~~ one or more portions of a first image~~displayed content~~ in a second region of the graphical user interface, wherein the second touch input is received during a second time interval;
detecting a respective edge associated with each of the one or more portions of the first image based on the second touch input;
refining the selection based on the detected edge associated with each of the one or more portions of the first image; and
~~computing~~ performing one or more operations ~~in connection with~~ to a portion of the first image that corresponds to the refined selection~~one or more portions of the displayed content~~, based on the one or more tools displayed in the first region associated with the first [[user]]touch input ~~and the second user input~~;

Applicant : Duelight Llc
Application No. : 14/547,077

Attorney's Docket No.: DUELP015/DL024
Page : 5 of 14

wherein the second time interval occurs during a portion of the first time interval.

20. (Currently amended) A method, comprising:
presenting a first presentation of a graphical user interface;
receiving a first [[user]]touch input in a first region of [[a]]the graphical user interface, wherein the first region displays one or more tools, and the first touch input is continuously received without interruption during a first time interval;
while ~~continually receiving the first user input~~maintaining presenting of the the first presentation, receiving a second [[user]]touch input that is a selection of ~~in connection with~~ one or more portions of a first image~~displayed content~~ in a second region of the graphical user interface, wherein the second touch input is received during a second time interval;
detecting a respective edge associated with each of the one or more portions of the first image based on the second touch input;
refining the selection based on the detected edge associated with each of the one or more portions of the first image; and
~~computing~~ performing one or more operations ~~in connection with~~ to a portion of the first image that corresponds to the refined selection~~one or more portions of the displayed content~~, based on the one or more tools displayed in the first region associated with the first [[user]]touch input ~~and the second user input~~;
wherein the second time interval occurs during a portion of the first time interval.

21. (Currently amended) The computer program product of Claim 1, wherein the computer program product is operable such that the first [[user]]touch input is continuously[[ally]] received even after the second [[user]]touch input has completed being received and the one or more operations are computed after the first [[user]]touch input has completed being received.

22. (Currently amended) The computer program product of Claim 21, wherein the computer program product is operable such that after the second [[user]]touch input has been received but while the first [[user]]touch input is still being received, a third [[user]]touch input is received via a sensor in connection with one or more portions of the first image~~displayed content~~ in a third region of the graphical user interface.

23. (Currently amended) The computer program product of Claim 22, wherein the computer program product is operable such that the one or more operations are computed based on the first [[user]]touch input, the second [[user]]touch input, and the third [[user]]touch input.

Applicant : Duelight Llc
Application No. : 14/547,077

Attorney's Docket No.: DUELP015/DL024

24. (New) The computer program product of Claim 1, further comprising code for combining the one or more portions of the first image based on the detection.

25. (New) The computer program product of Claim 1, further comprising:
code for selecting a union area based on the detection;
code for combining the one or more portions of the first image based on the detection;
code for creating a hue vector based on the combination; and
code for updating the first image based on the hue vector.

26. (New) The computer program product of Claim 1, wherein the second touch input is received, at least in part, simultaneously with the first touch input.

Applicant : Duelight Llc
Application No. : 14/547,077

Attorney's Docket No.: DUELP015/DL024
Page : 7 of 14

Remarks:

Summary

Claims 1-4, 6-23 were pending.

Claims 1, 7, 11–13, 15, and 17–23 have been amended, while claims 4, 5, and 16 have been cancelled. Claims 24-26 have been added. Support for such amendments is found, inter alia, in Figures 6-8 (and accompanying paragraphs [0112]-[0137]) of the present description. No new matter is introduced. Claims 1–3, 6–15, and 17–26 are now pending, including independent claims 1, 19, and 20.

Rejections Under 35 U.S.C. 103

Claims 1-4, 6-10, 12-13, 16-21 stand rejected under 35 U.S.C. § 103(a) in view of U.S. Pat. Pub. No. 2013/0235071 (UBILLOS) and U.S. Pat. Pub. No. 2014/0306899 (HICKS). Claim 11 stands rejected under 35 U.S.C. § 103(a) in view of U.S. Pat. Pub. No. 2013/0235071 (UBILLOS), U.S. Pat. Pub. No. 2014/0306899 (HICKS), and U.S. Pat. Pub. No. 2013/0287265 (NEPOMNIACHTCHI). Claim 14 stands rejected under 35 U.S.C. § 103(a) in view of U.S. Pat. Pub. No. 2013/0235071 (UBILLOS), U.S. Pat. Pub. No. 2014/0306899 (HICKS), and U.S. Pat. Pub. No. 2010/0010986 (ICHO). Claim 15 stands rejected under 35 U.S.C. § 103(a) in view of U.S. Pat. Pub. No. 2013/0235071 (UBILLOS), U.S. Pat. Pub. No. 2014/0306899 (HICKS), and U.S. Pat. Pub. No. 2004/0021701 (IWEMA). Claims 22, 23 stand rejected under 35 U.S.C. § 103(a) in view of U.S. Pat. Pub. No. 2013/0235071 (UBILLOS), U.S. Pat. Pub. No. 2014/0306899 (HICKS), and U.S. Pat. Pub. No. 2016/0196042 (LAUTE). Applicant respectfully disagrees with such rejection, especially in view of the amendments made hereinabove to each of the independent claims.

Specifically, applicant has amended the independent claims, as follows:

> code for presenting a first presentation of a graphical user interface;
> code for receiving a first [[user]]touch input in a first region of [[a]]the graphical user interface, wherein the first region displays one or more tools, and the first touch input is continuously received without interruption during a first time interval;
> code for, while continually receiving the first user input maintaining the presenting of the first presentation, receiving a second [[user]]touch input that is a selection of in connection with one or more portions of a first image displayed content in a second region of the graphical user interface, wherein the second touch input is received during a second time interval;
> code for detecting a respective edge associated with each of the one or more portions of the first image based on the second touch input;

Applicant : Duelight Llc
Application No. : 14/547,077

Attorney's Docket No.: DUELP015/DL024
Page : 8 of 14

<u>code for refining the selection based on the detected edge associated with each of the one or more portions of the first image;</u> and

code for ~~computing~~ <u>performing</u> one or more operations ~~in connection with~~<u>to a</u> portion of the ~~one or more portions of the displayed~~ <u>first image that corresponds to the refined selection</u>~~content~~, based on the <u>one or more tools displayed in the first region associated with the</u> first [[user]]<u>touch</u> input ~~and the second user input~~<u>;</u>

<u>wherein the second time interval occurs during a portion of the first time interval</u>.

(see this or similar, but not necessarily identical language in the independent claims – as amended).

With respect to the independent claims, the Examiner has relied on paragraphs [0178] and [0180] from the UBILLOS reference, in addition to paragraph [0049] from the HICKS reference.

Applicant respectfully notes that the UBILLOS reference, as relied upon by the Examiner, discloses:

> [0178] At stage 1202, the user then selects the icon 421 displayed in the tool selection pane 420. In response, the image editing application at stage 1203 activates the cropping and straightening tool. <u>The image editing application highlights the icon 421 to indicate that the cropping and straightening tool is activated.</u> The image editing application also displays the dial 435 in the tool display area 425 and the gridlines 450 in the image display area 410. The number pointed by the stationary knob 460 indicates that the dial 435 has not been turned to either direction at all.

UBILLOS. Paragraph [0178] – emphasis added.

Applicant : Duelight Llc
Application No. : 14/547,077

Attorney's Docket No.: DUELP015/DL024
Page : 9 of 14

[0180] At the next stage **1205**, the user has rotated the fingers **1235** and **1240** clockwise past the predefined threshold degrees. The cropping and straightening tool rotates the displayed image **445** accordingly. The user has rotated the fingers **1235** and **1240** until the bicycle displayed in image **445** is straightened. In this example, "–10" that is pointed by the stationary knob **460** indicates that the dial **435** and the displayed image **445** have rotated clockwise by 10 degrees. The stage **405** also illustrates that the straightening tool has zoomed in (hence, the bicycle in the image appears bigger) and cropped the image **445** in order to avoid displaying a part that falls outside the image **445** before being rotated. <u>Also, the cropping and straightening tool displays the gridlines **455** as soon as the rotation of the fingers **1235** goes over the predefined threshold.</u>

UBILLOS. Paragraph [0180] – emphasis added.

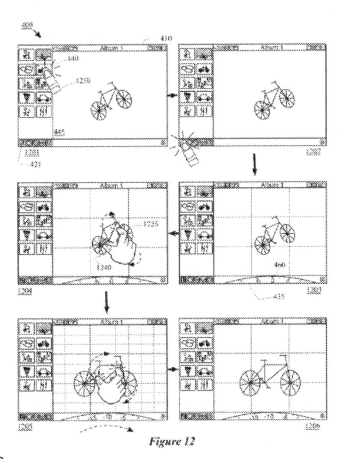

UBILLOS. Figure 12.

Applicant : Duelight Llc
Application No. : 14/547,077

Attorney's Docket No.: DUELP015/DL024

Applicant respectfully notes that the HICKS reference, as relied upon by the Examiner, discloses:

> [0049] FIG. 3f shows an example highlighting action in use with a multidirectional swipe key gesture, in accordance with an embodiment. <u>In this example case, the shift key is being held down (by the user's other hand) while making a swipe gesture from the multidirectional swipe key to cause the text to be highlighted and/or selected in combination with the cursor movement shown (from the initial cursor position in FIG. 3a)</u>. As previously described, the highlight activation action may include various actions such as selecting the shift key/function before performing multidirectional swipe key gestures for cursor movement, for example. Therefore, when using the highlighting feature, the multidirectional swipe key gesture causes cursor movement as described herein, but also performs the additional function of highlighting and/or selecting text as the cursor moves. In some embodiments, other actions or functions may be used in combination with the multidirectional swipe key gestures as variously described herein. For example, in one embodiment, multidirectional swipe key gestures may be used in combination with a copy key to copy selected text. In some such embodiments, the user may hold down the copy key, move the cursor and select text using the multidirectional swipe key, and release the copy key to copy the selected text. These example actions and functions are provided for illustrative purposes and are not intended to limit the claimed invention.

UBILLOS. Paragraph [0049] – emphasis added.

However, disclosing that an "image editing application highlights the icon 421 to indicate that the cropping and straightening tool is activated" as well as that "the cropping and straightening tool displays the gridlines...as soon as the rotation of the fingers 1235 goes over the predefined threshold", as in the UBILLOS excerpt(s) relied upon, in addition to teaching that a "shift key [may be] held down (by the user's other hand) while making a swipe gesture from the multidirectional swipe key to cause the text to be highlighted and/or selected" does not teach or suggest:

> code for presenting <u>a first presentation</u> of a graphical user interface;
> code for receiving <u>a first touch input</u> in a first region of the graphical user interface, wherein the first region displays one or more tools, and the <u>first touch input is continuously received without interruption during a first time interval</u>;
> code for, <u>while maintaining the presenting of the first presentation</u>, receiving <u>a second touch input</u> that is a selection of one or more portions of a first image in a second region of the graphical user interface, wherein <u>the second touch input is received during a second time interval</u>;

Applicant : Duelight Llc
Application No. : 14/547,077

Attorney's Docket No.: DUELP015/DL024

> code for <u>detecting a respective edge</u> associated with each of the one or more portions of the first image <u>based on the second touch input</u>;
> code for <u>refining the selection based on the detected edge</u> associated with each of the one or more portions of the first image; and
> code for performing one or more operations to a portion of the first image that corresponds to the refined selection, <u>based on the one or more tools</u> displayed in the first region associated with the first touch input;
> <u>wherein the second time interval occurs during a portion of the first time interval</u>.

(emphasis added), as claimed by applicant.

To establish a prima facie case of obviousness, three basic criteria must be met. First, there must be some suggestion or motivation, either in the references themselves or in the knowledge generally available to one of ordinary skill in the art, to modify the reference or to combine reference teachings. Second, there must be a reasonable expectation of success. Finally, the prior art reference (or references when combined) must teach or suggest all the claim limitations. The teaching or suggestion to make the claimed combination and the reasonable expectation of success must both be found in the prior art and not based on applicant's disclosure. *In re Vaeck*, 947 F.2d 488, 20 USPQ2d 1438 (Fed.Cir.1991).

Applicant respectfully asserts that at least the third element of the prima facie case of obviousness has not been met, since the prior art excerpts, as relied upon by the Examiner, fail to teach or suggest all of the claim limitations, as noted above.

Dependent Claims

Applicant further notes that the prior art is also deficient with respect to the dependent claims. For example, with respect to Claim 22, the Examiner has relied on paragraphs [0043]-[0045] from the LAUTE reference to make a prior art showing of applicant's claimed technique "wherein the computer program product is operable such that after the second touch input has been received but while the first touch input is still being received, a third touch input is received via a sensor in connection with one or more portions of the first image in a third region of the graphical user interface" (as amended).

Additionally, the Examiner has indicated on Page 13 of the Office Action that:

Applicant : Duelight Llc
Application No. : 14/547,077

Attorney's Docket No.: DUELP015/DL024
Page : 12 of 14

> However, Laute teaches after the second user input has been received *(i.e. fig. 6, the user uses a second finger 220 to create a second user input contact point 240 in the first element 620; para. [0045])* but while the first user input is still being received *(i.e. fig. 6, the first user input contact point 230; para. [0044])*, a third user input *(i.e. fig. 6, input contact point 240 to an area of the second element 630; para. [0045])* is received via a sensor in connection with one or more portions of displayed content in a third region of the graphical user interface *(i.e. fig. 6, the user interface on the touchscreen; para. [0043-0045])*.

Applicant respectfully notes that the LAUTE reference, as relied upon by the Examiner, discloses:

> [0044] FIG. 6A, 6B, 6C, 6D show multiple steps of a user providing as user input a value via a tablet computer 500 according to the method of the invention. In a first step (FIG. 6A) the tablet computer 500 provides, through the touch sensitive screen 510, a button 600. This button can be visible or invisible (e.g. a 'hot zone'). When the user touches the button 600 (FIG. 6B) the current value 610 is shown ("01: 45"). In this example, the current value 610 is a timer function set to count down from 1 hour and 45 minutes to zero (e.g. a cooking timer). Two elements are displayed 620, 630 on the touch sensitive screen 510, each element relating to a range of values. <u>The first element displayed 620 partially surrounds the button 600 where the first user input contact point 230 was detected</u>. The second element displayed 630 partially surrounds the first element 620. The first element 620 shows, in this example, four values relating to selecting minutes in increments of 15 minutes ("0 minutes", "15 minutes", "30 minutes" and "45 minutes"). The second element displayed shows, in this example, eight values relating to selecting hours ("0, 1 . . . 6, 7 hours").
>
> [0045] <u>In a next step (FIG. 6C) the user uses a second finger 220 to create a second user input contact point 240 in the first element 620. The first 230 and second 240 user input contact points are located in the imaginary plane 200 that is, in this example, (a part of) the surface of the touch sensitive screen 510.</u> In this example the user selects the value "30 minutes" from the range "minutes in 15 minute increments" that the

LAUTE. Paragraphs [0044]-[0045] – emphasis added.

Applicant : Duelight Llc
Application No. : 14/547,077

Attorney's Docket No.: DUELP015/DL024
Page : 13 of 14

However, disclosing a "first user input contact point" and a "second user input contact point", as in the LAUTE excerpt(s) relied upon, does not teach or suggest applicant's claimed technique "wherein the computer program product is operable such that after <u>the second touch input</u> has been received but <u>while the first touch input is still being received</u>, a <u>third touch input is received</u> via a sensor in connection with one or more portions of the first image in a third region of the graphical user interface" (emphasis added), as claimed by applicant. Clearly, merely teaching a "first" and "second" user input does not teach a "third" touch input as well.

Additionally, applicant respectfully notes that the Examiner relies on "second user input contact point 240" to teach both "second user input" and "third user input" as claimed by applicant. Clearly, a "second user input" cannot both be a "second user input" and "third user input" as suggested.

Again, as noted above, since at least the third element of the prima facie case of obviousness has not been met, a notice of allowance or specific prior art showing of each of the foregoing claim elements, in combination with the remaining claimed features, is respectfully requested.

New Claims

Still yet, applicant brings to the Examiner's attention the subject matter of new Claims 24-26 below, which are added for full consideration:

24. (New) The computer program product of Claim 1, further comprising code for combining the one or more portions of the first image based on the detection.

25. (New) The computer program product of Claim 1, further comprising:
code for selecting a union area based on the detection;
code for combining the one or more portions of the first image based on the detection;
code for creating a hue vector based on the combination; and
code for updating the first image based on the hue vector.

26. (New) The computer program product of Claim 1, wherein the second touch input is received, at least in part, simultaneously with the first touch input.

Again, a notice of allowance or a proper prior art showing of all of applicant's claim limitations, in combination with the remaining claim elements, is respectfully requested.

Applicant : Duelight Llc
Application No. : 14/547,077

Attorney's Docket No.: DUELP015/DL024
Page : 14 of 14

Conclusion

It is believed that all of the pending issues have been addressed. Claims 1–3, 6–15, and 17–26 are in condition for allowance per the claim amendments herein.

However, the absence of a reply to a specific rejection, issue, or comment does not signify agreement with or concession of that rejection, issue, or comment. In addition, because the arguments made above may not be exhaustive, there may be reasons for patentability of any or all pending claims (or other claims) that have not been expressed. Still yet, nothing in this reply should be construed as intention to concede any issue with regard to any claim, except as specifically stated in this reply. Finally, it should be noted that no claims are intended to be construed under 35 U.S.C. 112, paragraph 6.

In the event a telephone conversation would expedite the prosecution of this application, the Examiner may reach the undersigned at (408) 971-2573 or britten@zilkakotab.com. Applicant hereby requests an extension of time to respond and encloses the appropriate fee. Applicant does not believe that any additional fees are due. However, in the event that any other fees are due, the Director is hereby authorized to charge any required fees due (other than issue fees), and to credit any overpayment made, in connection with the filing of this paper to Deposit Account No. 50-1351 (Order No. DUELP015/DL024).

Respectfully submitted,

Zilka-Kotab, PC.

/BRITTENSESSIONS/

Britten Sessions
Reg. No. 68,278

1155 N. 1st Street, Suite 105
San Jose, CA 95112-4925
408-971-2573

LINCOLN LAW SCHOOL OF SAN JOSE
INTELLECTUAL PROPERTY SERIES

EXHIBIT: OFFICE ACTION

UNITED STATES PATENT AND TRADEMARK OFFICE

UNITED STATES DEPARTMENT OF COMMERCE
United States Patent and Trademark Office
Address: COMMISSIONER FOR PATENTS
P.O. Box 1450
Alexandria, Virginia 22313-1450
www.uspto.gov

APPLICATION NO.	FILING DATE	FIRST NAMED INVENTOR	ATTORNEY DOCKET NO.	CONFIRMATION NO.
14/547,079	11/18/2014	William Rivard	DUELP016	1119

28875	7590	03/15/2017

Zilka-Kotab, PC
1155 N. 1st St.
Suite 105
SAN JOSE, CA 95112

EXAMINER
TON, DANG T

ART UNIT	PAPER NUMBER
2476	

NOTIFICATION DATE	DELIVERY MODE
03/15/2017	ELECTRONIC

Please find below and/or attached an Office communication concerning this application or proceeding.

The time period for reply, if any, is set in the attached communication.

Notice of the Office communication was sent electronically on above-indicated "Notification Date" to the following e-mail address(es):

zk-uspto@zilkakotab.com
chrisc@zilkakotab.com

PTOL-90A (Rev. 04/07)

EXHIBITS 177

Office Action Summary	Application No. 14/547,079	Applicant(s) RIVARD ET AL.
	Examiner DANG TON	Art Unit 2476	AIA (First Inventor to File) Status Yes

-- *The MAILING DATE of this communication appears on the cover sheet with the correspondence address* --

Period for Reply

A SHORTENED STATUTORY PERIOD FOR REPLY IS SET TO EXPIRE **3** MONTHS FROM THE MAILING DATE OF THIS COMMUNICATION.
- Extensions of time may be available under the provisions of 37 CFR 1.136(a). In no event, however, may a reply be timely filed after SIX (6) MONTHS from the mailing date of this communication.
- If NO period for reply is specified above, the maximum statutory period will apply and will expire SIX (6) MONTHS from the mailing date of this communication.
- Failure to reply within the set or extended period for reply will, by statute, cause the application to become ABANDONED (35 U.S.C. § 133). Any reply received by the Office later than three months after the mailing date of this communication, even if timely filed, may reduce any earned patent term adjustment. See 37 CFR 1.704(b).

Status

1) ☒ Responsive to communication(s) filed on *2/7/2017*.
   ☐ A declaration(s)/affidavit(s) under **37 CFR 1.130(b)** was/were filed on _____.
2a) ☐ This action is **FINAL**.   2b) ☒ This action is non-final.
3) ☐ An election was made by the applicant in response to a restriction requirement set forth during the interview on _____; the restriction requirement and election have been incorporated into this action.
4) ☐ Since this application is in condition for allowance except for formal matters, prosecution as to the merits is closed in accordance with the practice under *Ex parte Quayle*, 1935 C.D. 11, 453 O.G. 213.

Disposition of Claims*

5) ☒ Claim(s) *1-26* is/are pending in the application.
   5a) Of the above claim(s) _____ is/are withdrawn from consideration.
6) ☐ Claim(s) _____ is/are allowed.
7) ☒ Claim(s) *1-24 and 26* is/are rejected.
8) ☒ Claim(s) *25* is/are objected to.
9) ☐ Claim(s) _____ are subject to restriction and/or election requirement.

* If any claims have been determined allowable, you may be eligible to benefit from the **Patent Prosecution Highway** program at a participating intellectual property office for the corresponding application. For more information, please see http://www.uspto.gov/patents/init_events/pph/index.jsp or send an inquiry to PPHfeedback@uspto.gov.

Application Papers

10) ☐ The specification is objected to by the Examiner.
11) ☐ The drawing(s) filed on _____ is/are: a) ☐ accepted or b) ☐ objected to by the Examiner.
    Applicant may not request that any objection to the drawing(s) be held in abeyance. See 37 CFR 1.85(a).
    Replacement drawing sheet(s) including the correction is required if the drawing(s) is objected to. See 37 CFR 1.121(d).

Priority under 35 U.S.C. § 119

12) ☐ Acknowledgment is made of a claim for foreign priority under 35 U.S.C. § 119(a)-(d) or (f).
   Certified copies:
      a) ☐ All   b) ☐ Some**   c) ☐ None of the:
      1. ☐ Certified copies of the priority documents have been received.
      2. ☐ Certified copies of the priority documents have been received in Application No. _____.
      3. ☐ Copies of the certified copies of the priority documents have been received in this National Stage application from the International Bureau (PCT Rule 17.2(a)).
** See the attached detailed Office action for a list of the certified copies not received.

Attachment(s)

1) ☐ Notice of References Cited (PTO-892)
2) ☐ Information Disclosure Statement(s) (PTO/SB/08a and/or PTO/SB/08b) Paper No(s)/Mail Date _____.
3) ☐ Interview Summary (PTO-413) Paper No(s)/Mail Date _____.
4) ☐ Other: _____.

U.S. Patent and Trademark Office
PTOL-326 (Rev. 11-13)   Office Action Summary   Part of Paper No./Mail Date 20170301

Application/Control Number: 14/547,079 Page 2
Art Unit: 2476

The present application, filed on or after March 16, 2013, is being examined under the first inventor to file provisions of the AIA.

1. The claimed invention is directed to a judicial exception (i.e., a law of nature, a natural phenomenon, or an abstract idea) without significantly more. Claim(s) 1-24 and 26 are directed to abstract ideas. The claim(s) does/do not include additional elements that are sufficient to amount to significantly more than the judicial exception because all limitations recited in claims 1-24 and 26 do not provide significant more than just abstract ideas.

2. Applicant's arguments with respect to claims 1-26 have been considered but are moot because the arguments do not apply to any of the references being used in the current rejection.

3. Claim 25 is objected to as being dependent upon a rejected base claim, but would be allowable if rewritten in independent form including all of the limitations of the base claim and any intervening claims.

4. Any inquiry concerning this communication or earlier communications from the examiner should be directed to DANG TON whose telephone number is (571)272-3171. The examiner can normally be reached on MON-Thurs, 5:30 AM-4:00 PM.

If attempts to reach the examiner by telephone are unsuccessful, the examiner's supervisor, Sheikl Ayaz can be reached on 571-272-3795. The fax phone number for the organization where this application or proceeding is assigned is 571-273-8300.

Application/Control Number: 14/547,079
Art Unit: 2476

Page 3

Information regarding the status of an application may be obtained from the Patent Application Information Retrieval (PAIR) system. Status information for published applications may be obtained from either Private PAIR or Public PAIR. Status information for unpublished applications is available through Private PAIR only. For more information about the PAIR system, see http://pair-direct.uspto.gov. Should you have questions on access to the Private PAIR system, contact the Electronic Business Center (EBC) at 866-217-9197 (toll-free). If you would like assistance from a USPTO Customer Service Representative or access to the automated information system, call 800-786-9199 (IN USA OR CANADA) or 571-272-1000.

/DANG TON/
Primary Examiner, Art Unit 2476/D. T./
Primary Examiner, Art Unit 2476

LINCOLN LAW SCHOOL OF SAN JOSE
INTELLECTUAL PROPERTY SERIES

EXHIBIT: OFFICE ACTION RESPONSE

IN THE UNITED STATES PATENT AND TRADEMARK OFFICE

In re Application of:	Confirmation No.: 1119
William Rivard	Examiner: Ton, Dang T
Application No.: 14/547,079	Art Unit: 2476
File Date: 11/18/2014	Docket No.: DUELP016
Title: SYSTEM AND METHOD FOR SHARING DATA BASED ON A COMBINED BANDWIDTH CONSUMPTION	Date: June 14, 2017

AMENDMENT B

Commissioner for Patents
P.O. Box 1450
Alexandria VA 22313-1450

Examiner:

In response to the communication mailed 2017-03-15 (hereafter "Non Final Office Action" or "NFOA"), please consider the following amendments believed to place the claims in condition for allowance, as follows:

— **Amendments to the Claims** are reflected in the listing of the claims that begins on page 2 of this paper.
— **Remarks/Arguments** begin on page 6 of this paper.

Applicant : William Rivard
Application No. : 14/547,079

Attorney's Docket No.: DUELP016
Page : 2 of 10

Amendments to the Claims:

This listing of claims replaces all prior versions and listings of claims in the application:

1. (Original) A computer program product embodied on a non-transitory computer readable medium, comprising:
    code for receiving a first sharing action;
    code for receiving a first bandwidth consumption;
    code for receiving a second bandwidth consumption;
    code for determining whether a combination of the first bandwidth consumption and the second bandwidth consumption surpasses a predefined threshold; and
    code for conditionally allowing the first sharing action based on the determination.

2. (Original) The computer program product of Claim 1, wherein the computer program product is operable such that the first bandwidth consumption is received from a network carrier.

3. (Original) The computer program product of Claim 1, wherein the computer program product is operable such that the second bandwidth consumption is received from a network carrier.

4. (Original) The computer program product of Claim 1, wherein the computer program product is operable such that the first bandwidth consumption is calculated from consumption information received from a peer-to-peer network.

5. (Original) The computer program product of Claim 2, wherein the network carrier provides the first bandwidth consumption in response to a query of usage associated with a first user.

6. (Original) The computer program product of Claim 3, wherein the network carrier provides the second bandwidth consumption in response to a query of usage associated with the first sharing action.

7. (Original) The computer program product of Claim 1, wherein the computer program product is operable such that specific types of data are not included in the first bandwidth consumption and second bandwidth consumption.

8. (Original) The computer program product of Claim 1, wherein the computer program product is operable such that the first bandwidth consumption reflects actual bandwidth consumption as calculated by a network carrier.

Applicant : William Rivard
Application No. : 14/547,079

Attorney's Docket No.: DUELP016
Page : 3 of 10

9. (Original) The computer program product of Claim 4, wherein the peer-to-peer network monitors bandwidth consumption associated with two or more devices.

10. (Original) The computer program product of Claim 1, wherein the computer program product is operable such that if the predefined threshold is surpassed, the first sharing action is denied.

11. (Original) The computer program product of Claim 1, wherein the computer program product is operable such that if the predefined threshold is not surpassed, the first sharing action is fully allowed.

12. (Original) The computer program product of Claim 1, wherein the computer program product is operable such that the conditionally allowing depends on an effect of the first sharing action.

13. (Original) The computer program product of Claim 12, wherein the computer program product is operable such that the effect includes a total amount of bandwidth utilized as a result of the first sharing action.

14. (Original) The computer program product of Claim 1, wherein the computer program product is operable such that the first bandwidth consumption comprises an amount of bandwidth consumed against a data allocation associated with a wireless data service, and the second bandwidth consumption comprises an amount of data associated with performing the first sharing action.

15. (Original) The computer program product of Claim 1, wherein the computer program product is operable such that the predefined threshold is associated with a predefined limit associated with a first account.

16. (Original) The computer program product of Claim 15, wherein the computer program product is operable such that the predefined threshold is adjusted.

17. (Original) The computer program product of Claim 16, wherein the computer program product is operable such that the adjustment includes purchasing additional bandwidth associated with the first account.

18. (Original) The computer program product of Claim 1, wherein the computer program product is operable such the first bandwidth consumption and second bandwidth consumption are received from a peer-to-peer network, the peer-to-peer network periodically

Applicant : William Rivard
Application No. : 14/547,079

Attorney's Docket No.: DUELP016
Page : 4 of 10

receiving updates from a network carrier regarding the first bandwidth consumption and the second bandwidth consumption.

19. (Previously presented) A mobile computing device, comprising:
a memory interface configured to store data; and
a processing unit in communication with the memory interface and configured to:
    receive a first sharing action;
    receive a first bandwidth consumption;
    receive a second bandwidth consumption;
    determine whether a combination of the first bandwidth consumption and the second bandwidth consumption surpasses a predefined threshold; and
    conditionally allow the first sharing action based on the determination.

20. (Original) A method, comprising:
    receiving a first sharing action;
    receiving a first bandwidth consumption;
    receiving a second bandwidth consumption;
    determining whether a combination of the first bandwidth consumption and the second bandwidth consumption surpasses a predefined threshold; and
    conditionally allowing the first sharing action based on the determination.

21. (Previously presented) The mobile computing device of Claim 19, wherein the mobile computing device is operable such that the first bandwidth consumption and the second bandwidth consumption are each received from a network carrier, where the first bandwidth consumption reflects actual bandwidth consumption as calculated by the network carrier, the actual bandwidth consumption including a total adjusted consumption that comprises one or more particular data items.

22. (Previously presented) The mobile computing device of Claim 21, wherein the conditionally allowing is based on the actual bandwidth consumption.

23. (Previously presented) The method of claim 20, wherein when it is determined that the combination of the first bandwidth consumption and the second bandwidth consumption surpasses the predefined threshold, data associated with the first sharing action is reduced and the first sharing action is allowed.

24. (Previously presented) The method of claim 23, wherein the data associated with the first sharing action is reduced by decreasing at least one of resolution, size, and quality.

25. (Previously presented) The method of claim 20, wherein when it is determined that the combination of the first bandwidth consumption and the second bandwidth

Applicant : William Rivard
Application No. : 14/547,079

Attorney's Docket No.: DUELP016
Page : 5 of 10

consumption surpasses the predefined threshold, performing at least one of: determining whether an additional amount of data is purchased; determining whether the first sharing action is delayed; and determining if a new network is detected separate from a network associated with the first bandwidth consumption and the second bandwidth consumption.

26. (Previously presented) The mobile computing device of Claim 19, wherein the mobile computing device is operable such that at least one of the first bandwidth consumption and the second bandwidth consumption is based on the data stored within the memory interface located on the mobile computing device.

Applicant : William Rivard
Application No. : 14/547,079

Attorney's Docket No.: DUELP016
Page : 6 of 10

Remarks:

Summary

Claims 1-26 were pending.

Claims 1–26 are pending, with claims 1, 19, and 20 being independent. No new subject matter has been added.

Allowable Subject Matter

The Examiner is thanked for the allowable subject matter of Claim 25. The Examiner has objected to such claim and noted that such claim would be allowable if rewritten in independent form including all of the limitations of the base claim and any intervening claims. Although applicant appreciates the indication of allowable subject matter, applicant asserts that Claims 1-26 are in condition for allowance per the arguments provided herein.

Rejections Under 35 U.S.C. 101

In the latest office action, the Examiner has indicated that:

> 1. The claimed invention is directed to a judicial exception (i.e., a law of nature, a natural phenomenon, or an abstract idea) without significantly more. Claim(s) 1-24 and 26 are directed to abstract ideas. The claim(s) does/do not include additional elements that are sufficient to amount to significantly more than the judicial exception because all limitations recited in claims 1-24 and 26 do not provide significant more than just abstract ideas.

As such, it is assumed that the Examiner has rejected Claims 1-24 and 26 under 35 U.S.C. 101 as being directed to non-statutory subject matter.

Applicant respectfully notes that per the recent USPTO's memorandum "Formulating a Subject Matter Eligibility Rejection and Evaluating the Applicant's Response to a Subject Matter Eligibility Rejection" ("Formulating Memo"), the USPTO has indicated that:

Applicant : William Rivard
Application No. : 14/547,079

Attorney's Docket No.: DUELP016
Page : 7 of 10

> "After determining what the applicant invented and establishing the broadest reasonable interpretation of the claimed invention, <u>the eligibility of each claim</u> should be evaluated as a whole using the two-step analysis detailed in the Interim Eligibility Guidance.
>
> When making the rejection, the Office action must provide an explanation as to why <u>each claim is unpatentable</u>, which must be sufficiently clear and specific to provide applicant sufficient notice of the reasons for ineligibility and enable the applicant to effectively respond."

Further, with respect to the first step of *Alice*, the Interim Eligibility Guidance Sheet indicates that the rejection should:

> "identify the judicial exception by referring to **what is recited** (i.e., set forth or described) in the claim and explain why it is considered an exception;
>
> identify any additional elements (**specifically point to claim features/limitations/steps**) recited in the claim beyond the identified judicial exception; and

With respect to the second step of *Alice*, the Interim Eligibility Guidance Sheet indicates that the rejection should:

> explain the reason(s) that the additional elements **taken individually, and also taken as a combination**, do not result in the claim as a whole amounting to significantly more than the judicial exception" (emphasis added).

<u>Step 1 of *Alice*</u>

The Examiner has indicated in relation to Claims 1-24 and 26 that such claims are directed to "abstract ideas." Applicant respectfully notes that no claim feature or element is recited in the office action as being abstract, nor is any analysis provided in the office action regarding how such claims are considered a judicial exception. Further, the Examiner has not provided any support from a court case to support the position of such claims being directed to a judicial exception.

Merely concluding that Claims 1-24 and 26 are "abstract ideas" fails to provide a reasoned rationale as to how such is a concept that the <u>courts</u> have identified as being an abstract idea.

In any case, Applicant respectfully notes that Claims 1-24 and 26 are not limited to an "abstract idea." For example, Claim 1 requires many tangible aspects:

> "code for receiving a <u>first sharing action</u>"

Applicant : William Rivard
Application No. : 14/547,079

Attorney's Docket No.: DUELP016
Page : 8 of 10

    "code for receiving a <u>first bandwidth consumption</u>"
    "code for receiving a <u>second bandwidth consumption</u>"
    "code for conditionally allowing the <u>first sharing action</u> based on the determination"

Additionally, Applicant brings to the Examiner's attention *Intellectual Ventures I LLC, Intellectual Ventures II LLC, v. Motorola Mobility LLC* (Memorandum Opinion) DED-1-11-cv-00908 where the claims related to "reallocating bandwidth based on the contents of packet headers." The court concluded that such was directed to "patent-eligible subject matter." In like manner, applicant respectfully asserts that the claims here are likewise patent eligible subject matter.

Step 2 of *Alice*

In the rejection, the Examiner fails to specifically point out claim limitations (in their entirety) and how such claim limitations relate to a judicial exception.

The Examiner is reminded that in the USPTO "July 2015 Update: Subject Matter Eligibility" memo, the USPTO has taught that "courts have held computer-implemented processes to be significantly more than an abstract idea (and thus eligible), where generic computer components are able in combination to perform functions that are not merely generic", including, for example, "digital image processing...GUI for relocating obscured textual information...and ...rubber manufacturing." Further, "[t]he importance of considering the additional elements in combination was emphasized in examiner training" including, for example, "digital image processing...global positioning system...transmission of stock quote data...and ...rubber manufacturing[] illustrate how generic computer components that individually perform merely generic computer functions (e.g., a CPU that performs mathematical calculations or a clock that produces time data) are able in combination to perform functions that are not generic computer functions and that amount to significantly more."

Further, the USPTO has indicated in the "Recent Subject Matter Eligibility Decision Memorandum" (November 2, 2016) that "an "improvement in computer-related technology" is not limited to improvements in the operation of a computer or a computer network per se, but may also be claimed as a set of "rules" (basically mathematical relationships) that improve computer-related technology by allowing computer performance of a function not previously performable by a computer."

Here, applicant respectfully notes that the Claims amount to more than just a mere use of a generic computer to perform generic computer functions. For example, the independent claims include, at a minimum, elements which are more than a mere generic recitation of computer components:

    "code for <u>receiving</u> a first sharing <u>action</u>"

Applicant: William Rivard
Application No.: 14/547,079

Attorney's Docket No.: DUELP016

> "code for <u>receiving</u> a <u>first bandwidth consumption</u>"
> "code for <u>receiving</u> a <u>second bandwidth consumption</u>"
> "code for <u>determining</u> whether a <u>combination</u> of the first bandwidth consumption and the second bandwidth consumption <u>surpasses</u> a <u>predefined threshold</u>"
> "code for <u>conditionally allowing</u> the first sharing <u>action</u> <u>based on</u> the <u>determination</u>"

(emphasis added), all of which convey a method which is much more than merely a generic recitation of computer components.

As such, the claim language is much more than a generic recitation of components. Further, the specificity and complexity of the claims, individually and collectively, rise to a level above a mere generic computer to perform generic computer functions. Therefore, since applicant's claim language is clearly not an abstract idea, and alternately includes unique functionality that constitutes more than an abstract idea, such language is statutory subject matter.

Conclusion

It is believed that all of the pending issues have been addressed. Claims 1-26 are in condition for allowance per the claim amendments herein.

However, the absence of a reply to a specific rejection, issue, or comment does not signify agreement with or concession of that rejection, issue, or comment. In addition, because the arguments made above may not be exhaustive, there may be reasons for patentability of any or all pending claims (or other claims) that have not been expressed. Still yet, nothing in this reply should be construed as intention to concede any issue with regard to any claim, except as specifically stated in this reply. Finally, it should be noted that no claims are intended to be construed under 35 U.S.C. 112, paragraph 6.

Applicant : William Rivard
Application No. : 14/547,079

Attorney's Docket No.: DUELP016
Page : 10 of 10

In the event a telephone conversation would expedite the prosecution of this application, the Examiner may reach the undersigned at (408) 971-2573 or britten@zilkakotab.com. Applicant does not believe that any additional fees are due. However, in the event that any other fees are due, the Director is hereby authorized to charge any required fees due (other than issue fees), and to credit any overpayment made, in connection with the filing of this paper to Deposit Account No. 50-1351 (Order No. DUELP016).

Respectfully submitted,

Zilka-Kotab, PC.

/BRITTENSESSIONS/

Britten Sessions
Reg. No. 68,278

1155 N. 1st Street, Suite 105
San Jose, CA 95112-4925
408-971-2573

LINCOLN LAW SCHOOL OF SAN JOSE
INTELLECTUAL PROPERTY SERIES

EXHIBIT: OFFICE ACTION

UNITED STATES PATENT AND TRADEMARK OFFICE

UNITED STATES DEPARTMENT OF COMMERCE
United States Patent and Trademark Office
Address: COMMISSIONER FOR PATENTS
P.O. Box 1450
Alexandria, Virginia 22313-1450
www.uspto.gov

APPLICATION NO.	FILING DATE	FIRST NAMED INVENTOR	ATTORNEY DOCKET NO.	CONFIRMATION NO.
14/582,178	12/23/2014	John Anthony Marsh	MARJ-P0001	2271

127633   7590   03/04/2016
Intellectual Property Clinic
Lincoln Law School of San Jose
384 S Second Street
San Jose, CA 95113

EXAMINER
KUMAR, KALYANAVENKA K

ART UNIT	PAPER NUMBER
3653	

NOTIFICATION DATE	DELIVERY MODE
03/04/2016	ELECTRONIC

Please find below and/or attached an Office communication concerning this application or proceeding.

The time period for reply, if any, is set in the attached communication.

Notice of the Office communication was sent electronically on above-indicated "Notification Date" to the following e-mail address(es):

director@lincolnipclinic.com
patent_docketing@lincolnipclinic.com
eofficeaction@appcoll.com

PTOL-90A (Rev. 04/07)

EXHIBITS 193

Office Action Summary

Application No.	Applicant(s)
14/582,178	MARSH, JOHN ANTHONY
Examiner	Art Unit	AIA (First Inventor to File) Status
KALYANAVENKATESHWARE KUMAR	3653	Yes

-- The MAILING DATE of this communication appears on the cover sheet with the correspondence address --

Period for Reply

A SHORTENED STATUTORY PERIOD FOR REPLY IS SET TO EXPIRE <u>3</u> MONTHS FROM THE MAILING DATE OF THIS COMMUNICATION.
- Extensions of time may be available under the provisions of 37 CFR 1.136(a). In no event, however, may a reply be timely filed after SIX (6) MONTHS from the mailing date of this communication.
- If NO period for reply is specified above, the maximum statutory period will apply and will expire SIX (6) MONTHS from the mailing date of this communication.
- Failure to reply within the set or extended period for reply will, by statute, cause the application to become ABANDONED (35 U.S.C. § 133). Any reply received by the Office later than three months after the mailing date of this communication, even if timely filed, may reduce any earned patent term adjustment. See 37 CFR 1.704(b).

Status

1) ☒ Responsive to communication(s) filed on *12/23/2004*.
   ☐ A declaration(s)/affidavit(s) under **37 CFR 1.130(b)** was/were filed on _____.
2a) ☐ This action is **FINAL**.   2b) ☒ This action is non-final.
3) ☐ An election was made by the applicant in response to a restriction requirement set forth during the interview on _____; the restriction requirement and election have been incorporated into this action.
4) ☐ Since this application is in condition for allowance except for formal matters, prosecution as to the merits is closed in accordance with the practice under *Ex parte Quayle*, 1935 C.D. 11, 453 O.G. 213.

Disposition of Claims*

5) ☒ Claim(s) *1-7* is/are pending in the application.
   5a) Of the above claim(s) _____ is/are withdrawn from consideration.
6) ☐ Claim(s) _____ is/are allowed.
7) ☒ Claim(s) *1-7* is/are rejected.
8) ☐ Claim(s) _____ is/are objected to.
9) ☐ Claim(s) _____ are subject to restriction and/or election requirement.

* If any claims have been determined <u>allowable</u>, you may be eligible to benefit from the **Patent Prosecution Highway** program at a participating intellectual property office for the corresponding application. For more information, please see http://www.uspto.gov/patents/init_events/pph/index.jsp or send an inquiry to PPHfeedback@uspto.gov.

Application Papers

10) ☐ The specification is objected to by the Examiner.
11) ☒ The drawing(s) filed on *12/23/2014* is/are: a)☒ accepted or b)☐ objected to by the Examiner.
   Applicant may not request that any objection to the drawing(s) be held in abeyance. See 37 CFR 1.85(a).
   Replacement drawing sheet(s) including the correction is required if the drawing(s) is objected to. See 37 CFR 1.121(d).

Priority under 35 U.S.C. § 119

12) ☐ Acknowledgment is made of a claim for foreign priority under 35 U.S.C. § 119(a)-(d) or (f).
   Certified copies:
   a)☐ All   b)☐ Some**   c)☐ None of the:
      1. ☐ Certified copies of the priority documents have been received.
      2. ☐ Certified copies of the priority documents have been received in Application No. _____.
      3. ☐ Copies of the certified copies of the priority documents have been received in this National Stage application from the International Bureau (PCT Rule 17.2(a)).
** See the attached detailed Office action for a list of the certified copies not received.

Attachment(s)
1) ☒ Notice of References Cited (PTO-892)
2) ☐ Information Disclosure Statement(s) (PTO/SB/08a and/or PTO/SB/08b) Paper No(s)/Mail Date _____.
3) ☐ Interview Summary (PTO-413) Paper No(s)/Mail Date. _____.
4) ☐ Other: _____.

Application/Control Number: 14/582,178 Page 2
Art Unit: 3653

The present application, filed on or after March 16, 2013, is being examined under the first inventor to file provisions of the AIA.

DETAILED ACTION

Claim Rejections - 35 USC § 103

1. In the event the determination of the status of the application as subject to AIA 35 U.S.C. 102 and 103 (or as subject to pre-AIA 35 U.S.C. 102 and 103) is incorrect, any correction of the statutory basis for the rejection will not be considered a new ground of rejection if the prior art relied upon, and the rationale supporting the rejection, would be the same under either status.

2. The following is a quotation of 35 U.S.C. 103 which forms the basis for all obviousness rejections set forth in this Office action:

> A patent for a claimed invention may not be obtained, notwithstanding that the claimed invention is not identically disclosed as set forth in section 102 of this title, if the differences between the claimed invention and the prior art are such that the claimed invention as a whole would have been obvious before the effective filing date of the claimed invention to a person having ordinary skill in the art to which the claimed invention pertains. Patentability shall not be negated by the manner in which the invention was made.

3. Claims 1-7 are rejected under 35 U.S.C. 103 as being unpatentable over **Young (USP 5,191,981)** in view of **Gobatti (USP 2,989,184)**.

4. Regarding claim 1, Young discloses an apparatus comprising: a sluice box (see Fig. 1) having a bottom panel (elements 26) and one or more of side walls (elements 28); riffles located at the bottom panel of the sluice box (see Fig. 2), wherein the riffles comprise: a first portion that is below the bottom panel of the sluice box (elements 30);

Application/Control Number: 14/582,178 Page 3
Art Unit: 3653

and a second portion that extends above the bottom panel of the sluice box (elements 30), but Young does not disclose the first portion extending from the bottom panel. Gobatti teaches as obvious riffles extending above and below the plane of the panel (elements 125, 129, and 131). All the claimed elements were known in the prior art and one skilled in the art could have combined the elements as claimed by known methods with no change in their respective functions, and the combination would have yielded predictable results to one of ordinary skill in the art at the time of the invention. In the present case, it would have been obvious to combine Gobatti's extension of riffles to Young to further control material separation along the riffles (col. 9, lines 1-35).

5. Regarding claim 2, Young/Gobatti discloses the first portion of each riffle that extends below the bottom panel of the sluice box extends downward from the bottom panel of the sluice box at an angle that is substantially forty-five degrees relative to the bottom panel of the sluice box, and extends upward at an angle of ninety degrees relative to the bottom panel of the sluice box (col. 9, lines 1-35; angled structure capable of rotation about element 131 changing the angle of the riffle).

6. Regarding claim 3, Young/Gobatti discloses the second portion of each riffle that extends above the bottom panel of the sluice box creates a sheer, wherein the sheer extends upward at an angle that is substantially ninety degrees relative to the bottom panel of the sluice box, and extends downward toward the bottom panel of the sluice box at an angle that is substantially forty-five degrees relative to the bottom panel of the sluice box (col. 9, lines 1-35; angled structure capable of rotation about element 131 changing the angle of the riffle).

Application/Control Number: 14/582,178 Page 4
Art Unit: 3653

7. Regarding claim 4, Young/Gobatti discloses the upward extension of the first portion is connected to the upward extension of the second portion such that their angles with respect to the bottom panel of the sluice box is a same angle (col. 9, lines 1-35; angled structure capable of rotation about element 131 changing the angle of the riffle).

8. Regarding claim 5, Young/Gobatti discloses the riffles are configured to cause the creation of placers by separating gold and sand (col. 1, lines 18-26).

9. Regarding claim 6, Young/Gobatti discloses the sluice box positioned at an angle based upon a speed of a flow (col. 6). Further, Applicant is respectfully reminded that claim language consisting of functional language and/or intended use phrasing is given little, if any, patentable weight as the apparatus must merely be capable of functioning, or being used, as claimed. See MPEP 2114. Here, Young/Gobatti is capable of angle change in order to influence feed flow speed.

10. Regarding claim 7, Young/Gobatti discloses the riffles are configured based at least in part upon a capture rate (col. 1, lines 18-26; it would have been obvious to configure the riffles shape and angle based on optimization of gold collection).

Conclusion

11. Any inquiry concerning this communication or earlier communications from the examiner should be directed to KALYAN KUMAR whose telephone number is (571)272-8102. The examiner can normally be reached on Mon-Fri 7:00AM-3:30PM.

Application/Control Number: 14/582,178 Page 5
Art Unit: 3653

12. If attempts to reach the examiner by telephone are unsuccessful, the examiner's supervisor, Stefanos Karmis can be reached on 571-272-6744. The fax phone number for the organization where this application or proceeding is assigned is 571-273-8300.

13. Information regarding the status of an application may be obtained from the Patent Application Information Retrieval (PAIR) system. Status information for published applications may be obtained from either Private PAIR or Public PAIR. Status information for unpublished applications is available through Private PAIR only. For more information about the PAIR system, see http://pair-direct.uspto.gov. Should you have questions on access to the Private PAIR system, contact the Electronic Business Center (EBC) at 866-217-9197 (toll-free). If you would like assistance from a USPTO Customer Service Representative or access to the automated information system, call 800-786-9199 (IN USA OR CANADA) or 571-272-1000.

Kalyan Kumar
Examiner
Art Unit 3653

/JOSEPH C RODRIGUEZ/
Primary Examiner, Art Unit 3653

LINCOLN LAW SCHOOL OF SAN JOSE
INTELLECTUAL PROPERTY SERIES

EXHIBIT: OFFICE ACTION RESPONSE

IN THE UNITED STATES PATENT AND TRADEMARK OFFICE

In re Application of:	Title: Kreeger Sluice
Application No.: 14/582,178	Examiner: Kalyanavenka K KUMAR
Applicant: John Anthony Marsh	Docket No.: MARJ-P0001
File Date: 2014-12-23	Confirmation No.: 2271

RESPONSE TO NON-FINAL OFFICE ACTION UNDER 37 C.F.R. § 1.111

MS Amendment
Commissioner for Patents
P.O. Box 1450
Alexandria VA 22313-1450

Dear Sir/Madam:

In response to the communication mailed 2016-03-04 (hereafter "Non Final Office Action" or "NFOA"), please enter the following amendments and reconsider the instant application in light of the remarks below.

Application No.: 14/582,178
Reply to Office Action of 2016-03-04

Amendments to the Claims:

The listing of amended claims follow:

1.   (Currently amended) An apparatus comprising:

<u>a</u> sluice box having a bottom panel ~~and one or more of side walls~~; and

a <u>plurality of</u> riffles located at the bottom panel ~~of the sluice box~~, wherein <u>a</u> [[the]]riffle[[s]] comprise<u>s</u>:

  a <u>descending wall having a first end and a second end, wherein the first end of the descending wall joins the bottom panel, and wherein the second end of the descending wall</u>~~first portion that~~ extends <u>downward</u> below the bottom panel <u>at a predetermined angle</u> ~~of the sluice box~~; and

  a <u>shear wall having a first end and a second end, wherein the first end of the shear wall joins the second end of the descending wall, and wherein the second end of the shear wall</u> ~~second portion that~~ extends <u>upward until</u> above the bottom panel ~~of the sluice box~~.

2.   (Currently amended) The apparatus of claim 1, wherein the <u>shear wall comprises a notch located at the second end of the shear wall, the notch including:</u>

  <u>a notch seat that is substantially orthogonal to the shear wall; and</u>

  <u>a notch shear wall that is substantially parallel to the shear wall.</u>

~~first portion of each riffle that extends below the bottom panel of the sluice box extends downward from the bottom panel of the sluice box at an angle that is substantially forty-five degrees relative to the bottom panel of the sluice box, and extends upward at an angle of ninety degrees relative to the bottom panel of the sluice box.~~

3.   (Currently amended) The apparatus of claim <u>1</u>[[2]], wherein <u>the riffle further comprises a gentle down ramp having a first end and a second end, wherein the first end of the gentle down ramp joins the second end of the shear wall, and wherein the second end of the gentle down ramp extends downward from the second end of the shear wall toward the bottom panel in a direction of a flow of slurry.</u>~~the second portion of each riffle that extends above the bottom panel of the sluice box creates a sheer, wherein the sheer extends upward at~~

Application No.: 14/582,178
Reply to Office Action of 2016-03-04

~~an angle that is substantially ninety degrees relative to the bottom panel of the sluice box, and extends downward toward the bottom panel of the sluice box at an angle that is substantially forty-five degrees relative to the bottom panel of the sluice box.~~

4. (Currently amended) The apparatus of claim 3, wherein the <u>shear wall comprises a notch located at the second end of the shear wall, the notch including:</u>

<u>a notch seat that is substantially orthogonal to the shear wall; and</u>

<u>a notch shear wall that is substantially parallel to the shear wall.</u>

~~upward extension of the first portion is connected to the upward extension of the second portion such that their angles with respect to the bottom panel of the sluice box is a same angle.~~

5. (Currently amended) The apparatus of claim 1, wherein ~~the riffles are configured to cause the creation of placers by~~ <u>a configuration of the descending wall and the shear wall creates a vortex for</u> separating [[gold]]<u>materials of different density</u> ~~and sand~~<u>in a slurry</u>.

6. (Currently amended) The apparatus of claim 1, wherein the sluice box <u>is configured</u> ~~positioned~~ <u>to operate</u> at an <u>incline</u> angle <u>of approximately five degrees from a horizontal axis</u> ~~based upon a speed of a flow~~.

7. (Currently amended) The apparatus of claim [[1]]<u>2</u>, wherein ~~the riffles are configured based at least in part upon a capture rate~~ <u>a configuration of the notch creates a high order vortex</u>.

8. (New) The apparatus of claim 1, wherein the predetermined angle is substantially forty-five degrees, measured from the bottom panel.

9. (New) The apparatus of claim 1, wherein the shear wall extends upward at an angle substantially orthogonal to the bottom panel.

Application No.: 14/582,178
Reply to Office Action of 2016-03-04

10. (New) The apparatus of claim 3, wherein the gentle down ramp is configured to create a high order flow.

11. (New) The apparatus of claim 3, wherein the gentle down ramp and the shear wall form an angle substantially forty-five degrees.

12. (New) The apparatus of claim 4, wherein the predetermined angle is substantially forty-five degrees, measured from the bottom panel, wherein the shear wall extends upward at an angle substantially orthogonal to the bottom panel, and wherein the gentle down ramp extends downward at an angle substantially forty-five degrees from the shear wall.

13. (New) The apparatus of claim 4, wherein the notch seat is substantially parallel to the bottom panel.

14. (New) The apparatus of claim 4, wherein the notch shear wall is substantially parallel to the shear wall.

15. (New) The apparatus of claim 4, wherein:
   the notch seat is substantially parallel to the bottom panel; and
   the notch shear wall is substantially parallel to the shear wall.

16. (New) The apparatus of claim 12, wherein:
   the notch seat is substantially parallel to the bottom panel; and
   the notch shear wall is substantially parallel to the shear wall.

17. (New) The apparatus of claim 1, wherein the sluice box further comprises a plurality of sidewalls, at least one sidewall configured to include a cleanup rail that also functions as a handle.

EXHIBITS

Application No.: 14/582,178
Reply to Office Action of 2016-03-04

18. (New) The apparatus of claim 4, wherein:

the descending wall is substantially between three-eighths and five-eighths of an inch in length;

the gentle down ramp is substantially one to three inches in length;

the notch seat is substantially one-eighth of an inch in length; and

the notch shear wall is substantially one-eighth of an inch in height.

19. (New) The apparatus of claim 17, wherein:

a height of the side walls are substantially three to five inches; and

a length of the cleanup rail is substantially between twenty-six and thirty inches.

20. (New) The apparatus of claim 1, wherein:

a width of the sluice box is substantially between five to ten inches; and

a length of the sluice box is substantially thirty-six inches.

Application No.: 14/582,178
Reply to Office Action of 2016-03-04

Remarks:

Summary of the Office Action

Rejections under 35 U.S.C. § 103

Claims 1-7 stand rejected under 35 U.S.C. § 103 over U.S. Patent No. 5,191,981 ("Young") in view of U.S. Patent No. 2,989,184 ("Gobatti").

Summary of this Response

In this response, claims 1-7 have been amended. Claims 8-20 have been added. Support for the amendments and the newly added claims can be found throughout the original specification as filed. No new matter has been introduced. Reconsideration of the present application is respectfully requested.

Interview Summary Statement

Applicant wishes to thank Examiner Kumar for engaging in a telephonic interview on May 13, 2016 to discuss the present Office Action, the applied references, and the proposed amendments to the pending claims.

The Examiner and Applicant agreed that proposed amendment can overcome cited references. A further search will be conducted after this formal submission. Applicant accordingly requests this submission constitute the Applicant's Interview Summary.

Detailed Remarks

Rejections under 35 U.S.C. § 103

It remains well settled law that the failure of an asserted combination to teach or suggest each and every feature of a claim is fatal to an obviousness rejection under 35 U.S.C. § 103.[1] The KSR decision in no way relieves the Patent Office of its obligations to "consider all

---

[1] See In re Royka, 490 F.2d 981, 180 USPQ 580 (CCPA 1974) (to establish *prima facie* obviousness of a claimed invention, all the claim features must be taught or suggested by the prior art).

Application No.: 14/582,178
Reply to Office Action of 2016-03-04

claim limitations when determining patentability of an invention over the prior art."[2] Accordingly, a finding of "obviousness requires a suggestion of **all limitations** in a claim."[3]

Applicant respectfully traverses the rejections, as discussed below with respect to the independent claim(s). Although Applicant's arguments here are directed to the cited combination of references, it is necessary to consider their individual disclosures, in order to ascertain what combination, if any, could be made from them.

Independent Claim 1

Applicant's claim 1 recites, in part:

> a plurality of riffles located at the bottom panel, wherein a riffle comprises:
> a descending wall having a first end and a second end, wherein the first end of the descending wall joins the bottom panel, and wherein the second end of the descending wall extends downward below the bottom panel at a predetermined angle; and
> a shear wall having a first end and a second end, wherein the first end of the shear wall joins the second end of the descending wall, and wherein the second end of the shear wall extends upward until above the bottom panel.

As agreed upon by the Examiner during the interview, Applicant submits that neither Young nor Gobatti discloses at least the aforementioned feature of independent claim 1. In particular, it is submitted that Young, whether viewed alone or in combination with Gobatti, does not disclose "a descending wall having a first end and a second end, wherein the first end of the descending wall joins the bottom panel, and wherein the second end of the descending wall extends downward below the bottom panel at a predetermined angle," or "a shear wall having a first end and a second end, wherein the first end of the shear wall joins the second end of the descending wall, and wherein the second end of the shear wall extends upward until above the bottom panel," as recited in Applicant's claim 1.

---

[2] KSR Int'l Co. v. Teleflex Inc., 127 S.Ct. 1727, 82 U.S.P.Q.2d 1385, 550 U.S. 398 (2007).
[3] CFMT, Inc. v. Yieldup Intern. Corp., 349 F.3d 1333, 1342 (Fed. Cir. 2003) (emphasis added) (cited in Ex Parte Wada, 2008 WL 142652, *4 (Bd. Pat. App. & Interf., Jan. 14, 2008)).

Application No.: 14/582,178
Reply to Office Action of 2016-03-04

Since Young, whether taken alone or in view of Gobatti, does not disclose or suggest each and every element recited in Applicant's claim 1 as required by 35 U.S.C. § 103(a), it is submitted that Applicant's claim 1 is patentable over the cited arts for at least the reasons stated above.

Disclaimer

Applicant has not necessarily discussed here every reason why every pending independent claim is patentable over the cited art; nonetheless, Applicant is not waiving any argument regarding any such reason or reasons. Applicant hereby reserves the right to raise any such additional argument(s) during the future prosecution of this application, if Applicant deems it necessary or appropriate to do so.

Dependent Claims

In view of the above remarks, a specific discussion of the dependent claims is considered to be unnecessary. Therefore, Applicant's silence regarding any dependent claim is not to be interpreted as agreement with, or acquiescence to, the rejection of such claim or as waiving any argument regarding that claim.

Reservation of Rights

For the sake of conciseness and clarity, Applicant may not have addressed every assertion or rejection made in the Office Action, particularly where Applicant has presented amendments or arguments that Applicant believes render such assertions/rejections moot. Therefore, Applicant's silence regarding any such assertions or rejections does not constitute an admission or acquiescence regarding such assertions/rejections or a waiver of any argument relating to such assertions/rejections. Applicant hereby reserves the right to challenge at a later time any rejection or any factual or legal assertion made by the Office in relation to the present application. Applicant does not admit that any of the references cited in the Office Action are prior art. Applicant reserves the right to swear behind any cited reference at a later date, to the extent permitted by law.

Application No.: 14/582,178
Reply to Office Action of 2016-03-04

Conclusion:

Accordingly, favorable reconsideration and withdrawal of the rejection of independent claim 1 under 35 U.S.C. §103 are respectfully requested. In the event a telephone conversation would expedite the prosecution of this application, the Examiner may reach the undersigned at (408) 977-7227.

Respectfully submitted,

IP Clinic at Lincoln Law School

By /Steven M. Studulski /
Date: June 6, 2016

Steven M Studulski
Reg. No. 67261
IP Clinic at Lincoln Law School
384 S Second St.
San Jose, California 95113
Phone (408) 977-7227
Fax (408) 977-7228

LINCOLN LAW SCHOOL OF SAN JOSE
INTELLECTUAL PROPERTY SERIES

EXHIBIT: OFFICE ACTION

UNITED STATES PATENT AND TRADEMARK OFFICE

UNITED STATES DEPARTMENT OF COMMERCE
United States Patent and Trademark Office
Address: COMMISSIONER FOR PATENTS
P.O. Box 1450
Alexandria, Virginia 22313-1450
www.uspto.gov

APPLICATION NO.	FILING DATE	FIRST NAMED INVENTOR	ATTORNEY DOCKET NO.	CONFIRMATION NO.
14/731,282	06/04/2015	Gerald J. Matson	MATG-P0001	3180

127633	7590	01/27/2017
Intellectual Property Clinic		
Lincoln Law School of San Jose		
384 S Second Street		
San Jose, CA 95113		

EXAMINER
LEE, NATHANIEL J.

ART UNIT	PAPER NUMBER
2875	

NOTIFICATION DATE	DELIVERY MODE
01/27/2017	ELECTRONIC

Please find below and/or attached an Office communication concerning this application or proceeding.

The time period for reply, if any, is set in the attached communication.

Notice of the Office communication was sent electronically on above-indicated "Notification Date" to the following e-mail address(es):

director@lincolnipclinic.com
patent_docketing@lincolnipclinic.com
eofficeaction@appcoll.com

PTOL-90A (Rev. 04/07)

210 PATENT PROSECUTION WORKBOOK

Office Action Summary	Application No. 14/731,282	Applicant(s) MATSON, GERALD J.		
	Examiner NATHANIEL LEE	Art Unit 2875	AIA (First Inventor to File) Status Yes	

-- The MAILING DATE of this communication appears on the cover sheet with the correspondence address --

Period for Reply

A SHORTENED STATUTORY PERIOD FOR REPLY IS SET TO EXPIRE **3** MONTHS FROM THE MAILING DATE OF THIS COMMUNICATION.
- Extensions of time may be available under the provisions of 37 CFR 1.136(a). In no event, however, may a reply be timely filed after SIX (6) MONTHS from the mailing date of this communication.
- If NO period for reply is specified above, the maximum statutory period will apply and will expire SIX (6) MONTHS from the mailing date of this communication.
- Failure to reply within the set or extended period for reply will, by statute, cause the application to become ABANDONED (35 U.S.C. § 133). Any reply received by the Office later than three months after the mailing date of this communication, even if timely filed, may reduce any earned patent term adjustment. See 37 CFR 1.704(b).

Status

1) ☒ Responsive to communication(s) filed on *June 4, 2015*.
   ☐ A declaration(s)/affidavit(s) under **37 CFR 1.130(b)** was/were filed on _____.
2a) ☐ This action is **FINAL.**   2b) ☒ This action is non-final.
3) ☐ An election was made by the applicant in response to a restriction requirement set forth during the interview on _____; the restriction requirement and election have been incorporated into this action.
4) ☐ Since this application is in condition for allowance except for formal matters, prosecution as to the merits is closed in accordance with the practice under *Ex parte Quayle*, 1935 C.D. 11, 453 O.G. 213.

Disposition of Claims*

5) ☒ Claim(s) *1-20* is/are pending in the application.
   5a) Of the above claim(s) _____ is/are withdrawn from consideration.
6) ☐ Claim(s) _____ is/are allowed.
7) ☒ Claim(s) *1-20* is/are rejected.
8) ☐ Claim(s) _____ is/are objected to.
9) ☐ Claim(s) _____ are subject to restriction and/or election requirement.

* If any claims have been determined allowable, you may be eligible to benefit from the **Patent Prosecution Highway** program at a participating intellectual property office for the corresponding application. For more information, please see http://www.uspto.gov/patents/init_events/pph/index.jsp or send an inquiry to PPHfeedback@uspto.gov.

Application Papers

10) ☐ The specification is objected to by the Examiner.
11) ☒ The drawing(s) filed on *June 4, 2015* is/are: a) ☒ accepted or b) ☐ objected to by the Examiner.
    Applicant may not request that any objection to the drawing(s) be held in abeyance. See 37 CFR 1.85(a).
    Replacement drawing sheet(s) including the correction is required if the drawing(s) is objected to. See 37 CFR 1.121(d).

Priority under 35 U.S.C. § 119

12) ☐ Acknowledgment is made of a claim for foreign priority under 35 U.S.C. § 119(a)-(d) or (f).
    Certified copies:
    a) ☐ All   b) ☐ Some**   c) ☐ None of the:
       1. ☐ Certified copies of the priority documents have been received.
       2. ☐ Certified copies of the priority documents have been received in Application No. _____.
       3. ☐ Copies of the certified copies of the priority documents have been received in this National Stage application from the International Bureau (PCT Rule 17.2(a)).
    ** See the attached detailed Office action for a list of the certified copies not received.

Attachment(s)

1) ☒ Notice of References Cited (PTO-892)
2) ☒ Information Disclosure Statement(s) (PTO/SB/08a and/or PTO/SB/08b) Paper No(s)/Mail Date *6/4/2015*.
3) ☐ Interview Summary (PTO-413) Paper No(s)/Mail Date. _____.
4) ☐ Other: _____.

U.S. Patent and Trademark Office
PTOL-326 (Rev. 11-13)   Office Action Summary   Part of Paper No./Mail Date 20170104

Application/Control Number: 14/731,282 Page 2
Art Unit: 2875

1. The present application, filed on or after March 16, 2013, is being examined under the first inventor to file provisions of the AIA.

DETAILED ACTION

Claim Rejections - 35 USC § 103

1. In the event the determination of the status of the application as subject to AIA 35 U.S.C. 102 and 103 (or as subject to pre-AIA 35 U.S.C. 102 and 103) is incorrect, any correction of the statutory basis for the rejection will not be considered a new ground of rejection if the prior art relied upon, and the rationale supporting the rejection, would be the same under either status.

2. The following is a quotation of 35 U.S.C. 103 which forms the basis for all obviousness rejections set forth in this Office action:

> A patent for a claimed invention may not be obtained, notwithstanding that the claimed invention is not identically disclosed as set forth in section 102, if the differences between the claimed invention and the prior art are such that the claimed invention as a whole would have been obvious before the effective filing date of the claimed invention to a person having ordinary skill in the art to which the claimed invention pertains. Patentability shall not be negated by the manner in which the invention was made.

3. Claims 1-20 are rejected under 35 U.S.C. 103 as being unpatentable over Howell (US 2014/0226319 A1) in view of Dueker et al. (US 7,088,222 B1).

4. With respect to claim 1: Howell teaches "an apparatus (10), comprising: a housing (28) including at least two principle sides (Fig. 2); an illumination structure protruding from each of the two principle sides (22); a stabilization pad protruding from each of the two principle sides (30); an electric circuit coupled to the housing (12); at least one orientation sensor coupled to the housing (14) and an electric power source coupled to the housing (20)".

5. Howell does not specifically teach "an antenna coupled to the housing".

Application/Control Number: 14/731,282 Page 3
Art Unit: 2875

6. However, Dueker teaches "an antenna (706) coupled to the housing (102)".

7. It would have been obvious at the time of the invention for one of ordinary skill in the art to modify the apparatus of Howell with the antenna of Dueker in order to synchronize with a plurality of devices (Dueker column 7 lines 3-12).

8. With respect to claim 2: Dueker teaches "wherein the antenna is configured to receive at least one radio frequency signal (Fig. 7) from a remote activation device (704)".

9. The motivation to combine is the same as in claim 1.

10. With respect to claim 3: Howell teaches "wherein the apparatus has a generally rectangular shape (Fig. 2), and wherein the at least two principle sides are parallel to one another (Fig. 2)".

11. With respect to claim 4: Howell teaches "wherein a cross sectional shape of at least one of the illumination structures is selected from a group consisting of: an octagon, a heptagon, a hexagon, a pentagon, a rectangle, a square, a triangle, a circle, and an ellipse (Fig. 2)".

12. With respect to claim 5: Howell teaches "wherein the illumination structures each comprise one or more light sources coupled thereto (paragraph 71)".

13. With respect to claim 6: Howell teaches "wherein the light sources are light emitting diodes (paragraph 71)".

14. With respect to claim 7: Dueker teaches "wherein the one or more light sources are controlled by a remote activation device (704)".

Application/Control Number: 14/731,282 Page 4
Art Unit: 2875

15. It would have been obvious at the time of the invention for one of ordinary skill in the art to modify the apparatus of Howell with the remote activation device of Dueker in order to allow field programming (Dueker column 6 lines 39-59).

16. With respect to claim 8: Howell teaches "wherein the one or light sources of each illumination structure are selectively powered based on an orientation of the apparatus at rest (paragraph 71)".

17. With respect to claim 9: Howell teaches "at least one of the illumination structures has a faceted side surface (Fig. 2), and wherein at least one light source is coupled to each facet thereof (Fig. 2)".

18. With respect to claim 10: Howell teaches "wherein the housing further comprises a front side and a back side (Fig. 2), wherein the front side and the back side are each oriented perpendicular to the at least two principle sides (Fig. 2)".

19. With respect to claim 11: Howell teaches "further comprising a reading light source protruding from the front side of the housing (22)".

20. With respect to claim 13: Dueker teaches "further comprising a charging connector on the front side of the housing (110a, 110b), and wherein the power source includes at least one rechargeable battery (112)".

21. It would have been obvious at the time of the invention for one of ordinary skill in the art to modify the apparatus of Howell with the charging connector of Dueker in order to recharge the battery (Dueker column 3 lines 36-39).

22. With respect to claim 14: Howell teaches "further comprising at least five selector switches (14, 18) on the front side of the housing".

Application/Control Number: 14/731,282 Page 5
Art Unit: 2875

23. Note: 14 and 18 may both be embodied as switches (paragraph 71) and Fig. 1 depicts 4 14's and 18 for 5 total switches.

24. With respect to claim 15: Dueker teaches "wherein one or more light sources coupled to each illumination structure are controlled by a unique signal transmitted from a remote activation device when one of the five selector switches is set to an on position (Dueker column 7 lines 3-12)".

25. It would have been obvious at the time of the invention for one of ordinary skill in the art to modify the apparatus of Howell with the remote activation device of Dueker in order to emit particular light patterns (Dueker column 7 lines 3-12).

26. With respect to claim 16: Dueker teaches "further comprising a protective cover coupled to at least one portion of the housing (104)".

27. It would have been obvious at the time of the invention for one of ordinary skill in the art to modify the apparatus of Howell with the protective cover of Dueker in order to protect the housing (column 4 lines 60-64).

28. With respect to claim 17: Dueker teaches "wherein the protective cover comprises rubber (column 4 lines 60-64)".

29. The motivation to combine is the same as in claim 16.

30. With respect to claim 18: Dueker teaches "further comprising an audio device (Fig. 7), a camera, and/or a gas dispensing device coupled to at least one of the principle sides of the housing".

Application/Control Number: 14/731,282
Art Unit: 2875

31. It would have been obvious at the time of the invention for one of ordinary skill in the art to modify the apparatus of Howell with the audio device of Dueker in order to deter theft (Dueker column 6 lines 65-66).

32. With respect to claim 19: Howell teaches "wherein a height of the stabilization pad is about equal to a height of the illumination structure (paragraph 64)".

33. With respect to claim 20: Dueker teaches "wherein a length of the housing is about 4.6 inches, and wherein a width of the housing is about 3 inches (column 3 lines 47-61)".

34. It would have been obvious at the time of the invention for one of ordinary skill in the art to modify the apparatus of Howell by making it in the size range taught by Dueker for improved ergonomics (Dueker column 1 lines 51-53).

1. Claim 12 is rejected under 35 U.S.C. 103 as being unpatentable over Howell and Dueker as applied to claims 1 and 10 above, and further in view of Mayo et al. (US 8,113,689 B2).

2. With respect to claim 12: Howell does not specifically teach "further comprising a status indicator light source protruding from the front side of the housing".

3. However, Mayo teaches "further comprising a status indicator light source protruding from the front side of the housing (116)".

4. It would have been obvious at the time of the invention for one of ordinary skill in the art to modify the apparatus of Howell with the status light of Mayo to give feedback to the user with regard to battery charge and operational mode (Mayo column 8 line 67 - column 9 line 2).

Application/Control Number: 14/731,282
Art Unit: 2875

Page 7

Contact Information

Any inquiry concerning this communication or earlier communications from the examiner should be directed to NATHANIEL LEE whose telephone number is (571)270-5721. The examiner can normally be reached on Monday-Thursday, 8:00 a.m.-5:00 p.m., EST.

If attempts to reach the examiner by telephone are unsuccessful, the examiner's supervisor, Anh Mai can be reached on (571)272-1995. The fax phone number for the organization where this application or proceeding is assigned is 571-273-8300.

Information regarding the status of an application may be obtained from the Patent Application Information Retrieval (PAIR) system. Status information for published applications may be obtained from either Private PAIR or Public PAIR. Status information for unpublished applications is available through Private PAIR only. For more information about the PAIR system, see http://pair-direct.uspto.gov. Should you have questions on access to the Private PAIR system, contact the Electronic Business Center (EBC) at 866-217-9197 (toll-free). If you would like assistance from a USPTO Customer Service Representative or access to the automated information system, call 800-786-9199 (IN USA OR CANADA) or 571-272-1000.

/NATHANIEL LEE/
Examiner, Art Unit 2875
/ANDREW COUGHLIN/
Primary Examiner, Art Unit 2875

LINCOLN LAW SCHOOL OF SAN JOSE
INTELLECTUAL PROPERTY SERIES

EXHIBIT: OFFICE ACTION RESPONSE

IN THE UNITED STATES PATENT AND TRADEMARK OFFICE

In re Application of:	Examiner: Nathaniel J. LEE
Gerald J. Matson	Docket No.: MATG-P0001
Application No.: 14/731,282	Confirmation No.: 3180
File Date: 2015-06-04	Date: April 27, 2017
Title: TACTICAL LIGHT APPARATUS	

AMENDMENT A

Commissioner for Patents
P.O. Box 1450
Alexandria VA 22313-1450

Examiner:

In response to the communication mailed 2017-01-27 (hereafter "Non Final Office Action" or "NFOA"), please consider the following amendments believed to place the claims in condition for allowance.

- Amendments to the Claims are reflected in the listing of claims which begins on page 2 of this paper.
- Remarks/Arguments begin on page 5 of this paper.

Application No.: 14/731,282
Date: Apr 27, 2017
Reply to Office Action of 2017-01-27

Amendments to the Claims:

The listing of amended claims follow:

1. (Original) An apparatus, comprising:

    a housing including at least two principle sides;

    an illumination structure protruding from each of the two principle sides;

    a stabilization pad protruding from each of the two principle sides;

    an electric circuit coupled to the housing;

    an antenna coupled to the housing;

    at least one orientation sensor coupled to the housing; and

    an electric power source coupled to the housing.

2. (Original) The apparatus as recited in claim 1, wherein the antenna is configured to receive at least one radio frequency signal from a remote activation device.

3. (Original) The apparatus as recited in claim 1, wherein the apparatus has a generally rectangular shape, and wherein the at least two principle sides are parallel to one another.

4. (Original) The apparatus as recited in claim 1, wherein a cross sectional shape of at least one of the illumination structures is selected from a group consisting of: an octagon, a heptagon, a hexagon, a pentagon, a rectangle, a square, a triangle, a circle, and an ellipse.

5. (Original) The apparatus as recited in claim 1, wherein the illumination structures each comprise one or more light sources coupled thereto.

6. (Currently Amended) The apparatus as recited in claim 5, wherein the <u>one or more</u> light sources are light emitting diodes.

Application No.: 14/731,282
Date: Apr 27, 2017
Reply to Office Action of 2017-01-27

7. (Original) The apparatus as recited in claim 5, wherein the one or more light sources are controlled by a remote activation device.

8. (Currently Amended) The apparatus as recited in claim 5, wherein the one or <u>more</u> light sources of each illumination structure are selectively powered based on an orientation of the apparatus at rest.

9. (Currently Amended) The apparatus as recited in claim 5, <u>wherein</u> at least one of the illumination structures has a faceted side surface, and wherein at least one light source is coupled to each facet thereof.

10. (Original) The apparatus as recited in claim 1, wherein the housing further comprises a front side and a back side, wherein the front side and the back side are each oriented perpendicular to the at least two principle sides.

11. (Original) The apparatus as recited in claim 10, further comprising a reading light source protruding from the front side of the housing.

12. (Original) The apparatus as recited in claim 10, further comprising a status indicator light source protruding from the front side of the housing.

13. (Original) The apparatus as recited in claim 10, further comprising a charging connector on the front side of the housing, and wherein the power source includes at least one rechargeable battery.

14. (Currently Amended) The apparatus as recited in claim 10, further comprising at least five selector switches on the front side of the housing<u>, wherein each switch is independently a rocker switch, a rotary switch, or a slide switch</u>.

3

EXHIBITS

Application No.: 14/731,282
Date: Apr 27, 2017
Reply to Office Action of 2017-01-27

15.   (Currently Amended) The apparatus as recited in claim 14, wherein the one or more light sources coupled to each illumination structure are controlled by a unique signal transmitted from a remote activation device when one of the five selector switches is set to an on position.

16.   (Original) The apparatus as recited in claim 1, further comprising a protective cover coupled to at least one portion of the housing.

17.   (Canceled)

18.   (Original) The apparatus as recited in claim 1, further comprising an audio device, a camera, and/or a gas dispensing device coupled to at least one of the principle sides of the housing.

19.   (Original) The apparatus as recited in claim 1, wherein a height of the stabilization pad is about equal to a height of the illumination structure.

20.   (Original) The apparatus as recited in claim 1, wherein a length of the housing is about 4.6 inches, and wherein a width of the housing is about 3 inches.

21.   (New) The apparatus as recited in claim 1, wherein each of the at least two principle sides correspond to exterior sides of the housing.

Application No.: 14/731,282
Date: Apr 27, 2017
Reply to Office Action of 2017-01-27

Remarks:

Summary

Claims 1-20 were pending.

Claims 6, 8, 9, 14, and 15 are currently amended, while claim 17 is canceled. New claim 21 is added herein. No new matter is introduced. Support for such amendments is found, inter alia, in paragraph [0132] and Figures 1A-1B and 8A-8D of the present application. Claims 1-16, and 18-21 are now pending, including independent claim 1.

The right to pursue the canceled subject matter in a continuing application is respectfully reserved.

Rejections Under 35 U.S.C. 103

Claims 1-11, 13, 15-20

Claims 1-11, 13, and 15-20 are rejected under 35 U.S.C. § 103(a) as allegedly being unpatentable over Howell (US 2014/0226319, herein "Howell") in view of Dueker et al. (US 7,088,222, herein "Dueker"). Applicant respectfully traverses this rejection for at least the following reasons.

> a. *The rejection of independent claim 1 fails to establish a prima facie case of obviousness over the art of record.*

Applicant respectfully submits that the Office fails to establish a proper *prima facie* case of obviousness with respect to independent claim 1, and particularly fails to establish that the Howell in view of Dueker teaches or suggests each and every feature thereof.

The framework for determining obviousness was set forth in *Graham v. John Deere Co.*, 383 U.S. 1 (1966), and reaffirmed in *KSR Int'l Co.*, 550 U.S. 398, 404 (2207). This well-established framework is premised on the following factual inquiries: (i) determining the scope and content of the prior art; (ii) ascertaining the differences between the claimed invention and the prior art; and (iii) resolving the level of ordinary skill in the pertinent art. *See Graham*, 383 at 17-18; *see also KSR Int' Co.*, 550 U.S. at 406-407. Resolution of such inquiries may warrant a rejection under 35 U.S.C. § 103 where the record reflects facts, supported by articulated reasoning, that the prior art teaches or suggests all the claim elements, and that a skilled artisan would not only be reasonably motivated to combine and/or modify the teachings of the prior art as proposed in the rejection, but also have a reasonable expectation that such combination and/or

Application No.: 14/731,282
Date: Apr 27, 2017
Reply to Office Action of 2017-01-27

modification would produce a successful result. *See CFMT, Inc. v. Yieldup Intern. Corp.*, 349 F.3d 1333; *see also* MPEP §§ 2143.01, 2143.02.

Moreover, the Office bears the initial burden of presenting, and supporting, a *prima facie* case of obviousness. *See* MPEP § 2141. The Office is obliged to both allege all the elements necessary for a *prima facie* case of obviousness, as well as explain the reasons why the facts of the record require the legal conclusion of obviousness. In particular, the key to supporting any rejection under 35 U.S.C. § 103 is the clear articulation of the reason(s) why the claimed invention would have been obvious. *See id.* at § 2142. "[R]ejections on obviousness cannot be sustained with mere conclusory statements; instead, there must be some articulated reasoning with some rational underpinning to support the legal conclusion of obviousness." *In re Kahn*, 441 F.3d 977, 988 (Fed. Cir. 2006). Accordingly, the analysis supporting a rejection under 35 U.S.C. § 103 should be made explicit. *KSR Int'l Co. v. Teleflex Inc.*, 550 U.S. 398, 418 (2007).

In the instant case, Applicant respectfully submits that the Office has not established that Howell and Dueker teach or suggest "an illumination structure protruding from each of the two principle sides." To allegedly show these limitations, the Officer alleges that Howell teaches "an illumination structure protruding from each of the two principle sides (22). . . ." Office Action at p. 2. However, Applicant respectfully submits that such allegation amounts to a conclusory statement insufficient to support a legal conclusion of obviousness. Merely reciting Applicant's claim limitation, and identifying a reference numeral of a component within the prior art does not provide articulated reasoning as to how said prior art component truly teaches or suggests the claim limitation. For instance, the Office has not provided a reasoned explanation as to why components 22 of Howell allegedly teaches or suggests the protruding illumination stabilization structure, as claimed.

In view of the above, Applicant respectfully submits that a proper *prima facie* case of obviousness has not been established with respect to independent claim 1, and, as such, has not been established with respect to claims depending therefrom.

    b. *The art of record fails to teach or suggest each and every limitation of independent claim 1.*

Notwithstanding the above, Applicant respectfully submits that Howell in view Dueker fails to teach or suggest each and every limitation of independent claim 1, and particularly "an illumination structure <u>protruding</u> from each of the two principle sides," and "a stabilization pad <u>protruding</u> from each of the two principle sides" (emphasis added). To allegedly show the protruding illumination structure and the protruding stabilization pad, the Office cites to

Application No.: 14/731,282
Date: Apr 27, 2017
Reply to Office Action of 2017-01-27

reference numerals 22 and 30, respectively of Howell's Figure 2, which is reproduced below for reference.

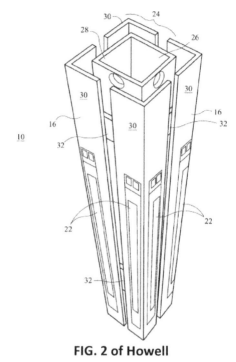

FIG. 2 of Howell

However, as evident from the structure above, Howell's illumination features 22 do not protrude from the sides of the light bar 10, but rather are flush (even) therewith.

Moreover, further reliance on Dueker fails to correct the aforementioned deficiency. Accordingly, Applicant respectfully submits that the combination of Howell and Dueker fails to teach or suggest each and every claim limitation claim 1, and thus fails to render obvious claim 1 (and claims depending therefrom).

Claim 14

Claim 14 is rejected under 35 U.S.C. § 103(a) as allegedly being unpatentable over Howell in view of Dueker. Without acquiescing to the propriety of this rejection, but in a sincere attempt to advance prosecution, claim 14 has been amended to specify that each of the at least five switches is interpedently a rocker switch, a rotary switch, or a slide switch. Review of Howell and Dueker fails to reveal any teaching or suggestion of the subject matter recited in claim 14, particularly as amended. Reconsideration and withdrawal of this rejection are therefore respectfully requested.

Application No.: 14/731,282
Date: Apr 27, 2017
Reply to Office Action of 2017-01-27

Claim 12

Claim 12 is rejected under 35 U.S.C. § 103(a) as allegedly being unpatentable over Howell and Dueker as applied to claims 1 and 10 above, and further in view of Mayo et al. (US 8,113,689, herein "Mayo"). Applicant respectfully traverses this rejection for at least the following reasons.

As noted herein, the combination of Howell and Dueker fails to teach or suggest each and every limitation of independent claim 1. Accordingly, the combination of Howell and Dueker fails to render obvious claim 1, and, for at least this reason, fails to render obvious claim 12 depending therefrom.

Further reliance on Mayo with respect to dependent claim 12 fails to correct the aforementioned deficiencies. As such, the combination of Howell, Dueker, and Mayo also fails to render obvious claim 12. Reconsideration and withdrawal of this rejection are therefore respectfully requested.

New Claims

Still yet, applicant brings to the Examiner's attention the subject matter of new Claim 21 below, which is added for full consideration:

> 21. (New) The apparatus as recited in claim 1, wherein each of the at least two principle sides correspond to exterior sides of the housing.

Again, a notice of allowance or a proper prior art showing of all of applicant's claim limitations, in combination with the remaining claim elements, is respectfully requested.

Conclusion

It is believed that all of the pending issues have been addressed. Claims 1-16, and 18-21 are in condition for allowance per the claim amendments herein.

However, the absence of a reply to a specific rejection, issue, or comment does not signify agreement with or concession of that rejection, issue, or comment. In addition, because the arguments made above may not be exhaustive, there may be reasons for patentability of any or all pending claims (or other claims) that have not been expressed. Still yet, nothing in this reply should be construed as intention to concede any issue with regard to any claim, except as specifically stated in this reply. Finally, it should be noted that no claims are intended to be construed under 35 U.S.C. 112, paragraph 6.

Application No.: 14/731,282
Date: Apr 27, 2017
Reply to Office Action of 2017-01-27

In the event a telephone conversation would expedite the prosecution of this application, the Examiner may reach the undersigned at (408) 977-7227.

Respectfully submitted,

IP Clinic at Lincoln Law School

By_____/Britten Sessions/_____

Britten Sessions
Reg. No. 68278
IP Clinic at Lincoln Law School
384 S Second St.
San Jose, California 95113
Phone (408) 977-7227
Fax (408) 977-7228

LINCOLN LAW SCHOOL OF SAN JOSE
INTELLECTUAL PROPERTY SERIES

EXHIBIT: OFFICE ACTION

UNITED STATES PATENT AND TRADEMARK OFFICE

UNITED STATES DEPARTMENT OF COMMERCE
United States Patent and Trademark Office
Address: COMMISSIONER FOR PATENTS
P.O. Box 1450
Alexandria, Virginia 22313-1450
www.uspto.gov

APPLICATION NO.	FILING DATE	FIRST NAMED INVENTOR	ATTORNEY DOCKET NO.	CONFIRMATION NO.
14/742,430	06/17/2015	Monte Phillip Dauer	DAUM-P0001	1086

127633	7590	02/04/2016

Intellectual Property Clinic
Lincoln Law School of San Jose
384 S Second Street
San Jose, CA 95113

EXAMINER
O'HERN, BRENT T

ART UNIT	PAPER NUMBER
1781	

NOTIFICATION DATE	DELIVERY MODE
02/04/2016	ELECTRONIC

Please find below and/or attached an Office communication concerning this application or proceeding.

The time period for reply, if any, is set in the attached communication.

Notice of the Office communication was sent electronically on above-indicated "Notification Date" to the following e-mail address(es):

director@lincolnipclinic.com
patent_docketing@lincolnipclinic.com
eofficeaction@appcoll.com

PTOL-90A (Rev. 04/07)

EXHIBITS 229

	Application No.	Applicant(s)
Office Action Summary	14/742,430	DAUER, MONTE PHILLIP
	Examiner	Art Unit	AIA (First Inventor to File) Status
	BRENT O'HERN	1781	Yes

-- The MAILING DATE of this communication appears on the cover sheet with the correspondence address --

Period for Reply

A SHORTENED STATUTORY PERIOD FOR REPLY IS SET TO EXPIRE <u>3</u> MONTHS FROM THE MAILING DATE OF THIS COMMUNICATION.
- Extensions of time may be available under the provisions of 37 CFR 1.136(a). In no event, however, may a reply be timely filed after SIX (6) MONTHS from the mailing date of this communication.
- If NO period for reply is specified above, the maximum statutory period will apply and will expire SIX (6) MONTHS from the mailing date of this communication.
- Failure to reply within the set or extended period for reply will, by statute, cause the application to become ABANDONED (35 U.S.C. § 133). Any reply received by the Office later than three months after the mailing date of this communication, even if timely filed, may reduce any earned patent term adjustment. See 37 CFR 1.704(b).

Status

1)☒ Responsive to communication(s) filed on <u>6/17/2015</u>.
    ☐ A declaration(s)/affidavit(s) under **37 CFR 1.130(b)** was/were filed on _____.
2a)☐ This action is **FINAL**.   2b)☒ This action is non-final.
3)☐ An election was made by the applicant in response to a restriction requirement set forth during the interview on _____; the restriction requirement and election have been incorporated into this action.
4)☐ Since this application is in condition for allowance except for formal matters, prosecution as to the merits is closed in accordance with the practice under *Ex parte Quayle*, 1935 C.D. 11, 453 O.G. 213.

Disposition of Claims*

5)☒ Claim(s) <u>1-6</u> is/are pending in the application.
    5a) Of the above claim(s) _____ is/are withdrawn from consideration.
6)☐ Claim(s) _____ is/are allowed.
7)☒ Claim(s) <u>1-6</u> is/are rejected.
8)☐ Claim(s) _____ is/are objected to.
9)☐ Claim(s) _____ are subject to restriction and/or election requirement.

* If any claims have been determined <u>allowable</u>, you may be eligible to benefit from the **Patent Prosecution Highway** program at a participating intellectual property office for the corresponding application. For more information, please see http://www.uspto.gov/patents/init_events/pph/index.jsp or send an inquiry to PPHfeedback@uspto.gov.

Application Papers

10)☐ The specification is objected to by the Examiner.
11)☒ The drawing(s) filed on <u>6/17/2016</u> is/are: a)☐ accepted or b)☒ objected to by the Examiner.
    Applicant may not request that any objection to the drawing(s) be held in abeyance. See 37 CFR 1.85(a).
    Replacement drawing sheet(s) including the correction is required if the drawing(s) is objected to. See 37 CFR 1.121(d).

Priority under 35 U.S.C. § 119

12)☐ Acknowledgment is made of a claim for foreign priority under 35 U.S.C. § 119(a)-(d) or (f).
    Certified copies:
      a)☐ All b)☐ Some** c)☐ None of the:
        1.☐ Certified copies of the priority documents have been received.
        2.☐ Certified copies of the priority documents have been received in Application No. _____.
        3.☐ Copies of the certified copies of the priority documents have been received in this National Stage application from the International Bureau (PCT Rule 17.2(a)).
** See the attached detailed Office action for a list of the certified copies not received.

Attachment(s)

1)☒ Notice of References Cited (PTO-892)
2)☒ Information Disclosure Statement(s) (PTO/SB/08a and/or PTO/SB/08b) Paper No(s)/Mail Date _____.
3)☐ Interview Summary (PTO-413) Paper No(s)/Mail Date. _____.
4)☐ Other: _____.

U.S. Patent and Trademark Office
PTOL-326 (Rev. 11-13)   Office Action Summary   Part of Paper No./Mail Date 20160130

Application/Control Number: 14/742,430 Page 2
Art Unit: 1781

The present application, filed on or after March 16, 2013, is being examined under the first inventor to file provisions of the AIA.

DETAILED ACTION

Drawings

1. The drawings are objected to as failing to comply with 37 CFR 1.84(p)(5) because they do not include the following reference sign(s) mentioned in the description: reference #100 described at paragraph #18 is not illustrated in the Drawings. Corrected drawing sheets in compliance with 37 CFR 1.121(d) are required in reply to the Office action to avoid abandonment of the application. Any amended replacement drawing sheet should include all of the figures appearing on the immediate prior version of the sheet, even if only one figure is being amended. Each drawing sheet submitted after the filing date of an application must be labeled in the top margin as either "Replacement Sheet" or "New Sheet" pursuant to 37 CFR 1.121(d). If the changes are not accepted by the examiner, the applicant will be notified and informed of any required corrective action in the next Office action. The objection to the drawings will not be held in abeyance.

Claim Rejections - 35 USC § 112

The following is a quotation of 35 U.S.C. 112(b):
(b) CONCLUSION.—The specification shall conclude with one or more claims particularly pointing out and distinctly claiming the subject matter which the inventor or a joint inventor regards as the invention.

The following is a quotation of 35 U.S.C. 112 (pre-AIA), second paragraph:
The specification shall conclude with one or more claims particularly pointing out and distinctly claiming the subject matter which the applicant regards as his invention.

Application/Control Number: 14/742,430 Page 3
Art Unit: 1781

2. Claims 2 and 4-6 are rejected under 35 U.S.C. 112(b) or 35 U.S.C. 112 (pre-AIA), second paragraph, as being indefinite for failing to particularly point out and distinctly claim the subject matter which the inventor or a joint inventor, or for pre-AIA the applicant regards as the invention.

3. The phrase "wherein the first sheet, the second sheet and the third sheet include, but not limited to, a material selected from the group consisting of: solid wood veneer sheets, bonded wood chip veneer sheets, laminate bamboo sheets. material selected from the group consisting of: solid wood veneer sheets, bonded wood chip veneer sheets, laminate bamboo sheets" in claim 2, lines 1-4 is vague and indefinite as it is unclear what is the scope of the material as the "but not limited to" language infers the scope is open while the "consisting of" language is closed.

4. Claim 4 recites the limitation "the metal" in line 1. There is insufficient antecedent basis for this limitation in the claim.

5. The phrase "wherein the second group of wires precede the first layer of wire mesh" in claim 5, lines 3-4 is vague and indefinite as it is unclear whether the wires are separate from the mesh or part of the mesh as claim 1 infers the panel only includes mesh while claim 5 appears to infer there are wires in addition to mesh.

6. Claim 6 recites the limitation "the first group" in line 1. There is insufficient antecedent basis for this limitation in the claim.

7. Claim 6 recites the limitation "the second group" in line 1. There is insufficient antecedent basis for this limitation in the claim.

Application/Control Number: 14/742,430 Page 4
Art Unit: 1781

8. The phrase "separated by a wood laminate sheet" in claim 6, line 2 is vague and indefinite as it is unclear whether the wood laminate sheet is the second sheet or an additional sheet. There is not an antecedent basis linking the members.

Clarification and/or correction required.

Claim Rejections - 35 USC § 102

The following is a quotation of the appropriate paragraphs of 35 U.S.C. 102 that form the basis for the rejections under this section made in this Office action:

A person shall be entitled to a patent unless –

(a)(2) the claimed invention was described in a patent issued under section 151, or in an application for patent published or deemed published under section 122(b), in which the patent or application, as the case may be, names another inventor and was effectively filed before the effective filing date of the claimed invention.

9. Claim 1 is rejected under 35 U.S.C. 102(a)(2) as being anticipated by Idestrup (US 2008/0152862).

Idestrup ('862) teaches a reinforced plywood panel comprising: a first sheet, a second sheet a third sheet; and a mesh bonded between the first sheet and the second sheet and the second sheet and third sheet *(See paras. 53-57 and FIG-6, plywood #30 with mesh #62 and #48 between veneer sheets #60, #48 and #46.).*

Application/Control Number: 14/742,430 Page 5
Art Unit: 1781

FIG.6.

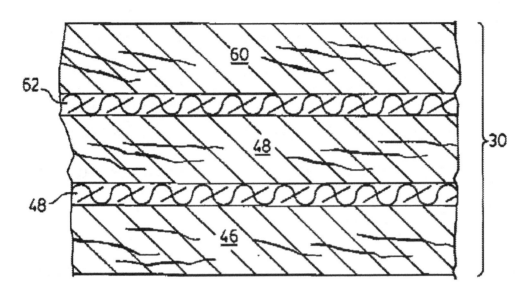

Claim Rejections - 35 USC § 103

The following is a quotation of 35 U.S.C. 103 which forms the basis for all obviousness rejections set forth in this Office action:

> A patent for a claimed invention may not be obtained, notwithstanding that the claimed invention is not identically disclosed as set forth in section 102 of this title, if the differences between the claimed invention and the prior art are such that the claimed invention as a whole would have been obvious before the effective filing date of the claimed invention to a person having ordinary skill in the art to which the claimed invention pertains. Patentability shall not be negated by the manner in which the invention was made.

10. Claims 2-6 are rejected under 35 U.S.C. 103 as being unpatentable over Idestrup (US 2008/0152862) in view of McIntire (US 2008/127587).

Idestrup ('862) teaches plywood discussed above, with three layers of wood veneer separated by two sheets of mesh and bonded by adhesive *(See paras. 53-57 and FIG-6, plywood #30 with mesh #62 and #48 between sheets #60, #48 and #46.)*,

Application/Control Number: 14/742,430 Page 6
Art Unit: 1781

where the mesh is made from various alternative materials including nylon *(See para. 57.)*, however, fails to expressly disclose the mesh being made of metal.

McIntire ('587) teaches building members alternatively being reinforced with nylon mesh or metal mesh *(See paras. 20, 40 and 42.)*. It would have been obvious to substitute one type of mesh a material for another based on strength, environmental and cost requirements. Metal mesh is known to be strong and stronger that non-metal mesh of the same dimensions and configurations. If a stronger panel is required then it would have been obvious to select a stronger mesh material, including metal, over a material that is not as strong.

It would have been obvious to a person having ordinary skill in the art at the time of Applicant's invention to substitute Idestrup's ('862) nylon mesh by metal mesh in order to provide a strong panel that is suitable for its intended use.

Conclusion

Any inquiry concerning this communication or earlier communications from the examiner should be directed to BRENT O'HERN whose telephone number is (571)272-6385. The examiner can normally be reached on Monday-Thursday, 9:00-6:00.

If attempts to reach the examiner by telephone are unsuccessful, the examiner's supervisor, Aaron Austin can be reached on (571) 272-8535. The fax phone number for the organization where this application or proceeding is assigned is 571-273-8300.

Application/Control Number: 14/742,430 Page 7
Art Unit: 1781

Information regarding the status of an application may be obtained from the Patent Application Information Retrieval (PAIR) system. Status information for published applications may be obtained from either Private PAIR or Public PAIR. Status information for unpublished applications is available through Private PAIR only. For more information about the PAIR system, see http://pair-direct.uspto.gov. Should you have questions on access to the Private PAIR system, contact the Electronic Business Center (EBC) at 866-217-9197 (toll-free). If you would like assistance from a USPTO Customer Service Representative or access to the automated information system, call 800-786-9199 (IN USA OR CANADA) or 571-272-1000.

/BRENT O'HERN/
Primary Examiner, Art Unit 1781
January 30, 2016

LINCOLN LAW SCHOOL OF SAN JOSE
INTELLECTUAL PROPERTY SERIES

EXHIBIT: OFFICE ACTION RESPONSE

IN THE UNITED STATES PATENT AND TRADEMARK OFFICE

In re Application of:	Title: Dauer Board
Monte Dauer	Examiner: Brent T O'HERN
Application No.: 14/742,430	Docket No.: DAUM-P0001
File Date: 2015-06-17	Confirmation No.: 1086

AMENDMENT A

Commissioner for Patents
P.O. Box 1450
Alexandria VA 22313-1450

Examiner:

In response to the communication mailed 2016-02-04 (hereafter "Non Final Office Action" or "NFOA"), please consider the following amendments believed to place the claims in condition for allowance.

Application No.: 14/742,430
Date: Apr 15, 2016
Reply to Office Action of 2016-02-04

Amendments to the Claims:

The listing of amended claims follow:

1. (Currently Amended) A reinforced plywood panel comprising:

    a first sheet;

    a second sheet;

    a third sheet; ~~and~~

    <u>a fourth sheet;</u>

    <u>a first mesh bonded with the first sheet and the second sheet using a first layer of glue;</u>

    <u>a second mesh bonded with the second sheet and the third sheet, wherein the material between the second sheet and the third sheet consists of the second mesh; and</u>

    <u>a third mesh bonded with the third sheet and the fourth sheet using a second layer of glue.</u>

    ~~a mesh bonded between the first sheet and the second sheet and the second sheet and third sheet.~~

2. (Currently Amended) The panel of claim 1, wherein the first sheet, the second sheet<u>,</u> [[and]] the third sheet <u>and the fourth sheet</u> include~~, but not limited to,~~ a material selected from the group consisting of:

    solid wood veneer sheets, bonded wood chip veneer sheets, laminate bamboo sheets.

3. (Currently Amended) The panel of claim 1, wherein the <u>first mesh, the second mesh and the third</u> mesh utilized between the first sheet, second sheet<u>,</u> [[and]] third sheet <u>and the fourth sheet</u> include a material selected from the group consisting of:

    steel, metal alloy, and aluminum.

4. (Cancel)

EXHIBITS

Application No.: 14/742,430
Date: Apr 15, 2016
Reply to Office Action of 2016-02-04

5. (Currently Amended) The panel of claim 1, wherein <u>each of</u> the <u>first mesh, the second mesh and the third</u> mesh comprises a first group of wires and a second group of wires, wherein the first group of wires are positioned such that the direction of the first group of the wires are in a different direction than the second group of wires.<s>, and wherein the second group of wires precede the first layer of wire mesh.</s>

6. (Canceled)

Application No.: 14/742,430
Date: Apr 15, 2016
Reply to Office Action of 2016-02-04

Amendments to the Drawings:

The Examiner has objected to the drawings. Such objection is deemed avoided by virtue of the replacement sheets submitted herewith. This sheet replaces the corresponding original sheet.

Application No.: 14/742,430
Date: Apr 15, 2016
Reply to Office Action of 2016-02-04

Remarks:

Claims 1, 2, 3, and 5 are pending. Claims 1, 2, 3, and 5 are amended in this response. Support for the amendments to claims can be found at least in at least paragraph [0020] and FIG. 4 in the application as originally filed. Claims 4 and 6 are canceled without prejudice or disclaimer. No new matter is added by this response. Applicant respectfully requests reconsideration and allowance of these claims in view of the following remarks. Applicant's silence as to assertions by the Examiner in the Office Action or certain requirements that may be applicable to such rejections (for example, assertions regarding dependent claims, whether a reference constitutes prior art, whether reference are legally combinable for obviousness purposes) is not a concession by Applicants that such assertions are accurate or such requirements have been met, and Applicants reserve the right to analyze and dispute such in the future.

Drawings

The drawings are objected to as failing to comply with 37 CFR 1.84(p)(5) because they do not include the following reference sign(s) mentioned in the description: reference #100 described at paragraph #18 is not illustrated in the Drawings.

In response, Applicant has added the label "100" in figures 1-2 and 4-5. Thus, this objection should be overcome.

Claim rejections under 35 U.S.C.§112

Claims 2 and 4-6 are rejected under 35 U.S.C. 112(b) or 35 U.S.C. 112(pre-AIA), second paragraph, as being indefinite for failing to particularly point out and distinctly claim the subject matter which the inventor or a joint inventor, or for pre-AIA the applicant regards as the invention.

Application No.: 14/742,430
Date: Apr 15, 2016
Reply to Office Action of 2016-02-04

While Applicant respectfully traverses the rejections, claims 4 and 6 have been canceled without prejudice or disclaimer, rendering the rejection thereof moot.

In addition, Applicant has amended claims 2 and 5 to clarify the scope of claims in order to expedite examination. In detail, the phrase ", but not limited to," in claim 2 is canceled, and the phrase ", and wherein the second group of wires precede the first layer of wire mesh" in claim 5 is also canceled.

Thus, Applicant respectfully requests that these rejections be reconsidered and withdrawn.

Claim rejections under 35 U.S.C. §102 &103

The Office Action recites that claim 1 is rejected under 35 U.S.C. §102 (a)(2) as being anticipated by U.S. Patent Application Publication No. 2008/0152862 to Idestrup (hereinafter "Idestrup").

The Office Action recites that claims 2-6 are rejected under 35 U.S.C. §103 (a) as being unpatentable over Idestrup in view of U.S. Patent Application Publication No. 2008/127587 to McIntire (hereinafter "McIntire").

Applicant respectfully traverses the rejections. The rejection of claims 4 and 6 are rendered moot as claims 4 and 6 have been canceled without prejudice or disclaimer.

<u>Regarding claims 1, 2, 3, and 5</u>

Claim 1, as currently amended, recites, in part:

> *A reinforced plywood panel comprising:*
>
> ...
>
> ***a first mesh bonded with the first sheet and the second sheet using a first layer of glue**; a second mesh bonded with the second sheet*

Application No.: 14/742,430
Date: Apr 15, 2016
Reply to Office Action of 2016-02-04

*and the third sheet, wherein **the material between the second sheet and the third sheet consists of the second mesh**; and **a third mesh bonded with the third sheet and the fourth sheet using a second layer of glue**.* (Emphases added).

The Office Action rejected claim 1 based on Idestrup. However, Applicant submits that amended claim 1 is patentable at least for the following reasons:

Idestrup describes a multi-ply plywood panel 24 including a backing veneer construct 30 and a decorative or facing veneer construct 32. The backing veneer construct 30 is bonded to the rear surface of the facing veneer construct 32 by an adhesive layer 34. The facing veneer construct 32 includes an inner veneer ply 38 and an outer veneer play 36 bonded to the inner veneer ply 38 by an adhesive layer 40. The backing veneer construct 30 includes a pair of rotary-cut veneer ply layers 44, 46, and the rotary-cut veneer ply layers 44, 46 are bonded on each lateral side of a flexible mesh layer 48 (see paras. [0047]-[0049], and FIG. 4).

In addition, the backing veneer construct 30 can include three veneer layers 46, 44, 60, and interposed between each of the veneer layers 46, 44 and 44, 60 is respectively a flexible mesh layer 48, 62(see para. [0053], and FIG. 6).

The Office Action, on pages 4-5, equates Idestrup's veneer layers 46, 44, 60 to the sheets of amended claim 1, and equates Idestrup's flexible mesh layer 48, 62 to the mesh of amended claim 1. Firstly, Idestrup only describes the backing veneer construct 30 including three veneer layers 46, 44, 60. However, claim 1 has been amended to "**a first mesh bonded with the first sheet and the second sheet using a first layer of glue, a third mesh bonded with the third sheet and the fourth sheet using a second layer of glue**". That is, the reinforced plywood panel of amended claim 1 includes four sheets, which is different from Idestrup.

Additionally, assuming that Idestrup's backing veneer construct 30 includes at least four veneer layers, Idestrup teaches or suggests that each two adjacent veneer layers are bonded by a mesh layer, and adhesives are provided in a sufficient amount to fully penetrate through the mesh layer (see para. [0053]). In other words, the mesh layer and the adhesives must be

Application No.: 14/742,430
Date: Apr 15, 2016
Reply to Office Action of 2016-02-04

simultaneously applied to each two adjacent veneer layers of Idestrup's backing veneer construct 30. However, the material interposed between the second sheet and the third sheet of amended claim 1 consists of the second mesh, and thus adhesives are not needed. Therefore, Idestrup also fails to disclose "**the material between the second sheet and the third sheet consists of the second mesh**" as recited in amended independent claim 1.

Furthermore, McIntire describes an external roofing surface. Throughout McIntire's detailed description and drawing, McIntire fails to disclose the above-features of amended claim 1. Thus, there is no motivation to use McIntire to meet the deficiencies of the base references.

The product described in amended claim 1 increases the strength of the material at the same time of reducing the weight of the end product, reducing the thickness of the panels needed and thus reducing the number of veneer sheets needed to produce panels of equivalent strength.

Therefore, Idestrup and McIntire, taken alone or in combination, cannot support a rejection under 35 U.S.C. §§102&103 for independent claim 1 and dependent claims 2, 3, and 5, and claim 1 and dependent claims 2, 3, and 5 should be allowable for at least these reasons. Thus, Applicant respectfully requests reconsideration and withdrawal of the rejection of claim 1 under 35 U.S.C. §102. and the rejection of claims 2, 3, and 5 under 35 U.S.C. §103.

8

Application No.: 14/742,430
Date: Apr 15, 2016
Reply to Office Action of 2016-02-04

Conclusion

In the event a telephone conversation would expedite the prosecution of this application, the Examiner may reach the undersigned at (408) 977-7227.

Respectfully submitted,

IP Clinic at Lincoln Law School

By____/Britten Sessions/____

Britten Sessions
Reg. No. 68278
IP Clinic at Lincoln Law School
384 S Second St.
San Jose, California 95113
Phone (408) 977-7227
Fax (408) 977-7228

LINCOLN LAW SCHOOL OF SAN JOSE
INTELLECTUAL PROPERTY SERIES

EXHIBIT: OFFICE ACTION

EXHIBITS 247

UNITED STATES PATENT AND TRADEMARK OFFICE

UNITED STATES DEPARTMENT OF COMMERCE
United States Patent and Trademark Office
Address: COMMISSIONER FOR PATENTS
P.O. Box 1450
Alexandria, Virginia 22313-1450
www.uspto.gov

APPLICATION NO.	FILING DATE	FIRST NAMED INVENTOR	ATTORNEY DOCKET NO.	CONFIRMATION NO.
14/796,998	07/10/2015	Dustin Grzesik	GRZD-P0001	8050

127633 7590 06/21/2017
Intellectual Property Clinic
Lincoln Law School of San Jose
384 S Second Street
San Jose, CA 95113

EXAMINER
MORAN, KATHERINE M

ART UNIT	PAPER NUMBER
3765	

NOTIFICATION DATE	DELIVERY MODE
06/21/2017	ELECTRONIC

Please find below and/or attached an Office communication concerning this application or proceeding.

The time period for reply, if any, is set in the attached communication.

Notice of the Office communication was sent electronically on above-indicated "Notification Date" to the following e-mail address(es):

director@lincolnipclinic.com
patent_docketing@lincolnipclinic.com
eofficeaction@appcoll.com

PTOL-90A (Rev. 04/07)

248 PATENT PROSECUTION WORKBOOK

Office Action Summary	Application No. 14/796,998	Applicant(s) GRZESIK, DUSTIN		
	Examiner KATHERINE MORAN	Art Unit 3765	AIA (First Inventor to File) Status Yes	

-- *The MAILING DATE of this communication appears on the cover sheet with the correspondence address* --

Period for Reply

A SHORTENED STATUTORY PERIOD FOR REPLY IS SET TO EXPIRE <u>3</u> MONTHS FROM THE MAILING DATE OF THIS COMMUNICATION.
- Extensions of time may be available under the provisions of 37 CFR 1.136(a). In no event, however, may a reply be timely filed after SIX (6) MONTHS from the mailing date of this communication.
- If NO period for reply is specified above, the maximum statutory period will apply and will expire SIX (6) MONTHS from the mailing date of this communication.
- Failure to reply within the set or extended period for reply will, by statute, cause the application to become ABANDONED (35 U.S.C. § 133). Any reply received by the Office later than three months after the mailing date of this communication, even if timely filed, may reduce any earned patent term adjustment. See 37 CFR 1.704(b).

Status

1) ☒ Responsive to communication(s) filed on <u>7/10/15</u>.
   ☐ A declaration(s)/affidavit(s) under **37 CFR 1.130(b)** was/were filed on _____.
2a) ☐ This action is **FINAL**.   2b) ☒ This action is non-final.
3) ☐ An election was made by the applicant in response to a restriction requirement set forth during the interview on _____; the restriction requirement and election have been incorporated into this action.
4) ☐ Since this application is in condition for allowance except for formal matters, prosecution as to the merits is closed in accordance with the practice under *Ex parte Quayle*, 1935 C.D. 11, 453 O.G. 213.

Disposition of Claims*

5) ☒ Claim(s) <u>1-20</u> is/are pending in the application.
   5a) Of the above claim(s) _____ is/are withdrawn from consideration.
6) ☐ Claim(s) _____ is/are allowed.
7) ☒ Claim(s) <u>1-20</u> is/are rejected.
8) ☐ Claim(s) _____ is/are objected to.
9) ☐ Claim(s) _____ are subject to restriction and/or election requirement.

* If any claims have been determined <u>allowable</u>, you may be eligible to benefit from the **Patent Prosecution Highway** program at a participating intellectual property office for the corresponding application. For more information, please see http://www.uspto.gov/patents/init_events/pph/index.jsp or send an inquiry to PPHfeedback@uspto.gov.

Application Papers

10) ☐ The specification is objected to by the Examiner.
11) ☒ The drawing(s) filed on <u>7/10/15</u> is/are: a) ☒ accepted or b) ☐ objected to by the Examiner.
    Applicant may not request that any objection to the drawing(s) be held in abeyance. See 37 CFR 1.85(a).
    Replacement drawing sheet(s) including the correction is required if the drawing(s) is objected to. See 37 CFR 1.121(d).

Priority under 35 U.S.C. § 119

12) ☐ Acknowledgment is made of a claim for foreign priority under 35 U.S.C. § 119(a)-(d) or (f).
    Certified copies:
    a) ☐ All   b) ☐ Some**   c) ☐ None of the:
       1. ☐ Certified copies of the priority documents have been received.
       2. ☐ Certified copies of the priority documents have been received in Application No. _____.
       3. ☐ Copies of the certified copies of the priority documents have been received in this National Stage application from the International Bureau (PCT Rule 17.2(a)).
** See the attached detailed Office action for a list of the certified copies not received.

Attachment(s)

1) ☒ Notice of References Cited (PTO-892)
2) ☒ Information Disclosure Statement(s) (PTO/SB/08a and/or PTO/SB/08b) Paper No(s)/Mail Date <u>10/26/15, 7/10/15</u>.
3) ☐ Interview Summary (PTO-413) Paper No(s)/Mail Date. _____.
4) ☐ Other: _____.

Application/Control Number: 14/796,998 Page 2
Art Unit: 3765

1. The present application, filed on or after March 16, 2013, is being examined under the first inventor to file provisions of the AIA.

DETAILED ACTION

Claim Objections

2. Claim 2 objected to because of the following informalities: line 1: delete "opening" and insert --openings--. Appropriate correction is required.

Claim Rejections - 35 USC § 112

3. The following is a quotation of 35 U.S.C. 112(b):
(b) CONCLUSION.—The specification shall conclude with one or more claims particularly pointing out and distinctly claiming the subject matter which the inventor or a joint inventor regards as the invention.

4. Claims 1-20 are rejected under 35 U.S.C. 112(b) being indefinite for failing to particularly point out and distinctly claim the subject matter which the inventor or a joint inventor, or for pre-AIA the applicant regards as the invention. Claim 1 is unclear in that the metes and bounds of "substantially equal dimensions" cannot be ascertained from the specification. A review of the specification doesn't provide further details as to what values would be considered as "substantially equal" to one another, this phrasing being a phrase of degree. For example, if one opening is 3 inches and the other two openings are 6 inches, are these considered substantially equal dimensions?

Claim Rejections - 35 USC § 103

5. In the event the determination of the status of the application as subject to AIA 35 U.S.C. 102 and 103 (or as subject to pre-AIA 35 U.S.C. 102 and 103) is incorrect, any correction of the statutory basis for the rejection will not be considered a new ground of

Application/Control Number: 14/796,998 Page 3
Art Unit: 3765

rejection if the prior art relied upon, and the rationale supporting the rejection, would be the same under either status.

6. The following is a quotation of 35 U.S.C. 103 which forms the basis for all obviousness rejections set forth in this Office action:

> A patent for a claimed invention may not be obtained, notwithstanding that the claimed invention is not identically disclosed as set forth in section 102, if the differences between the claimed invention and the prior art are such that the claimed invention as a whole would have been obvious before the effective filing date of the claimed invention to a person having ordinary skill in the art to which the claimed invention pertains. Patentability shall not be negated by the manner in which the invention was made.

7. Claims 1, 2, 9, 12, and 18-20 are rejected under 35 U.S.C. 103 as being unpatentable over Parbat (WO/012551) in view of Edenfield (U.S. 5,819,323). Parbat discloses the invention substantially as claimed. Parbat teaches an undergarment 10 comprising a main body comprising at least one panel of material 17, three openings (one waist opening at 24 and two leg openings 22,23) and three peripheral edges, whereon one peripheral edge is located between adjacent openings. The three openings and three peripheral edges define an outer periphery of the main body. The dimensions of the leg openings and waist opening appear to be substantially equal and all three peripheral edges have substantially equal dimensions as in Figures 1 and 2 and each peripheral edge includes three fastening poppers (snaps) 11,110 for attaching the panels. However, Parbat doesn't explicitly teach all three openings have substantially equal dimensions and all three peripheral edges have substantially equal dimensions, all three openings having a length in a range from about 1.5 inches to about 60 inches. Edenfield teaches an undergarment with leg openings 8 and waist opening 6 having substantially equal dimensions in that the leg openings have a circumference (the circumference is considered as a length around the openings) of

Application/Control Number: 14/796,998 Page 4
Art Unit: 3765

approximately 15 inches and the waist opening having a circumference of approximately 17.5 inches. Given this teaching, and Parbat's teaching of replacing one panel with another, one of ordinary skill could have arrived at a conclusion that forming the undergarment with leg openings and a waist opening having substantially equal dimensions would lend itself to the intended operation of Parbat. Parbat teaches the panels 17,18 are changeable such that one panel can be removed and replaced with another panel. Thus, it appears that the replacement panel would need to have substantially equal dimensions to the panel it is replacing, in order to align with and secure to the other panel. Therefore, it would have been obvious to modify Parbat to form all three openings with substantially equal dimensions in that this undergarment structure would be expected to accommodate circumferences of the waist and legs of a range of wearer sizes. It also would have been obvious to form all three peripheral edges with the same dimensions to accommodate the intended interchangeability of the panels. For claim 20, it would have been obvious to form all three peripheral edges with a length in the range of about 1 inch to about 30 inches in that the edges should be long enough to accommodate the three poppers and a length of 3-4 inches would accommodate the poppers while also adequately covering the wearer's crotch area.

8. Claims 3 and 4 are rejected under 35 U.S.C. 103 as being unpatentable over Parbat in view of Edenfield, and further in view of O'Leary (U.S. 2011/0023216). Parbat discloses the invention substantially as claimed but doesn't teach the at least one panel comprises a stretchable material, the material comprises one or more elastomeric fibers present in an amount ranging from about 10 wt% to about 100 wt.% or each of the two

Application/Control Number: 14/796,998 Page 5
Art Unit: 3765

panels comprise a multi-stretch material, the two panels having substantially equal dimensions. O'Leary teaches an undergarment 10 formed of elastic fibers present in an amount of 10wt% (par. 101). One of ordinary skill could have arrived at an ideal wt% for the elastomeric fibers based upon the degree of stretchability desired. Therefore, it would have been obvious to modify Long to provide stretchable material comprising one or more elastomeric fibers present in an amount ranging from about 10wt% to about 100 wt% to achieve a desired stretchability property for the undergarment.

9. Claim 5 is rejected under 35 U.S.C. 103 as being unpatentable over Parbat in view of Edenfield, and further in view of Braunstein et al. (U.S. 6,041,446). Parbat discloses the invention substantially as claimed. However, Parbat doesn't teach the main body comprises antimicrobial material. Braunstein teaches an undergarment formed from a material that is pre-treated with an antimicrobial composition to kill and inhibit the growth of bacteria and yeast. Therefore, it would have been obvious to form Parbat's main body from a material pre-treated with an antimicrobial material in that Braunstein teaches the composition kills and inhibits the grown of bacteria and yeast.

10. Claims 6-8 are rejected under 35 U.S.C. 103 as being unpatentable over Parbat in view of Edenfield, and further in view of Russano (U.S. 5,546,608). Parbat discloses the invention substantially as claimed. However, Parbat doesn't teach the main body comprises at least one cinching device near at least one of the openings, wherein the at least one cinching device is configured to alter a size of the opening or the main body comprises an additional stretchable material near at least one of the openings, the additional stretchable material includes an elastic band. Russano teaches an

Application/Control Number: 14/796,998
Art Unit: 3765

Page 6

undergarment with at least one cinching device (drawstring) near at least one of the openings (col.2, lines 45-49), the cinching device configured to alter a size of the opening. The leg openings include elastic bands 1,2. The cinching device allows for customized adjustment based on the wearer's size and the elastic bands hold the leg openings close to the wearer's skin to prevent debris from entering inside the undergarment. Therefore, it would have been obvious to modify Parbat to provide at least one cinching device near at least one of the openings and the elastic bands in that Russano teaches these are known elements in undergarments which allows for adjustment of the size of the leg and waist openings.

11. Claims 10 and 11 are rejected under 35 U.S.C. 103 as being unpatentable over Parbat in view of Edenfield, and further in view of Feinberg et al. (U.S. 5,398,346). Parbat discloses the invention substantially as claimed and the two panels 17,18 appear to have substantially equal dimensions as in Figure 1 and 2. However, Parbat doesn't teach each of the two panels of material comprise a multi-stretch material and each of the two panels of material have substantially equal dimensions. Feinberg teaches an undergarment formed of panels comprising multi-stretch material, the undergarment stretchable in a longitudinal direction, a transverse direction, and a bias direction. Feinberg teaches this multi-stretch material allows for the undergarment portions to move in unison with movements of the wearer's skin (col. 4, lines 60-65). Therefore, it would have been obvious to modify Parbat to form each of the two panels of a multi-stretch material, each of the two panels having substantially equal dimensions in that Feinberg teaches the material allows for the undergarment to move in unison with

Application/Control Number: 14/796,998 Page 7
Art Unit: 3765

movements of the wearer's skin. It also would have been obvious to form the panels with substantially equal dimensions in that the panels could be cut together in a single step to improve manufacturing efficiency.

12. Claims 13-16 are rejected under 35 U.S.C. 103 as being unpatentable over Parbat in view of Edenfield, and further in view of Pundyk (U.S. 4,538,615). Parbat discloses the invention substantially as claimed, including at least one of the panels of material connected to another panel via a hook and loop fastener (lines 14 and 15) but doesn't teach the main body comprises at least six panels of material, each of the panels comprise a multi-stretch material, the six panels have substantially equal dimensions. Pundyk teaches an undergarment comprising at least six panels of material (abstract), each of the panels comprise a multi-stretch material (Figs. 5-7 show arrows for the direction of stretch of each panel). As discussed above, forming the six panels with substantially equal dimensions would improve manufacturing efficiency in that the panels could be cut at the same time such that more undergarments could be made within a period of time. Therefore, it would have been obvious to modify Parbat's undergarment such that the main body comprises at least six panels of material, each panel comprising a multi-stretch material, the six panels having substantially equal dimensions in that Pundyk teaches this structure is known in the undergarment art.

13. Claim 17 is rejected under 35 U.S.C. 103 as being unpatentable over Parbat in view of Edenfield, and further in view of Pace et al. (U.S. 2012/0284895). Parbat discloses the invention substantially as claimed. However, Parbat doesn't teach at least one of the peripheral edges comprises an identification label coupled thereto. Pace

Application/Control Number: 14/796,998 Page 8
Art Unit: 3765

teaches in column 27 that labels have been attached to apparel items by stitching. Therefore, it would have been obvious to modify Parbat to provide at least one of the peripheral edges with an identification label coupled thereto in that Pace teaches the label provides decorative images or ornamentation.

Conclusion

14. Any inquiry concerning this communication or earlier communications should be directed to Primary Examiner Katherine Moran at (571) 272-4990. The examiner can be reached on Monday-Thursday from 8:30 am to 6:00 pm, and alternating Fridays.

If attempts to reach the examiner by telephone are unsuccessful, the examiner's supervisor, Khoa Huynh, may be reached at (571) 272-4888. The official and after final fax number for the organization where this application is assigned is (571) 273-8300.

General information regarding this application may be obtained by contacting the Group Receptionist at (571) 272-3700.

Information regarding the status of an application may be obtained from the Patent Application Information Retrieval (PAIR) system. Status information for published applications may be obtained from either Private PAIR or Public PAIR. Status information for unpublished applications is available through Private PAIR only. For more information about the PAIR system, see http://pair-direct.uspto.gov. Should you have questions on access to the Private PAIR system, contact the Electronic Business Center (EBC) at 866-217-9197 (toll-free).

/Katherine Moran/

Primary Examiner, AU 3765

LINCOLN LAW SCHOOL OF SAN JOSE
INTELLECTUAL PROPERTY SERIES

EXHIBIT: OFFICE ACTION RESPONSE

IN THE UNITED STATES PATENT AND TRADEMARK OFFICE

In re Application of:	Examiner: Katherine M MORAN
Dustin Grzesik	Docket No.: GRZD-P0001
Application No.: 14/796,998	Art Unit: 3765
File Date: 2015-07-10	Confirmation No.: 8050
Title: UNDERGARMENTS WITH EQUILATERAL DIMENSIONS	Date: Sept 21, 2017

AMENDMENT

Commissioner for Patents
P.O. Box 1450
Alexandria VA 22313-1450

Examiner:

In response to the communication mailed 2017-06-21 (hereafter "Non-Final Office Action" or "NFOA"), please consider the following amendments believed to place the claims in condition for allowance. Listing of the Claims begins on page 2 of this response. Remarks/Arguments begin on page 6 of this response.

Application No.: 14/796,998
Date: Sep 21, 2017

AMENDMENTS TO THE CLAIMS

What is claimed is:

1. (Currently Amended) An undergarment, comprising:

    a main body comprising at least one panel of material, <u>wherein the at least one panel of material comprises a stretchable material</u>;

    three openings, wherein all three openings have ~~substantially~~ equal dimensions<u>, and wherein the main body further comprises an additional stretchable material near at least one of the openings</u>; and

    three peripheral edges, whereon one peripheral edge is located between adjacent openings, <u>wherein the three peripheral edges have equal dimensions</u>.

2. (Currently Amended) The undergarment as recited in claim 1, wherein the three opening<u>s</u> and the three peripheral edges define an outer periphery of the main body.

3. (Canceled)

4. (Currently Amended) The undergarment as recited in claim [[3]] <u>1</u>, wherein the stretchable material comprises one or more elastomeric fibers present in an amount ranging from about 10 wt.% to about 100 wt.%, wherein the one or more elastomeric fibers are selected from the group consisting of: spandex, lastol, natural rubber, synthetic rubber, and combinations thereof.

EXHIBITS

Application No.: 14/796,998
Date: Sep 21, 2017

5. (Original) The undergarment as recited in claim 1, wherein the main body further comprises one or more additives selected from the group consisting of: colorants, pigments, crosslinking agents, phase change materials, antimicrobial materials, chlorine degradation resistant materials, fragrances, insect repellants, materials configured to provide UV protection, anti-static agents, wetting agents, and combinations thereof.

6. (Canceled)

7. (Currently Amended) The undergarment as recited in claim [[6]] 1, wherein the additional stretchable material includes an elastic band.

8. (Original) The undergarment as recited in claim 1, wherein the main body comprises at least one cinching device near at least one of the openings, wherein the at least one cinching device is configured to alter a size of the opening.

9. (Original) The undergarment as recited in claim 1, wherein the main body comprises at least two panels of material, wherein the two panels of material are attached at each of the peripheral edges via a closure.

10. (Original) The undergarment as recited in claim 9, wherein each of the two panels of material comprise a multi-stretch material.

Application No.: 14/796,998
Date: Sep 21, 2017

11. (Currently Amended) The undergarment as recited in claim 10, wherein the two panels of material have ~~substantially~~ equal dimensions.

12. (Original) The undergarment as recited in claim 9, wherein the closure is a hook and loop fastener.

13. (Original) The undergarment as recited in claim 1, wherein the main body comprises at least six panels of material.

14. (Original) The undergarment as recited in claim 13, wherein each of the six panels of material comprise a multi-stretch material.

15. (Currently Amended) The undergarment as recited in claim 14, wherein the six panels of material have ~~substantially~~ equal dimensions.

16. (Original) The undergarment as recited in claim 13, wherein at least one of the panels of material is connected to at least another of the panels of material via a hook and loop fastener.

17. (Original) The undergarment as recited in claim 1, wherein at least one of the peripheral edges comprises an identification label coupled thereto.

Application No.: 14/796,998
Date: Sep 21, 2017

18. (Original) The undergarment as recited in claim 1, wherein all three of the openings have a length in a range from about 1.5 inches to about 60 inches.

19. (Canceled)

20. (Currently Amended) The undergarment as recited in claim [[19]] 1, wherein all three of the peripheral edges have a length in a range from about 1 inch to about 30 inches.

Application No.: 14/796,998
Date: Sep 21, 2017

Summary

Claims 1, 2, 4, 7, 11, 15, and 20 are amended herein, and Claims 3, 6, and 19 are canceled. No new matter is introduced. Support for such amendments is found in the specification of the present application. See e.g. para. 35. Claims 1, 2, 4-5, 7-18, 20 are pending.

Applicant thanks Examiner for taking the time to speak and review possible amendments. Applicant has made a good faith effort to amend the claims in accordance with the direction provided in the Nonfinal Office Action and the Examiner Interview conducted on Sept. 19, 2017.

Rejections Under 35 U.S.C. 112

With respect to claim 1-20 rejected under 35 USC 112(b), the Examiner has cited that "Claim 1 Is unclear in that the metes and bounds of 'substantially equal dimensions' cannot be ascertained from the specification."

Applicant appreciates Examiner's comments, and in an effort to further prosecution, Applicant has removed the term "substantially" in the phrase "substantially equal dimensions" from the entire claim set, as follows:

> a main body comprising at least one panel of material, <u>wherein the at least one panel of material comprises a stretchable material;</u>
> three openings, wherein all three openings have ~~substantially~~ equal dimensions<u>, and wherein the main body further comprises an additional stretchable material near at least one of the openings</u>; and
> three peripheral edges, whereon one peripheral edge is located between adjacent openings, <u>wherein the three peripheral edges have equal dimensions</u>.

(see independent claim as amended).

Rejections Under 35 U.S.C. 103

Claims 1, 2, 9, 12, and 18-20 are rejected under 35 U.S.C. 103 as being unpatentable over Parbat (W0/012551) in view of Edenfield (U.S. 5,819,323). Claims 3 and 4 are rejected under 103 as being unpatentable over Parbat and Edenfield, in further view of O-Leary (U.S. 20110023216). Claim 5 is rejected under 103 as being unpatentable over Parbat and Edenfield, in further view of Braunstein (U.S. 6041446). Claims 6-8 are rejected under 103 as being unpatentable over Parbat and Edenfield, in further view of Russano (U.S. 5546608). Claims 10 and 11 are rejected under 103 as being unpatentable over Parbat and Edenfield, in further view of Feinberg (U.S. 5398346). Claims 13-16 are rejected under 103 as being unpatentable over Parbat and Edenfield, in further view of Pundyk (U.S. 4538615). Claim 17 is rejected under 103 as being unpatentable over Parbat and Edenfield, in further view of Pace (U.S. 20120284895).

Application No.: 14/796,998
Date: Sep 21, 2017

Applicant respectfully disagrees with such rejection, especially in view of the amendments made hereinabove to the independent claims, we combined Claims 3, 6, and 19 into 1 as a good faith effort to further prosecution. Specifically, applicant has amended the independent claim, as follows:

> "An undergarment, comprising:
> a main body comprising at least one panel of material, <u>wherein the at least one panel of material comprises a stretchable material</u>;
> three openings, wherein all three openings have ~~substantially~~ equal dimensions, <u>and wherein the main body further comprises an additional stretchable material near at least one of the openings</u>; and
> three peripheral edges, whereon one peripheral edge is located between adjacent openings, <u>wherein the three peripheral edges have equal dimensions</u>" (as amended). "

Examples of support for the current amendments to Claim 1 (as well as Claims 11 and 15), may be found throughout the Specification. See e.g. paragraph 25 line 2 ("Embodiments disclosed herein overcome the disadvantages by providing a novel undergarment having three openings with <u>equal</u> dimensions." (emphasis added)); paragraph 35 line 2 ("each of the openings 104 *a*, 104 *b*, 104 *c* may have <u>equal</u> dimensions…(e.g., $l_{O(a)}=l_{O(b)}=l_{O(c)}$)" (emphasis added)); and paragraph 37 line 2 ("As discussed previously, a configuration where each of the openings 104 *a*, 104 *b*, 104 *c* have e dimensions as one another (e.g., are of the <u>same size</u> and define the same size aperture) allows for simplified use because a human wearer need not determine a "front" or "back" of the undergarment 100 or determine which opening is designed to accept the waist or leg." (emphasis added)).

To establish a prima facie case of obviousness, three basic criteria must be met. First, there must be some suggestion or motivation, either in the references themselves or in the knowledge generally available to one of ordinary skill in the art, to modify the reference or to combine reference teachings. Second, there must be a reasonable expectation of success. Finally, the prior art reference (or references when combined) must teach or suggest all the claim limitations. The teaching or suggestion to make the claimed combination and the reasonable expectation of success must both be found in the prior art and not based on applicant's disclosure. *In re Vaeck*, 947 F.2d 488, 20 USPQ2d 1438 (Fed.Cir.1991).

Applicant respectfully asserts that at least the third element of the prima facie case of obviousness has not been met, since the prior art, as relied upon by the Examiner, fail to teach or suggest all of the claim limitations, as noted above. In particular, as amended, all of the prior art fails to teach "equal dimensions."

Application No.: 14/796,998
Date: Sep 21, 2017

Conclusion

Applicant believes that all of the pending issues have been addressed and requests that the Examiner amend Claims 1, 2, 4, 7, 11, 15, and 20; cancel Claims 3, 6, and 19; and allow Claims 1, 2, 4-5, 7-18, and 20.

However, the absence of a reply to a specific rejection, issue, or comment does not signify agreement with or concession of that rejection, issue, or comment. In addition, because the arguments made above may not be exhaustive, there may be reasons for patentability of any or all pending claims (or other claims) that have not been expressed. Still yet, nothing in this reply should be construed as intention to concede any issue with regard to any claim, except as specifically stated in this reply. Finally, it should be noted that no claims are intended to be construed under 35 U.S.C. 112, paragraph 6.

In the event a telephone conversation would expedite the prosecution of this application, the Examiner may reach the undersigned at (408) 977-7227. Additionally, as discussed in the Interview, the Examiner may also reach Camille Wilson, a mentor with the Clinic, at (904) 955-1975.

Respectfully submitted,

IP Clinic at Lincoln Law School

By____/Britten Sessions/____

Britten Sessions
Reg. No. 68278
IP Clinic at Lincoln Law School
384 S Second St.
San Jose, California 95113
Phone (408) 977-7227
Fax (408) 977-7228

LINCOLN LAW SCHOOL OF SAN JOSE
INTELLECTUAL PROPERTY SERIES

EXHIBIT: OFFICE ACTION

UNITED STATES PATENT AND TRADEMARK OFFICE

UNITED STATES DEPARTMENT OF COMMERCE
United States Patent and Trademark Office
Address: COMMISSIONER FOR PATENTS
P.O. Box 1450
Alexandria, Virginia 22313-1450
www.uspto.gov

APPLICATION NO.	FILING DATE	FIRST NAMED INVENTOR	ATTORNEY DOCKET NO.	CONFIRMATION NO.
14/806,548	07/22/2015	Kiran Vanjani	84448837US01/FUWEP002	1557

28875   7590   02/24/2017
Zilka-Kotab, PC
1155 N. 1st St.
Suite 105
SAN JOSE, CA 95112

EXAMINER
SALIH, AWAT M

ART UNIT	PAPER NUMBER
2845	

NOTIFICATION DATE	DELIVERY MODE
02/24/2017	ELECTRONIC

Please find below and/or attached an Office communication concerning this application or proceeding.

The time period for reply, if any, is set in the attached communication.

Notice of the Office communication was sent electronically on above-indicated "Notification Date" to the following e-mail address(es):

zk-uspto@zilkakotab.com
chrisc@zilkakotab.com

PTOL-90A (Rev. 04/07)

EXHIBITS 267

Office Action Summary	Application No. 14/806,548	Applicant(s) VANJANI ET AL.	
	Examiner AWAT SALIH	Art Unit 2845	AIA (First Inventor to File) Status Yes

-- The MAILING DATE of this communication appears on the cover sheet with the correspondence address --

Period for Reply

A SHORTENED STATUTORY PERIOD FOR REPLY IS SET TO EXPIRE <u>3</u> MONTHS FROM THE MAILING DATE OF THIS COMMUNICATION.
- Extensions of time may be available under the provisions of 37 CFR 1.136(a). In no event, however, may a reply be timely filed after SIX (6) MONTHS from the mailing date of this communication.
- If NO period for reply is specified above, the maximum statutory period will apply and will expire SIX (6) MONTHS from the mailing date of this communication.
- Failure to reply within the set or extended period for reply will, by statute, cause the application to become ABANDONED (35 U.S.C. § 133).
- Any reply received by the Office later than three months after the mailing date of this communication, even if timely filed, may reduce any earned patent term adjustment. See 37 CFR 1.704(b).

Status

1) ☒ Responsive to communication(s) filed on <u>07/22/2015</u>.
☐ A declaration(s)/affidavit(s) under **37 CFR 1.130(b)** was/were filed on _____.
2a) ☐ This action is **FINAL**. 2b) ☒ This action is non-final.
3) ☐ An election was made by the applicant in response to a restriction requirement set forth during the interview on _____; the restriction requirement and election have been incorporated into this action.
4) ☐ Since this application is in condition for allowance except for formal matters, prosecution as to the merits is closed in accordance with the practice under *Ex parte Quayle*, 1935 C.D. 11, 453 O.G. 213.

Disposition of Claims*

5) ☒ Claim(s) <u>1-22</u> is/are pending in the application.
5a) Of the above claim(s) _____ is/are withdrawn from consideration.
6) ☐ Claim(s) _____ is/are allowed.
7) ☒ Claim(s) <u>1-22</u> is/are rejected.
8) ☐ Claim(s) _____ is/are objected to.
9) ☐ Claim(s) _____ are subject to restriction and/or election requirement.

* If any claims have been determined <u>allowable</u>, you may be eligible to benefit from the **Patent Prosecution Highway** program at a participating intellectual property office for the corresponding application. For more information, please see http://www.uspto.gov/patents/init_events/pph/index.jsp or send an inquiry to PPHfeedback@uspto.gov.

Application Papers

10) ☐ The specification is objected to by the Examiner.
11) ☒ The drawing(s) filed on <u>07/22/2015</u> is/are: a) ☒ accepted or b) ☐ objected to by the Examiner.
Applicant may not request that any objection to the drawing(s) be held in abeyance. See 37 CFR 1.85(a).
Replacement drawing sheet(s) including the correction is required if the drawing(s) is objected to. See 37 CFR 1.121(d).

Priority under 35 U.S.C. § 119

12) ☐ Acknowledgment is made of a claim for foreign priority under 35 U.S.C. § 119(a)-(d) or (f).
Certified copies:
a) ☐ All b) ☐ Some** c) ☐ None of the:
1. ☐ Certified copies of the priority documents have been received.
2. ☐ Certified copies of the priority documents have been received in Application No. _____.
3. ☐ Copies of the certified copies of the priority documents have been received in this National Stage application from the International Bureau (PCT Rule 17.2(a)).
** See the attached detailed Office action for a list of the certified copies not received.

Attachment(s)
1) ☒ Notice of References Cited (PTO-892)
2) ☒ Information Disclosure Statement(s) (PTO/SB/08a and/or PTO/SB/08b) Paper No(s)/Mail Date <u>07/22/2015, 08/08/2016 and 01/17/2017</u>.
3) ☐ Interview Summary (PTO-413) Paper No(s)/Mail Date _____.
4) ☐ Other: _____.

U.S. Patent and Trademark Office
PTOL-326 (Rev. 11-13)   Office Action Summary   Part of Paper No./Mail Date 20170215

Application/Control Number: 14/806,548 Page 2
Art Unit: 2845

DETAILED ACTION

Notice of Pre-AIA or AIA Status

The present application, filed on or after March 16, 2013, is being examined under the first inventor to file provisions of the AIA.

Information Disclosure Statement

The information disclosure statement (IDS) submitted on 07/22/2015, 08/08/2016 and 01/17/2017 were filed after the mailing date of the 07/22/2015. The submission is in compliance with the provisions of 37 CFR 1.97. Accordingly, the information disclosure statement is being considered by the examiner.

Claim Rejections - 35 USC § 112

The following is a quotation of the first paragraph of 35 U.S.C. 112(a):

> (a) IN GENERAL.—The specification shall contain a written description of the invention, and of the manner and process of making and using it, in such full, clear, concise, and exact terms as to enable any person skilled in the art to which it pertains, or with which it is most nearly connected, to make and use the same, and shall set forth the best mode contemplated by the inventor or joint inventor of carrying out the invention.

The following is a quotation of the first paragraph of pre-AIA 35 U.S.C. 112:

> The specification shall contain a written description of the invention, and of the manner and process of making and using it, in such full, clear, concise, and exact terms as to enable any person skilled in the art to which it pertains, or with which it is most nearly connected, to make and use the same, and shall set forth the best mode contemplated by the inventor of carrying out his invention.

Claims 1 and 22 are rejected under 35 U.S.C. 112(a) or 35 U.S.C. 112 (pre-AIA), first paragraph, as failing to comply with the written description requirement. The

Application/Control Number: 14/806,548 Page 3
Art Unit: 2845

claim(s) contains subject matter which was not described in the specification in such a way as to reasonably convey to one skilled in the relevant art that the inventor or a joint inventor, or for pre-AIA the inventor(s), at the time the application was filed, had possession of the claimed invention. In this case,

Regarding claim 1,

Applicant cites (... <u>a component</u> coupled to the housing...). Applicant claimed all components (e.g. of components such as pusher for a watch, power supply for a computer...etc). For example, Applicant's figures 2-6 has the component as a pusher for a watch (see element 204). However, in the claim, Applicant claimed all components. Furthermore, Applicant does not have a clear definition or explanation in the specification to define a component. It would not be reasonable to have a component such as a power supply coupled to the housing in this case or invention. Therefore, Applicant has not possessed the claimed invention (see MPEP 2163). The Examiner suggests:

(a component includes a pusher and is configured for only aesthetic purposes coupled to the housing...)

Or

(a component includes a pusher <u>or</u> a component configured for only aesthetic purposes coupled to the housing...).

Regarding claim 22,

Application/Control Number: 14/806,548 Page 4
Art Unit: 2845

Applicant cites (... <u>a component</u> coupled to a housing...). Applicant claimed all components (e.g. of components such as pusher for a watch, power supply for a computer...etc). For example, Applicant's figures 2-6 has the component as a pusher for a watch (see element 204). However, in the claim, Applicant claimed all components. Furthermore, Applicant does not have a clear definition or explanation in the specification to define a component. It would not be reasonable to have a component such as a power supply coupled to the housing in this case or invention. Therefore, Applicant has not possessed the claimed invention (see MPEP 2163). The Examiner suggests:

(...a component includes a pusher and is configured for only aesthetic purposes coupled to a housing...)

Or

(...a component includes a pusher <u>or</u> a component configured for only aesthetic purposes coupled to a housing...).

Claims 2-21 are rejected under 35 U.S.C. 112(a) or 35 U.S.C. 112 (pre-AIA), first paragraph because of their dependency.

Additionally,

The following is a quotation of 35 U.S.C. 112(b):
(b) CONCLUSION.—the specification shall conclude with one or more claims particularly pointing out and distinctly claiming the subject matter which the inventor or a joint inventor regards as the invention.

The following is a quotation of 35 U.S.C. 112 (pre-AIA), second paragraph:

Application/Control Number: 14/806,548 Page 5
Art Unit: 2845

> The specification shall conclude with one or more claims particularly pointing out and distinctly
> claiming the subject matter which the applicant regards as his invention.

Claim 14 is rejected under 35 U.S.C. 112(b) or 35 U.S.C. 112 (pre-AIA), second paragraph, as being indefinite for failing to particularly point out and distinctly claim the subject matter which the inventor or a joint inventor, or for pre-AIA the applicant regards as the invention.

Applicant recites (wherein the <u>wrist band is constructed from a conductive material</u> that is in electrical communication with <u>a printed circuit board</u> positioned in the <u>housing</u> for <u>providing a ground plane</u> in connection with the helical antenna). It is nebulous to the Examiner because not certain which element provides or acts as a ground plane; is it the conductive wrist band? or is it the PCB has the grounding? or the housing portion of the watch acts as a grounding?. In addition, the all the three aforementioned elements can act as a grounding according to the specification. The Examiner interprets the claim as (further comprising a wrist band coupled to the housing, a printed circuit board positioned in the housing and a helical antenna positioned in the housing) for the purpose of examining.

Claim Rejections - 35 USC § 102

The following is a quotation of the appropriate paragraphs of 35 U.S.C. 102 that form the basis for the rejections under this section made in this Office action:

> A person shall be entitled to a patent unless –
>
> (a)(1) The claimed invention was patented, described in a printed publication, or in public use, on sale or otherwise available to the public before the effective filing date of the claimed invention.

Application/Control Number: 14/806,548 Page 6
Art Unit: 2845

Claims 1, 3-5, 10, 13-15, 21 are rejected under 35 U.S.C. 102(a) (1) as being anticipated by Pan et al. (US2015/0130666, hereby referred as Pan).

Regarding claim 1,

As best understood, Pan discloses (figure 5);

A housing (the housing for the watch or element 110); a component (element 112´) coupled to the housing; and a helical antenna (element 164) coupled to the component for communicating radio frequency (RMF) signals.

Regarding claim 3,

Pan discloses (figure 5);

Wherein the helical antenna (element 164´) is positioned at least partially in the component (element 112´).

Regarding claim 4,

Pan discloses (figure 5);

Wherein an end of the helical antenna (end of helical antenna 164) extends beyond a periphery of the housing (housing 110).

Regarding claim 5,

Pan discloses (figure 5);

Application/Control Number: 14/806,548 Page 7
Art Unit: 2845

Wherein the apparatus includes a wearable article (the device of figure 5 is a watch. See paragraph [0041], lines 1-2).

Regarding claim 10,

Pan discloses (figure 5);

Wherein the component is constructed from a conductive material (element 112′).

Regarding claim 13,

Pan discloses;

The apparatus of Claim 1, and further comprising a wrist band (the wrist band for the wearable/watch device (see paragraph [0003]).

Regarding claim 14,

As best understood, Pan discloses (figure 5);

Wherein the wrist band is constructed from a conductive material that is in electrical communication with a printed circuit board positioned in the housing for providing a ground plane in connection with the helical antenna (further comprising a wrist band (the wrist band for the wearable/watch device (see paragraph [0003]) coupled to the housing (the housing for the watch or element 110), a printed circuit board (element 170′) positioned in the housing and a helical antenna (element 164′) positioned in the housing).

Application/Control Number: 14/806,548
Art Unit: 2845

Page 8

Regarding claim 15,

Pan discloses (figure 2);

Wherein the housing includes a back plate configured for abutting a skin of a user (when the user wears the watch on his/her wrist, the back plate is abutting the skin of the user. See paragraph [0030]).

Regarding claim 21,

Pan discloses;

Wherein the apparatus includes a watch (see figure 2).

Claim Rejections - 35 USC § 103

The following is a quotation of 35 U.S.C. 103 which forms the basis for all obviousness rejections set forth in this Office action:

> A patent for a claimed invention may not be obtained, notwithstanding that the claimed invention is not identically disclosed as set forth in section 102, if the differences between the claimed invention and the prior art are such that the claimed invention as a whole would have been obvious before the effective filing date of the claimed invention to a person having ordinary skill in the art to which the claimed invention pertains. Patentability shall not be negated by the manner in which the invention was made.

Claims 1-2, 7, 20 are rejected under 35 U.S.C. 103 as being unpatentable over Pan et al. (US2015/0130666, hereby referred as Pan).

Regarding claim 1,

As best understood, Pan discloses (figure 5);

Application/Control Number: 14/806,548
Art Unit: 2845

A housing (element 110´ or the housing for the watch); and a helical antenna (helical antenna 164´) coupled to the component for communicating radio frequency (RMF) signals.

Pan, in the embodiment of figure 5, may not explicitly disclose;

A pusher component.

However, Pan, in another embodiment, teaches;

A component coupled to the housing (see the pusher element in figure 2 or see elements 130 in figure 3A).

Therefore, it would have been obvious to one of ordinary skill in the art before the effective filing date of the invention to combine the teaching of both embodiments to produce an antenna as claimed in order to have a protection for other elements (see paragraphs 0014) and to have the first and second body contact each other (see paragraph 0012). Moreover, in order to provide a mechanical movement to the device (see the pusher component as shown in figure 2).

Regarding claim 2,

Pan, in the embodiment of figure 5, may not explicitly disclose;

Wherein the component includes a pusher

However, Pan, in another embodiment, teaches;

Wherein the component includes a pusher (see the pusher element in figure 2 which is coupled to the housing of the watch or element 110).

Therefore, it would have been obvious to one of ordinary skill in the art before the effective filing date of the invention to combine the teaching of both embodiments to produce an antenna as claimed in order to provide a mechanical movement for the device (see the pusher component as shown in figure 2).

Regarding claim 7,

Pan, in the embodiment of figure 5, may not explicitly disclose;
Wherein the component is moveably coupled to the housing.

However, Pan, in another embodiment, teaches;
Wherein the component is moveably coupled to the housing (see the pusher button/element in figure 2 which coupled to the housing for the device or element 110. Further, the pusher element has capability of moving).

Therefore, it would have been obvious to one of ordinary skill in the art before the effective filing date of the invention to combine the teaching of both embodiments to produce an antenna as claimed in order to provide a mechanical movement for the device (see the pusher component as shown in figure 2).

Application/Control Number: 14/806,548 Page 11
Art Unit: 2845

Regarding claim 20,

Pan discloses (figure 5);

Another component (either element 112´ or element 162´ can be construed as the second/another component) coupled to the housing (element 110´);

Pan may not explicitly disclose;
Another helical antenna coupled to the another component.

However, Pan, in another embodiment figure 3A, does teach two components 130 coupled to the housing 110. Moreover, two helical shape elastic members 140 which are similar to the helical antenna 164´ of figure 5. Therefore, it would be obvious to have a second helical antenna in figure 5 to both sides of the watch as shown in the embodiment of figure 3A (see paragraphs [0018], [0019] and pargraph [0040]).

Therefore, it would have been obvious to one of ordinary skill in the art before the effective filing date of the invention to combine the teaching of both embodiments to produce an antenna as claimed in order to add or have an additional frequency bands

In addition, for clarity purpose, it would have been obvious to one of ordinary skill in the art before the effective filing date of the invention to add a second helical antenna, such as the antenna of figure 5, to the device in the same manner as the two elements 130 of figure 3A in both sides in order to add or have an additional frequency bands.

Application/Control Number: 14/806,548 Page 12
Art Unit: 2845

Moreover, it has been held that mere duplication of the essential working parts of a device involves only routine skill in the art. St Regis Paper Co. v. Bemis Co., 193 USPQ 8.

Claim 6 is rejected under 35 U.S.C. 103 as being unpatentable over Pan et al. (US2015/0130666, hereby referred as Pan) in view of Clerc et al. (US2009/0147630, hereby referred as Clerc).

Regarding claim 6,

Pan may not explicitly disclose;

Wherein the component is configured for only aesthetic purposes.

However, Clerc teaches;

Wherein the component is configured for only aesthetic purposes (see paragraph [0013] which the watch has a button for aesthetic appearance).

Therefore, it would have been obvious to one of ordinary skill in the art before the effective filing date of the invention to combine the teaching of Pan and Clerc to produce an antenna as claimed in order to gives the watch a new and attractive aesthetic appearance (Clerc, paragraph [0013]).

Claims 8-9, 22 are rejected under 35 U.S.C. 103 as being unpatentable over Pan et al. (US2015/0130666, hereby referred as Pan) in view of Moyer (US4120148).

Application/Control Number: 14/806,548 Page 13
Art Unit: 2845

Regarding claim 8,

Pan does not disclose;

Wherein the apparatus is configured such that a signal is generated in response to a depression of the component.

However, Moyer teaches;

Wherein the apparatus is configured such that a signal is generated in response to a depression of the component (signal is generated when pushing component/button 34. See Col. 3, Lines 36-45 and figures 1-2).

Therefore, it would have been obvious to one of ordinary skill in the art before the effective filing date of the invention to combine the teaching of Pan and Moyer to produce an antenna as claimed in order to have a digital button to provide a signal for the device in order to cause other circuitry to select the component/pushbutton response that is appropriate (Moyer, Col. 3, Lines 55-59).

Regarding claim 9,

Pan discloses (figure 5);

Wherein the helical antenna (antenna 164´) is configured to be springably-biased (Helical antenna 164´ is forms a spring shape as shown in figure 5. Further, it does function similar to the elastic member, see the teaching in paragraph [0040], lines 22-29) in response to the depression of the component (component 130 which disposed on

Application/Control Number: 14/806,548 Page 14
Art Unit: 2845

the opening 112a´. See paragraph [0040], Lines 16-22) so as to extend the component after the depression of the component.

Regarding claim 22,

As best understood, Pan discloses (figures 1 and 5);

Communicating radio frequency (RF) signals utilizing a helical antenna (figure 5, helical antenna 164´) coupled to the component (the pusher button of the watch as shown in figure 1).

Pan does not discloses;

Receiving a signal in response to manipulation of a component coupled to a housing.

However, Moyer teaches;

Receiving a signal in response to manipulation of a component coupled to a housing (signal is generated when pushing component/button 34. See Col. 3, Lines 36-45 and figures 1-2).

Therefore, it would have been obvious to one of ordinary skill in the art before the effective filing date of the invention to combine the teaching of Pan and Moyer to produce an antenna as claimed in order to have a digital button to provide a signal for the device in order to cause other circuitry to select the component/pushbutton response that is appropriate (Moyer, Col. 3, Lines 55-59).

Claims 11-12 are rejected under 35 U.S.C. 103 as being unpatentable over Pan et al. (US2015/0130666, hereby referred as Pan) in view of Shibuya et al. (US2004/0231159, hereby referred as Shibuya).

Regarding claim 11,

Pan does not disclose;

Wherein an outer surface of the component is lined with at least one material that is insulative, but has a metallic appearance.

However, Shibuya teaches (figures 17-18);

Wherein an outer surface of the component (outer surface of component 45 or 46) is lined with at least one material that is insulative, but has a metallic appearance (see paragraph [0179]. The insulating material 52 and metallic appearance 47 and 3).

Therefore, it would have been obvious to one of ordinary skill in the art before the effective filing date of the invention to combine the teaching of Pan and Shibuya to produce an antenna as claimed for the purpose of providing decoration for the wrist watch and in order to the smooth the surface (Shibuya, paragraph [0179]).

Regarding claim 12,

Application/Control Number: 14/806,548 Page 16
Art Unit: 2845

Pan does not disclose;

Wherein the at least one material with the metallic appearance compliments an appearance of the housing.

However, Shibuya teaches (figures 17-18);

Wherein the at least one material with the metallic appearance (material 52 with metallic appearance 47 and 3. Further, see paragraph [0179]) compliments an appearance of the housing (compliments an appearance of the housing for the watch as shown in figure 17).

Therefore, it would have been obvious to one of ordinary skill in the art before the effective filing date of the invention to combine the teaching of Pan and Shibuya to produce an antenna as claimed for the purpose of providing decoration for the wrist watch and in order to the smooth the surface (Shibuya, paragraph [0179]).

Claims 16-17 are rejected under 35 U.S.C. 103 as being unpatentable over Pan et al. (US2015/0130666, hereby referred as Pan) in view of Someya (US2009/0305657).

Regarding claim 16,

Pan does not disclose;

Wherein the back plate of the housing is constructed from an insulative material.

Application/Control Number: 14/806,548 Page 17
Art Unit: 2845

However, Someya teaches (figure 2 below);

Wherein the back plate (element 38. See paragraph [0056]) of the housing (see the housing below) is constructed from an insulative material (the housing is accommodating element 20).

Therefore, it would have been obvious to one of ordinary skill in the art before the effective filing date of the invention to combine the teaching of Pan and Someya to produce an antenna as claimed for the purpose of protection (Someya, paragraph [0056]).

Regarding claim 17,

Pan does not disclose;

Wherein the housing is configured with an insulative region between the back plate and a transceiver positioned in the housing.

However, Someya teaches (figure 2 below);

Wherein the housing (see the housing below) is configured with an insulative region (element 38) between the back plate (back plate 18) and a transceiver (the transceiver for the antenna 20) positioned in the housing.

Therefore, it would have been obvious to one of ordinary skill in the art before the effective filing date of the invention to combine the teaching of Pan and Someya to produce an antenna as claimed for the purpose of protection (Someya, paragraph [0056]).

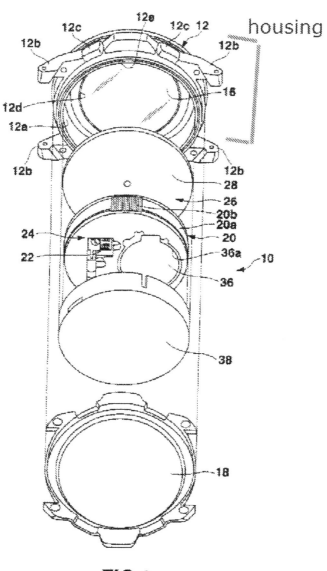

FIG.2

Application/Control Number: 14/806,548 Page 19
Art Unit: 2845

Claims 18-19 are rejected under 35 U.S.C. 103 as being unpatentable over Pan et al. (US2015/0130666, hereby referred as Pan) in view of DINallo et al. (US2014/0253410, hereby referred as DINallo).

Regarding claim 18,

Pan does not disclose;

Wherein the helical antenna is configured for communicating multi-band-multi-mode RF signals.

However, DINallo teaches;

Wherein the helical antenna is configured for communicating multi-band-multi-mode RF signals (the helical antenna. See the abstract).

Therefore, it would have been obvious to one of ordinary skill in the art before the effective filing date of the invention to combine the teaching of Pan and DINallo to produce an antenna as claimed in order to reduce the physical length and to support a certain frequency bands for a handheld wireless device (DINallo, see the abstract).

Regarding claim 19,

Pan does not disclose;

Wherein the helical antenna is configured for communicating cellular RF signals.

However, DINallo teaches (figures 1 and 4);

Application/Control Number: 14/806,548 Page 20
Art Unit: 2845

Wherein the helical antenna (figure 4, element 404) is configured for communicating cellular RF signals (figure 1, see paragraph [0023]).

Therefore, it would have been obvious to one of ordinary skill in the art before the effective filing date of the invention to combine the teaching of Pan and DINallo to produce an antenna as claimed in order to reduce the physical length and to support a certain frequency bands for a handheld wireless device (DINallo, see the abstract).

Conclusion

The prior art made of record and not relied upon is considered pertinent to applicant's disclosure. Applicant is directed to consider additional pertinent art that listed on the PTO-892 form.

Any inquiry concerning this communication or earlier communications from the examiner should be directed to AWAT SALIH whose telephone number is (571)270-5601. The examiner can normally be reached on Monday- Friday; 08:00 am - 05:00 pm EST.

Examiner interviews are available via telephone, in-person, and video conferencing using a USPTO supplied web-based collaboration tool. To schedule an interview, applicant is encouraged to use the USPTO Automated Interview Request (AIR) at http://www.uspto.gov/interviewpractice.

Application/Control Number: 14/806,548
Art Unit: 2845

If attempts to reach the examiner by telephone are unsuccessful, the examiner's supervisor, Dameon Levi can be reached on (571) 272-2105. The fax phone number for the organization where this application or proceeding is assigned is 571-273-8300.

Information regarding the status of an application may be obtained from the Patent Application Information Retrieval (PAIR) system. Status information for published applications may be obtained from either Private PAIR or Public PAIR. Status information for unpublished applications is available through Private PAIR only. For more information about the PAIR system, see http://pair-direct.uspto.gov. Should you have questions on access to the Private PAIR system, contact the Electronic Business Center (EBC) at 866-217-9197 (toll-free). If you would like assistance from a USPTO Customer Service Representative or access to the automated information system, call 800-786-9199 (IN USA OR CANADA) or 571-272-1000.

/DAMEON E LEVI/
Supervisory Patent Examiner, Art Unit 2845

/A. S./
Examiner, Art Unit 2845

LINCOLN LAW SCHOOL OF SAN JOSE
INTELLECTUAL PROPERTY SERIES

EXHIBIT: OFFICE ACTION RESPONSE

Serial No. : 14/806,548

In the Claims:

1. (Currently Amended) An apparatus, comprising:

   a housing;

   a component coupled to the housing; and

   a helical antenna coupled to the component for communicating radio frequency (RF) signals;

   wherein an end of the helical antenna extends beyond a periphery of the housing.

2. (Original) The apparatus of Claim 1, wherein the component includes a pusher.

3. (Original) The apparatus of Claim 1, wherein the helical antenna is positioned at least partially in the component.

4. (Canceled)

5. (Original) The apparatus of Claim 1, wherein the apparatus includes a wearable article.

6. (Original) The apparatus of Claim 1, wherein the component is configured for only aesthetic purposes.

7. (Original) The apparatus of Claim 1, wherein the component is moveably coupled to the housing.

8. (Original) The apparatus of Claim 1, wherein the apparatus is configured such that a signal is generated in response to a depression of the component.

Serial No. : 14/806,548   Page : 3 of 15

9. (Original) The apparatus of Claim 8, wherein the helical antenna is configured to be springably-biased in response to the depression of the component so as to extend the component after the depression of the component.

10. (Original) The apparatus of Claim 1, wherein the component is constructed from a conductive material.

11. (Original) The apparatus of Claim 1, wherein an outer surface of the component is lined with at least one material that is insulative, but has a metallic appearance.

12. (Original) The apparatus of Claim 11, wherein the at least one material with the metallic appearance compliments an appearance of the housing.

13. (Original) The apparatus of Claim 1, and further comprising a wrist band.

14. (Currently Amended) The apparatus of Claim 13, wherein the wrist band is constructed from a conductive material that is in electrical communication with a printed circuit board positioned in the housing, the housing configured for providing a ground plane in connection with the helical antenna.

15. (Original) The apparatus of Claim 1, wherein the housing includes a back plate configured for abutting a skin of a user.

16. (Original) The apparatus of Claim 15, wherein the back plate of the housing is constructed from an insulative material.

17. (Original) The apparatus of Claim 15, wherein the housing is configured with an insulative region between the back plate and a transceiver positioned in the housing.

Serial No. : 14/806,548   Page : 4 of 15

18. (Original) The apparatus of Claim 1, wherein the helical antenna is configured for communicating multi-band-multi-mode RF signals.

19. (Original) The apparatus of Claim 1, wherein the helical antenna is configured for communicating cellular RF signals.

20. (Original) The apparatus of Claim 1, and further comprising:
another component coupled to the housing; and
another helical antenna coupled to the another component.

21. (Original) The apparatus of Claim 1, wherein the apparatus includes a watch.

22. (Currently Amended) A method, comprising:
receiving a signal in response to manipulation of a component coupled to a housing; and
communicating radio frequency (RF) signals utilizing a helical antenna coupled to the component;
<u>wherein an end of the helical antenna extends beyond a periphery of the housing.</u>

23. (New) The apparatus of Claim 10, wherein the component is constructed from the conductive material for remaining RF transparent in connection with the communication of the RF signals from the helical antenna.

24. (New) The apparatus of Claim 1, wherein a majority of a length of the helical antenna extends beyond the periphery of the housing.

25. (New) The apparatus of Claim 1, wherein the end of the helical antenna extends beyond the periphery of the housing for enhancing the communication of the RF signals from the helical antenna.

Serial No. : 14/806,548

26. (New) The apparatus of Claim 14, wherein the wrist band extends a reference ground plane to enhance performance in connection with the communication of the RF signals from the helical antenna.

Serial No. : 14/806,548   Page : 6 of 15

Remarks:

Summary

Claims 1-22 were pending.

Claims 1, 14, and 22 have been amended, while claim 4 has been cancelled. Claims 23–26 are added herein. Support for such amendments is found, inter alia, in former dependent Claim 4, as well as paragraphs [0030], [0041], [0043] – [0046], and Figures 6 and 9 of the present description. No new matter is introduced. Claims 1–3 and 5–26 are now pending, including independent Claims 1 and 22.

Rejections Under 35 U.S.C. 112(a)

Claims 1-22 stand rejected under 35 U.S.C. § 112(a) or 35 U.S.C. 112 (pre-AIA), first paragraph, as failing to comply with the written description requirement. In particular, where claims 1-22 require "a component" the Examiner alleges that the written description supporting this limitation is insufficient to reasonably convey to one skilled in the art that Applicant possessed the claimed invention at the time the application was filed. Applicant respectfully disagrees.

For example, Applicant respectfully submits that the foregoing claim language is fully supported by the specification, as follows:

[0025] ... Further, the component 104 may refer to any mechanism that functions and/or simply looks like it functions (for aesthetics) as a component for controlling a device associated with the housing 102.

[0027] Still yet, in one possible embodiment, the component 104 may be moveably (e.g. slidably, etc.) coupled to the housing 102, as shown. For example, in one embodiment, the component 104 may be operable such that a signal is generated in response to a depression (e.g. manual depression, etc.) of the component 104. Such signal could, in various optional embodiments, control at least one aspect of a device housed by the housing 102. In such embodiment, the component 104 may optionally include a pusher. In other embodiments, the component 104 may be rotatably coupled (e.g. so as to be windable, etc.) to the housing 102, to generate a signal and/or interact with internal mechanical components (e.g. winding spring, etc.) in the housing 102. Of course, any combination of different movements may be implemented for allowing any type of manipulation, in various embodiments. Of course, as mentioned earlier, the component 104 may be configured for only aesthetic purposes (e.g. constitute a "mock," imitation, artificial, etc. pusher or other type of component).

As such, applicant respectfully suggests that the claimed term "component" is well defined in the specification with both a definition and a myriad of examples of what a "component" may be (e.g. pusher, winder, etc.). Accordingly, applicant respectfully requests favorable reconsideration and withdrawal of the rejection.

Rejections Under 35 U.S.C. 112(b)

Claim 14 stands rejected under 35 U.S.C. § 112(b) or 35 U.S.C. 112 (pre-AIA), second paragraph, as being indefinite for failing to particularly point out and distinctly claim the subject matter which the inventor or a joint inventor, or for pre-AIA the Applicant regards as the invention. Such rejection is deemed overcome by virtue of the amendments made hereinabove.

Rejections Under 35 U.S.C. 102

Claims 1, 3-5, 10, 13-15, 21 stand rejected under 35 U.S.C. § 102(a) in view of U.S. Patent Application Pub. No. 2015/0130666 [PAN]. Applicant respectfully disagrees with such rejection, especially in view of the amendments made hereinabove to each of the independent claims.

Specifically, applicant has amended the independent claims to at least substantially include the subject matter of former dependent Claim 4, as follows:

> a housing;
>
> a component coupled to the housing; and
>
> a helical antenna coupled to the component for communicating radio frequency (RF) signals;
>
> <u>wherein an end of the helical antenna extends beyond a periphery of the housing</u>.

Serial No. : 14/806,548

(see this or similar, but not necessarily identical language in the independent claims, as amended).

With respect to the subject matter of former Claim 4 (now at least substantially incorporated into each of the independent claims), the Examiner has relied on Figure 5 (including elements 110' and 164') from the PAN reference to make a prior art showing of applicant's claimed technique "wherein an end of the helical antenna extends beyond a periphery of the housing" (see this or similar, but not necessarily identical language in the independent claims).

Applicant respectfully notes that the PAN reference, as relied upon by the Examiner, discloses that:

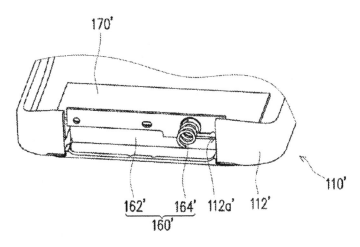

FIG. 5

PAN. See Figure 5.

Serial No. : 14/806,548

[0040] FIG. 5 is a diagram of the partial parts of a first body according to another embodiment of the invention. In the embodiment of FIG. 5, the layout and actions of a first body 110', a metal casing 112', an opening 112a' and a circuit board 170' are similar to the layout and actions of the first body 110, the metal casing 112, the opening 112a and the circuit board 170, which is omitted to describe. The unique of the embodiment of FIG. 5 from the embodiment of FIG. 4 rests in that the antenna module 160' includes a substrate 162' and a helical antenna 164', the substrate 162' is disposed in the metal casing 112' the helical antenna 164' is disposed on the substrate 162' and electrically connected to the circuit board 170' in the metal casing 112'. The helical antenna 164' is to transmit and receive wireless signal, wherein the length of the helical antenna 164' is, for example, equal to ¼ of the wavelength of the wireless signal. In addition, the engaging members 130

PAN. See Paragraph [0040] – emphasis added.

Serial No. : 14/806,548

Further, PAN discloses:

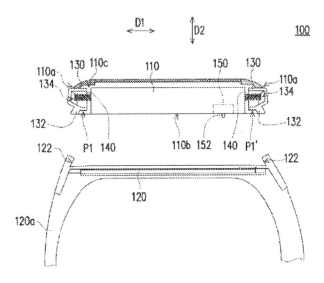

FIG. 3C

PAN. See Figure 3C.

[0038] In the embodiment, the first body 110 has a bottom surface 110b, and the bottom surface 110b is between the two sides 110a of the first body 110. The assembled wearable electronic device 100 includes an electrical connection module 150 disposed at the bottom surface 110b of the first body 110. When the first body 110 and the second body 120 are combined as shown by FIGS. 1 and 3A, the first body 110 is electrically connected to the second body 120 through the electrical connection module 150. The electrical connection module 150 of the embodiment can be, for example, a pogo

PAN. See Paragraph [0038] – emphasis added.

However, disclosing that a helical antenna is contained within an antenna module, as well as a first body which includes a bottom surface which "is between the two sides 110a of the first body 110," as in the PAN excerpt(s) relied upon, does not teach or suggest applicant's claimed technique "wherein <u>an end of the helical antenna</u> **extends beyond** <u>a periphery of the housing</u>" (emphasis added), as claimed by applicant.

Serial No. : 14/806,548 Page : 11 of 15

Further, disclosing that "helical antenna 164' is disposed on the substrate 162'" where such substrate 162' "is disposed in the metal casing 112'" as in the PAN excerpt(s) relied upon, does not teach or suggest applicant's claimed technique "wherein <u>an end of the helical antenna extends beyond</u> a <u>periphery of the housing</u>" (emphasis added), as claimed by applicant.

The Examiner is reminded that a claim is anticipated only if each and every element as set forth in the claim is found, either expressly or inherently described in a single prior art reference. Verdegaal Bros. v. Union Oil Co. Of California, 814 F.2d 628, 631, 2 USPQ2d 1051, 1053 (Fed. Cir. 1987). Moreover, the identical invention must be shown in as complete detail as contained in the claim. Richardson v. Suzuki Motor Co.868 F.2d 1226, 1236, 9USPQ2d 1913, 1920 (Fed. Cir. 1989). The elements must be arranged as required by the claim.

This criterion has simply not been met by the above reference excerpt(s), as noted above.

Rejections Under 35 U.S.C. 103

Claims 1-2, 7, 20 stand rejected under 35 U.S.C. § 103(a) in view of U.S. Patent Application Pub. No. 2015/0130666 [PAN]. Claim 6 stands rejected under 35 U.S.C. § 103(a) in view of U.S. Patent Application Pub. No. 2015/0130666 [PAN] and U.S. Patent Application Pub. No. 2009/0147630 [CLERC]. Claims 8-9, 22 stand rejected under 35 U.S.C. § 103(a) in view of U.S. Patent Application Pub. No. 2015/0130666 [PAN] and U.S. Patent No. 4,120,148 [MOYER]. Claims 11-12 stand rejected under 35 U.S.C. § 103(a) in view of U.S. Patent Application Pub. No. 2015/0130666 [PAN] and U.S. Patent Application Pub. No. 2004/0231159 [SHIBUYA]. Claims 16-17 stand rejected under 35 U.S.C. § 103(a) in view of U.S. Patent Application Pub. No. 2015/0130666 [PAN] and U.S. Patent Application Pub. No. 2009/0305657 [SOMEYA]. Claims 18-19 stand rejected under 35 U.S.C. § 103(a) in view of U.S. Patent Application Pub. No. 2015/0130666 [PAN] and U.S. Patent Application Pub. No. 2014/0253410 [DINALLO]. Applicant respectfully disagrees with such rejection, especially in view of the amendments made hereinabove to each of the independent claims, as argued hereinabove. Additionally, applicant respectfully notes each of the dependent Claims is allowable in view of its dependence on a respective allowable independent claim.

Serial No. : 14/806,548　　　　　　　　　　　　　　　　　　　　　　　　Page : 12 of 15

Dependent Claims

Applicant further notes that the prior art is also deficient with respect to the dependent claims. For example, with respect to Claim 14, the Examiner has relied on Figure 5 (including elements 110, 164', and 170') in addition to paragraph [0003] from the PAN reference to make a prior art showing of applicant's claimed technique "wherein the wrist band is constructed from a conductive material that is in electrical communication with a printed circuit board positioned in the housing, the housing configured for providing a ground plane in connection with the helical antenna."

Applicant respectfully notes that the PAN reference, as relied upon by the Examiner, discloses that:

> [0003] The invention generally relates to an electronic device, and more particularly, to an assembled wearable electronic device.

PAN. See Paragraph [0003].

> [0040] FIG. 5 is a diagram of the partial parts of a first body according to another embodiment of the invention. In the embodiment of FIG. 5, <u>the layout and actions of a first body 110'</u>, a metal casing 112', an opening 112a' and a circuit board 170' are similar to the layout and actions of the first body 110, the metal casing 112, the opening 112a and the circuit board 170, which is omitted to describe. The unique of the embodiment of FIG. 5 from the embodiment of FIG. 4 rests in that the antenna module 160' includes a substrate 162' and <u>a helical antenna 164'</u>, the substrate 162' is disposed in the metal casing 112' the helical antenna 164' is disposed on the substrate 162' and <u>electrically connected to the circuit board 170'</u> in the metal casing 112'. The helical antenna 164' is to transmit and receive wireless signal, wherein the length of the helical antenna 164' is, for example, equal to ¼ of the wavelength of the wireless signal. In addition, the engaging members 130

PAN. See Paragraph [0040] – emphasis added.

However, merely disclosing a "wearable electronic device" which includes a "first body 110'", "a helical antenna 164'", and a "circuit board 170'", as in the PAN excerpt(s) relied upon, does not teach or suggest, much less even mention, applicant's claimed technique "wherein the <u>wrist band is constructed from a conductive material</u> that is in <u>electrical communication with a</u>

Serial No. : 14/806,548 Page : 13 of 15

printed circuit board positioned in the housing, the housing configured for providing a ground plane in connection with the helical antenna" (emphasis added), as claimed by applicant. Clearly, merely listing components such as "first body 110'", "a helical antenna 164'", and a "circuit board 170'", as in the PAN excerpt(s) relied upon, fails to rise to the level of specificity required by the Claim, where "the wrist band is constructed from a conductive material that is in electrical communication with a printed circuit board positioned in the housing, the housing configured for providing a ground plane in connection with the helical antenna" (emphasis added), as claimed by applicant

Again, as noted above, since this anticipation criterion has simply not been met by the above reference excerpt(s), a notice of allowance or specific prior art showing of each of the foregoing claim elements, in combination with the remaining claimed features, is respectfully requested.

New Claims

Still yet, applicant brings to the Examiner's attention the subject matter of new Claims 23-26 below, which are added for full consideration:

23. (New) The apparatus of Claim 10, wherein the component is constructed from the conductive material for remaining RF transparent in connection with the communication of the RF signals from the helical antenna.

24. (New) The apparatus of Claim 1, wherein a majority of a length of the helical antenna extends beyond the periphery of the housing.

25. (New) The apparatus of Claim 1, wherein the end of the helical antenna extends beyond the periphery of the housing for enhancing the communication of the RF signals from the helical antenna.

Serial No. : 14/806,548 Page : 14 of 15

26. (New) The apparatus of Claim 14, wherein the wrist band extends a reference ground plane to enhance performance in connection with the communication of the RF signals from the helical antenna.

Again, a notice of allowance or a proper prior art showing of all of applicant's claim limitations, in combination with the remaining claim elements, is respectfully requested.

Conclusion:

It is believed that all of the pending issues have been addressed. Claims 1–3 and 5–26 are in condition for allowance per the claim amendments herein.

However, the absence of a reply to a specific rejection, issue, or comment does not signify agreement with or concession of that rejection, issue, or comment. In addition, because the arguments made above may not be exhaustive, there may be reasons for patentability of any or all pending claims (or other claims) that have not been expressed. Still yet, nothing in this reply should be construed as intention to concede any issue with regard to any claim, except as specifically stated in this reply. Finally, it should be noted that no claims are intended to be construed under 35 U.S.C. 112, paragraph 6.

Serial No. : 14/806,548

In the event a telephone conversation would expedite the prosecution of this application, the Examiner may reach the undersigned at (408) 971-2573 or kevin@zilkakotab.com. Applicant does not believe that any additional fees are due. However, in the event that any other fees are due, the Director is hereby authorized to charge any required fees due (other than issue fees), and to credit any overpayment made, in connection with the filing of this paper to Deposit Account No. 50-1351 (Order No. 84448837US01/FUWEP002).

Respectfully submitted,

Zilka-Kotab, PC.

/KEVINZILKA/

Kevin Zilka
Reg. No. 41,429

1155 N. 1st Street, Suite 105
San Jose, CA 95112-4925
408-971-2573

LINCOLN LAW SCHOOL OF SAN JOSE
INTELLECTUAL PROPERTY SERIES

EXHIBIT: OFFICE ACTION

UNITED STATES PATENT AND TRADEMARK OFFICE

UNITED STATES DEPARTMENT OF COMMERCE
United States Patent and Trademark Office
Address: COMMISSIONER FOR PATENTS
P.O. Box 1450
Alexandria, Virginia 22313-1450
www.uspto.gov

APPLICATION NO.	FILING DATE	FIRST NAMED INVENTOR	ATTORNEY DOCKET NO.	CONFIRMATION NO.
14/815,871	07/31/2015	Weizhong Chen	91030113US01/FUWEP003	4001

28875	7590	11/22/2016

Zilka-Kotab, PC
1155 N. 1st St.
Suite 105
SAN JOSE, CA 95112

EXAMINER
DO, STEVEN M

ART UNIT	PAPER NUMBER
2196	

NOTIFICATION DATE	DELIVERY MODE
11/22/2016	ELECTRONIC

Please find below and/or attached an Office communication concerning this application or proceeding.

The time period for reply, if any, is set in the attached communication.

Notice of the Office communication was sent electronically on above-indicated "Notification Date" to the following e-mail address(es):

zk-uspto@zilkakotab.com
chrisc@zilkakotab.com

PTOL-90A (Rev. 04/07)

EXHIBITS 305

Office Action Summary	Application No. 14/815,871	Applicant(s) CHEN ET AL.
	Examiner STEVEN DO	Art Unit 2196 / AIA (First Inventor to File) Status: Yes

-- The MAILING DATE of this communication appears on the cover sheet with the correspondence address --

Period for Reply

A SHORTENED STATUTORY PERIOD FOR REPLY IS SET TO EXPIRE 3 MONTHS FROM THE MAILING DATE OF THIS COMMUNICATION.
- Extensions of time may be available under the provisions of 37 CFR 1.136(a). In no event, however, may a reply be timely filed after SIX (6) MONTHS from the mailing date of this communication.
- If NO period for reply is specified above, the maximum statutory period will apply and will expire SIX (6) MONTHS from the mailing date of this communication.
- Failure to reply within the set or extended period for reply will, by statute, cause the application to become ABANDONED (35 U.S.C. § 133).
- Any reply received by the Office later than three months after the mailing date of this communication, even if timely filed, may reduce any earned patent term adjustment. See 37 CFR 1.704(b).

Status

1) ☒ Responsive to communication(s) filed on *31 July 2015*.
   ☐ A declaration(s)/affidavit(s) under **37 CFR 1.130(b)** was/were filed on _____.
2a) ☐ This action is **FINAL**.   2b) ☒ This action is non-final.
3) ☐ An election was made by the applicant in response to a restriction requirement set forth during the interview on _____; the restriction requirement and election have been incorporated into this action.
4) ☐ Since this application is in condition for allowance except for formal matters, prosecution as to the merits is closed in accordance with the practice under *Ex parte Quayle*, 1935 C.D. 11, 453 O.G. 213.

Disposition of Claims*

5) ☒ Claim(s) *1-20* is/are pending in the application.
   5a) Of the above claim(s) _____ is/are withdrawn from consideration.
6) ☐ Claim(s) _____ is/are allowed.
7) ☒ Claim(s) *1-20* is/are rejected.
8) ☐ Claim(s) _____ is/are objected to.
9) ☐ Claim(s) _____ are subject to restriction and/or election requirement.

* If any claims have been determined <u>allowable</u>, you may be eligible to benefit from the **Patent Prosecution Highway** program at a participating intellectual property office for the corresponding application. For more information, please see http://www.uspto.gov/patents/init_events/pph/index.jsp or send an inquiry to PPHfeedback@uspto.gov.

Application Papers

10) ☐ The specification is objected to by the Examiner.
11) ☒ The drawing(s) filed on *31 July 2015* is/are: a)☒ accepted or b)☐ objected to by the Examiner.
   Applicant may not request that any objection to the drawing(s) be held in abeyance. See 37 CFR 1.85(a).
   Replacement drawing sheet(s) including the correction is required if the drawing(s) is objected to. See 37 CFR 1.121(d).

Priority under 35 U.S.C. § 119

12) ☐ Acknowledgment is made of a claim for foreign priority under 35 U.S.C. § 119(a)-(d) or (f).
   Certified copies:
   a)☐ All   b)☐ Some**   c)☐ None of the:
   1. ☐ Certified copies of the priority documents have been received.
   2. ☐ Certified copies of the priority documents have been received in Application No. _____.
   3. ☐ Copies of the certified copies of the priority documents have been received in this National Stage application from the International Bureau (PCT Rule 17.2(a)).
** See the attached detailed Office action for a list of the certified copies not received.

Attachment(s)
1) ☒ Notice of References Cited (PTO-892)
2) ☒ Information Disclosure Statement(s) (PTO/SB/08a and/or PTO/SB/08b) Paper No(s)/Mail Date *7/31/2015; and 7/21/2016*.
3) ☐ Interview Summary (PTO-413) Paper No(s)/Mail Date. _____.
4) ☐ Other: _____.

Application/Control Number: 14/815,871 Page 2
Art Unit: 2196

The present application, filed on or after March 16, 2013, is being examined under the first inventor to file provisions of the AIA.

DETAILED ACTION

Claims 1-20 are pending and they are presented for examination.

Examiner's Notes

Examiner cites particular columns and line numbers in the references as applied to the claims below for the convenience of the applicant. Although the specified citations are representative of the teachings in the art and are applied to the specific limitations within the individual claim, other passages and figures may apply as well. It is respectfully requested that, in preparing responses, the applicant fully consider the references in entirety as potentially teaching all or part of the claimed invention, as well as the context of the passage as taught by the prior art or disclosed by the examiner.

Application/Control Number: 14/815,871 Page 3
Art Unit: 2196

Information Disclosure Statement

As required by M.P.E.P. 609, the applicant's submissions of the Information Disclosure Statement dated 31 July 2015; and 21 July 2016 are acknowledged by the examiner and the cited references have been considered in the examination of the claims now pending.

Claim Objections

Claims 3 and 16 are objected to because of the following informalities: Claims 3 line 3 and Claim 16 line 2 "VLIM" should be "VLIW". Appropriate correction is required.

Claim Rejections - 35 USC § 102

The following is a quotation of the appropriate paragraphs of 35 U.S.C. 102 that form the basis for the rejections under this section made in this Office action:

> A person shall be entitled to a patent unless –
>
> (a)(1) the claimed invention was patented, described in a printed publication, or in public use, on sale or otherwise available to the public before the effective filing date of the claimed invention.

Claims 1-6 and 8-20 are rejected under 35 U.S.C. 102(a)(1) as being anticipated by Winkel et al. (US 2016/0274944).

As per Claim 1, Winkel teaches **a baseband processor, comprising:**

a receiver to receive a request for service [Winkel Abstract, The front end includes circuitry to determine whether to apply an acyclical or cyclical thread assignment scheme to code received (i.e. receive a request for service) at the

Application/Control Number: 14/815,871 Page 4
Art Unit: 2196

processor, and to, based upon a determined thread assignment scheme, assign code to a static logical thread and to a rotating logical thread.];

a configuration unit to allocate at least one of a plurality of resources to a plurality of threads [Winkel ¶0101, allocate module 1282 may allocate resources of processor or other resources, such as registers or buffers, to execute a given instruction (i.e. thread).], **wherein the at least one of the plurality of resources is configurable** [Winkel ¶0050, System 100 may include a processor 102 for processing data signals. Processor 102 may include a complex instruction set computer (CISC) microprocessor, a reduced instruction set computing (RISC) microprocessor, a very long instruction word (VLIW) microprocessor, a processor implementing a combination of instruction sets (i.e. resources is configurable), or any other processor device, such as a digital signal processor, for example.]**; and**

a performing unit to perform the service with the threads, utilizing the allocated at least one resource [Winkel ¶0101, Resource schedulers may determine when an instruction (i.e. thread) is ready to execute based on the readiness of a given resource's sources and the availability of execution resources needed to execute an instruction.].

As per Claim 2, rejection of Claim 1 incorporated, Winkel teaches **wherein a number of the plurality of threads is configurable** [Winkel ¶0050, System 100 may include a processor 102 for processing data signals. Processor 102 may include a complex instruction set computer (CISC) microprocessor, a reduced instruction set

Application/Control Number: 14/815,871 Page 5
Art Unit: 2196

computing (RISC) microprocessor, a very long instruction word (VLIW) microprocessor, a processor implementing a combination of instruction sets (i.e. threads), or any other processor device, such as a digital signal processor, for example.; Note: Since the instruction sets are a combination of CISC, RISC, and VLIM then the threads are configurable to the different instruction sets].

As per Claim 3, rejection of Claim 1 incorporated, Winkel teaches **wherein the plurality of threads include very long instruction word (VLIW) processor instruction issuing slots, wherein a number of VLIW processor instruction issuing slots is configurable** [Winkel ¶0050, System 100 may include a processor 102 for processing data signals. Processor 102 may include a complex instruction set computer (CISC) microprocessor, a reduced instruction set computing (RISC) microprocessor, a very long instruction word (VLIW) microprocessor, a processor implementing a combination of instruction sets, or any other processor device, such as a digital signal processor, for example.].

As per Claim 4, rejection of Claim 3 incorporated, Winkel teaches **wherein the plurality of resources include at least one of scalar functional units and vector functional units** [Winkel ¶0085, Scheduler units 456 may be coupled to physical register file units 458. Each of physical register file units 458 represents one or more physical register files, different ones of which store one or more different data types, such as scalar integer, scalar floating point, packed integer, packed floating point,

Application/Control Number: 14/815,871 Page 6
Art Unit: 2196

vector integer, vector floating point, etc., status (e.g., an instruction pointer that is the address of the next instruction to be executed), etc.].

As per Claim 5, rejection of Claim 4 incorporated, Winkel teaches **wherein the plurality of resources include at least one of load or store functional units, memory or cache resources and vector units with configurable width** [Winkel ¶0086, memory access units 464 may include a load unit, a store address unit, and a store data unit, each of which may be coupled to data TLB unit 472 in memory unit 470. L2 cache unit 476 may be coupled to one or more other levels of cache and eventually to a main memory.].

As per Claim 6, rejection of Claim 5 incorporated, Winkel teaches **wherein the configuration unit to allocate at least one of the plurality of resources to the plurality of threads comprising grouping the plurality of resources in at least one of scalar functional units, vector functional units, load or store functional unites, memory or cache resources and vector units with configurable width** [Winkel ¶0091, cores 502 and system agent 510 may be communicatively coupled to one or more caches 506. Cores 502, system agent 510, and caches 506 may be communicatively coupled via one or more memory control units 552. Furthermore, cores 502, system agent 510, and caches 506 may be communicatively coupled to a graphics module 560 via memory control units 552.].

Application/Control Number: 14/815,871 Page 7
Art Unit: 2196

As per Claim 8, rejection of Claim 1 incorporated, Winkel teaches **wherein the configuration unit allocates at least one of the plurality of resources to the plurality of threads based on at least one of a power efficiency and processing capacity** [Winkel ¶0108, In other embodiments, additional or different processors may also be present in system 600. For example, additional processors 610, 615 may include additional processors that may be the same as processor 610, additional processors that may be heterogeneous or asymmetric to processor 610, accelerators (such as, e.g., graphics accelerators or digital signal processing (DSP) units), field programmable gate arrays, or any other processor. There may be a variety of differences between the physical resources 610, 615 in terms of a spectrum of metrics of merit including architectural, micro-architectural, thermal, power consumption characteristics, and the like. These differences may effectively manifest themselves as asymmetry and heterogeneity amongst processors 610, 615. For at least one embodiment, various processors 610, 615 may reside in the same die package.].

As per Claim 9, has similar limitations as Claim 1 and therefore rejected on the same rationale.

As per Claim 10, rejection of Claim 9 incorporated, Winkel teaches **wherein the plurality of resources include at least scalar functional units and vector functional units** [Winkel ¶0085, Scheduler units 456 may be coupled to physical register file units 458. Each of physical register file units 458 represents one or more physical register

Application/Control Number: 14/815,871 Page 8
Art Unit: 2196

files, different ones of which store one or more different data types, such as scalar integer, scalar floating point, packed integer, packed floating point, vector integer, vector floating point, etc., status (e.g., an instruction pointer that is the address of the next instruction to be executed), etc.].

As per Claim 11, rejection of Claim 10 incorporated, Winkel teaches **wherein the apparatus comprises a first baseband processor and a second baseband processor, wherein the first baseband processor includes a higher ratio of scalar functional units to vector functional units than the second baseband processor** [Winkel ¶0108, In other embodiments, additional or different processors may also be present in system 600. For example, additional processors 610, 615 may include additional processors that may be the same as processor 610, additional processors that may be heterogeneous or asymmetric to processor 610, accelerators (such as, e.g., graphics accelerators or digital signal processing (DSP) units), field programmable gate arrays, or any other processor. There may be a variety of differences between the physical resources 610, 615 in terms of a spectrum of metrics of merit including architectural, micro-architectural, thermal, power consumption characteristics, and the like. These differences may effectively manifest themselves as asymmetry and heterogeneity amongst processors 610, 615. For at least one embodiment, various processors 610, 615 may reside in the same die package.].

Application/Control Number: 14/815,871 Page 9
Art Unit: 2196

As per Claim 12, rejection of Claim 9 incorporated, Winkel teaches **wherein the apparatus comprises a general purpose processor and a hardware accelerator** [Winkel ¶0108, In other embodiments, additional or different processors may also be present in system 600. For example, additional processors 610, 615 may include additional processors that may be the same as processor 610, additional processors that may be heterogeneous or asymmetric to processor 610, accelerators (such as, e.g., graphics accelerators or digital signal processing (DSP) units), field programmable gate arrays, or any other processor. There may be a variety of differences between the physical resources 610, 615 in terms of a spectrum of metrics of merit including architectural, micro-architectural, thermal, power consumption characteristics, and the like. These differences may effectively manifest themselves as asymmetry and heterogeneity amongst processors 610, 615. For at least one embodiment, various processors 610, 615 may reside in the same die package.].

As per Claim 13, rejection of Claim 9 incorporated, Winkel teaches **wherein the service includes at least a wireless communication service** [Winkel ¶0123, the data representing the IP core design may be provided to storage 1130 via memory 1140 (e.g., hard disk), wired connection (e.g., internet) 1150 or wireless connection 1160.].

As per Claim 14, has similar limitations as Claim 1 and therefore rejected on the same rationale.

Application/Control Number: 14/815,871 Page 10
Art Unit: 2196

As per Claim 15, rejection of Claim 14 incorporated, has similar limitations as Claim 2 and therefore rejected on the same rationale.

As per Claim 16, rejection of Claim 14 incorporated, has similar limitations as Claim 3 and therefore rejected on the same rationale.

As per Claim 17, rejection of Claim 16 incorporated, has similar limitations as Claim 4 and therefore rejected on the same rationale.

As per Claim 18, rejection of Claim 17 incorporated, has similar limitations as Claim 5 and therefore rejected on the same rationale.

As per Claim 19, rejection of Claim 18 incorporated, has similar limitations as Claim 6 and therefore rejected on the same rationale.

As per Claim 20, rejection of Claim 14 incorporated, has similar limitations as Claim 8 and therefore rejected on the same rationale.

Claim Rejections - 35 USC § 103

The following is a quotation of 35 U.S.C. 103 which forms the basis for all obviousness rejections set forth in this Office action:

> A patent for a claimed invention may not be obtained, notwithstanding that the claimed invention is not identically disclosed as set forth in section 102, if the differences between the claimed invention and the prior art are such that the claimed invention as a whole would have been obvious before the effective filing date of the claimed invention to a person having ordinary skill in the art to which the claimed invention pertains. Patentability shall not be negated by the manner in which the invention was made.

Claim 7 is rejected under 35 U.S.C. 103 as being unpatentable over Winkel et al. (US 2016/0274944 in view of Oksanen et al. (US 2009/0079547).

Application/Control Number: 14/815,871 Page 11
Art Unit: 2196

As per Claim 7, rejection of Claim 1 incorporated, Winkel does not explicitly teach wherein unallocated resources of the plurality resources are configured for being powered down.

However Oksanen teaches **wherein unallocated resources of the plurality resources are configured for being powered down** [Oksanen ¶0052, processing resources to be powered down during periods of non-use.].

Winkel in view of Oksanen is analogous art because they are from the same field of endeavor, resource management.

Therefore, it would have been obvious to one of ordinary skill in the art at the time of filing was made to incorporate wherein unallocated resources of the plurality resources are configured for being powered down into the teaching of Winkel in view of Oksanen because doing so provides predictable results such as known method for saving power.

Conclusion

Any inquiry concerning this communication or earlier communications from the examiner should be directed to STEVEN DO whose telephone number is (571)270-3344. The examiner can normally be reached on Monday to Friday, 8am to 5pm EST.

Application/Control Number: 14/815,871 Page 12
Art Unit: 2196

If attempts to reach the examiner by telephone are unsuccessful, the examiner's supervisor, EMERSON PUENTE can be reached on 571-272-3652. The fax phone number for the organization where this application or proceeding is assigned is 571-273-8300.

Information regarding the status of an application may be obtained from the Patent Application Information Retrieval (PAIR) system. Status information for published applications may be obtained from either Private PAIR or Public PAIR. Status information for unpublished applications is available through Private PAIR only. For more information about the PAIR system, see http://pair-direct.uspto.gov. Should you have questions on access to the Private PAIR system, contact the Electronic Business Center (EBC) at 866-217-9197 (toll-free). If you would like assistance from a USPTO Customer Service Representative or access to the automated information system, call 800-786-9199 (IN USA OR CANADA) or 571-272-1000.

10/12/2016

/SD/
Steven Do
Examiner, Art Unit 2196

/EMERSON PUENTE/
Supervisory Patent Examiner, Art Unit 2196

LINCOLN LAW SCHOOL OF SAN JOSE
INTELLECTUAL PROPERTY SERIES

EXHIBIT: OFFICE ACTION RESPONSE

Application No.: 14/815,871   Page 2

In the Claims:

1.   (Currently Amended) An apparatus~~baseband processor~~, comprising:

a plurality of baseband processors comprising a first baseband processor and a second baseband processor, wherein the first baseband processor includes a higher ratio of scalar functional units to vector functional units than the second baseband processor;

wherein each baseband processor of the plurality of baseband processors comprises:

a receiving unit[[er]] to receive a request for a wireless communication service;

a configuration unit to allocate at least one of a plurality of resources to a plurality of threads, wherein the plurality of resources includes at least the scalar functional units and the vector functional units and the at least one of the plurality of resources is configurable; and

a performing unit to perform the wireless communication service with the threads, utilizing the allocated at least one of the plurality of resources.

2.   (Currently amended) The apparatus ~~baseband processor~~ of Claim 1, wherein a number of the plurality of threads is configurable.

3.   (Currently amended) The apparatus ~~baseband processor~~ of Claim 1, wherein the plurality of threads includes very long instruction word (VLIW) processor instruction issuing slots, wherein a number of VLI[[M]]W processor instruction issuing slots is configurable.

4.   (Cancelled)

5.   (Currently amended) The apparatus ~~baseband processor~~ of Claim 1[[4]], wherein the plurality of resources includes at least one of load or store functional units, memory or cache resources and vector units with configurable width.

6.   (Currently amended) The apparatus ~~baseband processor~~ of Claim 5, wherein the configuration unit to allocate at least one of the plurality of resources to the plurality of threads

Application No.: 14/815,871   Page 3

comprises[[ing]] grouping the plurality of resources in at least one of scalar functional units, vector functional units, load or store functional unit[[e]]s, memory or cache resources and vector units with configurable width.

7. (Currently amended) The apparatus ~~baseband processor~~ of Claim 1, wherein unallocated resources of the plurality of resources are configured for being powered down.

8. (Currently amended) The apparatus ~~baseband processor~~ of Claim 1, wherein the configuration unit allocates at least one of the plurality of resources to the plurality of threads based on at least one of a power efficiency and processing capacity.

9. (Cancelled)

10. (Cancelled)

11. (Cancelled)

12. (Cancelled)

13. (Cancelled)

14. (Currently Amended) A method, comprising:
   receiving, by an apparatus including a first baseband processor and a second baseband processor, a request for a wireless communication service, wherein the first baseband processor includes a higher ratio of scalar functional units to vector functional units than the second baseband processor;
   allocating, by the apparatus, at least one of a plurality of resources to a plurality of threads, wherein the plurality of resources includes at least the scalar functional units and the vector functional units, at least one of the plurality of resources is configurable; and

Application No.: 14/815,871   Page 4

performing the <u>wireless communication</u> service in connection with the threads, utilizing the allocated at least one <u>of the plurality of</u> resource<u>s</u>.

15. (Original) The method of Claim 14, wherein a number of the plurality of threads is configurable.

16. (Currently amended) The method of Claim 14, wherein the plurality of threads include<u>s</u> very long instruction word (VLIW) processor instruction issuing slots, wherein a number of VLI[[M]]<u>W</u> processor instruction issuing slots is configurable.

17. (Cancelled)

18. (Currently amended) The method of Claim 1<u>4</u>[[7]], wherein the plurality of resources include<u>s</u> at least one of load or store functional units, memory or cache resources and vector units with configurable width.

19. (Currently amended) The method of Claim 18, wherein the allocating the at least one of the plurality of resources to the plurality of threads compris<u>es</u>[[ing]] grouping the plurality of resources in at least one of scalar functional units, vector functional units, load or store functional units, memory or cache resources, and vector units with configurable width.

20. (Original) The method of Claim 14, wherein the allocating the at least one of the plurality of resources to the plurality of threads is based on at least one of a power efficiency and processing capacity.

21. (New) The apparatus of Claim 1, wherein the first baseband processor and the second baseband processor exhibit differing configurations of vector resources that overlap.

Application No.: 14/815,871   Page 5

22. (New) The apparatus of Claim 1, wherein the plurality of baseband processors is associated with a Layer 1 system-on-a-chip,

the request for the wireless communication service is received from a Layer 2/3 system-on-a-chip, and

a master processor of the Layer 1 system-on-a-chip that directs operation of the plurality of baseband processors and is configured for:

determining whether the request for the wireless communication service is capable of being completed within a predetermined margin,

performing the allocation among the plurality of baseband processors associated with the Layer 1 system-on-a-chip, if it is determined that the request for the wireless communication service is capable of being completed within the predetermined margin, and

performing a reconfiguration of the plurality of baseband processors of the Layer 1 system-on-a-chip, if it is determined that the request for the wireless communication service is not capable of being completed within the predetermined margin.

23. (New) The apparatus of Claim 22, wherein the master processor of the Layer 1 system-on-a-chip is further configured for:

determining whether the request for the wireless communication service is capable of being completed within the predetermined margin with the reconfiguration,

performing the allocation among the plurality of baseband processors associated with the Layer 1 system-on-a-chip, if it is determined that the request for the wireless

Application No.: 14/815,871   Page 6

communication service is capable of being completed within the predetermined margin with the reconfiguration, and

sending the Layer 2/3 system-on-a-chip a rejection, if it is determined that the request for the wireless communication service is not capable of being completed within the predetermined margin with the reconfiguration.

24. (New) The apparatus of Claim 1, wherein a frequency of the allocation is based on a cellular protocol.

25. (New) The apparatus of Claim 1, wherein the allocation accommodates use of different cellular protocols by different users.

Application No.: 14/815,871 Page 7

Remarks:

Summary

Claims 1-20 were pending.

Claims 1-3, 5-8, 14, 16, 18, and 19 have been amended herein, while claims 4, 9-13, and 17 are cancelled. Support for such amendments is found, inter alia, in Figures 4 and 5, as well as paragraph(s) [0039], [0042], and [0045] of the present description. Claims 21-25 are added herein. No new matter is introduced. Claims 1-3, 5-8, 14-16, and 18-25 are now pending, including independent claims 1, and 14.

Claim Objection

Claim 3 and 16 was objected because of informalities. Such objections are deemed overcome by virtue of the amendments made hereinabove.

Rejections Under 35 U.S.C. 102

Claims 1-6, 8-20 were rejected under 35 U.S.C. 102(a)(1) as being anticipated by WINKEL (U.S. Patent Pub. No. 2016/0274944). In response to this rejection, applicant herein amends Claims 1-3, 5-6, 14, 16, 18, and 19. Specifically, applicant has amended the independent claims, as follows:

1. An apparatus~~baseband processor~~, comprising:
a plurality of baseband processors comprising a first baseband processor and a second baseband processor, wherein the first baseband processor includes a higher ratio of scalar functional units to vector functional units than the second baseband processor;
    wherein each baseband processor of the plurality of baseband processors comprises:
        a receiving unit[[er]] to receive a request for a wireless communication service;
        a configuration unit to allocate at least one of a plurality of resources to a plurality of threads, wherein the plurality of resources includes at least the scalar functional units and the vector functional units and the at least one of the plurality of resources is configurable; and
a performing unit to perform the wireless communication service with the threads, utilizing the allocated at least one of the plurality of resources.

14. A method, comprising:

Application No.: 14/815,871   Page 8

receiving, by an apparatus including a first baseband processor and a second baseband processor, a request for a wireless communication service, wherein the first baseband processor includes a higher ratio of scalar functional units to vector functional units than the second baseband processor;

allocating, by the apparatus, at least one of a plurality of resources to a plurality of threads, wherein the plurality of resources includes at least the scalar functional units and the vector functional units, at least one of the plurality of resources is configurable; and

performing the wireless communication service in connection with the threads, utilizing the allocated at least one of the plurality of resources.

With respect to the independent claims, the Examiner has relied on paragraph [0108] from the WINKEL reference to make a prior art showing of applicant's claimed technique "a plurality of baseband processors" (see this or similar, but not necessarily identical language in the independent claims).

Applicant respectfully notes that the WINKEL reference, as relied upon by the Examiner, discloses that:

> [0108] In other embodiments, additional or different processors may also be present in system 600. For example, additional processors 610, 615 may include additional processors that may be the same as processor 610, additional processors that may be heterogeneous or asymmetric to processor 610, accelerators (such as, e.g., graphics accelerators or digital signal processing (DSP) units), field programmable gate arrays, or any other processor. There may be a variety of differences between the physical resources 610, 615 in terms of a spectrum of metrics of merit including architectural, micro-architectural, thermal, power consumption characteristics, and the like. These differences may effectively manifest themselves as asymmetry and heterogeneity amongst processors 610, 615. For at least one embodiment, various processors 610, 615 may reside in the same die package.

See WINKEL Paragraph [0108] – emphasis added.

However, disclosing that "additional processors [] may be heterogeneous or asymmetric to processor 610," as in the WINKEL excerpt(s) relied upon (emphasis added), fails to teach or suggest "a plurality of **baseband** processors" (emphasis added), as claimed by applicant. Clearly, merely disclosing "processor" and "additional processors," as in the WINKEL excerpt(s) relied upon, fails to specifically teach "**baseband** processors" as claimed by applicant. Additionally, disclosing that "additional processors" may be "asymmetric," as in the WINKEL

Application No.: 14/815,871   Page 9

excerpt(s) relied upon, fails to rise to the level of specificity claimed, namely, "a plurality of **baseband** processors" (emphasis added), as claimed by applicant.

With respect to former Claim 11, the subject matter of which is now incorporated into each of the independent claims, the Examiner has relied on paragraph [0108] from the WINKEL reference (excerpted above) to make a prior art showing of applicant's claimed technique "wherein the first baseband processor includes a higher ratio of scalar functional units to vector functional units than the second baseband processor" (see this or similar, but not necessarily identical language in the independent claims).

However, disclosing that "additional processors [] may be heterogeneous or asymmetric to processor 610," as in the WINKEL excerpt(s) relied upon (emphasis added), does not teach or suggest applicant's claimed technique "wherein the first baseband processor includes a higher ratio of scalar functional units to vector functional units than the second baseband processor" (emphasis added), as claimed by applicant.

The Examiner is reminded that a claim is anticipated only if each and every element as set forth in the claim is found, either expressly or inherently described in a single prior art reference. Verdegaal Bros. v. Union Oil Co. Of California, 814 F.2d 628, 631, 2 USPQ2d 1051, 1053 (Fed. Cir. 1987). Moreover, the identical invention must be shown in as complete detail as contained in the claim. Richardson v. Suzuki Motor Co.868 F.2d 1226, 1236, 9USPQ2d 1913, 1920 (Fed. Cir. 1989). The elements must be arranged as required by the claim.

This criterion has simply not been met by the above reference excerpt(s), as noted above.

Rejections Under 35 U.S.C. 103

Claim 7 was rejected under 35 U.S.C. 103(a) as being obvious over WINKEL in view of OKSANEN (U.S. Patent Pub. No. 2009/0079547). Applicant respectfully notes that dependent Claim 7 is allowable in view of its dependence on a respective allowable independent claim (Claim 1, amended and argued hereinabove).

Application No.: 14/815,871   Page 10

Dependent Claims

Applicant further notes that the prior art is also deficient with respect to the dependent claims. For example, with respect to Claims 8 and 20, the Examiner has relied on paragraph [0108] from the WINKEL reference (excerpted above) to make a prior art showing of applicant's claimed technique "wherein the configuration unit allocates at least one of the plurality of resources to the plurality of threads based on at least one of a power efficiency and processing capacity" (see this or similar, but not necessarily identical language in Claim 20).

However, disclosing that "additional processors [] may be heterogeneous or asymmetric to processor 610," as in the WINKEL excerpt(s) relied upon (emphasis added), does not teach or suggest applicant's claimed technique "wherein the configuration unit allocates at least one of the plurality of resources to the plurality of threads **based on** at least one of a power efficiency and processing capacity" (emphasis added), as claimed by applicant.

Again, as noted above, since this anticipation criterion has simply not been met by the above reference excerpt(s), a notice of allowance or specific prior art showing of each of the foregoing claim elements, in combination with the remaining claimed features, is respectfully requested.

New Claims

Still yet, applicant brings to the Examiner's attention the subject matter of new Claims 21-25, which are added for full consideration. No new matter is added.

Again, a notice of allowance or a proper prior art showing of all of applicant's claim limitations, in combination with the remaining claim elements, is respectfully requested.

Conclusion

It is believed that all of the pending issues have been addressed. Claims 1-3, 5-8, 14-16, and 18-25 are in condition for allowance per the claim amendments herein.

However, the absence of a reply to a specific rejection, issue, or comment does not signify agreement with or concession of that rejection, issue, or comment. In addition, because the arguments made above may not be exhaustive, there may be reasons for patentability of

Application No.: 14/815,871								Page 11

any or all pending claims (or other claims) that have not been expressed. Still yet, nothing in this reply should be construed as intention to concede any issue with regard to any claim, except as specifically stated in this reply. Finally, it should be noted that no claims are intended to be construed under 35 U.S.C. 112, paragraph 6.

In the event a telephone conversation would expedite the prosecution of this application, the Examiner may reach the undersigned at (408) 971-2573 or kevin@zilkakotab.com. Applicant does not believe that any additional fees are due. However, in the event that any other fees are due, the Director is hereby authorized to charge any required fees due (other than issue fees), and to credit any overpayment made, in connection with the filing of this paper to Deposit Account No. 50-1351 (Order No. 91030113US01/FUWEP003).

Respectfully submitted,

Zilka-Kotab, PC.

/KEVINZILKA/

Kevin Zilka
Reg. No. 41,429

1155 N. 1st Street, Suite 105
San Jose, CA 95112-4925
408-971-2573

LINCOLN LAW SCHOOL OF SAN JOSE
INTELLECTUAL PROPERTY SERIES

EXHIBIT: OFFICE ACTION

EXHIBITS   329

UNITED STATES PATENT AND TRADEMARK OFFICE

UNITED STATES DEPARTMENT OF COMMERCE
United States Patent and Trademark Office
Address: COMMISSIONER FOR PATENTS
P.O. Box 1450
Alexandria, Virginia 22313-1450
www.uspto.gov

APPLICATION NO.	FILING DATE	FIRST NAMED INVENTOR	ATTORNEY DOCKET NO.	CONFIRMATION NO.
14/823,993	08/11/2015	William Rivard	DUELP019	5351

28875   7590   02/10/2017
Zilka-Kotab, PC
1155 N. 1st St.
Suite 105
SAN JOSE, CA 95112

EXAMINER
JERABEK, KELLY L

ART UNIT	PAPER NUMBER
2662	

NOTIFICATION DATE	DELIVERY MODE
02/10/2017	ELECTRONIC

Please find below and/or attached an Office communication concerning this application or proceeding.

The time period for reply, if any, is set in the attached communication.

Notice of the Office communication was sent electronically on above-indicated "Notification Date" to the following e-mail address(es):

zk-uspto@zilkakotab.com
chrisc@zilkakotab.com

PTOL-90A (Rev. 04/07)

330 | PATENT PROSECUTION WORKBOOK

Office Action Summary	Application No. 14/823,993	Applicant(s) RIVARD ET AL.
	Examiner KELLY L. JERABEK	Art Unit 2662 — AIA (First Inventor to File) Status: Yes

-- The MAILING DATE of this communication appears on the cover sheet with the correspondence address --

Period for Reply

A SHORTENED STATUTORY PERIOD FOR REPLY IS SET TO EXPIRE **3** MONTHS FROM THE MAILING DATE OF THIS COMMUNICATION.
- Extensions of time may be available under the provisions of 37 CFR 1.136(a). In no event, however, may a reply be timely filed after SIX (6) MONTHS from the mailing date of this communication.
- If NO period for reply is specified above, the maximum statutory period will apply and will expire SIX (6) MONTHS from the mailing date of this communication.
- Failure to reply within the set or extended period for reply will, by statute, cause the application to become ABANDONED (35 U.S.C. § 133). Any reply received by the Office later than three months after the mailing date of this communication, even if timely filed, may reduce any earned patent term adjustment. See 37 CFR 1.704(b).

Status

1) ☒ Responsive to communication(s) filed on *11/28/2016*.
   ☐ A declaration(s)/affidavit(s) under **37 CFR 1.130(b)** was/were filed on _____.
2a) ☒ This action is **FINAL**.   2b) ☐ This action is non-final.
3) ☐ An election was made by the applicant in response to a restriction requirement set forth during the interview on _____; the restriction requirement and election have been incorporated into this action.
4) ☐ Since this application is in condition for allowance except for formal matters, prosecution as to the merits is closed in accordance with the practice under *Ex parte Quayle*, 1935 C.D. 11, 453 O.G. 213.

Disposition of Claims*

5) ☒ Claim(s) *1-20* is/are pending in the application.
   5a) Of the above claim(s) _____ is/are withdrawn from consideration.
6) ☐ Claim(s) _____ is/are allowed.
7) ☒ Claim(s) *1-20* is/are rejected.
8) ☐ Claim(s) _____ is/are objected to.
9) ☐ Claim(s) _____ are subject to restriction and/or election requirement.

* If any claims have been determined allowable, you may be eligible to benefit from the **Patent Prosecution Highway** program at a participating intellectual property office for the corresponding application. For more information, please see http://www.uspto.gov/patents/init_events/pph/index.jsp or send an inquiry to PPHfeedback@uspto.gov.

Application Papers

10) ☐ The specification is objected to by the Examiner.
11) ☒ The drawing(s) filed on *8/11/2015* is/are: a) ☒ accepted or b) ☐ objected to by the Examiner.
   Applicant may not request that any objection to the drawing(s) be held in abeyance. See 37 CFR 1.85(a).
   Replacement drawing sheet(s) including the correction is required if the drawing(s) is objected to. See 37 CFR 1.121(d).

Priority under 35 U.S.C. § 119

12) ☐ Acknowledgment is made of a claim for foreign priority under 35 U.S.C. § 119(a)-(d) or (f).
   Certified copies:
   a) ☐ All b) ☐ Some** c) ☐ None of the:
   1. ☐ Certified copies of the priority documents have been received.
   2. ☐ Certified copies of the priority documents have been received in Application No. _____.
   3. ☐ Copies of the certified copies of the priority documents have been received in this National Stage application from the International Bureau (PCT Rule 17.2(a)).

** See the attached detailed Office action for a list of the certified copies not received.

Attachment(s)

1) ☐ Notice of References Cited (PTO-892)
2) ☒ Information Disclosure Statement(s) (PTO/SB/08a and/or PTO/SB/08b) Paper No(s)/Mail Date _____.
3) ☐ Interview Summary (PTO-413) Paper No(s)/Mail Date _____.
4) ☐ Other: _____.

U.S. Patent and Trademark Office
PTOL-326 (Rev. 11-13) — Office Action Summary — Part of Paper No./Mail Date 20170206

Application/Control Number: 14/823,993
Art Unit: 2662

Page 2

DETAILED ACTION

The present application, filed on or after March 16, 2013, is being examined under the first inventor to file provisions of the AIA.

Information Disclosure Statement

The information disclosure statement (IDS) submitted on 11/28/2016 is in compliance with the provisions of 37 CFR 1.97. Accordingly, the information disclosure statement is being considered by the examiner.

Response to Arguments

Applicant's arguments filed 11/28/2016 have been fully considered but they are not persuasive.

Response to Remarks:

Applicant's arguments regarding claims 1-7, 10-12, 14-15 and 19-20 (amendment pages 6-8) state that the McMahon reference fails to teach or suggest, "generating a first amplified analog signal associated with each pixel by amplifying the analog signal utilizing a first gain, the first amplified analog signal including first gain-adjusted analog pixel data representative of **a first common analog value from each pixel** and generating a second amplified analog signal associated with each pixel by amplifying the analog signal utilizing a second gain, the second amplified analog signal including second gain-adjusted analog pixel data representative of **a second common**

Application/Control Number: 14/823,993 Page 3
Art Unit: 2662

analog value from each pixel". The examiner respectfully disagrees. McMahon discloses an apparatus (image sensor array – figure 4) and a method comprising: circuitry for: receiving an analog signal associated with at least one pixel of an image sensor (AFE 416 receives an analog signal output from array 410) (paragraphs 109-111; figure 4J); generating a first amplified analog signal associated with the at least one pixel by amplifying the analog signal utilizing a first gain (first AFE processing channel 420 amplifies the analog signal) (paragraphs 109-111; figure 4J); generating a second amplified analog signal associated with the at least one pixel by amplifying the analog signal utilizing a second gain (paragraphs 109-111; figure 4J); and transmitting the first amplified analog signal and the second amplified analog signal (outputs of AFE processing channels 420, 422 are output to ADC 418) (paragraphs 109-111; figure 4J). **McMahon discloses that specific amplification gains are applied to predetermined sets of pixels (paragraph 109). In addition, the examiner maintains that McMahon teaches that the amplified analog value of each pixel in the selected set of pixels is a common analog value because each pixel is part of the same (common) pixel array (410) (paragraphs 109-111).** Therefore, the examiner maintains that the **broadest reasonable interpretation of the terms "the first amplified analog signal including first gain-adjusted analog pixel data representative of a first common analog value from each pixel" and "the second amplified analog signal including second gain-adjusted analog pixel data representative of a second common analog value from each pixel" are met by the McMahon reference and therefore**

Application/Control Number: 14/823,993 Page 4
Art Unit: 2662

the McMahon reference discloses all of the limitations of claims 1-7, 10-12, 14-15 and 19-20.

Applicant's arguments regarding claims 8-9, 13 and 16-18 (amendment page 8) state that claims 8-9, 13 and 16-18 are allowable due to their dependency on claim 1 above. Therefore, the response above regarding claim 1 also applies to claims 8-9, 13 and 16-18.

Claim Rejections - 35 USC § 102

In the event the determination of the status of the application as subject to AIA 35 U.S.C. 102 and 103 (or as subject to pre-AIA 35 U.S.C. 102 and 103) is incorrect, any correction of the statutory basis for the rejection will not be considered a new ground of rejection if the prior art relied upon, and the rationale supporting the rejection, would be the same under either status.

The following is a quotation of the appropriate paragraphs of 35 U.S.C. 102 that form the basis for the rejections under this section made in this Office action:

> A person shall be entitled to a patent unless –
>
> (a)(1) the claimed invention was patented, described in a printed publication, or in public use, on sale or otherwise available to the public before the effective filing date of the claimed invention.

Claims 1-7, 10-12, 14-15 and 19-20 are rejected under 35 U.S.C. 102(a)(1) as being anticipated by McMahon et al. US 2013/0147979.

Application/Control Number: 14/823,993　　　　　　　　　　　　　　　　　　　　　Page 5
Art Unit: 2662

Re claims 1 and 19-20, McMahon discloses an apparatus (image sensor array – figure 4) and a method comprising: circuitry for: receiving an analog signal associated with at least one pixel of an image sensor (AFE 416 receives an analog signal output from array 410) (paragraphs 109-111; figure 4J); generating a first amplified analog signal associated with the at least one pixel by amplifying the analog signal utilizing a first gain (first AFE processing channel 420 amplifies the analog signal) (paragraphs 109-111; figure 4J); generating a second amplified analog signal associated with the at least one pixel by amplifying the analog signal utilizing a second gain (paragraphs 109-111; figure 4J); and transmitting the first amplified analog signal and the second amplified analog signal (outputs of AFE processing channels 420, 422 are output to ADC 418) (paragraphs 109-111; figure 4J). McMahon discloses that specific amplification gains are applied to predetermined sets of pixels (paragraph 109). In addition, the examiner maintains that McMahon teaches that the amplified analog value of each pixel in the selected set of pixels is a common analog value because each pixel is part of the same (common) pixel array (410) (paragraphs 109-111). Therefore, the examiner maintains that the broadest reasonable interpretation of the terms "the first amplified analog signal including first gain-adjusted analog pixel data representative of a first common analog value from each pixel" and "the second amplified analog signal including second gain-adjusted analog pixel data representative of a second common analog value from each pixel" are met by the McMahon reference

Application/Control Number: 14/823,993 Page 6
Art Unit: 2662

Re claim 2, McMahon further discloses that the apparatus is operable such that the analog signal is amplified utilizing the first gain simultaneously with the amplification of the analog signal utilizing a second gain (analog information read out from pixels is provided to parallel AFE processing channels that apply different gains) (paragraphs 106-108).

Re claim 3, McMahon further discloses that the apparatus is operable such that the analog signal is amplified utilizing the first gain in serial with the amplification of the analog signal utilizing the second gain (different gains can be applied by AFE 416 to the analog signal as it is read out from column circuit 414) (figure 4I; paragraphs 106-108).

Re claim 4, McMahon further discloses that the apparatus is operable such that the first amplified analog signal is converted to a first digital signal (a first amplified analog signal output by the first AFE channel 420 is converted to a first digital signal by ADC 418) (paragraph 111), and the second amplified analog signal is converted to a second digital signal (a second amplified analog signal output by the second AFE channel 422 is converted to a second digital signal by ADC 419) (paragraph 112).

Re claim 5, McMahon further discloses that the first amplified analog signal is converted to the first digital signal concurrent with the conversion of the second amplified analog signal to the second digital signal (ADCs 418, 419 perform AD conversion in parallel) (figure 4JA; paragraph 112).

Application/Control Number: 14/823,993
Art Unit: 2662

Page 7

Re claim 6, McMahon further discloses that the apparatus is operable such that the first digital signal has a first light sensitivity value associated therewith (different gain for "fast" pixels) and the second digital signal has a second light sensitivity value associated therewith (different gain for "normal" pixels) (paragraphs 104-106).

Re claim 7, McMahon further discloses that the apparatus is operable such that the first digital signal and the second digital signal are blended (figure 4P; paragraph 127).

Re claim 10, McMahon further discloses that the apparatus is operable such that the first digital signal and the second digital signal are combined, resulting in at least a portion of a high dynamic range (HDR) image (figure 4P; paragraph 127).

Re claim 11, McMahon further discloses that the apparatus is operable such that at least one of the first digital signal or the second digital signal is further combined with at least a portion of another image array (first and second signals are combined to create high dynamic range data) (figure 4P; paragraph 127).

Re claim 12, McMahon further discloses that a first digital value specifies the first gain, and a second digital value specifies the second gain (each AFE circuit is controlled by circuitry 454 to specify a gain) (figure 4N; paragraphs 122-123).

Application/Control Number: 14/823,993 Page 8
Art Unit: 2662

Re claim 14, McMahon further discloses that the apparatus is operable such that the other array is associated with a high dynamic range (HDR) image (the image data is an amplified high dynamic range image information that is digitized by ADCs) (paragraph 127).

Re claim 15, McMahon further discloses that the first amplified analog signal and the second amplified analog signal each include gain-adjusted analog pixel data representative of a common analog value from each pixel of the image sensor (the data from each analog signal is gain-adjusted such that the resulting images are created with overall uniform analog gain and the gains of the first and second analog signals are independently controlled such that the pixel levels are the same) (paragraphs 111, 124).

Claim Rejections - 35 USC § 103

In the event the determination of the status of the application as subject to AIA 35 U.S.C. 102 and 103 (or as subject to pre-AIA 35 U.S.C. 102 and 103) is incorrect, any correction of the statutory basis for the rejection will not be considered a new ground of rejection if the prior art relied upon, and the rationale supporting the rejection, would be the same under either status.

The following is a quotation of 35 U.S.C. 103 which forms the basis for all obviousness rejections set forth in this Office action:

> A patent for a claimed invention may not be obtained, notwithstanding that the claimed invention is not identically disclosed as set forth in section 102, if the differences between the claimed invention and the prior art are such that the claimed invention as a whole would have

Application/Control Number: 14/823,993 Page 9
Art Unit: 2662

been obvious before the effective filing date of the claimed invention to a person having ordinary skill in the art to which the claimed invention pertains. Patentability shall not be negated by the manner in which the invention was made.

Claims 8-9 are rejected under 35 U.S.C. 103 as being unpatentable over McMahon et al. US 2013/0147979 in view of Jannard US 2012/0069213.

Re claims 8 and 9, McMahon discloses all of the limitations of claim 4 above. In addition, McMahon further discloses that the first and second digital signals may be blended (paragraphs 127, 132). However, McMahon fails to specifically disclose that the first and second digital signals are blended in response to user input and the apparatus is operable such that sliding indicia is displayed and the first digital signal and the second digital signal are blended, in response to the sliding indicia being manipulated by a user.

Jannard discloses that it is well known in the digital imaging art for a first digital signal and a second digital signal to be blended in response to a user input (a user interface is provided to allow a user to set blending parameters) (paragraph 114) and that a sliding indicia may be displayed and the first and second digital signals may be blended in response to a manipulation of the sliding indicia (the GUI includes a slider or icons that a user can manipulate to adjust blending parameters) (paragraph 115). Therefore, it would have been obvious for one skilled in the art to have been motivated to include a user interface for allowing a user of a device to adjust blending parameters as disclosed by the Jannard reference in the apparatus disclosed by the McMahon reference. Doing so would provide a means for allowing a user to easily adjust the blending parameters of signals captured by an image sensor array.

Application/Control Number: 14/823,993 Page 10
Art Unit: 2662

Claim 13 is rejected under 35 U.S.C. 103 as being unpatentable over McMahon et al. US 2013/0147979 in view of Furuya US 2011/0115971.

Re claim 13, McMahon discloses all of the limitations of claim 12 above. However, McMahon fails to specifically disclose that at least one of the first digital value and the second digital value is selected based on a mapping from the at least one of the first digital value and the second digital value to an ISO value, and the ISO value is selected by at least one of software executing on the apparatus and a user.

Furuya discloses that it is well known in the digital imaging art for a digital value to be selected based on a mapping from a digital value to an ISO value (controller 7 calculates an amplification gain based on the ISO sensitivity obtained in the processing step 16 and the table shown in figure 3 and sets the gain for the AFE 3) (paragraph 87); and also discloses that the ISO value is selected by at least one of software executing on the apparatus and a user (the user may set the ISO sensitivity of the digital camera by operating a user interface) (paragraph 101). Therefore, it would have been obvious for one skilled in the art to have been motivated to include a user interface for allowing a user of a device to adjust ISO sensitivity of an image capturing device as disclosed by the Furuya reference in the apparatus disclosed by the McMahon reference. Doing so would provide a means for allowing a user to easily adjust the ISO sensitivity of a camera in order to improve image quality and signal-to-noise ratio of captured images.

Application/Control Number: 14/823,993 Page 11
Art Unit: 2662

Claims 16-18 are rejected under 35 U.S.C. 103 as being unpatentable over McMahon et al. US 2013/0147979 in view of Levien US 2007/0030357.

Re claims 16-18, McMahon discloses all of the limitations of claim 4 above. In addition, McMahon further discloses that image processing may result in at least a portion of a high dynamic range (HDR) image (paragraph 127). However, McMahon fails to specifically disclose that the apparatus is operable for transferring at least one of the first digital signal or the second digital signal over a network for being combined remotely.

Levien discloses that it is well known in the digital imaging art for an image capture apparatus to be operable for transferring digital images over a network (paragraph 44) and for transferred digital images to be combined remotely (a portion of an image may be substituted or replaced by another image or image portion) (paragraph 76). Therefore, it would have been obvious for one skilled in the art to have been motivated to include the teaching of transferring images over a network and combining transferred images remotely as disclosed by the Levien reference in the apparatus disclosed by the McMahon reference. Doing so would provide a means for performing image processing remotely on images that have been transmitted to a remote image processing device.

Application/Control Number: 14/823,993 Page 12
Art Unit: 2662

Conclusion

Applicant's amendment necessitated the new ground(s) of rejection presented in this Office action. Accordingly, **THIS ACTION IS MADE FINAL.** See MPEP § 706.07(a). Applicant is reminded of the extension of time policy as set forth in 37 CFR 1.136(a).

A shortened statutory period for reply to this final action is set to expire THREE MONTHS from the mailing date of this action. In the event a first reply is filed within TWO MONTHS of the mailing date of this final action and the advisory action is not mailed until after the end of the THREE-MONTH shortened statutory period, then the shortened statutory period will expire on the date the advisory action is mailed, and any extension fee pursuant to 37 CFR 1.136(a) will be calculated from the mailing date of the advisory action. In no event, however, will the statutory period for reply expire later than SIX MONTHS from the date of this final action.

Contacts

Any inquiry concerning this communication or earlier communications from the examiner should be directed to Kelly L. Jerabek whose telephone number is **(571) 272-7312**. The examiner can normally be reached on Monday - Friday (8:00 AM - 5:00 PM).

If attempts to reach the examiner by telephone are unsuccessful, the examiner's supervisor, Roberto Velez can be reached at **(571) 272-8597**. The fax phone number for submitting all Official communications is **(571) 273-7300**. The fax phone number for submitting informal communications such as drafts, proposed amendments, etc., may

Application/Control Number: 14/823,993
Art Unit: 2662

Page 13

be faxed directly to the Examiner at (571) 273-7312.

Information regarding the status of an application may be obtained from the Patent Application Information Retrieval (PAIR) system. Status information for published applications may be obtained from either Private PAIR or Public PAIR. Status information for unpublished applications is available through Private PAIR only. For more information about the PAIR system, see http://pair-direct.uspto.gov. Should you have questions on access to the Private PAIR system, contact the Electronic Business Center (EBC) at 866-217-9197 (toll-free).

/KELLY L JERABEK/

Primary Examiner, Art Unit 2662

LINCOLN LAW SCHOOL OF SAN JOSE
INTELLECTUAL PROPERTY SERIES

EXHIBIT: OFFICE ACTION RESPONSE

IN THE UNITED STATES PATENT AND TRADEMARK OFFICE

In re Application of:	Confirmation No.: 5351
William Rivard	Examiner: Jerabek, Kelly L
Application No.: 14/823,993	Art Unit: 2662
File Date: 08/11/2015	Docket No.: DUELP019
Title: IMAGE SENSOR APPARATUS AND METHOD FOR OBTAINING MULTIPLE EXPOSURES WITH ZERO INTERFRAME TIME	Date: May 24, 2017

AMENDMENT B (37 CFR 1.112) WITH RCE (37 CFR 1.114)

Commissioner for Patents
P.O. Box 1450
Alexandria VA 22313-1450

Examiner:

In response to the communication mailed 2017-02-10 (hereafter "Final Office Action" or "FOA"), please consider the following amendments believed to place the claims in condition for allowance, as follows:

— **Amendments to the Claims** are reflected in the listing of the claims that begins on page 2 of this paper.
— **Remarks/Arguments** begin on page 8 of this paper.

Inventor: William Rivard et al.
Application No. : 14/823,993

Attorney's Docket No.: DUELP019
Page : 2 of 15

Amendments to the Claims:

This listing of claims replaces all prior versions and listings of claims in the application:

1. (Currently amended) An apparatus, comprising:

    a[[n]] pixel array [[of]]within an image sensor, the pixel array including pixels located in one or more rows; and

    circuitry for:

    receiving an analog signal associated with each pixel of a first set of pixels of the pixel array;

    generating, for each pixel of the first set of pixels, a first amplified analog signal based on the received analog signal ~~associated with each pixel~~ by amplifying the analog signal utilizing a first gain~~, the first amplified analog signal including first gain-adjusted analog pixel data representative of a first common analog value from each pixel~~;

    generating, for each pixel of the first set of pixels, a second amplified analog signal based on the received analog signal ~~associated with each pixel~~ by amplifying the analog signal utilizing a second gain~~, the second amplified analog signal including second gain-adjusted analog pixel data representative of a second common analog value from each pixel~~; and

    transmitting the first amplified analog signal and the second amplified analog signal to an analog-to-digital converter circuit;

    wherein the first gain and the second gain are applied to each pixel of the first set of pixels.

2. (Original) The apparatus of Claim 1, wherein the apparatus is operable such that the analog signal is amplified utilizing the first gain simultaneously with the amplification of the analog signal utilizing the second gain.

Inventor: William Rivard et al.
Application No. : 14/823,993

Attorney's Docket No.: DUELP019
Page : 3 of 15

3. (Original) The apparatus of Claim 1, wherein the apparatus is operable such that the analog signal is amplified utilizing the first gain in serial with the amplification of the analog signal utilizing the second gain.

4. (Previously presented) The apparatus of Claim 1, wherein the apparatus is operable such that the first amplified analog signal is converted to a first digital signal, and the second amplified analog signal is converted to a second digital signal.

5. (Original) The apparatus of Claim 4, wherein the first amplified analog signal is converted to the first digital signal concurrent with the conversion of the second amplified analog signal to the second digital signal.

6. (Original) The apparatus of Claim 4, wherein the apparatus is operable such that the first digital signal has a first light sensitivity value associated therewith and the second digital signal has a second light sensitivity value associated therewith.

7. (Original) The apparatus of Claim 4, wherein the apparatus is operable such that the first digital signal and the second digital signal are blended.

8. (Original) The apparatus of Claim 4, wherein the apparatus is operable such that the first digital signal and the second digital signal are blended, in response to user input.

9. (Original) The apparatus of Claim 4, wherein the apparatus is operable such that sliding indicia is displayed and the first digital signal and the second digital signal are blended, in response to the sliding indicia being manipulated by a user.

10. (Original) The apparatus of Claim 4, wherein the apparatus is operable such that the first digital signal and the second digital signal are combined, resulting in at least a portion of a high dynamic range (HDR) image.

Inventor: William Rivard et al.
Application No. : 14/823,993

Attorney's Docket No.: DUELP019
Page : 4 of 15

11. (Previously presented) The apparatus of Claim 4, wherein the apparatus is operable such that at least one of the first digital signal or the second digital signal is further combined with at least a portion of another array.

12. (Original) The apparatus of Claim 1, wherein a first digital value specifies the first gain, and a second digital value specifies the second gain.

13. (Original) The apparatus of Claim 12, wherein at least one of the first digital value and the second digital value is selected based on a mapping from the at least one of the first digital value and the second digital value to an ISO value, and the ISO value is selected by at least one of software executing on the apparatus and a user.

14. (Previously presented) The apparatus of Claim 11, wherein the apparatus is operable such that the another array is associated with a high dynamic range (HDR) image.

15. (Currently amended) The apparatus of Claim 1, wherein the first amplified analog signal and the second amplified analog signal each include gain-adjusted analog pixel data representative of a common analog value <u>based on the first set of pixels</u><s>from each pixel of the image sensor</s>.

16. (Previously presented) The apparatus of Claim 4, wherein the apparatus is operable for transferring at least one of the first digital signal or the second digital signal over a network.

17. (Previously presented) The apparatus of Claim 4, wherein the apparatus is operable for transferring at least one of the first digital signal or the second digital signal over a network for being combined remotely, resulting in at least a portion of a high dynamic range (HDR) image.

Inventor: William Rivard et al.
Application No. : 14/823,993

Attorney's Docket No.: DUELP019
Page : 5 of 15

18.   (Previously presented)   The apparatus of Claim 4, wherein the apparatus is operable for transferring at least one of the first digital signal or the second digital signal over a network for being combined remotely, and receiving at least a portion of a high dynamic range (HDR) image resulting from the combination.

19.   (Currently amended)   A computer program product embodied on a non-transitory computer readable medium, comprising:

code for allowing receipt of an analog signal associated with each pixel of <u>a first set of pixels of</u>[[n]] <u>a pixel</u> array <u>within</u>[[of]] an image sensor;

code for generating, <u>for each pixel of the first set of pixels,</u> a first amplified analog signal <u>based on the received analog signal</u> ~~associated with each pixel~~ by amplifying the analog signal utilizing a first gain~~, the first amplified analog signal including first gain-adjusted analog pixel data representative of a first common analog value from each pixel~~;

code for generating, <u>for each pixel of the first set of pixels,</u> a second amplified analog signal <u>based on the received analog signal</u> ~~associated with each pixel~~ by amplifying the analog signal utilizing a second gain~~, the second amplified analog signal including second gain-adjusted analog pixel data representative of a second common analog value from each pixel~~; and

code for transmitting the first amplified analog signal and the second amplified analog signal <u>to an analog-to-digital converter circuit;</u>

<u>wherein the first gain and the second gain are applied to each pixel of the first set of pixels</u>.

20.   (Currently amended)   A method, comprising:

receiving an analog signal associated with each pixel of <u>a first set of pixels of</u>[[n]] <u>a pixel</u> array [[of]]<u>within</u> an image sensor;

amplifying the analog signal utilizing a first gain resulting in a first amplified analog signal <u>for each pixel of the first set of pixels</u>~~associated with each pixel, the first amplified analog~~

Inventor: William Rivard et al.
Application No. : 14/823,993
Attorney's Docket No.: DUELP019
Page : 6 of 15

~~signal including first gain-adjusted analog pixel data representative of a first common analog value from each pixel~~;

amplifying the analog signal utilizing a second gain resulting in a second amplified analog signal <u>for each pixel of the first set of pixels</u>~~associated with each pixel, the second amplified analog signal including second gain-adjusted analog pixel data representative of a second common analog value from each pixel~~; and

transmitting the first amplified analog signal and the second amplified analog signal <u>to an analog-to-digital converter circuit;</u>

<u>wherein the first gain and the second gain are applied to each pixel of the first set of pixels</u>.

21. (New) The apparatus of Claim 1, wherein the second gain is based, at least in part, on the first gain and the second gain is at least one of a half stop, one stop, or two stops away from the first gain

22. (New) The apparatus of Claim 4, further comprising circuitry for:
generating, for each pixel of the first set of pixels, a third amplified analog signal based on the received analog signal by amplifying the analog signal utilizing a third gain; and
transmitting the third amplified analog signal to the analog-to-digital convert circuit, wherein the apparatus is operable such that the third amplified signal is converted to a third digital signal,
wherein at least a portion of the first digital signal, the second digital signal, and the third digital signal are combined.

23. (New) The apparatus of Claim 1, wherein the first gain and the second gain are applied to a second set of pixels of the pixel array.

24. (New) The apparatus of Claim 1, wherein first gain-adjusted analog pixel data results from the analog-to-digital converter circuit applying the first gain to the analog signal, and

Inventor: William Rivard et al.
Application No. : 14/823,993

Attorney's Docket No.: DUELP019
Page : 7 of 15

second gain-adjusted analog pixel data results from the analog-to-digital converter circuit applying the second gain to the analog signal.

25. (New) The apparatus of Claim 1, wherein first gain-adjusted analog pixel data is converted by the analog-to-digital converter circuit, and second gain-adjusted analog pixel data is subsequently converted by the analog-to-digital converter circuit.

26. (New) The apparatus of Claim 1, wherein at least one of first gain-adjusted analog pixel data or second gain-adjusted analog pixel data includes brightness corrected pixel data based on a specified ISO.

Inventor: William Rivard et al.
Application No. : 14/823,993

Attorney's Docket No.: DUELP019
Page : 8 of 15

Remarks:

Summary

Claims 1-20 were pending.

Claims 1, 15, 19, and 20 have been amended. Claims 21–26 are added herein. Support for such amendments is found, inter alia, in paragraphs [0119], [0125], [0128], [0133] – [0134], [0139], and [0140] of the present description. No new matter is introduced. Claims 1–26 are now pending, including independent claims 1, 19, and 20.

Rejections Under 35 U.S.C. 102

Claims 1-7, 10-12, 14-15, 19-20 stand rejected under 35 U.S.C. § 102(a) in view of U.S. Patent Application Pub. No. 2013/0147979 [MCMAHON]. Applicant respectfully disagrees with such rejection, especially in view of the amendments made hereinabove to each of the independent claims.

Specifically, applicant has amended the independent claims, as follows:

a[[n]] pixel array [[of]]within an image sensor, the pixel array including pixels located in one or more rows; and

circuitry for:

receiving an analog signal associated with each pixel of a first set of pixels of the pixel array;

generating, for each pixel of the first set of pixels, a first amplified analog signal based on the received analog signal associated with each pixel by amplifying the analog signal utilizing a first gain, the first amplified analog signal including first gain-adjusted analog pixel data representative of a first common analog value from each pixel;

generating, for each pixel of the first set of pixels, a second amplified analog signal based on the received analog signal associated with each pixel by amplifying the analog signal utilizing a second gain, the second amplified analog signal including second gain-adjusted analog pixel data representative of a second common analog value from each pixel; and

Inventor: William Rivard et al.
Application No.: 14/823,993

Attorney's Docket No.: DUELP019

transmitting the first amplified analog signal and the second amplified analog signal <u>to an analog-to-digital converter circuit</u>;

<u>wherein the first gain and the second gain are applied to each pixel of the first set of pixels.</u>

(see this or similar, but not necessarily identical language in the independent claims, as amended.)

With respect to the independent claims, the Examiner has relied on Figure 4J as well as paragraphs [109]-[111] from the MCMAHON reference to make a prior art showing of applicant's claimed technique "generating, for each pixel of the first set of pixels, a first amplified analog signal based on the received analog signal by amplifying the analog signal utilizing a first gain" (see this or similar, but not necessarily identical language in the independent claims).

Applicant respectfully notes that the MCMAHON reference, as relied upon by the Examiner, discloses the following:

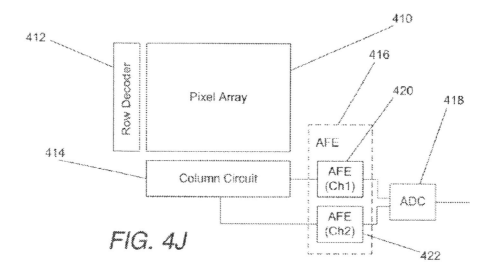

MCMAHON. Figure 4J.

[0109] A focal plane within an imager array in accordance with an embodiment of the invention can be provided with a dedicated or shared AFE. In addition, the AFE can provide amplified analog image information to a dedicated or shared ADC. The number of AFE processing channels per focal

Inventor: William Rivard et al.
Application No.: 14/823,993

Attorney's Docket No.: DUELP019

> plane and the type of analog amplifier incorporated within the AFE largely depend upon the requirements of a specific application. A focal plane including a dedicated AFE and ADC configured to enable the capture of high dynamic range image data in accordance with an embodiment of the invention is illustrated in FIG. 4I. The focal plane **410**, which can be one of many in an imager array, includes a row decoder **412** and a column circuit **414** that are configured to select pixels from which analog image information is read out. The analog image information is provided to an AFE **416** that amplifies the analog image information using different amplification gains to create amplified high dynamic range analog image information. <u>In many embodiments, specific amplification gains are applied to predetermined sets of pixels</u>. In a number of embodiments, the amplification gains are applied to the same analog image information in parallel to provide multiple versions of the analog image information that can be selected for digital conversion and/or digitally converted and selected by a processor for use in the synthesis of a high resolution image. In several embodiments, <u>the AFE applies amplification gains determined on a pixel by pixel basis</u>. The amplified high dynamic range analog image information is provided by the AFE to the ADC and the ADC digitizes the amplified high dynamic range analog image information to create high dynamic range digital image data. In embodiments where <u>the amplification gain applied to analog image information is determined on a pixel by pixel basis</u>, the high dynamic range digital image data can include a number of data bits determined by digitizing the amplified high dynamic range analog image information and at least one additional bit that indicates the amplification gain applied to create the amplified high dynamic range analog image information.

MCMAHON. Paragraph [109] – emphasis added.

> [0064] <u>In a number of embodiments, the use of programmable gain analog amplifiers enables the imager array to be configurable to operate in a standard image capture mode in which a uniform amplification gain is applied to the pixels read out from a given focal plane or a high dynamic range image capture mode in which different amplification gains are applied to the analog image information read out from the pixels in a given focal plane</u>. Where the focal planes form part of an array camera configured to synthesize a high resolution image based on captured image data using super-resolution processing, greater increases in resolution can be achieved in

MCMAHON. Paragraph [064] – emphasis added.

Inventor: William Rivard et al.
Application No. : 14/823,993

Attorney's Docket No.: DUELP019
Page : 11 of 15

However, disclosing that "amplification gains are applied to <u>predetermined sets of pixels</u>" and that "the AFE applies amplification gains determined on a pixel by pixel basis," as well as teaching that "a <u>uniform amplification gain</u> is applied to the pixels read out from a given focal plane or a high dynamic range image capture mode in which <u>different amplification gains are applied to the analog image information read out from the pixels</u> in a given focal plane" (emphasis added), as in the MCMAHON excerpt(s) relied upon, does not teach or suggest "generating, for <u>each pixel</u> of the <u>first set of pixels</u>, a <u>first amplified analog signal based</u> on the received analog signal by amplifying the analog signal utilizing a first gain" (emphasis added), as claimed by applicant.

With respect to the independent claims, the Examiner has relied on Figure 4J as well as paragraphs [109]-[111] from the MCMAHON reference to make a prior art showing of applicant's claimed technique "generating, for each pixel of the first set of pixels, a second amplified analog signal based on the received analog signal by amplifying the analog signal utilizing a second gain" (see this or similar, but not necessarily identical language in the independent claims).

However, disclosing that "amplification gains are applied to <u>predetermined sets of pixels</u>" and that "the AFE applies amplification gains determined on a pixel by pixel basis," as well as teaching that "a <u>uniform amplification gain</u> is applied to the pixels read out from a given focal plane or a high dynamic range image capture mode in which <u>different amplification gains are applied to the analog image information read out from the pixels</u> in a given focal plane" (emphasis added), as in the MCMAHON excerpt(s) relied upon, does not teach or suggest "generating, for <u>each pixel</u> of the <u>first set of pixels</u>, a <u>second amplified analog signal based</u> on the <u>received analog signal</u> by amplifying the analog signal utilizing a second gain" (emphasis added), as claimed by applicant.

Additionally, within the context of the independent claims, teaching generally that "amplification gains [are] determined on a pixel by pixel basis" as well as that "different amplification gains are applied to analog image information," as in the MCMAHON excerpt(s) relied upon, fails to teach applicant's claimed technique "wherein <u>the first gain</u> and <u>the second gain</u> are applied to <u>each pixel of the first set of pixels</u>" (emphasis added), as claimed by applicant.

The Examiner is reminded that a claim is anticipated only if each and every element as set forth in the claim is found, either expressly or inherently described in a single prior art reference. Verdegaal Bros. v. Union Oil Co. Of California, 814 F.2d 628, 631, 2 USPQ2d 1051, 1053 (Fed. Cir. 1987). Moreover, the identical invention must be shown in as complete detail as contained

Inventor: William Rivard et al.
Application No. : 14/823,993

Attorney's Docket No.: DUELP019
Page : 12 of 15

in the claim. Richardson v. Suzuki Motor Co.868 F.2d 1226, 1236, 9USPQ2d 1913, 1920 (Fed. Cir. 1989). The elements must be arranged as required by the claim.

This criterion has simply not been met by the above reference excerpt(s), as noted above.

Rejections Under 35 U.S.C. 103

Claims 8-9 stand rejected under 35 U.S.C. § 103(a) in view of U.S. Patent Application Pub. No. 2013/0147979 [MCMAHON] and U.S. Patent Application Pub. No. 2012/0069213 [JANNARD]. Additionally, Claim 13 stands rejected under 35 U.S.C. § 103(a) in view of U.S. Patent Application Pub. No. 2013/0147979 [MCMAHON] and U.S. Patent Application Pub. No. 2011/0115971 [FURUYA]. Further, Claims 16-18 stand rejected under 35 U.S.C. § 103(a) in view of U.S. Patent Application Pub. No. 2013/0147979 [MCMAHON] and U.S. Patent Application Pub. No. 2007/0030357 [LEVIEN]. Applicant respectfully disagrees and notes that such dependent claims are each allowable in view of their dependence on a respective allowable independent claim (as argued hereinabove).

Dependent Claims

Applicant further notes that the prior art is also deficient with respect to the dependent claims. For example, with respect to Claim 15, the Examiner has relied on paragraph [111] and [124] from the MCMAHON reference to make a prior art showing of applicant's claimed technique "wherein the first amplified analog signal and the second amplified analog signal each include gain-adjusted analog pixel data representative of a common analog value based on the first set of pixels" (as amended).

Applicant respectfully notes that the MCMAHON reference, as relied upon by the Examiner, discloses the following:

Inventor: William Rivard et al.
Application No. : 14/823,993

Attorney's Docket No.: DUELP019
Page : 13 of 15

> [0111] A focal plane including a dedicated AFE including two AFE channels and a dedicated ADC that are configured to generate high dynamic range digital image data in accordance with an embodiment of the invention is illustrated in FIG. 4J. The system illustrated in FIG. 4J is similar to that illustrated in FIG. 4I. The AFE illustrated in FIG. 4J includes a first AFE processing channel **420** and a second AFE processing channel **422**. The two AFE processing channels can both provide amplified high dynamic range analog image information to the dedicated ADC **418**. The presence of two AFE processing channels means that predetermined sets of pixels can be read out and provided to each of the first and second AFE processing channels **420** and **422**. The number of pixels per row (or column) that are connected to each AFE processing channel can be evenly divided or can be unevenly divided depending upon the requirements of a specific application. As discussed above, the gain of the analog amplifier in each of the AFE processing channels associated with a focal plane can be independently controlled to enable the capture of images <u>with uniform analog gain or with increased dynamic range</u>.

MCMAHON. Paragraph [0111] – emphasis added.

However, disclosing that "the capture of images" occurs "with uniform analog gain," as in MCMAHON, does not teach or suggest applicant's claimed technique "wherein the <u>first amplified analog signal</u> and the <u>second amplified analog signal</u> each include gain-adjusted analog pixel data representative of <u>a common analog value **based** on the first set of pixels</u>" (emphasis added), as claimed by applicant.

Again, as noted above, since this anticipation criterion has simply not been met by the above reference excerpt(s), a notice of allowance or specific prior art showing of each of the foregoing claim elements, in combination with the remaining claimed features, is respectfully requested.

<u>New Claims</u>

Still yet, applicant brings to the Examiner's attention the subject matter of new Claims 21-26 below, which are added for full consideration:

> 21. (New) The apparatus of Claim 1, wherein the second gain is based, at least in part, on the first gain and the second gain is at least one of a half stop, one stop, or two stops away from the first gain
>
> 22. (New) The apparatus of Claim 4, further comprising circuitry for:

Inventor: William Rivard et al.
Application No. : 14/823,993

Attorney's Docket No.: DUELP019
Page : 14 of 15

generating, for each pixel of the first set of pixels, a third amplified analog signal based on the received analog signal by amplifying the analog signal utilizing a third gain; and

transmitting the third amplified analog signal to the analog-to-digital convert circuit, wherein the apparatus is operable such that the third amplified signal is converted to a third digital signal,

wherein at least a portion of the first digital signal, the second digital signal, and the third digital signal are combined.

23. (New) The apparatus of Claim 1, wherein the first gain and the second gain are applied to a second set of pixels of the pixel array.

24. (New) The apparatus of Claim 1, wherein first gain-adjusted analog pixel data results from the analog-to-digital converter circuit applying the first gain to the analog signal, and second gain-adjusted analog pixel data results from the analog-to-digital converter circuit applying the second gain to the analog signal.

25. (New) The apparatus of Claim 1, wherein first gain-adjusted analog pixel data is converted by the analog-to-digital converter circuit, and second gain-adjusted analog pixel data is subsequently converted by the analog-to-digital converter circuit.

26. (New) The apparatus of Claim 1, wherein at least one of first gain-adjusted analog pixel data or second gain-adjusted analog pixel data includes brightness corrected pixel data based on a specified ISO.

Again, a notice of allowance or a proper prior art showing of all of applicant's claim limitations, in combination with the remaining claim elements, is respectfully requested.

Conclusion

It is believed that all of the pending issues have been addressed. Claims 1-26 are in condition for allowance per the claim amendments herein.

However, the absence of a reply to a specific rejection, issue, or comment does not signify agreement with or concession of that rejection, issue, or comment. In addition, because the arguments made above may not be exhaustive, there may be reasons for patentability of any or all pending claims (or other claims) that have not been expressed. Still yet, nothing in this reply should be construed as intention to concede any issue with regard to any claim, except as specifically stated in this reply. Finally, it should be noted that no claims are intended to be construed under 35 U.S.C. 112, paragraph 6.

In the event a telephone conversation would expedite the prosecution of this application, the Examiner may reach the undersigned at (408) 971-2573 or britten@zilkakotab.com. Applicant

Inventor: William Rivard et al.
Application No. : 14/823,993

Attorney's Docket No.: DUELP019
Page : 15 of 15

does not believe that any additional fees are due. However, in the event that any other fees are due, the Director is hereby authorized to charge any required fees due (other than issue fees), and to credit any overpayment made, in connection with the filing of this paper to Deposit Account No. 50-1351 (Order No. DUELP019).

Respectfully submitted,

Zilka-Kotab, PC.

/BRITTENSESSIONS/

Britten Sessions
Reg. No. 68,278

1155 N. 1st Street, Suite 105
San Jose, CA 95112-4925
408-971-2573

LINCOLN LAW SCHOOL OF SAN JOSE
INTELLECTUAL PROPERTY SERIES

EXHIBIT: OFFICE ACTION

UNITED STATES PATENT AND TRADEMARK OFFICE

UNITED STATES DEPARTMENT OF COMMERCE
United States Patent and Trademark Office
Address: COMMISSIONER FOR PATENTS
P.O. Box 1450
Alexandria, Virginia 22313-1450
www.uspto.gov

APPLICATION NO.	FILING DATE	FIRST NAMED INVENTOR	ATTORNEY DOCKET NO.	CONFIRMATION NO.
14/859,501	09/21/2015	Rohit Priyadarshi	PRIR-P0001D1	3121

127633	7590	03/01/2017

Intellectual Property Clinic
Lincoln Law School of San Jose
384 S Second Street
San Jose, CA 95113

EXAMINER
NGUYEN, THINH H

ART UNIT	PAPER NUMBER
2853	

NOTIFICATION DATE	DELIVERY MODE
03/01/2017	ELECTRONIC

Please find below and/or attached an Office communication concerning this application or proceeding.

The time period for reply, if any, is set in the attached communication.

Notice of the Office communication was sent electronically on above-indicated "Notification Date" to the following e-mail address(es):

director@lincolnipclinic.com
patent_docketing@lincolnipclinic.com
eofficeaction@appcoll.com

PTOL-90A (Rev. 04/07)

EXHIBITS 361

Office Action Summary

Application No.	Applicant(s)
14/859,501	PRIYADARSHI, ROHIT
Examiner	Art Unit	AIA (First Inventor to File) Status
THINH NGUYEN	2853	Yes

-- *The MAILING DATE of this communication appears on the cover sheet with the correspondence address* --

Period for Reply

A SHORTENED STATUTORY PERIOD FOR REPLY IS SET TO EXPIRE <u>3</u> MONTHS FROM THE MAILING DATE OF THIS COMMUNICATION.
- Extensions of time may be available under the provisions of 37 CFR 1.136(a). In no event, however, may a reply be timely filed after SIX (6) MONTHS from the mailing date of this communication.
- If NO period for reply is specified above, the maximum statutory period will apply and will expire SIX (6) MONTHS from the mailing date of this communication.
- Failure to reply within the set or extended period for reply will, by statute, cause the application to become ABANDONED (35 U.S.C. § 133).
- Any reply received by the Office later than three months after the mailing date of this communication, even if timely filed, may reduce any earned patent term adjustment. See 37 CFR 1.704(b).

Status

1) ☐ Responsive to communication(s) filed on _____.
   ☐ A declaration(s)/affidavit(s) under **37 CFR 1.130(b)** was/were filed on _____.
2a) ☐ This action is **FINAL**.   2b) ☒ This action is non-final.
3) ☐ An election was made by the applicant in response to a restriction requirement set forth during the interview on _____; the restriction requirement and election have been incorporated into this action.
4) ☐ Since this application is in condition for allowance except for formal matters, prosecution as to the merits is closed in accordance with the practice under *Ex parte Quayle*, 1935 C.D. 11, 453 O.G. 213.

Disposition of Claims*

5) ☒ Claim(s) *1-8* is/are pending in the application.
   5a) Of the above claim(s) _____ is/are withdrawn from consideration.
6) ☐ Claim(s) _____ is/are allowed.
7) ☒ Claim(s) *1-8* is/are rejected.
8) ☐ Claim(s) _____ is/are objected to.
9) ☐ Claim(s) _____ are subject to restriction and/or election requirement.

* If any claims have been determined <u>allowable</u>, you may be eligible to benefit from the **Patent Prosecution Highway** program at a participating intellectual property office for the corresponding application. For more information, please see http://www.uspto.gov/patents/init_events/pph/index.jsp or send an inquiry to PPHfeedback@uspto.gov.

Application Papers

10) ☐ The specification is objected to by the Examiner.
11) ☒ The drawing(s) filed on <u>09/21/15</u> is/are: a) ☒ accepted or b) ☐ objected to by the Examiner.
    Applicant may not request that any objection to the drawing(s) be held in abeyance. See 37 CFR 1.85(a).
    Replacement drawing sheet(s) including the correction is required if the drawing(s) is objected to. See 37 CFR 1.121(d).

Priority under 35 U.S.C. § 119

12) ☐ Acknowledgment is made of a claim for foreign priority under 35 U.S.C. § 119(a)-(d) or (f).
    Certified copies:
    a) ☐ All   b) ☐ Some**   c) ☐ None of the:
      1. ☐ Certified copies of the priority documents have been received.
      2. ☐ Certified copies of the priority documents have been received in Application No. _____.
      3. ☐ Copies of the certified copies of the priority documents have been received in this National Stage application from the International Bureau (PCT Rule 17.2(a)).
** See the attached detailed Office action for a list of the certified copies not received.

Attachment(s)
1) ☒ Notice of References Cited (PTO-892)
2) ☒ Information Disclosure Statement(s) (PTO/SB/08a and/or PTO/SB/08b) Paper No(s)/Mail Date <u>09/24/15</u>.
3) ☐ Interview Summary (PTO-413) Paper No(s)/Mail Date _____.
4) ☐ Other: _____.

U.S. Patent and Trademark Office
PTOL-326 (Rev. 11-13)   Office Action Summary   Part of Paper No./Mail Date 20151102

Application/Control Number: 14/859,501 Page 2
Art Unit: 2853

DETAILED ACTION

Notice of Pre-AIA or AIA Status

1. The present application, filed on or after March 16, 2013, is being examined under the first inventor to file provisions of the AIA.

Claim Rejections - 35 USC § 103

2. The following is a quotation of 35 U.S.C. 103 which forms the basis for all obviousness rejections set forth in this Office action:

> A patent for a claimed invention may not be obtained, notwithstanding that the claimed invention is not identically disclosed as set forth in section 102 of this title, if the differences between the claimed invention and the prior art are such that the claimed invention as a whole would have been obvious before the effective filing date of the claimed invention to a person having ordinary skill in the art to which the claimed invention pertains. Patentability shall not be negated by the manner in which the invention was made.

3. Claims 1-6 are rejected under 35 U.S.C. 103 as being unpatentable over Matsumoto (U.S. Patent 6,543,874) in view of Cook et al. (U.S. Patent 7,938,532)

Re-claim 1, Matsumoto (see fig.1C, 4A, 4B) discloses elements of the instant claimed method, comprising:

performing one or more multi-pass printing operations on an arbitrary surface using an untethered printing device to create markings on the arbitrary surface, wherein the multi-pass printing operation(s) comprise(s):

moving the untethered printing device along the arbitrary surface; and

creating the markings by either:

Application/Control Number: 14/859,501   Page 3
Art Unit: 2853

engaging the arbitrary surface with a stylus; or depositing a printing material on the arbitrary surface. (see col.4, line 52-col.5, line 30)

Re-claim 2, 3, wherein the one or more multi-pass printing operation(s) further comprise(s) moving a print head of the untethered printing device within a housing of the untethered printing device; wherein the print head moves within the housing in a different direction than a direction along which the untethered printing device moves along the arbitrary surface during at least one of the one or more multi-pass printing operation(s). (see col.8, lines 24-43; by way of the printer structure (frame 62) and the head (70) arrangement, the printer is more than capable executing relative movement of the printer by the user in one direction while moving the printhead in other direction based on the print pattern detection and position information of the head/nozzle.)

Re-claim 4, wherein creating the markings on the arbitrary surface further comprises positioning the print head within a 1-millimeter threshold vertical distance of the arbitrary surface. (col.7, lines 10-22)

Re-claim 5, receiving a predetermined print pattern, wherein moving the untethered printing device along the arbitrary surface and creating the markings on the arbitrary surface are each based on the predetermined print pattern. (inherently disclosed by the printer)

Re-claim 6, the method further comprising cooperatively creating the markings based on the predetermined print pattern using a plurality of the untethered printing devices, wherein each of the plurality of untethered printing devices is configured to simultaneously perform one or more multi-pass printing operations corresponding to a

Application/Control Number: 14/859,501 Page 4
Art Unit: 2853

unique portion of the predetermined print pattern. (the manner in which the printhead performed by either simultaneously or sequentially is well-known and well capable by any printer in the art)

Re-claim 1, Matsumoto discloses the printhead (18) having a large number of nozzles as noted above (see col.4, lines 56-61) with the exception of the markings are characterized by a resolution of at least 300 dots per inch (DPI).

Cook et al. (col.4, lines 36-49) discloses the handheld printhead having a nozzle row comprising 300 nozzles where the printhead height having a vertical resolution at 600dpi. Therefore, it would have been obvious to one of ordinary skill in the art at the time the invention was made to modify the number of nozzles in Matsumoto according to the basic teachings of Cook et al. for the purpose of increasing printing resolution.

4. Claims 7-8 are rejected under 35 U.S.C. 103 as being unpatentable over Matsumoto (U.S. Patent 6,543,874) in view of Cook et al. (U.S. Patent 7,938,532), as applied to claims 1-6 above, and further in view of Noe et al. (U.S. Patent 7,748,839)

Matsumoto, as modified by Cook et al. discloses the instant claimed subject matter as noted above with the exception of suspending operation of the device during at least one of the multi-pass printing operation(s):

removing the device from the arbitrary surface;

replacing the device on the arbitrary surface in at least one of:

a different position than a position from which the device was removed from the arbitrary surface; and

Application/Control Number: 14/859,501 Page 5
Art Unit: 2853

a different orientation than an orientation from which the device was removed from the arbitrary surface; and

navigating the device to the position from which the device was removed from the arbitrary surface and the orientation from which the device was removed from the arbitrary surface; and

resuming the suspended operation of the device; wherein the navigating further comprises:

detecting a last-printed position using one or more optical sensors; and

positioning and orienting the device based on the detected last-printed position.

Noe et al. generally discloses a robust and random method for printing with a handheld printer utilizing reference, a location pattern (40), and a guide pattern (41) (see col.4, line 42-col.6, line 29) for validating or recalibrating position during printing and/or reacquire position to complete an interrupted or lost print job. It would have been obvious to one of ordinary skill in the art at the time the invention was made to apply the teachings of Noe et al. in the printer structure of Matsumoto. The reasons for doing such would have been to provide a robust technique to assume or continue printing when printer location is lost or interrupted.

Application/Control Number: 14/859,501 Page 6
Art Unit: 2853

Pertinent Prior art

5. The prior art made of record and not relied upon is considered pertinent to applicant's disclosure.

U.S. Patent 6,310,640 to Askeland discloses multipass printmodes (see abs)

U.S. Patent 9,205,671 to Simmon discloses utilizing for calibrating the positioning (col.6, lines 33-43)

Patent Application Information Retrieval (PAIR)

6. Information regarding the status of an application may be obtained from the Patent Application Information Retrieval (PAIR) system. Status information for published applications may be obtained from either Private PAIR or Public PAIR. Status information for unpublished applications is available through Private PAIR only. For more information about the PAIR system, see http://pair-direct.uspto.gov. Should you have questions on access to the Private PAIR system, contact the Electronic Business Center (EBC) at 866-217-9197 (toll-free).

Contact Information

7. Any inquiry concerning this communication should be directed to examiner Thinh Nguyen at telephone number (571) 272-2257. The examiner can generally be reached Mon-Thurs 7:30A – 5:00P (first week); Mon-Thurs 7:30AM – 5:00PM; Fri 7:30AM – 4PM (second week). The official fax phone number for the organization is (571) 273-8300. The examiner supervisor, Matthew Luu, can also be reached at (571) 272-7663.

Application/Control Number: 14/859,501
Art Unit: 2853

/Thinh H Nguyen/

Primary Examiner, Art Unit 2861
February 2, 2017

LINCOLN LAW SCHOOL OF SAN JOSE
INTELLECTUAL PROPERTY SERIES

EXHIBIT: OFFICE ACTION RESPONSE

IN THE UNITED STATES PATENT AND TRADEMARK OFFICE

Application No.: 14/859,501	Examiner: Thinh H NGUYEN
Applicant: Rohit Priyadarshi	Docket No.: PRIR-P0001D1
File Date: 2015-09-21	Confirmation No.: 3121
Title: Arbitrary Surface Printing Device for Untethered Multi-Pass Printing	Date: May 24 2017

AMENDMENT A

Commissioner for Patents
P.O. Box 1450
Alexandria VA 22313-1450

Examiner:

In response to the communication mailed 2017-03-01 (hereafter "Non Final Office Action" or "NFOA"), please consider the following amendments believed to place the claims in condition for allowance.

Application No.: 14/859,501
Date: Apr 13, 2017
Reply to Office Action of 2017-03-01

Amendments to the Claims:

The listing of amended claims follow:

1. (Currently amended) A method, comprising:

    performing one or more multi-pass printing operations on an arbitrary surface using an untethered printing device to create markings on the arbitrary surface,

    wherein the multi-pass printing operation(s) comprise(s):

    moving the untethered printing device along the arbitrary surface, <u>wherein the untethered printing device is capable of rotating around a central axis</u>; and

    creating the markings by either: engaging the arbitrary surface with a stylus; or depositing a printing material on the arbitrary surface, and

    wherein the markings are characterized by a resolution of at least 300 dots per inch (DPI).

2. (original) The method as recited in claim 1, wherein the one or more multi-pass printing operation(s) further comprise(s) moving a print head of the untethered printing device within a housing of the untethered printing device.

3. (original) The method as recited in claim 2, wherein the print head moves within the housing in a different direction than a direction along which the untethered printing device moves along the arbitrary surface during at least one of the one or more multi-pass printing operation(s).

4. (original) The method as recited in claim 1, wherein creating the markings on the arbitrary surface further comprises positioning the print head within a 1-millimeter threshold vertical distance of the arbitrary surface.

5. (original) The method as recited in claim 1, further comprising: receiving a predetermined print pattern,

Application No.: 14/859,501
Date: Apr 13, 2017
Reply to Office Action of 2017-03-01

wherein moving the untethered printing device along the arbitrary surface and creating the markings on the arbitrary surface are each based on the predetermined print pattern.

6. (original) The method as recited in claim 5, further comprising cooperatively creating the markings based on the predetermined print pattern using a plurality of the untethered printing devices, wherein each of the plurality of untethered printing devices is configured to simultaneously perform one or more multi-pass printing operations corresponding to a unique portion of the predetermined print pattern.

7. (original) The method as recited in claim 1, further comprising:
suspending operation of the device during at least one of the multi-pass printing operation(s):
removing the device from the arbitrary surface;
replacing the device on the arbitrary surface in at least one of:
a different position than a position from which the device was removed from the arbitrary surface; and
a different orientation than an orientation from which the device was removed from the arbitrary surface; and navigating the device to the position from which the device was removed from the arbitrary surface and the orientation from which the device was removed from the arbitrary surface; and resuming the suspended operation of the device.

8. (original) The method as recited in claim 7, wherein the navigating further comprises:
detecting a last-printed position using one or more optical sensors; and
positioning and orienting the device based on the detected last-printed position.

Application No.: 14/859,501
Date: Apr 13, 2017
Reply to Office Action of 2017-03-01

Remarks:

Summary

Claims 1-8 were pending.

Claim 1 is amended herein. No new matter is introduced. Support for such amendments is found, inter alia, in paragraph(s) [0063] of the present application. Claims 1-8 are now pending, including independent claim 1.

Rejections Under 35 U.S.C. 103

Claims 1-6 stand rejected under 35 U.S.C. § 103(a) in view of U.S. Patent No. 6,543,874 [MATSUMOTO] and U.S. Patent No. 7,938,532 [COOK]. Additionally, Claims 7-8 stand rejected under 35 U.S.C. § 103(a) in view of U.S. Patent No. 6,543,874 [MATSUMOTO] and U.S. Patent No. 7,938,532 [COOK] and further in view of U.S. Patent No. 7,748,839 [Noe]. Applicant respectfully disagrees with such rejection, especially in view of the amendments made hereinabove to the independent claims.

Specifically, applicant has amended the independent claim, as follows: "moving the untethered printing device along the arbitrary surface, wherein the untethered printing device is capable of rotating around a central axis" (as amended).

With respect to the independent claims, the Examiner has relied on Figures 1C, 4A, and 4B from the MATSUMOTO reference to make a prior art showing of applicant's claimed technique "moving the untethered printing device along the arbitrary surface, wherein the untethered printing device is capable of rotating around a central axis."

Applicant respectfully notes that the MATSUMOTO reference, as relied upon by the Examiner, discloses that:

Application No.: 14/859,501
Date: Apr 13, 2017
Reply to Office Action of 2017-03-01

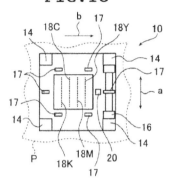

MATSUMOTO, Figure 1C

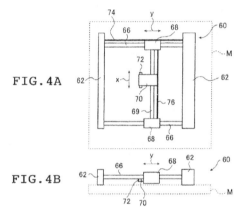

MATSUMOTO, Figures 4A and 4B

Further, MATSUMOTO discloses that:

> The printer **10** records images on a recording medium other than a human body (a recording sheet P in the example shown). The user brings the leg portions of the printer **10** into contact with the recording medium (the recording sheet P), with the ink ejecting surface facing the medium, and manually moves the printer **10** (performs scanning) in a <u>predetermined direction</u> indicated by the arrow b (hereinafter referred to as the scanning direction) which is perpendicular to the direction of nozzle arrangement in the recording head **18** (direction indicated by the arrow a and hereinafter referred to as the nozzle row direction) to record thereby a full-color image on the recording medium (the recording sheet P).

MATSUMOTO, Col. 3, lines 51-64 (emphasis added).

However, disclosing that the printer is moved into a "predetermined direction", as in the MATSUMOTO excerpt(s) relied upon, does not teach or suggest "moving the **untethered**

Application No.: 14/859,501
Date: Apr 13, 2017
Reply to Office Action of 2017-03-01

<u>printing device</u> along the arbitrary surface, wherein the untethered printing device is capable of <u>rotating around a central axis</u>" (emphasis added), as claimed by applicant.

With respect to the independent claims, the Examiner has relied on Figures 1C, 4A, and 4B from the MATSUMOTO reference to make a prior art showing of applicant's claimed technique "performing one or more multi-pass printing operations on an arbitrary surface using an untethered printing device to create markings on the arbitrary surface."

In addition to the excerpts provided above, applicant respectfully notes that MATSUMOTO discloses:

> The liquid droplet ejecting apparatus includes an ejecting head having a plurality of nozzles for ejecting liquid droplets and a plurality of liquid droplet ejecting devices arranged in correspondence with the plurality of nozzles, respectively, and driven with modulation in response to signals, a detection unit for detecting a condition of a virtual surface opposed to the ejecting head or an angle detection unit for detecting an angle made by a direction, in which liquid droplets are ejected from at least a part of the plurality of nozzles of the ejecting head, and a preset reference direction, and <u>a unit for prohibiting liquid droplet ejection from at least a part of the plurality of nozzles of the ejecting head depending on a result of detection by the detection unit</u> or an angle detected by the angle detection unit.

MATSUMOTO, Abstract (emphasis added).

However, merely teaching that "liquid droplets are ejected" and that the printer includes "a unit for prohibiting liquid droplet ejection…depending on a result of detection by the detection unit," as in the MATSUMOTO excerpt(s) relied upon, does not teach or suggest "performing one or more **multi-pass** printing operations on an arbitrary surface using an untethered printing device to create markings on the arbitrary surface" (emphasis added), as claimed by applicant.

To establish a prima facie case of obviousness, three basic criteria must be met. First, there must be some suggestion or motivation, either in the references themselves or in the knowledge generally available to one of ordinary skill in the art, to modify the reference or to combine reference teachings. Second, there must be a reasonable expectation of success. Finally, the prior art reference (or references when combined) must teach or suggest all the claim limitations. The teaching or suggestion to make the claimed combination and the reasonable expectation of success must both be found in the prior art and not based on applicant's disclosure. *In re Vaeck*, 947 F.2d 488, 20 USPQ2d 1438 (Fed.Cir.1991).

Application No.: 14/859,501
Date: Apr 13, 2017
Reply to Office Action of 2017-03-01

Applicant respectfully asserts that at least the third element of the prima facie case of obviousness has not been met, since the prior art excerpts, as relied upon by the Examiner, fail to teach or suggest all of the claim limitations, as noted above.

Additionally, applicant respectfully notes that each of the dependent claims is allowable in view of their dependence on a respective allowable independent claim (Claim 1, amended and argued hereinabove).

Conclusion

It is believed that all of the pending issues have been addressed. Claims 1-8 are in condition for allowance per the claim amendments herein.

However, the absence of a reply to a specific rejection, issue, or comment does not signify agreement with or concession of that rejection, issue, or comment. In addition, because the arguments made above may not be exhaustive, there may be reasons for patentability of any or all pending claims (or other claims) that have not been expressed. Still yet, nothing in this reply should be construed as intention to concede any issue with regard to any claim, except as specifically stated in this reply. Finally, it should be noted that no claims are intended to be construed under 35 U.S.C. 112, paragraph 6.

In the event a telephone conversation would expedite the prosecution of this application, the Examiner may reach the undersigned at (408) 977-7227.

Respectfully submitted,

IP Clinic at Lincoln Law School

By_____/Britten Sessions/_____

Britten Sessions
Reg. No. 68278
IP Clinic at Lincoln Law School
384 S Second St.
San Jose, California 95113
Phone (408) 977-7227
Fax (408) 977-7228

LINCOLN LAW SCHOOL OF SAN JOSE
INTELLECTUAL PROPERTY SERIES

EXHIBIT: OFFICE ACTION

EXHIBITS

UNITED STATES PATENT AND TRADEMARK OFFICE

UNITED STATES DEPARTMENT OF COMMERCE
United States Patent and Trademark Office
Address: COMMISSIONER FOR PATENTS
P.O. Box 1450
Alexandria, Virginia 22313-1450
www.uspto.gov

APPLICATION NO.	FILING DATE	FIRST NAMED INVENTOR	ATTORNEY DOCKET NO.	CONFIRMATION NO.
14/887,211	10/19/2015	William Guie Rivard	DUELP021A	8388

135841   7590   01/17/2017
Zilka-Kotab, PC - DUEL
1155 N. 1st St.
Suite 105
SAN JOSE, CA 95112

EXAMINER
DAGNEW, MEKONNEN D

ART UNIT	PAPER NUMBER
2664	

NOTIFICATION DATE	DELIVERY MODE
01/17/2017	ELECTRONIC

Please find below and/or attached an Office communication concerning this application or proceeding.

The time period for reply, if any, is set in the attached communication.

Notice of the Office communication was sent electronically on above-indicated "Notification Date" to the following e-mail address(es):

zk-uspto@zilkakotab.com
eofficeaction@appcoll.com

PTOL-90A (Rev. 04/07)

378   PATENT PROSECUTION WORKBOOK

Office Action Summary	Application No. 14/887,211	Applicant(s) RIVARD ET AL.
	Examiner MEKONNEN DAGNEW	Art Unit 2664 AIA (First Inventor to File) Status Yes

-- *The MAILING DATE of this communication appears on the cover sheet with the correspondence address* --

Period for Reply

A SHORTENED STATUTORY PERIOD FOR REPLY IS SET TO EXPIRE <u>3</u> MONTHS FROM THE MAILING DATE OF THIS COMMUNICATION.
- Extensions of time may be available under the provisions of 37 CFR 1.136(a). In no event, however, may a reply be timely filed after SIX (6) MONTHS from the mailing date of this communication.
- If NO period for reply is specified above, the maximum statutory period will apply and will expire SIX (6) MONTHS from the mailing date of this communication.
- Failure to reply within the set or extended period for reply will, by statute, cause the application to become ABANDONED (35 U.S.C. § 133). Any reply received by the Office later than three months after the mailing date of this communication, even if timely filed, may reduce any earned patent term adjustment. See 37 CFR 1.704(b).

Status

1) ☒ Responsive to communication(s) filed on <u>12/01/2016</u>.
   ☐ A declaration(s)/affidavit(s) under **37 CFR 1.130(b)** was/were filed on _____.
2a) ☐ This action is **FINAL**.   2b) ☒ This action is non-final.
3) ☐ An election was made by the applicant in response to a restriction requirement set forth during the interview on _____; the restriction requirement and election have been incorporated into this action.
4) ☐ Since this application is in condition for allowance except for formal matters, prosecution as to the merits is closed in accordance with the practice under *Ex parte Quayle*, 1935 C.D. 11, 453 O.G. 213.

Disposition of Claims*

5) ☒ Claim(s) <u>1-20</u> is/are pending in the application.
   5a) Of the above claim(s) _____ is/are withdrawn from consideration.
6) ☐ Claim(s) _____ is/are allowed.
7) ☒ Claim(s) <u>1-20</u> is/are rejected.
8) ☐ Claim(s) _____ is/are objected to.
9) ☐ Claim(s) _____ are subject to restriction and/or election requirement.

* If any claims have been determined <u>allowable</u>, you may be eligible to benefit from the **Patent Prosecution Highway** program at a participating intellectual property office for the corresponding application. For more information, please see http://www.uspto.gov/patents/init_events/pph/index.jsp or send an inquiry to PPHfeedback@uspto.gov.

Application Papers

10) ☐ The specification is objected to by the Examiner.
11) ☐ The drawing(s) filed on _____ is/are: a) ☐ accepted or b) ☐ objected to by the Examiner.
      Applicant may not request that any objection to the drawing(s) be held in abeyance. See 37 CFR 1.85(a).
      Replacement drawing sheet(s) including the correction is required if the drawing(s) is objected to. See 37 CFR 1.121(d).

Priority under 35 U.S.C. § 119

12) ☐ Acknowledgment is made of a claim for foreign priority under 35 U.S.C. § 119(a)-(d) or (f).
  Certified copies:
    a) ☐ All   b) ☐ Some**   c) ☐ None of the:
    1. ☐ Certified copies of the priority documents have been received.
    2. ☐ Certified copies of the priority documents have been received in Application No. _____.
    3. ☐ Copies of the certified copies of the priority documents have been received in this National Stage application from the International Bureau (PCT Rule 17.2(a)).

** See the attached detailed Office action for a list of the certified copies not received.

Attachment(s)

1) ☐ Notice of References Cited (PTO-892)
2) ☐ Information Disclosure Statement(s) (PTO/SB/08a and/or PTO/SB/08b) Paper No(s)/Mail Date _____.
3) ☐ Interview Summary (PTO-413) Paper No(s)/Mail Date. _____.
4) ☐ Other: _____.

U.S. Patent and Trademark Office
PTOL-326 (Rev. 11-13)   Office Action Summary   Part of Paper No./Mail Date 20170109

Application/Control Number: 14/887,211
Art Unit: 2664

Page 2

DETAILED ACTION

1. The present application, filed on or after March 16, 2013, is being examined under the first inventor to file provisions of the AIA.

Continued Examination Under 37 CFR 1.114

2. A request for continued examination under 37 CFR 1.114, including the fee set forth in 37 CFR 1.17(e), was filed in this application after final rejection. Since this application is eligible for continued examination under 37 CFR 1.114, and the fee set forth in 37 CFR 1.17(e) has been timely paid, the finality of the previous Office action has been withdrawn pursuant to 37 CFR 1.114. Applicant's submission filed on 12/01/2016 has been entered.

Claim Rejections - 35 USC § 101

3. 35 U.S.C. 101 reads as follows:

> Whoever invents or discovers any new and useful process, machine, manufacture, or composition of matter, or any new and useful improvement thereof, may obtain a patent therefor, subject to the conditions and requirements of this title.

the claimed invention is directed to a judicial exception (i.e., a law of nature, a natural phenomenon, or an abstract idea) without significantly more. Claim(s) 1, 9, 17 is/are directed to an abstract idea of sampling images, determining exposure, generating exposure parameters, and storing the parameters. The claim(s) does/do not include additional elements that are sufficient to amount to significantly more than the judicial exception because each of the steps recited n claims 1, 9, 17 are done by a computer to pre-compute the data for the camera for future capture of an image. These steps are identified which corresponds to concepts identified as abstract ideas by the courts, such as Obtaining and comparing intangible

Application/Control Number: 14/887,211 Page 3
Art Unit: 2664

data and Organizing information through mathematical correlations (Example Digitech Image Tech., LLC v. Electronics for Imaging, Inc). This concept relates to a process of organizing information through mathematical correlations and is not tied to a specific structure or machine. The concept described in claim 1 is not meaningfully different than those process of comparing intangible data using mathematical relationship concepts found by the courts to be abstract ideas. As such, the description in claims 1, 9, 17 of sampling images, determining exposure, generating exposure parameters, and storing the parameters is an abstract idea.

Claims 1, 9, 17 do not include additional elements that are sufficient to amount to significantly more than the judicial exception because the additional elements when considered both individually and as an ordered combination do not amount to significantly more than the abstract idea. Generic electronic device recited as performing generic functions that are well-understood, routine and conventional activities amount to no more than implementing the abstract idea with a computerized system. Thus, taken alone, the additional element do not amount to significantly more than the above-identified judicial exception (the abstract idea). Looking at the limitations as an ordered combination adds nothing that is not already present when looking at the elements taken individually. There is no indication that the combination of elements improves the functioning of a computer or improves any other technology. Their collective functions merely provide conventional computer implementation.

Claims 2-8, 10-16, 18-20 are similarly rejected because they are directed to an abstract idea without significantly more.

Application/Control Number: 14/887,211 Page 4
Art Unit: 2664

NOTE: There is no prior art rejection made for the claims. However, the 101 rejection has to be overcomed for the claims to be in condition for Allowance.

Conclusion

4. Any inquiry concerning this communication or earlier communications from the examiner should be directed to MEKONNEN DAGNEW whose telephone number is (571)270-5092. The examiner can normally be reached on Monday-Thursday, 8AM-5PM EST.

If attempts to reach the examiner by telephone are unsuccessful, the examiner's supervisor, Lin Ye can be reached on (571)272-7372. The fax phone number for the organization where this application or proceeding is assigned is 571-273-8300.

Information regarding the status of an application may be obtained from the Patent Application Information Retrieval (PAIR) system. Status information for published applications may be obtained from either Private PAIR or Public PAIR. Status information for unpublished applications is available through Private PAIR only. For more information about the PAIR system, see http://pair-direct.uspto.gov. Should you have questions on access to the Private PAIR system, contact the Electronic Business Center (EBC) at 866-217-9197 (toll-free). If you would like assistance from a USPTO Customer Service Representative or access to the automated information system, call 800-786-9199 (IN USA OR CANADA) or 571-272-1000.

/MEKONNEN DAGNEW/
Primary Examiner, Art Unit 2664

LINCOLN LAW SCHOOL OF SAN JOSE
INTELLECTUAL PROPERTY SERIES

EXHIBIT: OFFICE ACTION RESPONSE

Inventor: William Guie Rivard
Application No. : 14/887,211

Attorney's Docket No.: DUELP021A
Page : 2 of 12

Amendments to the Claims:

This listing of claims replaces all prior versions and listings of claims in the application:

1. (Previously presented) A method, comprising:

    causing a camera to sample one or more evaluation images, using a processor, wherein the one or more evaluation images are sampled at a lower resolution than images in an image set;

    selecting one or more image coordinates associated with the sampled one or more evaluation images, based on at least one of:

    a histogram of pixel intensity values within at least one of the evaluation images;

    a user tap gesture; and

    an object identification;

    determining an exposure target associated with each of the one or more image coordinates;

    generating camera subsystem exposure parameters for each image in the image set based on the exposure target associated with each of the one or more image coordinates, the camera subsystem exposure parameters comprising at least one of a sensitivity, exposure time, and aperture;

    storing the camera subsystem exposure parameters for each image in the image set;

    causing the camera to sample each image in the image set based on the camera subsystem exposure parameters for each of the images in the image set; and

    storing each sampled image in the image set.

2. (Previously presented) The method of claim 1, wherein the one or more image coordinates satisfy a corresponding exposure requirement.

3. (Previously presented) The method of claim 1, wherein the histogram of pixel intensity values includes a median of pixel intensity values representative of an ambient evaluation image.

Inventor: William Guie Rivard
Application No.: 14/887,211

Attorney's Docket No.: DUELP021A
Page: 3 of 12

4. (Previously presented) The method of claim 1, wherein the exposure target is defined by a user selected coordinate and a requirement to illuminate a scene with strobe illumination.

5. (Previously presented) The method of claim 1, further comprising determining exposure time and exposure sensitivity for the selected one or more image coordinates.

6. (Previously presented) The method of claim 1, further comprising adding the camera subsystem exposure parameters to a data structure entry for a corresponding image within the image set.

7. (Original) The method of claim 1, wherein the image set comprises one ambient image and one strobe image.

8. (Original) The method of claim 1, wherein the image set comprises two ambient images and one strobe image.

9. (Previously presented) A computer program product embodied in a non-transitory computer-readable medium that, when executed by a processor, causes the processor to perform the steps of:

    causing a camera to sample one or more evaluation images, wherein the one or more evaluation images are sampled at a lower resolution than images in the image set;

    selecting one or more image coordinates associated with the sampled one or more evaluation images, based on at least one of:

        a histogram of pixel intensity values within at least one of the evaluation images;
        a user tap gesture; and
        an object identification;

determining an exposure target associated with each of the one or more image coordinates;

generating camera subsystem exposure parameters for each image in the image set based on the exposure target associated with each of the one or more image coordinates, the camera subsystem exposure parameters comprising at least one of a sensitivity, exposure time, and aperture;

storing the camera subsystem exposure parameters for each image in the image set;

causing the camera to sample each image in the image set based on the camera subsystem exposure parameters for each of the images in the image set; and

storing each sampled image in the image set.

10. (Previously presented) The computer program product of claim 9, wherein the one or more image coordinates satisfy a corresponding exposure requirement.

11. (Previously presented) The computer program product of claim 9, wherein the histogram of pixel intensity values includes a median of pixel intensity values representative of an ambient evaluation image.

12. (Previously presented) The computer program product of claim 9, wherein the exposure target is defined by a user selected coordinate and a requirement to illuminate a scene with strobe illumination.

13. (Original) The computer program product of claim 9, further comprising determining exposure time and exposure sensitivity for the selected one or more image coordinates.

14. (Previously presented) The computer program product of claim 9, further comprising adding the camera subsystem exposure parameters to a data structure entry for a corresponding image within the image set.

Inventor: William Guie Rivard
Application No. : 14/887,211

Attorney's Docket No.: DUELP021A
Page : 5 of 12

15. (Original) The computer program product of claim 9, wherein the image set comprises one ambient image and one strobe image.

16. (Original) The computer program product of claim 9, wherein the image set comprises two ambient images and one strobe image.

17. (Previously presented) A photographic system, comprising:

a camera, configured to sample a photographic scene according to exposure parameters;

a processing unit in communication with the camera configured to:

cause the camera to sample one or more evaluation images, wherein the one or more evaluation images are sampled at a lower resolution than images in the image set;

select one or more image coordinates associated with the sampled one or more evaluation images, based on at least one of:

a histogram of pixel intensity values within at least one of the evaluation images;

a user tap gesture; and

an object identification;

determine an exposure target associated with each of the one or more image coordinates;

generate camera subsystem exposure parameters for each image in the image set based on the exposure target associated with each of the one or more image coordinates, the camera subsystem exposure parameters comprising at least one of a sensitivity, exposure time, and aperture;

store the camera subsystem exposure parameters for each image in the image set;

cause the camera to sample each image in the image set based on the camera subsystem exposure parameters for each of the images in the image set; and store each sampled image in the image set.

18. (Original) The photographic system of claim 17, wherein the one or more image coordinates satisfy a corresponding exposure requirement.

19. (Original) The photographic system of claim 17, further comprising determining exposure time and exposure sensitivity for the selected one or more image coordinates.

20. (Previously presented) The photographic system of claim 17, further comprising adding the camera subsystem exposure parameters to a data structure entry for a corresponding image within the image set.

Inventor: William Guie Rivard
Application No. : 14/887,211

Attorney's Docket No.: DUELP021A

Remarks:

Summary

Claims 1-20 were pending.

Claims 1-20 are pending, with claims 1, 9, and 17 being independent.

Rejections Under 35 U.S.C. 101

The Examiner has rejected Claims 1-20 under 35 U.S.C. 101 as being directed to non-statutory subject matter.

Applicant respectfully notes that per the recent USPTO's memorandum "Formulating a Subject Matter Eligibility Rejection and Evaluating the Applicant's Response to a Subject Matter Eligibility Rejection" ("Formulating Memo"), the USPTO has indicated that:

> "After determining what the applicant invented and establishing the broadest reasonable interpretation of the claimed invention, the eligibility of each claim should be evaluated as a whole using the two-step analysis detailed in the Interim Eligibility Guidance.

> When making the rejection, the Office action must provide an explanation as to why each claim is unpatentable, which must be sufficiently clear and specific to provide applicant sufficient notice of the reasons for ineligibility and enable the applicant to effectively respond."

Further, with respect to the first step of *Alice*, the Interim Eligibility Guidance Sheet indicates that the rejection should:

> "identify the judicial exception by referring to **what is recited** (i.e., set forth or described) in the claim and explain why it is considered an exception;

> identify any additional elements (**specifically point to claim features/limitations/steps**) recited in the claim beyond the identified judicial exception" (emphasis added).

With respect to the second step of *Alice*, the Interim Eligibility Guidance Sheet indicates that the rejection should:

Inventor: William Guie Rivard
Application No. : 14/887,211

Attorney's Docket No.: DUELP021A
Page : 8 of 12

"explain the reason(s) that the additional elements **taken individually, and also taken as a combination**, do not result in the claim as a whole amounting to significantly more than the judicial exception" (emphasis added).

Step 1 of *Alice*

The Examiner has indicated in relation to Claims 1, 9, and 17 that such claims are directed to "an abstract idea of sampling images, determining exposure, generating exposure parameters, and storing the parameters" and "[t]he claim (s) does/ do not include additional elements that are sufficient to amount to significantly more than the judicial exception because each of the steps recited in claims 1, 9, 17 are done by a computer to pre-compute the data for the camera for future capture of an image." Specifically, the Examiner has relied on support such as "[o]btaining and comparing intangible data and organizing information through mathematical correlations" from the *Example Digitech Image Tech., LLC v. Electronics for Imaging, Inc* case to support the conclusion that "claim 1 is not meaningfully different than those process of comparing intangible data using mathematical relationship concepts found by the courts to be abstract ideas."

However, merely concluding that a Claims 1, 9, and 17 may be summarized as "sampling images, determining exposure, generating exposure parameters, and storing the parameters " which the Examiner interprets as being akin to "comparing intangible data using mathematical relationship concepts" fails to provide a reasoned rationale as to how the claimed subject matter is a concept that the courts have identified as being an abstract idea. Clearly, the independent Claims 1, 9, and 17 amount more to merely "comparing intangible data using mathematical relationship concepts." For example, Claim 1 recites:

> causing a camera to sample one or more evaluation images, using a processor, wherein the one or more evaluation images are sampled at a lower resolution than images in an image set;
> selecting one or more image coordinates associated with the sampled one or more evaluation images, based on at least one of:
> > a histogram of pixel intensity values within at least one of the evaluation images;
> > a user tap gesture; and
> > an object identification;
> determining an exposure target associated with each of the one or more image coordinates;
> generating camera subsystem exposure parameters for each image in the image set based on the exposure target associated with each of the one or more image coordinates, the camera subsystem exposure parameters comprising at least one of a sensitivity, exposure time, and aperture;

Inventor: William Guie Rivard
Application No. : 14/887,211

Attorney's Docket No.: DUELP021A
Page : 9 of 12

>> storing the camera subsystem exposure parameters for each image in the image set;
>> causing the camera to sample each image in the image set based on the camera subsystem exposure parameters for each of the images in the image set; and
>> storing each sampled image in the image set.

(emphasis added — see this or similar, but not necessarily identical language in the independent claims).

At a minimum, therefore, the independent Claims include specific limitations that are vastly more than merely "comparing intangible data" using "mathematical relationship concepts."

Further, the independent Claims include aspects that are clearly more than "intangible" components. For example, Claim 1 recites:

> "causing a camera to sample one or more evaluation images, using a processor, wherein the one or more evaluation images are sampled at a lower resolution than images in an image set;"

> "generating camera subsystem exposure parameters for each image in the image set based on the exposure target associated with each of the one or more image coordinates, the camera subsystem exposure parameters comprising at least one of a sensitivity, exposure time, and aperture;"

> "storing the camera subsystem exposure parameters for each image in the image set;"

> "causing the camera to sample each image in the image set based on the camera subsystem exposure parameters for each of the images in the image set;"

> "storing each sampled image in the image set"

(emphasis added — see this or similar, but not necessarily identical language in the independent claims).

Step 2 of *Alice*

In the rejection, the Examiner has focused on one or two words of only some of the limitations (e.g. sampling images, determining exposure, generating exposure parameters, storing the parameters, etc.), which fails to specifically point out claim limitations (in their entirety) and how

Inventor: William Guie Rivard
Application No. : 14/887,211
Attorney's Docket No.: DUELP021A

such claim limitations relate to a judicial exception. Clearly, merely selecting one or two words from a few limitations fails to show how each limitation specifically is directed to a judicial exception, and fails to consider how the claim as a whole may amount to something significantly more than the judicial exception.

The Examiner is reminded that in the USPTO "July 2015 Update: Subject Matter Eligibility" memo, the USPTO has taught that "courts have held computer-implemented processes to be significantly more than an abstract idea (and thus eligible), where generic computer components are able in combination to perform functions that are not merely generic", including, for example, "digital image processing…GUI for relocating obscured textual information…and …rubber manufacturing." Further, "[t]he importance of considering the additional elements in combination was emphasized in examiner training" including, for example, "digital image processing…global positioning system…transmission of stock quote data…and …rubber manufacturing[] illustrate how generic computer components that individually perform merely generic computer functions (e.g., a CPU that performs mathematical calculations or a clock that produces time data) are able in combination to perform functions that are not generic computer functions and that amount to significantly more."

Further, the USPTO has indicated in the "Recent Subject Matter Eligibility Decision Memorandum" (November 2, 2016) that "an "improvement in computer-related technology" is not limited to improvements in the operation of a computer or a computer network per se, but may also be claimed as a set of "rules" (basically mathematical relationships) that improve computer-related technology by allowing computer performance of a function not previously performable by a computer."

Further, concluding that the dependent claims "are similarly rejected because they are directed to an abstract idea without significantly more" fails to provide sufficient details as to how such a limitation relates to a judicial exception.

Here, applicant respectfully notes that the Claims amount to more than just a mere "[g]eneric electronic device recited as performing generic functions" as indicated by the Examiner. For example, the independent claims include, at a minimum, elements which are more than a mere generic recitation of computer components:

> "<u>causing a camera to sample</u> one or more evaluation images, <u>using a processor</u>, wherein the one or more <u>evaluation images are sampled at a lower resolution than images in an image set</u>;"

> "selecting one or more <u>image coordinates associated with the sampled one or more evaluation images,</u> based on at least one of:

Inventor: William Guie Rivard
Application No. : 14/887,211

Attorney's Docket No.: DUELP021A
Page : 11 of 12

> a histogram of pixel intensity values within at least one of the evaluation images;
>> a user tap gesture; and
>> an object identification"

"determining an exposure target associated with each of the one or more image coordinates"

"generating camera subsystem exposure parameters for each image in the image set based on the exposure target associated with each of the one or more image coordinates, the camera subsystem exposure parameters comprising at least one of a sensitivity, exposure time, and aperture"

"storing the camera subsystem exposure parameters for each image in the image set"

"causing the camera to sample each image in the image set based on the camera subsystem exposure parameters for each of the images in the image set"

"storing each sampled image in the image set"

(emphasis added), all of which convey a method which is much more than merely a generic recitation of computer components.

As such, the claim language is much more than a generic recitation of components. Further, the specificity and complexity of the claims, individually and collectively, rise to a level above a mere "generic computer to perform generic computer functions." Therefore, since applicant's claim language is clearly not an abstract idea, and alternately includes unique functionality that constitutes more than an abstract idea, such language is statutory subject matter.

Conclusion

It is believed that all of the pending issues have been addressed. Claims 1-20 are in condition for allowance per the claim amendments herein.

However, the absence of a reply to a specific rejection, issue, or comment does not signify agreement with or concession of that rejection, issue, or comment. In addition, because the arguments made above may not be exhaustive, there may be reasons for patentability of any or all pending claims (or other claims) that have not been expressed. Still yet, nothing in this reply should be construed as intention to concede any issue with regard to any claim, except as

Inventor: William Guie Rivard
Application No. : 14/887,211

Attorney's Docket No.: DUELP021A

specifically stated in this reply. Finally, it should be noted that no claims are intended to be construed under 35 U.S.C. 112, paragraph 6.

In the event a telephone conversation would expedite the prosecution of this application, the Examiner may reach the undersigned at (408) 971-2573 or britten@zilkakotab.com. Applicant does not believe that any additional fees are due. However, in the event that any other fees are due, the Director is hereby authorized to charge any required fees due (other than issue fees), and to credit any overpayment made, in connection with the filing of this paper to Deposit Account No. 50-1351 (Order No. DUELP021A).

Respectfully submitted,

Zilka-Kotab, PC.

/BRITTENSESSIONS/

Britten Sessions
Reg. No. 68,278

1155 N. 1st Street, Suite 105
San Jose, CA 95112-4925
408-971-2573

LINCOLN LAW SCHOOL OF SAN JOSE
INTELLECTUAL PROPERTY SERIES

EXHIBIT: OFFICE ACTION

EXHIBITS

UNITED STATES PATENT AND TRADEMARK OFFICE

UNITED STATES DEPARTMENT OF COMMERCE
United States Patent and Trademark Office
Address: COMMISSIONER FOR PATENTS
P.O. Box 1450
Alexandria, Virginia 22313-1450
www.uspto.gov

APPLICATION NO.	FILING DATE	FIRST NAMED INVENTOR	ATTORNEY DOCKET NO.	CONFIRMATION NO.
15/145,757	05/03/2016	Risto Juhani Lempiainen	85019948US01/FUWEP013	1521

140463   7590   11/01/2016
Zilka-Kotab, PC - Futurewei
1155 N. 1st St.
Suite 105
SAN JOSE, CA 95112

EXAMINER
HARCUM, MARCUS E

ART UNIT	PAPER NUMBER
2831	

NOTIFICATION DATE	DELIVERY MODE
11/01/2016	ELECTRONIC

Please find below and/or attached an Office communication concerning this application or proceeding.

The time period for reply, if any, is set in the attached communication.

Notice of the Office communication was sent electronically on above-indicated "Notification Date" to the following e-mail address(es):

zk-uspto@zilkakotab.com

PTOL-90A (Rev. 04/07)

396 PATENT PROSECUTION WORKBOOK

Office Action Summary	Application No. 15/145,757	Applicant(s) LEMPIAINEN, RISTO JUHANI		
	Examiner MARCUS HARCUM	Art Unit 2831	AIA (First Inventor to File) Status Yes	

-- The MAILING DATE of this communication appears on the cover sheet with the correspondence address --

Period for Reply

A SHORTENED STATUTORY PERIOD FOR REPLY IS SET TO EXPIRE <u>3</u> MONTHS FROM THE MAILING DATE OF THIS COMMUNICATION.
- Extensions of time may be available under the provisions of 37 CFR 1.136(a). In no event, however, may a reply be timely filed after SIX (6) MONTHS from the mailing date of this communication.
- If NO period for reply is specified above, the maximum statutory period will apply and will expire SIX (6) MONTHS from the mailing date of this communication.
- Failure to reply within the set or extended period for reply will, by statute, cause the application to become ABANDONED (35 U.S.C. § 133). Any reply received by the Office later than three months after the mailing date of this communication, even if timely filed, may reduce any earned patent term adjustment. See 37 CFR 1.704(b).

Status

1)☒ Responsive to communication(s) filed on <u>05/03/2016</u>.
☐ A declaration(s)/affidavit(s) under **37 CFR 1.130(b)** was/were filed on _____.
2a)☐ This action is **FINAL**. 2b)☒ This action is non-final.
3)☐ An election was made by the applicant in response to a restriction requirement set forth during the interview on _____; the restriction requirement and election have been incorporated into this action.
4)☐ Since this application is in condition for allowance except for formal matters, prosecution as to the merits is closed in accordance with the practice under *Ex parte Quayle*, 1935 C.D. 11, 453 O.G. 213.

Disposition of Claims*

5)☒ Claim(s) <u>1-20</u> is/are pending in the application.
5a) Of the above claim(s) _____ is/are withdrawn from consideration.
6)☐ Claim(s) _____ is/are allowed.
7)☒ Claim(s) <u>1-20</u> is/are rejected.
8)☐ Claim(s) _____ is/are objected to.
9)☐ Claim(s) _____ are subject to restriction and/or election requirement.

* If any claims have been determined <u>allowable</u>, you may be eligible to benefit from the **Patent Prosecution Highway** program at a participating intellectual property office for the corresponding application. For more information, please see http://www.uspto.gov/patents/init_events/pph/index.jsp or send an inquiry to PPHfeedback@uspto.gov.

Application Papers

10)☐ The specification is objected to by the Examiner.
11)☒ The drawing(s) filed on <u>05/03/2016</u> is/are: a)☒ accepted or b)☐ objected to by the Examiner.
Applicant may not request that any objection to the drawing(s) be held in abeyance. See 37 CFR 1.85(a).
Replacement drawing sheet(s) including the correction is required if the drawing(s) is objected to. See 37 CFR 1.121(d).

Priority under 35 U.S.C. § 119

12)☐ Acknowledgment is made of a claim for foreign priority under 35 U.S.C. § 119(a)-(d) or (f).
Certified copies:
a)☐ All b)☐ Some** c)☐ None of the:
1.☐ Certified copies of the priority documents have been received.
2.☐ Certified copies of the priority documents have been received in Application No. _____.
3.☐ Copies of the certified copies of the priority documents have been received in this National Stage application from the International Bureau (PCT Rule 17.2(a)).

** See the attached detailed Office action for a list of the certified copies not received.

Attachment(s)

1) ☒ Notice of References Cited (PTO-892)
2) ☒ Information Disclosure Statement(s) (PTO/SB/08a and/or PTO/SB/08b) Paper No(s)/Mail Date <u>05/03/2016</u>.
3) ☐ Interview Summary (PTO-413) Paper No(s)/Mail Date. _____.
4) ☐ Other: _____.

U.S. Patent and Trademark Office
PTOL-326 (Rev. 11-13) Office Action Summary Part of Paper No./Mail Date 20161025

Application/Control Number: 15/145,757 Page 2
Art Unit: 2831

DETAILED ACTION

Notice of Pre-AIA or AIA Status

1. The present application, filed on or after March 16, 2013, is being examined under the first inventor to file provisions of the AIA.

Information Disclosure Statement

2. The information disclosure statement (IDS) submitted on 05/03/2016 was filed on the mailing date of the application on 05/03/2016. The submission is in compliance with the provisions of 37 CFR 1.97. Accordingly, the information disclosure statement is being considered by the examiner.

Claim Rejections - 35 USC § 112

3. The following is a quotation of 35 U.S.C. 112(d):

> (d) REFERENCE IN DEPENDENT FORMS.—Subject to subsection (e), a claim in dependent form shall contain a reference to a claim previously set forth and then specify a further limitation of the subject matter claimed. A claim in dependent form shall be construed to incorporate by reference all the limitations of the claim to which it refers.

The following is a quotation of pre-AIA 35 U.S.C. 112, fourth paragraph:

> Subject to the following paragraph [i.e., the fifth paragraph of pre-AIA 35 U.S.C. 112], a claim in dependent form shall contain a reference to a claim previously set forth and then specify a further limitation of the subject matter claimed. A claim in dependent form shall be construed to incorporate by reference all the limitations of the claim to which it refers.

4. Claim 19 is rejected under 35 U.S.C. 112(d) or pre-AIA 35 U.S.C. 112, 4th paragraph, as being of improper dependent form for failing to further limit the subject matter of the claim upon which it depends, or for failing to include all the limitations of the claim upon which it depends.

Application/Control Number: 15/145,757 Page 3
Art Unit: 2831

Claim 19 recites, "a system including the connector housing of claim 16, and further comprising the device that incorporates the connector housing." Claim 16 positively claims 'the connector housing' (*line 2*) and 'the device' (*line 10*) and how each limitation is related to each other. Therefore claim 19 is an improper dependent claim because the relation of the limitations 'connector housing' and 'device' explained in claim 19, are not further limiting claim 16.

Applicant may cancel the claim(s), amend the claim(s) to place the claim(s) in proper dependent form, rewrite the claim(s) in independent form, or present a sufficient showing that the dependent claim(s) complies with the statutory requirements.

Claim Rejections - 35 USC § 102

5. In the event the determination of the status of the application as subject to AIA 35 U.S.C. 102 and 103 (or as subject to pre-AIA 35 U.S.C. 102 and 103) is incorrect, any correction of the statutory basis for the rejection will not be considered a new ground of rejection if the prior art relied upon, and the rationale supporting the rejection, would be the same under either status.

6. The following is a quotation of the appropriate paragraphs of 35 U.S.C. 102 that form the basis for the rejections under this section made in this Office action:

> A person shall be entitled to a patent unless –
>
> (a)(1) the claimed invention was patented, described in a printed publication, or in public use, on sale or otherwise available to the public before the effective filing date of the claimed invention.

7. Claim(s) 1-13 and 20 are rejected under 35 U.S.C. 102(a)(1) as being anticipated by Scuteri et al. [U.S. 6,896,548].

Application/Control Number: 15/145,757 Page 4
Art Unit: 2831

Regarding claim 1, Scuteri discloses, an apparatus, comprising: a connector (fig. 4) including a first portion (fig. 1, 10) and a second portion (fig. 4, 50), and configured for being manipulated to have: a first orientation (fig. 5) where at least one of: the first portion (10) of the connector (fig. 4) is positioned for removably receiving a first card (fig. 5, 72) of a first size, or the second portion of the connector is positioned for removably receiving a second card of a second size; and a second orientation (fig. 6) where the first card (72) is stacked with the second card (fig. 5, 70) for being removably inserted in a device (fig. 7, 100) to permit electrical communication between the device (100) and the first card (72) when the first card (72) is removably received in the first portion (10) of the connector (fig. 4), and further to permit electrical communication between the device (100) and the second card (70) when the second card (70) is removably received in the second portion (50) of the connector (fig. 4).

Regarding claim 2, Scuteri discloses, wherein, in the first orientation (fig. 5), the first portion (10) of the connector (fig. 4) is positioned for removably receiving the first card (72).

Regarding claim 3, Scuteri discloses, wherein, in the second orientation (fig. 6), the second portion (50) of the connector (fig. 4) is positioned for removably receiving the second card (70).

Application/Control Number: 15/145,757 Page 5
Art Unit: 2831

Regarding claim 4, Scuteri discloses, wherein the first portion (10) of the connector (fig. 4) is movably coupled to the second portion (50) of the connector (fig. 4) such that the first portion (10) of the connector (fig. 4) and the second portion (50) of the connector (fig. 4) are movable between the first orientation (fig. 5) and the second orientation (fig. 6).

Regarding claim 5, Scuteri discloses, wherein the first portion (10) of the connector (fig. 4) is movably coupled to the second portion (50) of the connector (fig. 4) via at least one hinge (fig. 4: 38, 57).

Regarding claim 6, Scuteri discloses, wherein the connector (fig. 4) includes at least one lock (fig. 6: 522, 122) for maintaining the first portion (10) of the connector (fig. 4) and the second portion (50) of the connector in the second orientation (fig. 6).

Regarding claim 7, Scuteri discloses, wherein the at least one lock (522, 122) maintains the first portion (10) and the second portion (50) of the connector in the second orientation (fig. 6) utilizing friction.

Regarding claim 8, Scuteri discloses, wherein, in the second orientation (fig. 6) and when the first card (72) is removably received in the first portion (10) of the connector (fig. 4), the connector (fig. 6) is configured such that the first card (72) is locked in the first portion (10) of the connector (fig. 4).

Application/Control Number: 15/145,757 Page 6
Art Unit: 2831

Regarding claim 9, Scuteri discloses, wherein, in the second orientation (fig. 6) and when the first card (72) is removably received in the first portion (10) of the connector (fig. 4), the connector (fig. 4) is configured such that the first card (72) is locked in the first portion (10) of the connector (fig. 6), regardless as to whether the second card (70) is removably received in the second portion (50) of the connector (fig. 4).

Regarding claim 10, Scuteri discloses, wherein, in the second orientation (fig. 6) and when the first card (72) is removably received in the first portion (10) of the connector (fig. 4), the connector (fig. 4) is configured such that electrical communication is permitted between the device (100) and the first card (72), regardless as to whether the second card (70) is removably received in the second portion (50) of the connector (fig. 4).

Regarding claim 11, Scuteri discloses, wherein the connector (fig. 4) is configured for being removed from the device (100) without powering down the device (100).

Regarding claim 12, Scuteri discloses, wherein the first portion (10) of the connector (fig. 4) is shaped to preclude removably receiving the first card (72) in an improper orientation.

Application/Control Number: 15/145,757
Art Unit: 2831

Page 7

Regarding claim 13, Scuteri discloses, wherein the second portion (50) of the connector (fig. 4) is shaped to preclude removably receiving the second card (70) in an improper orientation.

Regarding claim 20, Scuteri discloses, a method, comprising: providing a connector (fig. 4) including a first portion (10) and a second portion (50); manipulating the connector (fig. 4) into a first orientation (fig. 5) where at least one of: the first portion (10) of the connector (fig. 4) is positioned for removably receiving a first card (72) of a first size, or the second portion of the connector is positioned for removably receiving a second card of a second size; and manipulating the connector into a second orientation (fig. 6) where the first card (72) is stacked with the second card (70) for being removably inserted in a device (100) to permit electrical communication between the device (100) and the first card (72) when the first card (72) is removably received in the first portion (10) of the connector (fig. 4), and further to permit electrical communication between the device (100) and the second card (70) when the second card (70) is removably received in the second portion (50) of the connector (fig. 4).

8. **Claim(s) 1 is rejected under 35 U.S.C. 102(a)(1) as being anticipated by Lim et al. [2014/0113495].**

Regarding claim 1, Lim discloses, an apparatus, comprising: a connector (fig. 1, 100) including a first portion (fig. 3, 151) and a second portion (fig. 3, 161), and

Application/Control Number: 15/145,757 Page 8
Art Unit: 2831

configured for being manipulated to have: a first orientation (fig. 3) where at least one of: the first portion (151) of the connector (100) is positioned for removably receiving a first card (fig. 3, 91) of a first size, or the second portion of the connector is positioned for removably receiving a second card of a second size; and a second orientation (fig. 4) where the first card (91) is stacked with the second card (fig. 4, 92, *stacked in longitudinal direction*) for being removably inserted in a device (fig. 1, 200) to permit electrical communication between the device and the first card (91) when the first card (91) is removably received in the first portion (151) of the connector (100), and further to permit electrical communication between the device (200) and the second card (92) when the second card (92) is removably received in the second portion (161) of the connector (100).

Claim Rejections - 35 USC § 103

9. The following is a quotation of 35 U.S.C. 103 which forms the basis for all obviousness rejections set forth in this Office action:

> A patent for a claimed invention may not be obtained, notwithstanding that the claimed invention is not identically disclosed as set forth in section 102, if the differences between the claimed invention and the prior art are such that the claimed invention as a whole would have been obvious before the effective filing date of the claimed invention to a person having ordinary skill in the art to which the claimed invention pertains. Patentability shall not be negated by the manner in which the invention was made.

10. **Claim 14 is rejected under 35 U.S.C. 103 as being unpatentable over Lim et al. [2014/0113495] (*Lim '495*) in view of Lim et al. [U.S. 8,961,207] (*Lim '207*).**

Lim '495 discloses, wherein the connector (100) includes hand-gripping portion (fig. 1, 102) formed thereon for receiving a manual force of the user to remove the connector (100) from the device (200).

Application/Control Number: 15/145,757 Page 9
Art Unit: 2831

Lim '495 does not disclose, wherein the connector includes an aperture formed therein for receiving a pin to remove the connector from the device.

However Lim '207 teaches, wherein the connector (fig. 4, 36) includes an aperture (fig. 4, 362) formed therein for receiving a pin (fig. 14, 6) to remove the connector (36) from the device (fig. 3, 3).

Therefore it would have been obvious to one of ordinary skill in the art before the effective filling date of the invention to incorporate an aperture formed therein for receiving a pin to remove the connector from the device as suggested by Lim '207 for the benefit of improving ejection of a connector to avoid force being directly on the connector from the user.

11.   Claim 15 is rejected under 35 U.S.C. 103 as being unpatentable over Scuteri et al. [U.S. 6,896,548] in view of You et al. [U.S. 2013/0288535].

Scuteri discloses wherein the first portion (10) is configured for removably receiving the first card (72) in a form of a subscriber identity module [Col. 4 Ln. 20], and the second portion (50) is configured for removably receiving the second card (70) in a form of a subscriber identity module [Col. 4 Ln. 20] also.

Scuteri does not disclose the second card being in a form of a memory card.

However You teaches the second card (fig. 1, 20) being in a form of a memory card (fig. 1, *micro sd*).

Therefore it would have been obvious to one of ordinary skill in the art before the effective filling date of the invention to incorporate the second card being in a form of a

Application/Control Number: 15/145,757 Page 10
Art Unit: 2831

memory card as suggested by You for the benefit of expanding the application of use of the connector and allow the connector to be used in multiple electronic devices.

12. Claims 16 and 19 are rejected under 35 U.S.C. 103 as being unpatentable over Lim et al. [2014/0113495].

Regarding claim 16, Lim discloses, an apparatus, comprising: a connector housing (fig. 1, 200) configured for removably receiving a connector (fig. 1, 100), the connector including a first portion (fig. 3, 151) and a second portion (fig. 3, 161) and configured for being manipulated to have: a first orientation (fig. 3) where at least one of: the first portion (151) of the connector (100) is positioned for removably receiving a first card (fig. 3, 91) of a first size, or the second portion (fig. 4, 92, *stacked in longitudinal direction*) of the connector is positioned for removably receiving a second card of a second size; and a second orientation (fig. 4) where the first card (91) is stacked with the second card (fig. 4, 92, *stacked in longitudinal direction*) for being removably inserted in a device (*it is known for sim card connectors to be inside electrical devices; see citations in PTO-892 form*) to permit electrical communication between the device and the first card (91) when the first card (91) is removably received in the first portion (151) of the connector (100), and further to permit electrical communication between the device and the second card (92) when the second card (92) is removably received in the second portion (161) of the connector (100).

Application/Control Number: 15/145,757 Page 11
Art Unit: 2831

Regarding claim 19, Lim discloses, further comprising the device (*it is known for sim card connectors to be inside electrical devices; see citations in PTO-892 form*) that incorporates the connector housing (200).

13. **Claim 17 is rejected under 35 U.S.C. 103 as being unpatentable over Lim et al. [2014/0113495] in view of Suzuki et al. [2011/0122030].**

Lim discloses, wherein the connector housing (200) includes a switch (fig. 8: 71, 72) for detecting whether the connector (100) the connector is removably inserted in the connector housing (200).

Lim does not disclose switch for detecting whether the first card is in the first portion of the connector.

However Suzuki teaches a switch (fig. 9, 55) for detecting whether the first card (fig. 2, 30) is in the first portion (fig. 1, *opening of 13*) of the connector (fig. 1, 13).

Therefore it would have been obvious to one of ordinary skill in the art before the effective filling date of the invention to incorporate the switch for detecting whether the first card is in the first portion of the connector as suggested by Suzuki for the benefit improving detection of a mating card inside a connector to avoid unwanted signal/power consumption.

14. **Claim 18 is rejected under 35 U.S.C. 103 as being unpatentable over Lim et al. [2014/0113495] in view of Lu et al. [2016/0006158].**

Application/Control Number: 15/145,757 Page 12
Art Unit: 2831

Lim discloses all the claim limitations except wherein the connector housing includes a lever positioned between first card contacts and second card contacts for ejecting the connector from the connector housing.

However Lu teaches, wherein the connector housing (fig. 3) includes a lever (fig. 3, 42) positioned between first card contacts (fig. 2, *top 203*) and second card contacts (fig. 2, *bottom card 200 also has contacts 203*) for ejecting the connector (fig. 2, 5) from the connector housing (fig. 3).

Therefore it would have been obvious to one of ordinary skill in the art before the effective filling date of the invention to incorporate the connector housing including a lever positioned between first card contacts and second card contacts for ejecting the connector from the connector housing for the benefit of avoiding unwanted disengagement of the connector while is connected with connector housing.

Conclusion

The prior art made of record and not relied upon is considered pertinent to applicant's disclosure. *See PTO-892 form.*

Any inquiry concerning this communication or earlier communications from the examiner should be directed to MARCUS HARCUM whose telephone number is (571)272-9986. The examiner can normally be reached on Mon-Fri. (8am-5pm) est..

Application/Control Number: 15/145,757　　　　　　　　　　　　　　　　　　　　Page 13
Art Unit: 2831

If attempts to reach the examiner by telephone are unsuccessful, the examiner's supervisor, Tulsidas C. Patel can be reached on 571-272-2098. The fax phone number for the organization where this application or proceeding is assigned is 571-273-8300.

Information regarding the status of an application may be obtained from the Patent Application Information Retrieval (PAIR) system. Status information for published applications may be obtained from either Private PAIR or Public PAIR. Status information for unpublished applications is available through Private PAIR only. For more information about the PAIR system, see http://pair-direct.uspto.gov. Should you have questions on access to the Private PAIR system, contact the Electronic Business Center (EBC) at 866-217-9197 (toll-free). If you would like assistance from a USPTO Customer Service Representative or access to the automated information system, call 800-786-9199 (IN USA OR CANADA) or 571-272-1000.

/MARCUS HARCUM/
Examiner, Art Unit 2831

/Tulsidas C Patel/
Supervisory Patent Examiner, Art Unit 2831

LINCOLN LAW SCHOOL OF SAN JOSE
INTELLECTUAL PROPERTY SERIES

EXHIBIT: OFFICE ACTION RESPONSE

Application No.: 15145757

In the Claims:

1. (Currently amended) An apparatus, comprising:

a connector including a first portion and a second portion, and configured for <u>receiving both a first card of a first size and a second card of a second size, and</u> being manipulated <u>such that the first portion is moveable with respect to the second portion so as</u> to have:

a first orientation where at least one of: the first portion of the connector is positioned for removably receiving [[a]]<u>the </u>first card of [[a]]<u>the </u>first size, or the second portion of the connector is positioned for removably receiving [[a]]<u>the </u>second card of [[a]]<u>the </u>second size; and

a second orientation where the first card is stacked with the second card for being removably inserted in a device to permit electrical communication between the device and the first card when the first card is removably received in the first portion of the connector, and further to permit electrical communication between the device and the second card when the second card is removably received in the second portion of the connector.

2. (Original) The apparatus of claim 1, wherein, in the first orientation, the first portion of the connector is positioned for removably receiving the first card.

3. (Original) The apparatus of claim 2, wherein, in the second orientation, the second portion of the connector is positioned for removably receiving the second card.

4. (Original) The apparatus of claim 1, wherein the first portion of the connector is movably coupled to the second portion of the connector such that the first portion of the connector and the second portion of the connector are movable between the first orientation and the second orientation.

Application No.: 15145757

5. (Original) The apparatus of claim 4, wherein the first portion of the connector is movably coupled to the second portion of the connector via at least one hinge.

6. (Original) The apparatus of claim 1, wherein the connector includes at least one lock for maintaining the first portion of the connector and the second portion of the connector in the second orientation.

7. (Original) The apparatus of claim 6, wherein the at least one lock maintains the first portion and the second portion of the connector in the second orientation utilizing friction.

8. (Original) The apparatus of claim 1, wherein, in the second orientation and when the first card is removably received in the first portion of the connector, the connector is configured such that the first card is locked in the first portion of the connector.

9. (Original) The apparatus of claim 8, wherein, in the second orientation and when the first card is removably received in the first portion of the connector, the connector is configured such that the first card is locked in the first portion of the connector, regardless as to whether the second card is removably received in the second portion of the connector.

10. (Original) The apparatus of claim 1, wherein, in the second orientation and when the first card is removably received in the first portion of the connector, the connector is configured such that electrical communication is permitted between the device and the first card, regardless as to whether the second card is removably received in the second portion of the connector.

11. (Original) The apparatus of claim 1, wherein the connector is configured for being removed from the device without powering down the device.

Application No.: 15145757

12. (Original) The apparatus of claim 1, wherein the first portion of the connector is shaped to preclude removably receiving the first card in an improper orientation.

13. (Original) The apparatus of claim 1, wherein the second portion of the connector is shaped to preclude removably receiving the second card in an improper orientation.

14. (Original) The apparatus of claim 1, wherein the connector includes an aperture formed therein for receiving a pin to remove the connector from the device.

15. (Original) The apparatus of claim 1, wherein the first portion is configured for removably receiving the first card in a form of a subscriber identity module, and the second portion is configured for removably receiving the second card in a form of a memory card.

16. (Currently amended) An apparatus, comprising:

a connector housing configured for removably receiving a connector, the connector including a first portion and a second portion and configured for <u>receiving both a first card of a first size and a second card of a second size, and</u> being manipulated <u>such that the first portion is moveable with respect to the second portion so as</u> to have:

a first orientation where at least one of: the first portion of the connector is positioned for removably receiving [[a]]<u>the</u> first card of [[a]]<u>the</u> first size, or the second portion of the connector is positioned for removably receiving [[a]]<u>the</u> second card of [[a]]<u>the</u> second size; and

a second orientation where the first card is stacked with the second card for being removably inserted in a device to permit electrical communication between the device and the first card when the first card is removably received in the first portion of the connector, and further to permit electrical communication between the device and the second card when the second card is removably received in the second portion of the connector.

Application No.: 15145757

17. (Original) The apparatus of claim 16, wherein the connector housing includes a switch for detecting whether the first card is in the first portion of the connector when the connector is removably inserted in the connector housing.

18. (Original) The apparatus of claim 16, wherein the connector housing includes a lever positioned between first card contacts and second card contacts for ejecting the connector from the connector housing.

19. (Canceled)

20. (Currently amended) A method, comprising:
providing a connector including a first portion and a second portion, the connector configured to receive both a first card of a first size and a second card of a second size, and to be manipulated such that the first portion is moveable with respect to the second portion;
manipulating the connector into a first orientation where at least one of: the first portion of the connector is positioned for removably receiving [[a]]the first card of [[a]]the first size, or the second portion of the connector is positioned for removably receiving [[a]]the second card of [[a]]the second size; and
manipulating the connector into a second orientation where the first card is stacked with the second card for being removably inserted in a device to permit electrical communication between the device and the first card when the first card is removably received in the first portion of the connector, and further to permit electrical communication between the device and the second card when the second card is removably received in the second portion of the connector.

21. (New) The apparatus of claim 1, wherein the first portion of the connector is hingably coupled to the second portion of the connector such that the first portion of the connector and the second portion of the connector are movable between the first orientation and the second orientation, such that:

Application No.: 15145757

in the first orientation, the first portion of the connector is positioned for removably receiving the first card; and

in the second orientation, the second portion of the connector is positioned for: engaging the first portion of the connector, while removably receiving the second card, wherein the second card extends beyond the first card to further permit electrical communication between the device and the second card when the second card is removably received in the second portion of the connector.

Application No.: 15145757

Remarks:

Summary

Claims 1-20 were pending.

Claims 1, 16, and 20 have been amended herein; claim 21 has been added; and claim 19 is cancelled. Support for such amendments is found, inter alia, in paragraph(s) 17 and 34, as well as Figs 1A and 2A-C (and the description thereof), of the present description. No new matter is introduced. Claims 1-18, and 20-21 are now pending, including independent claims 1, 16, and 20.

Rejections Under 35 U.S.C. 112(d)

Claim 19 was rejected under 35 U.S.C. 112 (d) or 35 U.S.C. 112 (pre-AIA), fourth paragraph, as failing to further limit the subject matter of the claim upon which it depends, or for failing to include all the limitations of the claim upon which it depends. Such rejection is deemed overcome by virtue of the cancellation of the claim.

Rejections Under 35 U.S.C. 102

Claims 1-13, and 20 were rejected under 35 U.S.C. 102(a) as being anticipated by SCUTERI (U.S. Patent No. 6,896,548). Further, Claim 1 was rejected under 35 U.S.C. 102(a) as being anticipated by LIM (U.S. Publ. No. 2014/0113495). Applicant respectfully disagrees, particularly in view of the amendments made hereinabove to Claims 1, 16, and 20. Specifically, applicant has amended the independent claims, as follows: "a connector including a first portion and a second portion, and configured for receiving both a first card of a first size and a second card of a second size, and being manipulated such that the first portion is moveable with respect to the second portion so as to have: a first orientation where at least one of: the first portion of the connector is positioned for removably receiving [[a]]the first card of [[a]]the first size, or the second portion of the connector is positioned for removably receiving [[a]]the second card of [[a]]the second size;" in the context claimed (see this or similar, but not necessarily identical language in the independent claims, as amended).

Application No.: 15145757

With respect to the independent claims, the Examiner has relied on Fig 1 (item 1) and Fig 4 (item 50) from the Scuteri reference, in order to make a prior art showing of the foregoing claim limitations. Applicant respectfully notes that the Scuteri reference, as relied upon by the Examiner, discloses the following:

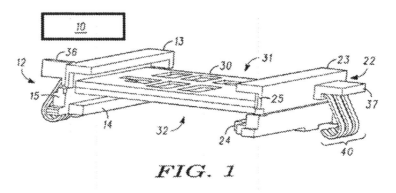

See Scuteri Fig 1 (emphasis added).

Application No.: 15145757

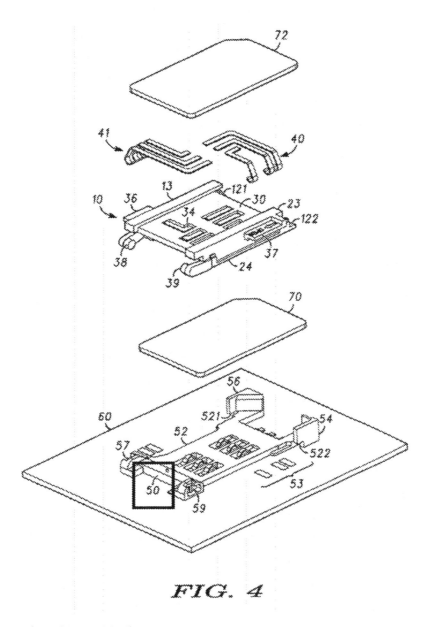

FIG. 4

See Scuteri Fig 4 (emphasis added).

Further, the description relating to such figure items indicates:

Application No.: 15145757

> An exemplary embodiment of the present invention will now be described with reference to FIGS. 1-7. FIG. 1 is a perspective view of the card holding apparatus according to the present invention, represented as a dual subscriber identity module (SIM) card holder **10**. The card holder **10** includes a first bracket structure **12**, a second bracket structure **22**, oriented parallel to and in opposition to the first bracket structure **12** and a separation member **30** contiguously disposed between the first bracket structure **12** and the second bracket structure **22**. The separation member **30**, together with the first bracket structure **12** and the second bracket structure **22** defines a first holding region **31** and a second holding region **32** that are in-line and configured to slidingly engage a corresponding SIM card or suitable electronic element.

See Scuteri Col. 2, lines 26-40 (emphasis added).

> The bottom portion **14** of the first bracket structure **12**, includes an attachment member **38** at one end thereof configured to slidingly engage a corresponding connection portion **57** of <u>a base connector **50**</u>. The bottom portion **24** of

See Scuteri Col. 3, lines 49-52 (emphasis added).

However, disclosing a "dual subscriber identity module (SIM) card holder" and "a base connector," as in the Scuteri excerpt(s) relied upon, does not teach or suggest "a connector including a first portion and a second portion, and configured for <u>receiving **both** a first card of a first size and a second card of a second size</u>, and being manipulated such that the first portion is moveable with respect to the second portion so as to have: a first orientation where at least one of: the first portion of the connector is positioned for removably receiving the first card of the first size, or the second portion of the connector is positioned for removably receiving the second card of the second size" (emphasis added), as claimed by applicant.

With respect to Claim 1, the Examiner has also relied on Fig. 1 (item 100) and Fig. 3 (items 91, 151 and 161) from the Lim reference, in order to make a prior art showing of the aforementioned claim limitations. Applicant respectfully notes that the Lim reference, as relied upon by the Examiner, discloses the following:

Application No.: 15145757

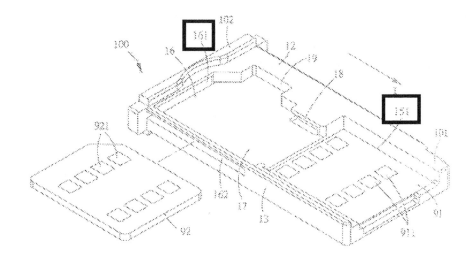

FIG. 3

See Lim Fig. 3 (emphasis added).

Further, the description relating to such figure items indicates:

> [0034] Referring to FIG. 2, FIG. 3 and FIG. 4, the tray 100 comprises a main body 101, a hand-gripping portion 102 and a polarizing portion 103. The main body 101 has a top side 11, a bottom side 12, a first side surface 13, a second side surface 14, a first receiving groove 15, a second receiving groove 16, <u>a first window 151, a second window 161</u> and a spacer 17. The bottom side 12 is positioned at an opposing side of the top side 11; the first side surface 13 and the second side surface 14 are respectively connected to the top side 11 at two opposing sides and the bottom side 12 at two opposing sides and are parallel to a lengthwise direction I of the tray 100. The first

See Lim Paragraph [0034] (emphasis added).

However, disclosing a "a first window" and "a second window," as in the Lim excerpt(s) relied upon, does not teach or suggest "a connector including a first portion and a second portion, and configured for receiving both a first card of a first size and a second card of a second size, and being manipulated such that <u>the first portion is **moveable** with respect to the second portion</u> so as to have: a first orientation where at least one of: the first portion of the connector is positioned for removably receiving the first card of the first size, or the second

11

Application No.: 15145757

portion of the connector is positioned for removably receiving the second card of the second size" (emphasis added), as claimed by applicant.

The Examiner is reminded that a claim is anticipated only if each and every element as set forth in the claim is found, either expressly or inherently described in a single prior art reference. Verdegaal Bros. v. Union Oil Co. Of California, 814 F.2d 628, 631, 2 USPQ2d 1051, 1053 (Fed. Cir. 1987). Moreover, the identical invention must be shown in as complete detail as contained in the claim. Richardson v. Suzuki Motor Co.868 F.2d 1226, 1236, 9USPQ2d 1913, 1920 (Fed. Cir. 1989). The elements must be arranged as required by the claim.

This criterion has simply not been met by the above reference excerpt(s), as noted above.

Rejections Under 35 U.S.C. 103

Claim 14 was rejected under 35 U.S.C. 103(a) as being obvious over Lim '495 (U.S. Appl. Publ. No. 2014/0113495), in view of Lim '207 (U.S. Patent No. 8,961,207). Claim 15 was rejected under 35 U.S.C. 103(a) as being obvious over Scuteri in view of You (U.S. Appl. Publ. No. 2013/0288535). Claims 16 and 19 were rejected under 35 U.S.C. 103(a) as being obvious over Lim '495. Claim 17 was rejected under 35 U.S.C. 103(a) as being obvious over Lim '495, in view of Suzuki (U.S. Appl. Publ. No. 2011/0122030). Claim 18 was rejected under 35 U.S.C. 103(a) as being obvious over Lim '495, in view of Lu (U.S. Appl. Publ. No. 2016/0006158).

Applicant respectfully disagrees, particularly in view of the amendments made hereinabove to Claim 16. Specifically, applicant has amended Claim 16, as follows: "a connector housing configured for removably receiving a connector, the connector including a first portion and a second portion and configured for receiving both a first card of a first size and a second card of a second size, and being manipulated such that the first portion is moveable with respect to the second portion so as to have: a first orientation where at least one of: the first portion of the connector is positioned for removably receiving [[a]]the first card of [[a]]the first size, or the second portion of the connector is positioned for removably receiving [[a]]the second card of [[a]]the second size," in the context claimed (see this or similar, but not necessarily identical language in the independent claims, as amended).

12

Application No.: 15145757

With respect to independent Claim 16, the Examiner has relied on Fig. 1 (items 100 and 200), Fig. 3 (items 91, 151 and 161), and Fig 4 (item 92) from the Lim reference, in order to make a prior art showing of the foregoing claim limitations. Applicant respectfully notes that the Lim reference, as relied upon by the Examiner, discloses the following:

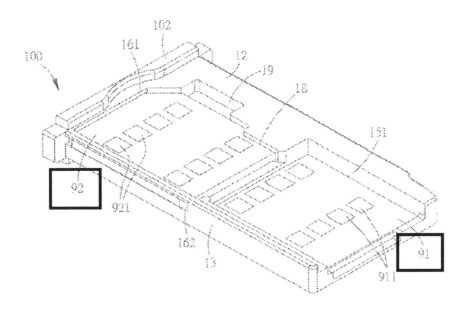

FIG. 4

See Lim Fig. 4 (emphasis added).

Further, the description relating to such figure items indicates:

> [0033] Referring to FIG. 1 and FIG. 2, a first embodiment of an electrical connector device that is applicable to load a mini-SIM card 91 and a micro-SIM card 92 and the embodiment comprises a tray 100 and a connector module 200.

See Lim Paragraph [0034] (emphasis added).

However, as indicated hereinabove, disclosing a "a first window" and "a second window," as well as a "mini-SIM card" and a "micro-SIM card," as in the Lim excerpt(s) relied upon, does not teach or suggest "a connector housing configured for removably receiving a connector, the connector including a first portion and a second portion and configured for receiving both a first card of a first size and a second card of a second size, and being

Application No.: 15145757

manipulated such that the first portion is **moveable** with respect to the second portion so as to have: a first orientation where at least one of: the first portion of the connector is positioned for removably receiving the first card of the first size, or the second portion of the connector is positioned for removably receiving the second card of the second size" (emphasis added), as claimed by applicant.

To establish a prima facie case of obviousness, three basic criteria must be met. First, there must be some suggestion or motivation, either in the references themselves or in the knowledge generally available to one of ordinary skill in the art, to modify the reference or to combine reference teachings. Second, there must be a reasonable expectation of success. Finally, the prior art reference (or references when combined) must teach or suggest all the claim limitations. The teaching or suggestion to make the claimed combination and the reasonable expectation of success must both be found in the prior art and not based on applicant's disclosure. *In re Vaeck*, 947 F.2d 488, 20 USPQ2d 1438 (Fed.Cir.1991).

Applicant respectfully asserts that at least the third element of the prima facie case of obviousness has not been met, since the prior art excerpts, as relied upon by the Examiner, fail to teach or suggest all of the claim limitations, as noted above.

Application No.: 15145757

Dependent Claims

Applicant further notes that the prior art is also deficient with respect to the dependent claims. For example, with respect to Claim 3, the Examiner has relied on items 50 and 70, as well as Figs 4 and 6 from the Scuteri reference, in order to make a prior art showing of applicant's claimed apparatus "wherein, in the second orientation, the second portion of the connector is positioned for removably receiving the second card."

Applicant respectfully notes that the Scuteri reference, as relied upon by the Examiner, discloses the following:

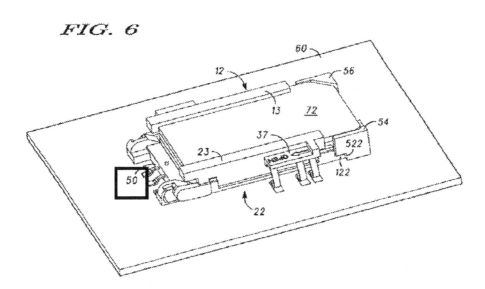

See Scuteri Fig. 6 (emphasis added).

Application No.: 15145757

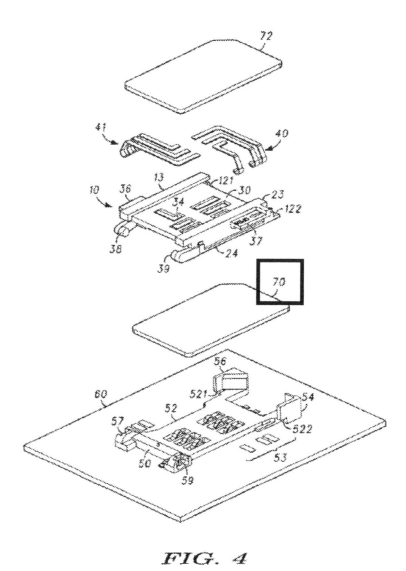

FIG. 4

See Scuteri Fig. 4 (emphasis added).

Further, the description relating to such figure items indicates:

> FIG. 6 is a schematic block diagram of the card holder 10 in operating (e.g. engaged) position relative to the printed circuit board 60. As illustrated, at least one of the SIM cards

See Scuteri Col. 4, lines 44-46 (emphasis added).

Application No.: 15145757

> Additionally, although described as having <u>the base connector 50 located along a first bottom edge of the card holder 10</u>, one of ordinary skill in the art will recognize and appreciate that a suitable base connector can be located substantially along the length of either the first bracket structure 12 or the second bracket structure 22 of the card holder 10, thereby providing for rotation along the length of the card holder. Such an alternate embodiment, and those

See Scuteri Col. 5, lines 29-36 (emphasis added).

> FIG. 5 is a schematic block diagram of the card holder 10 in an open (e.g. non-operating) position relative to a printed circuit board 60. The base 52 is located on the printed circuit board 60, and is configured to maintain the SIM cards held within the card holder 10. As illustrated, the base 52 includes a first holding portion 54 having a lip 522 formed therein. The base 52 also includes a second holding portion 56 having a lip 521 (FIG. 4) formed therein. The first and second holding portions 54, 56 each have a corresponding height (h) sufficient enough to maintain the corresponding edges of the <u>SIM cards 70, 72</u> on the printed circuit board 60. Also shown is at least one third contact member 55, which provides an electrical connection, for example, to the <u>SIM card 70</u> maintained within the second holding region 32.

See Scuteri Col. 4, lines 10-24 (emphasis added).

However, disclosing that "the card holder...in operating (e.g. engaged) position relative to the printed circuit board," including a "base connector" and a "SIM card" as in the Scuteri excerpt(s) relied upon, does not teach or suggest applicant's claimed technique "wherein, in the **<u>second orientation</u>**, the <u>second portion of the</u> **<u>connector</u>** is positioned for **<u>removably</u>** receiving <u>the second card</u>" (emphasis added), much less in the context claimed in Claims 1 and 2, where the "connector" is "<u>configured</u> for <u>receiving</u> **<u>both</u>** <u>a first card of a first size and a second card of a second size</u>" and "wherein, in the **<u>first orientation</u>**, the <u>first portion of the</u> **<u>connector</u>** is positioned for **<u>removably</u>** receiving <u>the first card</u>" (emphasis added), as claimed by applicant.

With respect to Claim 11, the Examiner has relied on Fig. 4 and item 100 from the Scuteri reference, in order to make a prior art showing of applicant's claimed apparatus

Application No.: 15145757

"wherein the connector is configured for being removed from the device without powering down the device."

In addition to the excerpts already shown hereinabove, Applicant respectfully notes that the Scuteri reference, as relied upon by the Examiner, discloses that:

> the card holder **10**. <u>FIG. 4 shows the first and second contact members **40, 41** being external to the separation member **30**, to illustrate that the first and second contact members **40, 41** provide an electrical contact between the SIM card **72** maintained within the first holding region **31** and the electrical interconnectors **53**.</u> However, in application, the first

See Scuteri Col. 3, lines 40-45 (emphasis added).

Application No.: 15145757

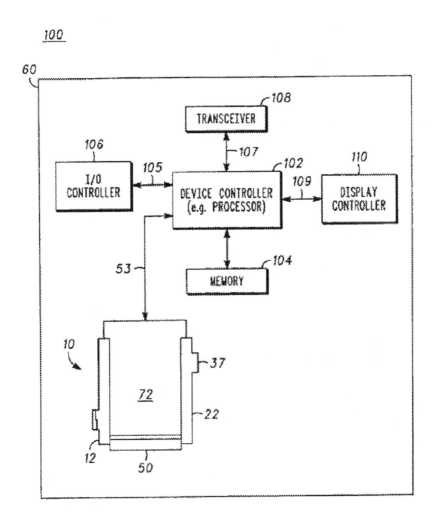

FIG. 7

See Scuteri Fig. 7 (emphasis added).

Further, the description relating to such figure items indicates:

Application No.: 15145757

> FIG. 7 is a schematic block diagram of a mobile communication device 100 incorporating the card holder 10 of the present invention. The mobile communication device 100 can be embodied as any device, such as portable electronic devices, cellular telephones, pagers, palm top computers, lap top computers, or the like that require an electronic card, such as SIM card 72, a smart card, memory card or the like, or a combination of such cards. The card holder 10 is particularly advantageous in a cellular telephone because cellular telephones are very compact communication devices wherein it is desirable to accommodate more than one card to enable maximum flexibility in the smallest possible volume for a very compact form factor. The mobile communication device 100 includes the card holder 10, a device controller 102, a memory 104, an input/output (I/O) controller 106, and a transceiver 108. The mobile communication device 100 may include a display controller 110 which is operable to control the formatting and display of data on a suitable display (not shown) based on display control signals 109 provided by the device controller 102. Each of the aforementioned components is illustrated as being maintained (e.g. carried) on a single printed circuit board 60 that is carried within a device housing (not shown). However, it will be appreciated by those of ordinary skill in the art that the components may be maintained on several printed circuit boards or other suitable mechanisms.

See Scuteri Col. 5, lines 40-65 (emphasis added).

However, merely disclosing "first and second contact members...[which] provide an electrical contact," as well as disclosing "a mobile communication device" as in the Scuteri excerpt(s) relied upon, does not teach or suggest applicant's claimed apparatus "wherein the connector is configured for being removed from the device without powering down the device" (emphasis added), as claimed by applicant.

Again, as noted above, since this anticipation criterion has simply not been met by the above reference excerpt(s), a notice of allowance or specific prior art showing of each of the foregoing claim elements, in combination with the remaining claimed features, is respectfully requested.

Application No.: 15145757

New Claims

Still yet, applicant brings to the Examiner's attention the subject matter of new Claim 21 below, which is added for full consideration:

21. (New) The apparatus of claim 1, wherein the first portion of the connector is hingably coupled to the second portion of the connector such that the first portion of the connector and the second portion of the connector are movable between the first orientation and the second orientation, such that:

in the first orientation, the first portion of the connector is positioned for removably receiving the first card; and

in the second orientation, the second portion of the connector is positioned for: engaging the first portion of the connector, while removably receiving the second card, wherein the second card extends beyond the first card to further permit electrical communication between the device and the second card when the second card is removably received in the second portion of the connector.

Conclusion

It is believed that all of the pending issues have been addressed. Claims 1-18, and 20 are in condition for allowance per the claim amendments herein.

However, the absence of a reply to a specific rejection, issue, or comment does not signify agreement with or concession of that rejection, issue, or comment. In addition, because the arguments made above may not be exhaustive, there may be reasons for patentability of any or all pending claims (or other claims) that have not been expressed. Still yet, nothing in this reply should be construed as intention to concede any issue with regard to any claim, except as specifically stated in this reply. Finally, it should be noted that no claims are intended to be construed under 35 U.S.C. 112, paragraph 6.

In the event a telephone conversation would expedite the prosecution of this application, the Examiner may reach the undersigned at (408) 971-2573 or

Application No.: 15145757

kevin@zilkakotab.com. Applicant does not believe that any fees are due. However, in the event that any fees are due, the Director is hereby authorized to charge any required fees due (other than issue fees), and to credit any overpayment made, in connection with the filing of this paper to Deposit Account No. 50-1351 (Order No. 85019948US01/FUWEP013).

Respectfully submitted,

Zilka-Kotab, PC.

/KEVINZILKA/

Kevin Zilka
Reg. No. 41,429

1155 N. 1st Street, Suite 105
San Jose, CA 95112-4925
408-971-2573

LINCOLN LAW SCHOOL OF SAN JOSE
INTELLECTUAL PROPERTY SERIES

EXHIBIT: OFFICE ACTION

UNITED STATES PATENT AND TRADEMARK OFFICE

UNITED STATES DEPARTMENT OF COMMERCE
United States Patent and Trademark Office
Address: COMMISSIONER FOR PATENTS
P.O. Box 1450
Alexandria, Virginia 22313-1450
www.uspto.gov

APPLICATION NO.	FILING DATE	FIRST NAMED INVENTOR	ATTORNEY DOCKET NO.	CONFIRMATION NO.
15/201,283	07/01/2016	William Guie Rivard	DUELP024	9478

135841	7590	12/07/2016

Zilka-Kotab, PC - DUEL
1155 N. 1st St.
Suite 105
SAN JOSE, CA 95112

EXAMINER
TEJANO, DWIGHT ALEX C

ART UNIT	PAPER NUMBER
2663	

NOTIFICATION DATE	DELIVERY MODE
12/07/2016	ELECTRONIC

Please find below and/or attached an Office communication concerning this application or proceeding.

The time period for reply, if any, is set in the attached communication.

Notice of the Office communication was sent electronically on above-indicated "Notification Date" to the following e-mail address(es):

zk-uspto@zilkakotab.com
eofficeaction@appcoll.com

PTOL-90A (Rev. 04/07)

EXHIBITS 433

Office Action Summary	Application No. 15/201,283	Applicant(s) RIVARD ET AL.
	Examiner Dwight Alex C. Tejano	Art Unit 2663	AIA (First Inventor to File) Status Yes

-- The MAILING DATE of this communication appears on the cover sheet with the correspondence address --

Period for Reply

A SHORTENED STATUTORY PERIOD FOR REPLY IS SET TO EXPIRE **3** MONTHS FROM THE MAILING DATE OF THIS COMMUNICATION.
- Extensions of time may be available under the provisions of 37 CFR 1.136(a). In no event, however, may a reply be timely filed after SIX (6) MONTHS from the mailing date of this communication.
- If NO period for reply is specified above, the maximum statutory period will apply and will expire SIX (6) MONTHS from the mailing date of this communication.
- Failure to reply within the set or extended period for reply will, by statute, cause the application to become ABANDONED (35 U.S.C. § 133).
- Any reply received by the Office later than three months after the mailing date of this communication, even if timely filed, may reduce any earned patent term adjustment. See 37 CFR 1.704(b).

Status

1) ☒ Responsive to communication(s) filed on *08 August 2016*.
   ☐ A declaration(s)/affidavit(s) under **37 CFR 1.130(b)** was/were filed on _____.
2a) ☐ This action is **FINAL**.   2b) ☒ This action is non-final.
3) ☐ An election was made by the applicant in response to a restriction requirement set forth during the interview on _____; the restriction requirement and election have been incorporated into this action.
4) ☐ Since this application is in condition for allowance except for formal matters, prosecution as to the merits is closed in accordance with the practice under *Ex parte Quayle*, 1935 C.D. 11, 453 O.G. 213.

Disposition of Claims*

5) ☒ Claim(s) *1-20* is/are pending in the application.
   5a) Of the above claim(s) _____ is/are withdrawn from consideration.
6) ☐ Claim(s) _____ is/are allowed.
7) ☒ Claim(s) *1,8,9,13,14,17 and 18* is/are rejected.
8) ☒ Claim(s) *2-7,10-12,15,16,19 and 20* is/are objected to.
9) ☐ Claim(s) _____ are subject to restriction and/or election requirement.

* If any claims have been determined allowable, you may be eligible to benefit from the **Patent Prosecution Highway** program at a participating intellectual property office for the corresponding application. For more information, please see http://www.uspto.gov/patents/init_events/pph/index.jsp or send an inquiry to PPHfeedback@uspto.gov.

Application Papers

10) ☐ The specification is objected to by the Examiner.
11) ☒ The drawing(s) filed on *07 July 2016* is/are: a) ☒ accepted or b) ☐ objected to by the Examiner.
    Applicant may not request that any objection to the drawing(s) be held in abeyance. See 37 CFR 1.85(a).
    Replacement drawing sheet(s) including the correction is required if the drawing(s) is objected to. See 37 CFR 1.121(d).

Priority under 35 U.S.C. § 119

12) ☐ Acknowledgment is made of a claim for foreign priority under 35 U.S.C. § 119(a)-(d) or (f).
    Certified copies:
    a) ☐ All   b) ☐ Some**   c) ☐ None of the:
    1. ☐ Certified copies of the priority documents have been received.
    2. ☐ Certified copies of the priority documents have been received in Application No. _____.
    3. ☐ Copies of the certified copies of the priority documents have been received in this National Stage application from the International Bureau (PCT Rule 17.2(a)).
** See the attached detailed Office action for a list of the certified copies not received.

Attachment(s)

1) ☒ Notice of References Cited (PTO-892)
2) ☒ Information Disclosure Statement(s) (PTO/SB/08a and/or PTO/SB/08b) Paper No(s)/Mail Date *08 Aug 16*.
3) ☐ Interview Summary (PTO-413) Paper No(s)/Mail Date. _____.
4) ☐ Other: _____.

U.S. Patent and Trademark Office
PTOL-326 (Rev. 11-13)   Office Action Summary   Part of Paper No./Mail Date 20161114

Application/Control Number: 15/201,283 Page 2
Art Unit: 2663

DETAILED ACTION

The present application, filed on or after March 16, 2013, is being examined under the first inventor to file provisions of the AIA.

In the event the determination of the status of the application as subject to AIA 35 U.S.C. 102 and 103 (or as subject to pre-AIA 35 U.S.C. 102 and 103) is incorrect, any correction of the statutory basis for the rejection will not be considered a new ground of rejection if the prior art relied upon, and the rationale supporting the rejection, would be the same under either status.

Claim Rejections - 35 USC § 102

The following is a quotation of the appropriate paragraphs of 35 U.S.C. 102 that form the basis for the rejections under this section made in this Office action:

> A person shall be entitled to a patent unless –
>
> (a)(1) the claimed invention was patented, described in a printed publication, or in public use, on sale or otherwise available to the public before the effective filing date of the claimed invention.

Claim(s) 1, 8, 9, 13, 14, 17, and 18 is/are rejected under 35 U.S.C. 102(a)(1) as being anticipated by Wilburn, et al. (US 20110242334 A1.)

Regarding **claim 1**, Wilburn, et al. (hereafter, "Wilburn") discloses a method (Fig. 11), comprising:

capturing, via at least one camera module (102), an ambient image comprising a plurality of ambient pixels (1104) and a flash image comprising a plurality of flash pixels (1102);

generating at least one de-noised pixel based on the ambient image (1108); and

Application/Control Number: 15/201,283 Page 3
Art Unit: 2663

generating a resulting image comprising a resulting pixel generated by combining the at least one de-noised pixel and a corresponding flash pixel (1112),

wherein the flash image is captured while an associated strobe unit is enabled and the ambient image is captured while the associated strobe unit is disabled (1102 occurs with flash; 1104 occurs when illumination discontinued.)

Regarding **claim 8**, Wilburn discloses claim 1, wherein the at least one de-noised pixel is further based on a pixel noise estimate, which is a function of at least an ambient image ISO value, an ambient pixel intensity, and a corresponding flash pixel intensity [0081 - 0089.]

Regarding **claim 9**, Wilburn discloses claim 1, wherein the at least one de-noised pixel is further based on a pixel noise estimate associated with a pixel location, wherein the pixel location is selected to correspond to an ambient pixel and a corresponding flash pixel [0084.]

Regarding **claim 13**, Wilburn discloses claim 1, further comprising using a de-noising weight to define an amount by which at least one of the at least one ambient pixel and the at least one flash pixel is made to appear visually similar to a plurality of pixels surrounding either the at least one ambient pixel or the at least one flash pixel [0028, 0087.]

Application/Control Number: 15/201,283 Page 4
Art Unit: 2663

Regarding **claim 14**, Wilburn discloses claim 1, wherein the combining of each of the at least one flash pixel with a corresponding de-noised pixel of the at least one de-noised pixel includes blending the at least one flash pixel with the corresponding de-noised pixel of the at least one de-noised pixel, the blending being performed by a mix function [0042, 0097.]

Claims 17 and 18 are variants of claim 1 and are similarly interpreted and rejected.

Allowable Subject Matter

Claims 2-7, 10-12, 15, 16, 19, and 20 are objected to as being dependent upon a rejected base claim, but would be allowable if rewritten in independent form including all of the limitations of the base claim and any intervening claims.

Citation of Pertinent Art

The prior art made of record is considered pertinent to the applicant's disclosure, but is not relied upon as a reference for the preceding sections:

- Shirakawa (US 20030090577 A1) discloses an imaging apparatus.
- Hofflinger, et al. (US 20040135912 A1) discloses a camera module.
- Ouchi (US 20050264688 A1) discloses a solid image pickup device.
- Tamaru, et al. (US 20060038899 A1) discloses a noise reduction apparatus.

Application/Control Number: 15/201,283 Page 5
Art Unit: 2663

- Wen (US 20070206885 A1) discloses an imaging system.

- Tanaka, et al. (US 20070263106 A1) discloses a photographic apparatus.

- Murayama (US 20080122933 A1) discloses a range image system.

- Terashima (US 20100194963 A1) discloses a display control apparatus.

- Furuya, et al. (US 20110115971 A1) discloses an imaging device.

- Atkinson (US 20110317005 A1) discloses a depth sensing camera system.

- Sugie (US 20150015774 A1) discloses an image control apparatus.

- Asano, et al. (US 20150092019 A1) discloses an image capture device.

Conclusion

Any inquiry concerning this communication or earlier communications from the examiner should be directed to Dwight Alex C. Tejano whose telephone number is (571)270-7200. The examiner can normally be reached on Monday through Friday 11:00-6:00 with alternate Fridays off.

If attempts to reach the examiner by telephone are unsuccessful, the examiner's supervisor, Twyler Haskins can be reached on (571) 272-7406. The fax phone number for the organization where this application or proceeding is assigned is 571-273-8300.

Application/Control Number: 15/201,283 Page 6
Art Unit: 2663

Information regarding the status of an application may be obtained from the Patent Application Information Retrieval (PAIR) system. Status information for published applications may be obtained from either Private PAIR or Public PAIR. Status information for unpublished applications is available through Private PAIR only. For more information about the PAIR system, see http://pair-direct.uspto.gov. Should you have questions on access to the Private PAIR system, contact the Electronic Business Center (EBC) at 866-217-9197 (toll-free). If you would like assistance from a USPTO Customer Service Representative or access to the automated information system, call 800-786-9199 (IN USA OR CANADA) or 571-272-1000.

/Dwight Alex C Tejano/
Examiner
Art Unit 2663

/TWYLER HASKINS/
Supervisory Patent Examiner, Art Unit 2663

LINCOLN LAW SCHOOL OF SAN JOSE
INTELLECTUAL PROPERTY SERIES

EXHIBIT: OFFICE ACTION RESPONSE

Application No.: 15/201,283
Filing Date: 2016-07-01

Amendments to the Claims:

What is claimed is:

1. (Currently amended) A method, comprising:

    capturing, via at least one camera module, an ambient image comprising a plurality of ambient pixels and a flash image comprising a plurality of flash pixels;

    generating at least one de-noised pixel based on the ambient image; and

    generating a resulting image comprising a resulting pixel generated by combining the at least one de-noised pixel and a corresponding flash pixel,

    wherein the flash image is captured while an associated strobe unit is enabled and the ambient image is captured while the associated strobe unit is disabled;

    wherein the at least one de-noised pixel is further based on a pixel noise estimate calculated by performing the steps of:

    calculating a first intermediate noise estimate based on an ambient image ISO value;

    calculating a second intermediate noise estimate based on the ambient image ISO value and an ambient pixel intensity;

    calculating a third intermediate noise estimate based on the ambient pixel intensity and a flash pixel intensity; and

    combining the first intermediate noise estimate, the second intermediate noise estimate, and the third intermediate noise estimate to create an overall pixel noise estimate.

2. (Canceled)

3. (Currently amended) The method of claim [[2]]1, wherein the first intermediate noise estimate is calculated as a smoothstep function configured to receive the ambient image ISO value as an input, a first ISO value as a left edge value, and a second ISO value as a right edge value.

4. (Currently amended) The method of claim [[2]]1, wherein the second intermediate noise estimate is calculated as a smoothstep function configured to receive the ambient pixel

Application No.: 15/201,283
Filing Date: 2016-07-01

intensity as an input, a left edge value that is a function of the ambient image ISO, and a right edge value that is an offset from the left edge value.

5. (Currently amended) The method of claim [[2]]1, wherein the third intermediate noise estimate is calculated according to a blend surface configured to receive the ambient pixel intensity and the flash pixel intensity.

6. (Currently amended) The method of claim [[2]]1, wherein generating each of the at least one de-noised pixel comprises:

   computing a patch-space sample at a location in patch-space that corresponds to a location of the de-noised pixel in a pixel-space;

   upon determining that a pixel noise estimate is above a predefined threshold, assigning the value of the patch-space sample to the de-noised pixel; and

   upon determining that a pixel noise estimate is below a predefined threshold, assigning the value of the ambient pixel to the de-noised pixel.

7. (Currently amended) A method, comprising:

   capturing, via at least one camera module, an ambient image comprising a plurality of ambient pixels and a flash image comprising a plurality of flash pixels;

   generating at least one de-noised pixel based on the ambient image; and

   generating a resulting image comprising a resulting pixel generated by combining the at least one de-noised pixel and a corresponding flash pixel,

   wherein the flash image is captured while an associated strobe unit is enabled and the ambient image is captured while the associated strobe unit is disabled;

   The method of claim 1, wherein at least one of the flash image and the ambient image is generated by combining a visible light image with an infrared image, and wherein the associated strobe unit is configured to generate at least infrared illumination for exposing the infrared image.

8. (Canceled)

Application No.: 15/201,283
Filing Date: 2016-07-01

9. (Currently amended) The method of claim 1, wherein the ~~at least one de-noised pixel is further based on a~~ pixel noise estimate is associated with a pixel location, wherein the pixel location is selected to correspond to an ambient pixel and a corresponding flash pixel.

10. (Currently amended) The method of claim [[2]]1, wherein the pixel noise estimate is calculated using a fourth intermediate noise estimate including at least one of a user input term or an image feature.

11. (Original) The method of claim 10, wherein the fourth intermediate noise estimate is used to create an overall pixel noise estimate.

12. (Currently amended) The method of claim 10, wherein [[an]]the overall pixel noise estimate is created by combined a first intermediate noise estimate, a second intermediate noise estimate, a third intermediate noise estimate, and the fourth intermediate noise estimate.

13. (Original) The method of claim 1, further comprising using a de-noising weight to define an amount by which at least one of the at least one ambient pixel and the at least one flash pixel is made to appear visually similar to a plurality of pixels surrounding either the at least one ambient pixel or the at least one flash pixel.

14. (Canceled)

15. (Currently amended) A method, comprising:

  capturing, via at least one camera module, an ambient image comprising a plurality of ambient pixels and a flash image comprising a plurality of flash pixels;

  generating at least one de-noised pixel based on the ambient image; and

  generating a resulting image comprising a resulting pixel generated by combining the at least one de-noised pixel and a corresponding flash pixel,

  wherein the flash image is captured while an associated strobe unit is enabled and the ambient image is captured while the associated strobe unit is disabled;

  wherein the combining of each of the at least one flash pixel with a corresponding de-noised pixel of the at least one de-noised pixel includes blending the at least one flash pixel

Application No.: 15/201,283
Filing Date: 2016-07-01

<u>with the corresponding de-noised pixel of the at least one de-noised pixel, the blending being performed by a mix function;</u>

~~The method of claim 14,~~ <u>wherein the mix function includes a mix function weight that is calculated according to a blend surface, the blend surface including a flash dominant region and an ambient dominant region, and the blend surface being further defined by an ambient intensity, a flash intensity, and an alpha value.</u>

16.   (Currently amended) <u>A method, comprising:</u>

<u>capturing, via at least one camera module, an ambient image comprising a plurality of ambient pixels and a flash image comprising a plurality of flash pixels;</u>

<u>performing an edge detection pass on the at least one ambient pixels of the ambient image to generate an edge-enhanced image, wherein the edge-enhanced image is used to assign de-noising weights</u>

<u>generating at least one de-noised pixel based on the ambient image; and</u>

<u>generating a resulting image comprising a resulting pixel generated by combining the at least one de-noised pixel and a corresponding flash pixel,</u>

<u>wherein the flash image is captured while an associated strobe unit is enabled and the ambient image is captured while the associated strobe unit is disabled</u>~~The method of claim 1, further comprising performing an edge detection pass on the at least one ambient pixels of the ambient image to generate an edge-enhanced image, wherein the edge-enhanced image is used to assign de-noising weights.~~

17.   (Currently amended) A computer program product embodied on a non-transitory computer readable medium, comprising:

code for capturing, via at least one camera module, an ambient image comprising a plurality of ambient pixels and a flash image comprising a plurality of flash pixels;

code for generating at least one de-noised pixel based on the ambient image; and

code for generating a resulting image comprising a resulting pixel generated by combining the at least one de-noised pixel and a corresponding flash pixel<u>;</u>

<u>wherein the flash image is captured while an associated strobe unit is enabled and the ambient image is captured while the associated strobe unit is disabled;</u>

<u>wherein the at least one de-noised pixel is further based on a pixel noise estimate calculated by performing the steps of:</u>

Application No.: 15/201,283
Filing Date: 2016-07-01

> calculating a first intermediate noise estimate based on an ambient image ISO value;
>
> calculating a second intermediate noise estimate based on the ambient image ISO value and an ambient pixel intensity;
>
> calculating a third intermediate noise estimate based on the ambient pixel intensity and a flash pixel intensity; and
>
> combining the first intermediate noise estimate, the second intermediate noise estimate, and the third intermediate noise estimate to create an overall pixel noise estimate.

18. (Currently amended) An apparatus, comprising:

    circuitry for:

    capturing, via at least one camera module, an ambient image comprising a plurality of ambient pixels and a flash image comprising a plurality of flash pixels;

    generating at least one de-noised pixel based on the ambient image; and

    generating a resulting image comprising a resulting pixel generated by combining the at least one de-noised pixel and a corresponding flash pixel;

    wherein the apparatus is configured such that the flash image is captured while an associated strobe unit is enabled and the ambient image is captured while the associated strobe unit is disabled;

    wherein the apparatus is configured such that the at least one de-noised pixel is further based on a pixel noise estimate calculated by performing the steps of:

    calculating a first intermediate noise estimate based on an ambient image ISO value;

    calculating a second intermediate noise estimate based on the ambient image ISO value and an ambient pixel intensity;

    calculating a third intermediate noise estimate based on the ambient pixel intensity and a flash pixel intensity; and

    combining the first intermediate noise estimate, the second intermediate noise estimate, and the third intermediate noise estimate to create an overall pixel noise estimate.

19. (Currently amended) A method, comprising:

EXHIBITS 445

Application No.: 15/201,283
Filing Date: 2016-07-01

> capturing, via at least one camera module, an ambient image comprising a plurality of ambient pixels and a flash image comprising a plurality of flash pixels;
>
> generating at least one de-noised pixel based on the ambient image; and
>
> generating a resulting image comprising a resulting pixel generated by combining the at least one de-noised pixel and a corresponding flash pixel,
>
> wherein the flash image is captured while an associated strobe unit is enabled and the ambient image is captured while the associated strobe unit is disabled;

~~The method of claim 1,~~ wherein a first camera module is configured to capture the ambient image, and a second camera module is configured to capture the flash image, wherein the ambient image is generated by combining two or more images by the first camera module, and the flash image is generated by combining two or more images by the second camera module.

20. (Currently amended) <u>A method, comprising:</u>

> capturing, via at least one camera module, an ambient image comprising a plurality of ambient pixels and a flash image comprising a plurality of flash pixels;
>
> generating at least one de-noised pixel based on the ambient image; and
>
> generating a resulting image comprising a resulting pixel generated by combining the at least one de-noised pixel and a corresponding flash pixel,
>
> wherein the flash image is captured while an associated strobe unit is enabled and the ambient image is captured while the associated strobe unit is disabled;

~~The method of claim 1,~~ wherein the at least one de-noised pixel is generated based on a contribution zone around each of the plurality of ambient pixels associated with the ambient image, the contribution zone being used to control the weight of each of the plurality of ambient pixels associated with the ambient image.

Application No.: 15/201,283
Filing Date: 2016-07-01

Remarks:

Summary

Claims 1-20 were pending.

Claims 1, 3-7, 9-13, and 15-20 are pending, with claims 1, 7, and 15-20 being independent. Claims 2, 8 and 14 have been cancelled. Claims 1, 3-7, 9, 10, 12, and 15-20 have been amended. No new subject matter has been added.

Allowable Subject Matter

The Examiner is thanked for the allowable subject matter of Claims 2-8, 10-12, 15-16, and 19-20. The Examiner has noted that such claims would be allowable if rewritten in independent form including all of the limitations of the base claim and any intervening claims. Applicant respectfully asserts that such allowable claims have been amended to include the subject matter of the base claim and any intervening claims. Further, any rejected claims have either been made to depend from an allowable independent claim, or canceled. Allowance of all pending claims is respectfully requested.

Rejections Under 35 U.S.C. 102

Claims 1, 8-9, 13-14, and 17-18 stand rejected under 35 U.S.C. § 102(a) in view of U.S. Patent Application Pub. No. 2011/0242334 [WILBURN]. Applicant respectfully disagrees with such rejection, especially in view of the amendments made hereinabove to each of the independent claims.

Conclusion

It is believed that all of the pending issues have been addressed. Claims 1, 3-7, 9-13, and 15-20 are in condition for allowance per the claim amendments herein.

However, the absence of a reply to a specific rejection, issue, or comment does not signify agreement with or concession of that rejection, issue, or comment. In addition, because the arguments made above may not be exhaustive, there may be reasons for patentability of any or all pending claims (or other claims) that have not been expressed. Still yet, nothing in this reply should be construed as intention to concede any issue with regard to any claim, except as specifically stated in this reply. Finally, it should be noted that no claims are intended to be construed under 35 U.S.C. 112, paragraph 6.

Application No.: 15/201,283
Filing Date: 2016-07-01

In the event a telephone conversation would expedite the prosecution of this application, the Examiner may reach the undersigned at (408) 971-2573 or Britten@zilkakotab.com. Applicant does not believe that any additional fees are due. However, in the event that any other fees are due, the Director is hereby authorized to charge any required fees due (other than issue fees), and to credit any overpayment made, in connection with the filing of this paper to Deposit Account No. 50-1351 (Order No. DUELP024).

Respectfully submitted,

Zilka-Kotab, PC.

_____/Britten Sessions/_____

Britten Sessions
Reg. No. 68278

1155 N. 1st Street, Suite 105
San Jose, CA 95112-4925
408-971-2573

LINCOLN LAW SCHOOL OF SAN JOSE
INTELLECTUAL PROPERTY SERIES

EXHIBIT: OFFICE ACTION

EXHIBITS 449

UNITED STATES PATENT AND TRADEMARK OFFICE

UNITED STATES DEPARTMENT OF COMMERCE
United States Patent and Trademark Office
Address: COMMISSIONER FOR PATENTS
P.O. Box 1450
Alexandria, Virginia 22313-1450
www.uspto.gov

APPLICATION NO.	FILING DATE	FIRST NAMED INVENTOR	ATTORNEY DOCKET NO.	CONFIRMATION NO.
15/253,721	08/31/2016	Adam Feder	DUELP020A	4612

135841	7590	11/03/2017

Zilka-Kotab, PC - DUEL
1155 N. 1st St.
Suite 105
SAN JOSE, CA 95112

EXAMINER
WU, JINGGE

ART UNIT	PAPER NUMBER
2665	

NOTIFICATION DATE	DELIVERY MODE
11/03/2017	ELECTRONIC

Please find below and/or attached an Office communication concerning this application or proceeding.

The time period for reply, if any, is set in the attached communication.

Notice of the Office communication was sent electronically on above-indicated "Notification Date" to the following e-mail address(es):

zk-uspto@zilkakotab.com
eofficeaction@appcoll.com

PTOL-90A (Rev. 04/07)

450 PATENT PROSECUTION WORKBOOK

Office Action Summary	Application No. 15/253,721	Applicant(s) FEDER ET AL.		
	Examiner JINGGE WU	Art Unit 2665	AIA (First Inventor to File) Status Yes	

-- *The MAILING DATE of this communication appears on the cover sheet with the correspondence address* --

Period for Reply

A SHORTENED STATUTORY PERIOD FOR REPLY IS SET TO EXPIRE 3 MONTHS FROM THE MAILING DATE OF THIS COMMUNICATION.
- Extensions of time may be available under the provisions of 37 CFR 1.136(a). In no event, however, may a reply be timely filed after SIX (6) MONTHS from the mailing date of this communication.
- If NO period for reply is specified above, the maximum statutory period will apply and will expire SIX (6) MONTHS from the mailing date of this communication.
- Failure to reply within the set or extended period for reply will, by statute, cause the application to become ABANDONED (35 U.S.C. § 133). Any reply received by the Office later than three months after the mailing date of this communication, even if timely filed, may reduce any earned patent term adjustment. See 37 CFR 1.704(b).

Status

1) ☒ Responsive to communication(s) filed on 9/11/2017.
☐ A declaration(s)/affidavit(s) under **37 CFR 1.130(b)** was/were filed on _____.
2a) ☒ This action is **FINAL**. 2b) ☐ This action is non-final.
3) ☐ An election was made by the applicant in response to a restriction requirement set forth during the interview on _____; the restriction requirement and election have been incorporated into this action.
4) ☐ Since this application is in condition for allowance except for formal matters, prosecution as to the merits is closed in accordance with the practice under *Ex parte Quayle*, 1935 C.D. 11, 453 O.G. 213.

Disposition of Claims*

5) ☒ Claim(s) *1-25* is/are pending in the application.
5a) Of the above claim(s) _____ is/are withdrawn from consideration.
6) ☐ Claim(s) _____ is/are allowed.
7) ☒ Claim(s) *1-25* is/are rejected.
8) ☐ Claim(s) _____ is/are objected to.
9) ☐ Claim(s) _____ are subject to restriction and/or election requirement.

* If any claims have been determined allowable, you may be eligible to benefit from the **Patent Prosecution Highway** program at a participating intellectual property office for the corresponding application. For more information, please see http://www.uspto.gov/patents/init_events/pph/index.jsp or send an inquiry to PPHfeedback@uspto.gov.

Application Papers

10) ☐ The specification is objected to by the Examiner.
11) ☐ The drawing(s) filed on _____ is/are: a) ☐ accepted or b) ☐ objected to by the Examiner.
Applicant may not request that any objection to the drawing(s) be held in abeyance. See 37 CFR 1.85(a).
Replacement drawing sheet(s) including the correction is required if the drawing(s) is objected to. See 37 CFR 1.121(d).

Priority under 35 U.S.C. § 119

12) ☐ Acknowledgment is made of a claim for foreign priority under 35 U.S.C. § 119(a)-(d) or (f).
Certified copies:
a) ☐ All b) ☐ Some** c) ☐ None of the:
1. ☐ Certified copies of the priority documents have been received.
2. ☐ Certified copies of the priority documents have been received in Application No. _____.
3. ☐ Copies of the certified copies of the priority documents have been received in this National Stage application from the International Bureau (PCT Rule 17.2(a)).

** See the attached detailed Office action for a list of the certified copies not received.

Attachment(s)

1) ☒ Notice of References Cited (PTO-892)
2) ☐ Information Disclosure Statement(s) (PTO/SB/08a and/or PTO/SB/08b) Paper No(s)/Mail Date _____.
3) ☐ Interview Summary (PTO-413) Paper No(s)/Mail Date. _____.
4) ☐ Other: _____.

U.S. Patent and Trademark Office
PTOL-326 (Rev. 11-13)   Office Action Summary   Part of Paper No./Mail Date 20171025

Application/Control Number: 15/253,721 Page 2
Art Unit: 2665

The present application, filed on or after March 16, 2013, is being examined under the first inventor to file provisions of the AIA.

Response to Amendment

1. Applicants' response to the last Office Action, filed on Sept. 11 2017, has been entered and made of record.

2. In view of the Applicant amendments/arguments, the rejection under 35 USC §101 is expressly withdrawn

3. Applicants' amendment has required new grounds of rejection. New grounds rejection are therefore presented in the Office Action. Applicant's arguments have been fully considered but are moot in view of the new ground(s) of rejection. Examiner would like to clarify his position as follows:

A. Interpretation of claimed term "specification" and Labour reference.

In the specification, Applicant mentions the term "specification" in Fig. 1, and paragraphs [0039], [0044]-[0045], [0111], none of them mentions that the specification is a data structure, and there is no definition for the term "term". Therefore, the term "specification" shall be interpreted under broadest reasonable interpretation. In a plain meaning, the specification is a detailed description or assessment of requirements, dimensions, materials, etc. In addition, in [0045], Applicant describes two embodiments of specification, one is the specification can have a filer, other one is the specification

Application/Control Number: 15/253,721 Page 3
Art Unit: 2665

can associate weighted value. Thus, Examiner read Labour's set of parameters on the claimed term is corrected.

Claim Rejections - 35 USC § 112

4. The following is a quotation of the second paragraph of 35 U.S.C. 112:

The following is a quotation of 35 U.S.C. 112(b):
> (b) CONCLUSION.—The specification shall conclude with one or more claims particularly pointing out and distinctly claiming the subject matter which the inventor or a joint inventor regards as the invention.

> The following is a quotation of 35 U.S.C. 112 (pre-AIA), second paragraph:
> The specification shall conclude with one or more claims particularly pointing out and distinctly claiming the subject matter which the applicant regards as his invention.

5 Claims 1, 19, and 20 recite the limitation "the identification is a data structure". There is insufficient antecedent basis for this limitation in the claim. Examiner did not find any express wording nor implication in the Specification for the added limitation. "the specification is a data structure", "configuration settings associated with a user interface of a viewer application", and "an order for the at least one filter", which are not defined in the Specification. In the Specification, [0039]-[0045] which describes "specification", [118]-[119] and [157]-[159] which describes "setting", Examiner does not find such descriptions could read on the claimed limitation under the broadest reasonable interpretation. Thus, the newly added limitations are not supported by the specification. The dependent claims are also rejected because all dependent claims contain the same limitation.

6. The following is a quotation of the first paragraph of 35 U.S.C. 112:

Application/Control Number: 15/253,721 Page 4
Art Unit: 2665

The following is a quotation of the first paragraph of 35 U.S.C. 112(a):

(a) IN GENERAL.—The specification shall contain a written description of the invention, and of the manner and process of making and using it, in such full, clear, concise, and exact terms as to enable any person skilled in the art to which it pertains, or with which it is most nearly connected, to make and use the same, and shall set forth the best mode contemplated by the inventor or joint inventor of carrying out the invention.

The following is a quotation of the first paragraph of pre-AIA 35 U.S.C. 112:

The specification shall contain a written description of the invention, and of the manner and process of making and using it, in such full, clear, concise, and exact terms as to enable any person skilled in the art to which it pertains, or with which it is most nearly connected, to make and use the same, and shall set forth the best mode contemplated by the inventor of carrying out his invention.

7. Claims 1, 19 and 20 are rejected under 35 U.S.C. 112, first paragraph, as failing to comply with the written description requirement. The claims contain subject matter, "the specification is a data structure", "configuration settings associated with a user interface of a viewer application", and "an order for the at least one filter", which are not described in the specification in such a way as to reasonably convey to one skilled in the relevant art that the inventor(s), at the time the application was filed, had possession of the claimed invention. The dependent claims are also rejected because all dependent claims contain the same limitation

Double Patenting

8. The nonstatutory double patenting rejection is based on a judicially created doctrine grounded in public policy (a policy reflected in the statute) so as to prevent the unjustified or improper timewise extension of the "right to exclude" granted by a patent and to prevent possible harassment by multiple assignees. See *In re Goodman*, 11 F.3d 1046, 29 USPQ2d 2010 (Fed. Cir. 1993); *In re Longi*, 759 F.2d 887, 225 USPQ

Application/Control Number: 15/253,721 Page 5
Art Unit: 2665

645 (Fed. Cir. 1985); In re Van Ornum, 686 F.2d 937, 214 USPQ 761 (CCPA 1982); In re Vogel, 422 F.2d 438, 164 USPQ 619 (CCPA 1970); and, In re Thorington, 418 F.2d 528, 163 USPQ 644 (CCPA 1969).

A timely filed terminal disclaimer in compliance with 37 CFR 1.321(c) may be used to overcome an actual or provisional rejection based on a nonstatutory double patenting ground provided the conflicting application or patent is shown to be commonly owned with this application. See 37 CFR 1.130(b).

Effective January 1, 1994, a registered attorney or agent of record may sign a terminal disclaimer. A terminal disclaimer signed by the assignee must fully comply with 37 CFR 3.73(b).

Claims 1, and 19-20 (as Examiner's best understanding through 112 rejection) are rejected on the ground of nonstatutory obviousness-type double patenting as being unpatentable over claims 1-20 of US 9448771 (copending Application No. 14/517731), and/or claims 1-20 of 9460118 (copending Application 14/843896). Although the conflicting claims are not identical, they are not patentably distinct from each other because the claimed subject matter of claims 1-20 of the instant invention is the **broader version** of above mentioned claims 1-20 of 9448771 and claims 1-20 of 9460118 such as specification referencing at least one image, outputting image processing code referencing images, creating HDR image, etc.

Claim Rejections - 35 USC § 103

Application/Control Number: 15/253,721 Page 6
Art Unit: 2665

9. The following is a quotation of 35 U.S.C. 103(a) which forms the basis for all obviousness rejections set forth in this Office action:

> (a) A patent may not be obtained though the invention is not identically disclosed or described as set forth in section 102 of this title, if the differences between the subject matter sought to be patented and the prior art are such that the subject matter as a whole would have been obvious before the effective filing date of the claimed invention to a person having ordinary skill in the art to which said subject matter pertains. Patentability shall not be negatived by the manner in which before the effective filing date of the claimed invention.

10. The factual inquiries set forth in *Graham v. John Deere Co.*, 383 U.S. 1, 148 USPQ 459 (1966), that are applied for establishing a background for determining obviousness under pre-AIA 35 U.S.C. 103(a) are summarized as follows:

   1). Determining the scope and contents of the prior art.

   2). Ascertaining the differences between the prior art and the claims at issue.

   3). Resolving the level of ordinary skill in the pertinent art.

   4). Considering objective evidence present in the application indicating obviousness or nonobviousness.

In the event the determination of the status of the application as subject to AIA 35 U.S.C. 102 and 103 (or as subject to pre-AIA 35 U.S.C. 102 and 103) is incorrect, any correction of the statutory basis for the rejection will not be considered a new ground of rejection if the prior art relied upon, and the rationale supporting the rejection, would be the same under either status.

Application/Control Number: 15/253,721 Page 7
Art Unit: 2665

11. Claims 1-4, 7-11, 19-25 are rejected under 35 U.S.C. 103(a) as being unpatentable over Labour et al. (US 2010/0118038 A1, a reference of PTO 1449, hereafter Labour) in view of Kramer et al. (US 2015/0077326 A1, hereinafter Kramer).

As to claim 20 (as Examiner's best understanding through 112 rejection), Labour discloses that a method, comprising:

receiving one or more images at a server (Fig. 1, [0032], [0068]);

analyzing the one or more images(Fig. 4 [0055], [0071]-[0076]);

creating a specification referencing at least the one or more images ([0055], [0070]-[0076], parameters specified and used in the rendering image)

outputting image processing code (rendering commands) referencing the specification and the one or more images, based on the analysis of the one or more images (Fig. 3-4 [0067]-[0076]).

Labour does not mention input filter into specification.

Kramer, in an analogous environment, discloses that combining the filters with the specifications ([0579]-[0582]).

The knowledge that inputting/combining filters into specifications is a desirable way to subject that would have been within the skill in the art, as evidenced by Kramer. Therefore, it would have been obvious to one having ordinary skill in the art at the

Application/Control Number: 15/253,721 Page 8
Art Unit: 2665

effective filing date of the invention to combine the well-known elements of Kramer with the well-known technique in image processing of Labour because the combination is nothing more than a "predictable use of prior art elements according to their established functions." *KSR*, 550 U.S., at 417.

As to claims 1 and 19, the claims are corresponding medium and apparatus claims to claim 20, the discussions are addressed with respect to claim 20.

As to claim 2, Labour further discloses that the apparatus of Claim 1, wherein the apparatus is operable such that the analyzing includes at least one of creating the one or more images, creating a high dynamic range (HDR) image, or processing at least one image ([0053]-[0055], [0070]-[0076]).

As to claim 3, Labour further discloses that the apparatus of Claim 1, wherein the apparatus is operable such that the image processing code includes one or more images ([0053], [0071]).

As to claim 4, Labour further discloses that the apparatus of Claim 1, wherein the apparatus is operable such that the outputting includes at least one of providing access to a constructed web application associated with the one or more images, or pushing the web application associated with the one or more images to a recipient ([0053]-[0055], [0071]-[0076]).

As to claim 7, Labour further discloses that the apparatus of Claim 1, wherein the apparatus is operable such that the outputting includes at least one of providing access

Application/Control Number: 15/253,721 Page 9
Art Unit: 2665

to code created for rendering vector graphics in a web application, or providing access to a created resulting image which references one or more assets not stored on the server ([0051]-[0055], [0071]-[0076]).

As to claims 8-9, Labour further discloses that The apparatus of Claim 7, wherein the apparatus is operable such that the outputting includes providing access to a created resulting image which references one or more assets not stored on the server, and the apparatus is further operable such that the one or more assets are stored locally on a mobile device as well as in the server ([0026]-[0036], [0071]-[0076]).

As to claim 10, Labour further discloses that the apparatus of Claim 1, wherein the apparatus is operable for generating a resulting image based on the one or more images, the resulting image being stored on the server (Fig. 1 and 3 9[0071]-[0076]).

As to claim 11, Labour further discloses that the apparatus of Claim 1, wherein the apparatus is operable for constructing two or more versions of a web application associated with the one or more images ([0053]-[0064], [0068]-[0076]).

As to claim 21, Kramer further discloses that the apparatus of claim 1, wherein the server is further configured to:

generate a resulting image, based on the one or more images and the at least one filter ([1067]-[1072]);

update the image processing code to include the resulting image ([1090]-[1094]);

Application/Control Number: 15/253,721 Page 10
Art Unit: 2665

wherein the image processing code includes code for manipulating the resulting image ([1088]-[1094]).

As to claim 22, Labour further discloses that the apparatus of claim 1, wherein the image processing code is sent to a client device ([0032]-[33], [0045], [0068]).

As to claim 23, Labour further discloses that the apparatus of claim 22, wherein the analysis displaces processing demands from the client device to the server ([0026]-[0032]).

As to claim 24, Labour further discloses that the apparatus of claim 1, wherein the server is further configured to:

generate a resulting image based on the one or more images ([0029]; and

construct a web application based on the resulting image, the specification, and the image processing code.

As to claim 25, Kramer further disclose that the apparatus of claim 24, wherein the server is further configured to:

create a reduced package based on the web application ([1084]-[1094]); and

send the reduced package to a client device ([1094]).

Application/Control Number: 15/253,721 Page 11
Art Unit: 2665

12. Claims 12-16 are rejected under 35 U.S.C. 103(a) as being unpatentable over the combination of Labour and Kramer, further in view of Knibbeler (US 2014/0210847 A1, a reference of PTO 1449, hereafter Knibbeler)

As to claim 16, Labour does not mention HDR, which is well known in the art.

Knibbeler, in an analogous environment, further discloses that the apparatus of Claim 1, wherein the apparatus is operable such that analyzing the one or more images includes at least one of correcting white balance, correcting exposure levels, creating a high dynamic range (HDR) image, setting a black point, setting a white point, performing a function, or adjusting a HDR strength ([0041], [0096], [0292]-[0311]).

The knowledge that creating HDR image object is a desirable way to subject that would have been within the skill in the art, as evidenced by Knibbeler. Therefore, it would have been obvious to one having ordinary skill in the art at the effective filing date of the invention to combine the well-known elements of Knibbeler with the well-known technique in image processing of Labour because the combination is nothing more than a "predictable use of prior art elements according to their established functions." *KSR*, 550 U.S., at 417.

As to claims 12-14, Labour does not mention paying account or user account (free or pay), which is well known in the art.

Examiner takes Official Notice that those features are well known in the art.

Application/Control Number: 15/253,721 Page 12
Art Unit: 2665

The knowledge that utilizing paying or free user account is a desirable way to subject that would have been within the skill in the art, as evidenced by Official Notice. Therefore, it would have been obvious to one having ordinary skill in the art at the effective filing date of the invention to combine the well-known elements of Official Notice with the well-known technique in image processing of the combination of Labour because the combination is nothing more than a "predictable use of prior art elements according to their established functions." *Id.*, at 417.

As to claim 15, Labour further discloses that The apparatus of Claim 11, wherein the apparatus is operable such that each version of the web application provides a different set of features, at least in part, by which the one or more images are capable of being manipulated utilizing the web application ([0053]-[0055],[0068]-[0076]).

13. Claims 5-6, 17-18 are rejected under 35 U.S.C. 103(a) as being unpatentable over the combination of Labour, Kramer and Knibbeler, further in view of Kishino et al. (US 2014/0043628 A1, a reference of PTO 1449, hereafter Kishino)

As to claim 5, Labour does not mention sliding indicia which is well known in the art.

Kishino, in an analogous environment, further discloses that the apparatus of Claim 4, wherein the apparatus is operable such that sliding indicia is displayed utilizing the web application and the one or more images are blended based on a first aspect, in response to the sliding indicia being manipulated by a user (Fig. 21).

Application/Control Number: 15/253,721 Page 13
Art Unit: 2665

The knowledge that utilizing a sliding indicia to adjust black point/whit point is a desirable way to subject that would have been within the skill in the art, as evidenced by Kishino. Therefore, it would have been obvious to one having ordinary skill in the art at the effective filing date of the invention to combine the well-known elements of Kishino with the well-known technique in image processing of the combination of the combination of Labour and Knibbeler because the combination is nothing more than a "predictable use of prior art elements according to their established functions." *Id.*, at 417.

As to claim 6, Labour further discloses that the apparatus of Claim 5, wherein the apparatus is operable such that the first aspect includes at least one of a white balance, a focus, an exposure, a color correction, or an intensity ([0055]).

As to claims 17 and 18, Knibbeler further discloses the apparatus of Claim 16, wherein the apparatus is operable such that analyzing the one or more images includes setting a black point, and the apparatus is further operable such that the black point/white is capable of being adjusted based on input by a user (Fig. 21, [0008], [0054]-[0059], [0086]-[0090]).

Examiner Notes

Application/Control Number: 15/253,721 Page 14
Art Unit: 2665

Examiner cites particular figures, paragraphs, columns and line numbers in the references as applied to the claims for the convenience of the applicant. Although the specified citations are representative of the teachings in the art and are applied to the specific limitations within the individual claim, other passages and figures may apply as well. It is respectfully requested that, in preparing responses, the applicant fully consider the references in entirety as potentially teaching all or part of the claimed invention, as well as the context of the passage as taught by the prior art or disclosed by the examiner.

Conclusion

14. Applicant's amendment necessitated the new ground(s) of rejection presented in this Office action. Accordingly, **THIS ACTION IS MADE FINAL**. See MPEP § 706.07(a). Applicant is reminded of the extension of time policy as set forth in 37 CFR 1.136(a).

A shortened statutory period for reply to this final action is set to expire THREE MONTHS from the mailing date of this action. In the event a first reply is filed within TWO MONTHS of the mailing date of this final action and the advisory action is not mailed until after the end of the THREE-MONTH shortened statutory period, then the shortened statutory period will expire on the date the advisory action is mailed, and any extension fee pursuant to 37 CFR 1.136(a) will be calculated from the mailing date of

Application/Control Number: 15/253,721 Page 15
Art Unit: 2665

the advisory action. In no event, however, will the statutory period for reply expire later than SIX MONTHS from the date of this final action.

Contact Information

Any inquiry concerning this communication or earlier communications should be directed to Jingge Wu whose telephone number is (571) 272-7429. He can normally be reached Monday through Thursday from 8:00 am to 5:30 pm. The examiner can be also reached on second alternate Fridays.

If attempts to reach the Examiner by telephone are unsuccessful, the Examiner's supervisor, Bhavesh Mehta, can be reached at (571) 272-7453.

/Jingge Wu/
Primary Patent Examiner Au 2665

EXHIBITS 465

LINCOLN LAW SCHOOL OF SAN JOSE
INTELLECTUAL PROPERTY SERIES

EXHIBIT: OFFICE ACTION RESPONSE

IN THE UNITED STATES PATENT AND TRADEMARK OFFICE

In re Application of:	Confirmation No.: 4612
Adam Feder	Examiner: Wu, Jingge
Application No.: 15/253,721	Art Unit: 2665
File Date: 08/31/2016	Docket No.: DUELP020A
Title: SYSTEM, METHOD, AND COMPUTER PROGRAM PRODUCT FOR EXCHANGING IMAGES	Date: December 8, 2017

AMENDMENT B

Commissioner for Patents
P.O. Box 1450
Alexandria VA 22313-1450

Examiner:

In response to the communication mailed 2017-11-03 (hereafter "Final Office Action" or "FOA"), please consider the following amendments believed to place the claims in condition for allowance, as follows:

— **Amendments to the Claims** are reflected in the listing of the claims that begins on page 2 of this paper.

— **Remarks/Arguments** begin on page 7 of this paper.

Applicant : Duelight LLC
Application No. : 15/253,721

Attorney's Docket No.: DUELP020A

Amendments to the Claims:

This listing of claims replaces all prior versions and listings of claims in the application:

1. (Previously presented) An apparatus, comprising:

    a server configured to:

    receive one or more images;

    analyze the one or more images;

    based on the analysis, create a specification, wherein the specification is a data structure that identifies at least three of:

    the one or more images,

    at least one filter associated with the one or more images,

    configuration settings associated with a user interface of a viewer application, and

    an order for the at least one filter;

    generate image processing code based on the specification; and

    output the image processing code.

2. (Previously presented) The apparatus of Claim 1, wherein the apparatus is operable such that the analysis includes at least one of creating a second image based on the one or more images, creating a high dynamic range (HDR) image, or processing at least one image of the one or more images.

3. (Previously presented) The apparatus of Claim 1, wherein the apparatus is operable such that the image processing code includes the one or more images.

4. (Previously presented) The apparatus of Claim 1, wherein the apparatus is operable such that the output of the image processing code includes at least one of providing access to a constructed web application associated with the one or more images, or pushing the web application associated with the one or more images to a recipient.

Applicant : Duelight LLC
Application No. : 15/253,721

Attorney's Docket No.: DUELP020A
Page : 3 of 14

5. (Original) The apparatus of Claim 4, wherein the apparatus is operable such that sliding indicia is displayed utilizing the web application and the one or more images are blended based on a first aspect, in response to the sliding indicia being manipulated by a user.

6. (Original) The apparatus of Claim 5, wherein the apparatus is operable such that the first aspect includes at least one of a white balance, a focus, an exposure, a color correction, or an intensity.

7. (Previously presented) The apparatus of Claim 1, wherein the apparatus is operable such that the output of the image processing code includes at least one of providing access to code created for rendering vector graphics in a web application, or providing access to a created resulting image which references one or more assets not stored on the server.

8. (Previously presented) The apparatus of Claim 7, wherein the apparatus is operable such that the output of the image processing code includes providing access to a created resulting image which references one or more assets not stored on the server, and the apparatus is further operable such that the one or more assets are stored remotely to the server.

9. (Original) The apparatus of Claim 8, wherein the apparatus is operable such that the image processing code references the one or more assets stored remotely to the server, as well as a resulting image stored on the server.

10. (Original) The apparatus of Claim 1, wherein the apparatus is operable for generating a resulting image based on the one or more images, the resulting image being stored on the server.

Applicant : Duelight LLC
Application No. : 15/253,721

Attorney's Docket No.: DUELP020A
Page : 4 of 14

11. (Original) The apparatus of Claim 1, wherein the apparatus is operable for constructing two or more versions of a web application associated with the one or more images.

12. (Original) The apparatus of Claim 11, wherein the apparatus is operable such that at least one of the two or more versions is associated with a paying account.

13. (Original) The apparatus of Claim 12, wherein the apparatus is operable such that the paying account is associated with a user identifier or a user account.

14. (Original) The apparatus of Claim 11, wherein the apparatus is operable such that at least one of the two or more versions is associated with a free account.

15. (Original) The apparatus of Claim 11, wherein the apparatus is operable such that each version of the web application provides a different set of features, at least in part, by which the one or more images are capable of being manipulated utilizing the web application.

16. (Original) The apparatus of Claim 1, wherein the apparatus is operable such that analyzing the one or more images includes at least one of correcting white balance, correcting exposure levels, creating a high dynamic range (HDR) image, setting a black point, setting a white point, performing a dehaze function, or adjusting a HDR strength.

17. (Original) The apparatus of Claim 16, wherein the apparatus is operable such that analyzing the one or more images includes setting the black point, and the apparatus is further operable such that the black point is capable of being adjusted based on input by a user.

18. (Original) The apparatus of Claim 16, wherein the apparatus is operable such that analyzing the one or more images includes setting the white point, and the apparatus is further operable such that the white point is capable of being adjusted based on input by a user.

Applicant : Duelight LLC
Application No. : 15/253,721

Attorney's Docket No.: DUELP020A
Page : 5 of 14

19. (Currently Amended) A computer program product <ins>comprising computer executable instructions stored on a non-transitory computer readable medium that when executed by a processor instruct the processor to</ins><del>embodied on a non-transitory computer readable medium, comprising</del>:

 <del>code for</del> receiv<ins>e</ins>[[ing]] one or more images at a server;

 <del>code for</del> analyz<ins>e</ins>[[ing]] the one or more images;

 based on the analysis, <del>code for</del> creat<ins>e</ins>[[ing]] a specification, wherein the specification is a data structure that identifies at least three of:

  the one or more images,

  at least one filter associated with the one or more images,

  configuration settings associated with a user interface of a viewer application, and

  an order for the at least one filter;

 <del>code for</del> generat<ins>e</ins>[[ing]] image processing code based on the specification and one or more images; and

 <del>code for</del> output[[ting]] the image processing code.

20. (Previously presented) A method, comprising:

 receiving one or more images at a server;

 analyzing the one or more images;

 based on the analysis, creating a specification, wherein the specification is a data structure that identifies at least three of:

  the one or more images,

  at least one filter associated with the one or more images,

  configuration settings associated with a user interface of a viewer application, and

  an order for the at least one filter;

Applicant : Duelight LLC
Application No. : 15/253,721

Attorney's Docket No.: DUELP020A
Page : 6 of 14

generating image processing code based on the specification and one or more images; and

outputting the image processing code.

21. (Previously presented) The apparatus of claim 1, wherein the server is further configured to:

generate a resulting image, based on the one or more images and the at least one filter;
update the image processing code to include the resulting image;
wherein the image processing code includes code for manipulating the resulting image.

22. (Previously presented) The apparatus of claim 1, wherein the image processing code is sent to a client device.

23. (Previously presented) The apparatus of claim 22, wherein the analysis displaces processing demands from the client device to the server.

24. (Previously presented) The apparatus of claim 1, wherein the server is further configured to:

generate a resulting image based on the one or more images; and
construct a web application based on the resulting image, the specification, and the image processing code.

25. (Previously presented) The apparatus of claim 24, wherein the server is further configured to:

create a reduced package based on the web application; and
send the reduced package to a client device.

Applicant : Duelight LLC
Application No. : 15/253,721

Attorney's Docket No.: DUELP020A
Page : 7 of 14

Remarks:

Summary

Claims 1-25 were pending.

Claims 1–25 are pending, with claims 1, 19, and 20 being independent. Claim 19 has been amended. No new subject matter has been added.

Double Patenting Rejection

Claims 1 and 19-20 have been provisionally rejected on the ground of nonstatutory obviousness type double patenting as being unpatentable over claims 1-20 of Application No. 14/517,731. Although this is a provisional rejection, to assist in moving this case along, Applicant asserts that such provisional rejection is overcome in view of the filing of the terminal disclaimer submitted herewith.

Rejections Under 35 U.S.C. 112(a)

The Examiner has rejected Claims 1, 19, and 20 under 35 U.S.C. 112 (a) or 35 U.S.C. 112 (pre-AIA), first paragraph, as failing to comply with the written description requirement. In particular, the Examiner has indicated:

> 5   Claims 1, 19, and 20 recite the limitation "the identification is a data structure". There is insufficient antecedent basis for this limitation in the claim. Examiner did not find any express wording nor implication in the Specification for the added limitation, "the specification is a data structure", "configuration settings associated with a user interface of a viewer application", and "an order for the at least one filter", which are not defined in the Specification. In the Specification, [0039]-[0045] which describes "specification", [118]-[119] and [157]-[159] which describes "setting", Examiner does not find such descriptions could read on the claimed limitation under the broadest reasonable interpretation. Thus, the newly added limitations are not supported by the specification. The dependent claims are also rejected because all dependent claims contain the same limitation.

Applicant : Duelight LLC
Application No. : 15/253,721

Attorney's Docket No.: DUELP020A

Applicant respectfully disagrees. In particular, as indicated on page 1 of the Office Action Response dated 2017-09-11 (and as discussed during Examiner Interviews held on 2017-11-03 and 2017-11-20):

> Support for such amendments is found, inter alia, in paragraphs [0032]-[0034], [0043], and [0127], as well as Figures 5-7 of the present description, **as well as Col. 2, lines 42-53 and Col. 5, lines 45-53 from US 9,448,771 to which priority is claimed (and whose subject matter is incorporated by reference)**. No new matter is introduced. Claims 1–25 are now pending, including independent claims 1, 19, and 20.

(emphasis added). As such, such rejection is deemed overcome by virtue of the previously provided support (and conversations) made hereinabove.

Rejections Under 35 U.S.C. 103

Claims 1-4, 7-11, 19-25 stand rejected under 35 U.S.C. § 103(a) in view of U.S. Pat. Pub. No. 2010/0118038 (LABOUR) and U.S. Pat. Pub. No. 2015/0077326 (KRAMER). Additionally, Claims 12-16 stand rejected under 35 U.S.C. § 103(a) in view of U.S. Pat. Pub. No. 2010/0118038 (LABOUR), U.S. Pat. Pub. No. 2015/0077326 (KRAMER), and U.S. Pat. Pub. No. 2014/0210847 (KNIBBELER).

With respect to the independent claims, the Examiner has relied on paragraphs [0070]-[0076] from the LABOUR reference to make a prior art showing of applicant's claimed technique "based on the analysis, create a specification, wherein the specification is a data structure that identifies at least three of: the one or more images, the at least one filter associated with the one or more images, configuration settings associated with a user interface of a viewer application, and an order for the at least one filter" (see this or similar, but not necessarily identical language in the independent claims, as amended).

Applicant respectfully notes that the LABOUR reference, as relied upon by the Examiner, discloses:

> [0074] A set of parameters associated with the component is also obtained (operation 406). For example, the component may correspond to a shape in a scenegraph or render graph with parameters that include vertex, index, texture, effect, and/or other data. The parameters may be obtained from the command buffer and/or a shared memory buffer. The rendering commands are then executed using the parameters (operation 408) to render the component in the image.

Applicant : Duelight LLC
Application No. : 15/253,721

Attorney's Docket No.: DUELP020A
Page : 9 of 14

LABOUR Paragraph [0074] – emphasis added.

However, disclosing that a "set of parameters" may be obtained which include "vertex, index, texture, effect, and/or other data," as in the LABOUR excerpt(s) relied upon, does not teach or suggest that "the specification is a data structure," much less applicant's claimed "based on the analysis, create a specification, wherein the specification is a data structure that identifies at least three of: the one or more images, the at least one filter associated with the one or more images, configuration settings associated with a user interface of a viewer application, and an order for the at least one filter" (emphasis added), as claimed by applicant.

Applicant notes that the above arguments were previously provided in the Response to Office Action dated 2017-09-11 and which have not been specifically addressed. Additionally, applicant notes that the claim language used on page 7 of the Office Action dated 2017-11-03 does not exactly correspond with the claim amendments made in the Response to Office Action dated 2017-09-11.

With respect to the independent claims, the Examiner has relied on paragraphs [0067]-[0076] in addition to Figures 3-4 from the LABOUR reference to make a prior art showing of applicant's claimed technique "generate image processing code based on the specification; and output the image processing code" (see this or similar, but not necessarily identical language in the independent claims, as amended).

Applicant respectfully notes that the LABOUR reference, as relied upon by the Examiner, discloses:

> [0074] A set of parameters associated with the component is also obtained (operation 406). For example, the component may correspond to a shape in a scenegraph or render graph with parameters that include vertex, index, texture, effect, and/or other data. The parameters may be obtained from the command buffer and/or a shared memory buffer. The rendering commands are then executed using the parameters (operation 408) to render the component in the image.
>
> [0075] The parameters may also be updated (operation 410) for subsequent renderings of the component. For example, the parameters may be updated to animate the component in successive frames of the image. If the parameters are updated, the updated parameters are obtained (operation 406), and the stored rendering commands are executed using the updated parameters (operation 408). In other words, the updated parameters may be inserted into the stored command buffer structure associated with the rendering commands in lieu of recalculating the rendering commands with the updated parameters from the command buffer.

Applicant : Duelight LLC
Application No. : 15/253,721

Attorney's Docket No.: DUELP020A
Page : 10 of 14

LABOUR. Paragraphs [0074]-[0075] – emphasis added.

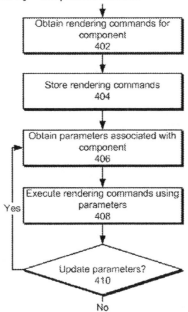

LABOUR. Figure 4.

However, merely disclosing that a "commands are then executed using the parameters" and that "rendering commands are executed using the updated parameters," as in the LABOUR excerpt(s) relied upon, does not teach or suggest "generate <u>image processing code</u> **based on** the <u>specification</u>; and output the <u>image processing code</u>" (emphasis added), as claimed by applicant.

Applicant notes that the above arguments were previously provided in the Response to Office Action dated 2017-09-11 and which have not been specifically addressed. Additionally, applicant notes that the claim language used on page 7 of the Office Action dated 2017-11-03 does not exactly correspond with the claim amendments made in the Response to Office Action dated 2017-09-11.

Additionally, with respect to the independent claims, the Examiner has relied on paragraphs [0579]-[0582] from the KRAMER reference. The Examiner asserts that such prior art reference "discloses that combining the filters with specification." Applicant respectfully notes that such claim language is not found in the claim set.

For purposes of responding, applicant will assume that the prior art is to be applied to the following claim language "generate image processing code based on the specification" (see this or similar, but not necessarily identical language in the independent claims, as amended).

Applicant : Duelight LLC
Application No. : 15/253,721

Attorney's Docket No.: DUELP020A

Applicant respectfully notes that the KRAMER reference, as relied upon by the Examiner, discloses:

> [0579] Using relative joint orientations allows the system described here to avoid problems associated with differing hand sizes and geometries. No "operator calibration" is required with this system. In addition, <u>specifying poses as a string or collection of relative orientations allows more complex gesture specifications</u> to be easily created by combining pose representations with further filters and specifications.
> [0580] Using a small number of discrete states for pose specification makes it possible to specify poses compactly as well as to ensure accurate pose recognition using a variety of underlying tracking technologies (for example, passive optical tracking using cameras, active optical tracking using lighted dots and cameras, electromagnetic field tracking, etc).
> [0581] Gestures in every category (1a) to (1f) may be partially (or minimally) specified, so that non-critical data is ignored. For example, a gesture in which the position of two fingers is definitive, and other finger positions are unimportant, may be represented by a single specification in which the operative positions of the two relevant fingers is given and, within the same string, "wild cards" or generic "ignore these" indicators are listed for the other fingers.
> [0582] All of the innovations described here for <u>gesture recognition</u>, including but not limited to the multi-layered specification technique, use of relative orientations, quantization of data, and allowance for partial or minimal specifi-

KRAMER. Paragraphs [0579] – [0582] (emphasis added).

Additionally, KRAMER generally discloses:

> Embodiments described herein includes a system comprising a processor coupled to display devices, sensors, remote client devices, and computer applications. The computer applications orchestrate content of the remote client devices simultaneously across the display devices and the remote client devices, and allow simultaneous control of the display devices. The simultaneous control includes automatically detecting a gesture of at least one object from gesture data received via the sensors. The detecting comprises identifying the gesture using only the gesture data. The computer applications translate the gesture to a gesture signal, and control the display devices in response to the gesture signal.

KRAMER. Abstract.

Applicant : Duelight LLC
Application No. : 15/253,721

Attorney's Docket No.: DUELP020A

However, merely disclosing a generic "gesture specification" which may include "specifying poses as a string or collection of relative orientations," as in the KRAMER excerpt(s) relied upon, does not teach or suggest "generate image processing code **based on** the specification" (emphasis added), as claimed by applicant. Further, KRAMER relates specifically to "gesture signal" and "simultaneous control of the display devices" which does not even mention, let alone teach, "image processing code" consistent with the context of the language as claimed:

> receive one or more images;
> analyze the one or more images;
> based on the analysis, create a specification, wherein the specification is a data structure that identifies at least three of:
> > the one or more images,
> > at least one filter associated with the one or more images,
> > configuration settings associated with a user interface of a viewer application, and
> > an order for the at least one filter;
> generate image processing code based on the specification; and
> output the image processing code.

To establish a prima facie case of obviousness, three basic criteria must be met. First, there must be some suggestion or motivation, either in the references themselves or in the knowledge generally available to one of ordinary skill in the art, to modify the reference or to combine reference teachings. Second, there must be a reasonable expectation of success. Finally, the prior art reference (or references when combined) must teach or suggest all the claim limitations. The teaching or suggestion to make the claimed combination and the reasonable expectation of success must both be found in the prior art and not based on applicant's disclosure. *In re Vaeck*, 947 F.2d 488, 20 USPQ2d 1438 (Fed.Cir.1991).

Applicant respectfully asserts that at least the third element of the prima facie case of obviousness has not been met, since the prior art excerpts, as relied upon by the Examiner, fail to teach or suggest all of the claim limitations, as noted above.

Rejections Under Official Notice

In addition, with respect to Claims 12-14, the Examiner has simply dismissed the same under Official Notice. Specifically, the Examiner has stated that it would have been obvious for one of ordinary skill in the art at the time the invention was made to "utilize[e] paying or free user account." Applicant respectfully disagrees. In particular, applicant respectfully asserts that the "at least one of the two or more versions is associated with a paying account" and the "at least one of the two or more versions is associated with a free account" (as claimed) is not obvious in view of "constructing two or more versions of a web application associated with the one or

Applicant : Duelight LLC
Application No. : 15/253,721
Attorney's Docket No.: DUELP020A
Page : 13 of 14

more images" (claim 11) where the "one or more images" (claim 1) are associated with the independent claim language, as follows:

>receive one or more images;
>analyze the one or more images;
>based on the analysis, create a specification, <u>wherein the specification is a data structure that identifies at least three of</u>:
>>
>><u>the one or more images</u>,
>><u>at least one filter associated with the one or more images</u>,
>><u>configuration settings associated with a user interface of a viewer application</u>, and
>><u>an order for the at least one filter</u>;
>
>generate image processing code based on the specification; and
>output the image processing code.

Applicant notes that such claims are therefore allowable per the claim amendments herein and/or dependence on a now allowable independent claim.

Therefore, applicant has adequately traversed the Examiner's assertion of obviousness, and thus formally requests a specific showing of the subject matter in ALL of the claims in any future action. Note excerpts from MPEP below.

> "It is never appropriate to rely solely on common knowledge in the art without evidentiary support in the record as the principal evidence upon which a rejection was based." See MPEP 2144.03(E), as well as *Zurko*, 258 F.3d at 1386, 59 USPQ2d at 1697; *Ahlert*, 424 F.2d at 1092, 165 USPQ 421.

> "If the applicant traverses such an [Official Notice] assertion the examiner should cite a reference in support of his or her position." See MPEP 2144.03.

Dependent Claims

Applicant further notes that the prior art is also deficient with respect to the dependent claims. Applicant notes that such claims are allowable per the claim amendments herein and/or dependence on a now allowable independent claim.

Conclusion

It is believed that all of the pending issues have been addressed. Claims 1-24 are in condition for allowance per the claim amendments herein.

Applicant : Duelight LLC
Application No. : 15/253,721

Attorney's Docket No.: DUELP020A

However, the absence of a reply to a specific rejection, issue, or comment does not signify agreement with or concession of that rejection, issue, or comment. In addition, because the arguments made above may not be exhaustive, there may be reasons for patentability of any or all pending claims (or other claims) that have not been expressed. Still yet, nothing in this reply should be construed as intention to concede any issue with regard to any claim, except as specifically stated in this reply. Finally, it should be noted that no claims are intended to be construed under 35 U.S.C. 112, paragraph 6.

In the event a telephone conversation would expedite the prosecution of this application, the Examiner may reach the undersigned at (408) 971-2573 or britten@zilkakotab.com. Applicant does not believe that any additional fees are due. However, in the event that any other fees are due, the Director is hereby authorized to charge any required fees due (other than issue fees), and to credit any overpayment made, in connection with the filing of this paper to Deposit Account No. 50-1351 (Order No. DUELP020A).

Respectfully submitted,

Zilka-Kotab, PC.

/BRITTENSESSIONS/

Britten Sessions
Reg. No. 68,278

1155 N. 1st Street, Suite 105
San Jose, CA 95112-4925
408-971-2573

LINCOLN LAW SCHOOL OF SAN JOSE
INTELLECTUAL PROPERTY SERIES

EXHIBIT: OFFICE ACTION

EXHIBITS 481

UNITED STATES PATENT AND TRADEMARK OFFICE

UNITED STATES DEPARTMENT OF COMMERCE
United States Patent and Trademark Office
Address: COMMISSIONER FOR PATENTS
P.O. Box 1450
Alexandria, Virginia 22313-1450
www.uspto.gov

APPLICATION NO.	FILING DATE	FIRST NAMED INVENTOR	ATTORNEY DOCKET NO.	CONFIRMATION NO.
15/289,039	10/07/2016	William Rivard	DUELP006A	6486

135841	7590	05/11/2017

Zilka-Kotab, PC - DUEL
1155 N. 1st St.
Suite 105
SAN JOSE, CA 95112

EXAMINER
MOREHEAD III, JOHN H

ART UNIT	PAPER NUMBER
2664	

NOTIFICATION DATE	DELIVERY MODE
05/11/2017	ELECTRONIC

Please find below and/or attached an Office communication concerning this application or proceeding.

The time period for reply, if any, is set in the attached communication.

Notice of the Office communication was sent electronically on above-indicated "Notification Date" to the following e-mail address(es):

zk-uspto@zilkakotab.com
eofficeaction@appcoll.com

PTOL-90A (Rev. 04/07)

	Application No.	Applicant(s)
Office Action Summary	15/289,039	RIVARD ET AL.
	Examiner	Art Unit	AIA (First Inventor to File) Status
	JOHN H. MOREHEAD III	2664	Yes

-- The MAILING DATE of this communication appears on the cover sheet with the correspondence address --

Period for Reply

A SHORTENED STATUTORY PERIOD FOR REPLY IS SET TO EXPIRE <u>3</u> MONTHS FROM THE MAILING DATE OF THIS COMMUNICATION.
- Extensions of time may be available under the provisions of 37 CFR 1.136(a). In no event, however, may a reply be timely filed after SIX (6) MONTHS from the mailing date of this communication.
- If NO period for reply is specified above, the maximum statutory period will apply and will expire SIX (6) MONTHS from the mailing date of this communication.
- Failure to reply within the set or extended period for reply will, by statute, cause the application to become ABANDONED (35 U.S.C. § 133). Any reply received by the Office later than three months after the mailing date of this communication, even if timely filed, may reduce any earned patent term adjustment. See 37 CFR 1.704(b).

Status

1)☒ Responsive to communication(s) filed on <u>10/07/2016</u>.
☐ A declaration(s)/affidavit(s) under **37 CFR 1.130(b)** was/were filed on _____.
2a)☐ This action is **FINAL**.   2b)☒ This action is non-final.
3)☐ An election was made by the applicant in response to a restriction requirement set forth during the interview on _____; the restriction requirement and election have been incorporated into this action.
4)☐ Since this application is in condition for allowance except for formal matters, prosecution as to the merits is closed in accordance with the practice under *Ex parte Quayle*, 1935 C.D. 11, 453 O.G. 213.

Disposition of Claims*

5)☒ Claim(s) <u>1-20</u> is/are pending in the application.
  5a) Of the above claim(s) _____ is/are withdrawn from consideration.
6)☐ Claim(s) _____ is/are allowed.
7)☒ Claim(s) <u>1-20</u> is/are rejected.
8)☒ Claim(s) _____ is/are objected to.
9)☐ Claim(s) _____ are subject to restriction and/or election requirement.

* If any claims have been determined <u>allowable</u>, you may be eligible to benefit from the **Patent Prosecution Highway** program at a participating intellectual property office for the corresponding application. For more information, please see http://www.uspto.gov/patents/init_events/pph/index.jsp or send an inquiry to PPHfeedback@uspto.gov.

Application Papers

10)☐ The specification is objected to by the Examiner.
11)☒ The drawing(s) filed on <u>10/07/2016</u> is/are: a)☒ accepted or b)☐ objected to by the Examiner.
  Applicant may not request that any objection to the drawing(s) be held in abeyance. See 37 CFR 1.85(a).
  Replacement drawing sheet(s) including the correction is required if the drawing(s) is objected to. See 37 CFR 1.121(d).

Priority under 35 U.S.C. § 119

12)☐ Acknowledgment is made of a claim for foreign priority under 35 U.S.C. § 119(a)-(d) or (f).
  Certified copies:
    a)☐ All   b)☐ Some** c)☐ None of the:
      1.☐ Certified copies of the priority documents have been received.
      2.☐ Certified copies of the priority documents have been received in Application No. _____.
      3.☐ Copies of the certified copies of the priority documents have been received in this National Stage application from the International Bureau (PCT Rule 17.2(a)).
** See the attached detailed Office action for a list of the certified copies not received.

Attachment(s)

1) ☒ Notice of References Cited (PTO-892)
2) ☐ Information Disclosure Statement(s) (PTO/SB/08a and/or PTO/SB/08b) Paper No(s)/Mail Date _____.
3) ☐ Interview Summary (PTO-413) Paper No(s)/Mail Date. _____.
4) ☐ Other: _____.

Application/Control Number: 15/289,039 Page 2
Art Unit: 2664

DETAILED ACTION

1. Claims 1-20 are pending in the application.

Notice of Pre-AIA or AIA Status

2. The present application, filed on or after March 16, 2013, is being examined under the first inventor to file provisions of the AIA.

Claim Interpretation

The following is a quotation of 35 U.S.C. 112(f):

> (f) Element in Claim for a Combination. – An element in a claim for a combination may be expressed as a means or step for performing a specified function without the recital of structure, material, or acts in support thereof, and such claim shall be construed to cover the corresponding structure, material, or acts described in the specification and equivalents thereof.

The following is a quotation of pre-AIA 35 U.S.C. 112, sixth paragraph:

> An element in a claim for a combination may be expressed as a means or step for performing a specified function without the recital of structure, material, or acts in support thereof, and such claim shall be construed to cover the corresponding structure, material, or acts described in the specification and equivalents thereof.

Use of the word "means" (or "step for") in a claim with functional language creates a rebuttable presumption that the claim element is to be treated in accordance with 35 U.S.C. 112(f) (pre-AIA 35 U.S.C. 112, sixth paragraph). The presumption that 35 U.S.C. 112(f) (pre-AIA 35 U.S.C. 112, sixth paragraph) is invoked is rebutted when the function is recited with sufficient structure, material, or acts within the claim itself to entirely perform the recited function.

Application/Control Number: 15/289,039 Page 3
Art Unit: 2664

Absence of the word "means" (or "step for") in a claim creates a rebuttable presumption that the claim element **is not** to be treated in accordance with 35 U.S.C. 112(f) (pre-AIA 35 U.S.C. 112, sixth paragraph). The presumption that 35 U.S.C. 112(f) (pre-AIA 35 U.S.C. 112, sixth paragraph) is not invoked is rebutted when the claim element recites function but fails to recite sufficiently definite structure, material or acts to perform that function.

Claim elements in this application that use the word "means" (or "step for") are presumed to invoke 35 U.S.C. 112(f) except as otherwise indicated in an Office action. Similarly, claim elements that do not use the word "means" (or "step for") are presumed not to invoke 35 U.S.C. 112(f) except as otherwise indicated in an Office action.

3. Claim limitation "strobe unit", and "processing unit" has/have been interpreted under 35 U.S.C. 112(f) or pre-AIA 35 U.S.C. 112, sixth paragraph, because it uses/they use a generic placeholder "unit" coupled with functional language without reciting sufficient structure to achieve the function:

"strobe unit" coupled with functional language "generate strobe".

"processing unit" coupled with functional language "receive".

Furthermore, the generic placeholder is not preceded by a structural modifier.

Since the claim limitation(s) invokes 35 U.S.C. 112(f) or pre-AIA 35 U.S.C. 112, sixth paragraph, claim(s) 1-20 has/have been interpreted to cover the corresponding

Application/Control Number: 15/289,039 Page 4
Art Unit: 2664

structure described in the specification that achieves the claimed function, and equivalents thereof.

A review of the specification shows that the following appears to be the corresponding structure described in the specification for the 35 U.S.C. 112(f) or pre-AIA 35 U.S.C. 112, sixth paragraph limitation:

For limitation "a strobe unit", corresponding structure is strobe unit 336 shown in fig. 3a.

For limitation "a processing unit", corresponding structure is processor complex 310 shown in figs. 3a and 3b also see para 0071 wherein processor complex 310 is tied to non-volatile (NV) memory 316 comprising of one or more flash memory devices.

If applicant wishes to provide further explanation or dispute the examiner's interpretation of the corresponding structure, applicant must identify the corresponding structure with reference to the specification by page and line number, and to the drawing, if any, by reference characters in response to this Office action.

If applicant does not intend to have the claim limitation(s) treated under 35 U.S.C. 112(f) or pre-AIA 35 U.S.C. 112, sixth paragraph, applicant may amend the claim(s) so that it/they will clearly not invoke 35 U.S.C. 112(f) or pre-AIA 35 U.S.C. 112, sixth paragraph, or present a sufficient showing that the claim recites/recite sufficient structure, material, or acts for performing the claimed function to preclude application of 35 U.S.C. 112(f) or pre-AIA 35 U.S.C. 112, sixth paragraph.

Application/Control Number: 15/289,039 Page 5
Art Unit: 2664

For more information, see MPEP § 2173 *et seq.* and *Supplementary Examination Guidelines for Determining Compliance With 35 U.S.C. 112 and for Treatment of Related Issues in Patent Applications*, 76 FR 7162, 7167 (Feb. 9, 2011).

Claim Rejections - 35 USC § 102

4. In the event the determination of the status of the application as subject to AIA 35 U.S.C. 102 and 103 (or as subject to pre-AIA 35 U.S.C. 102 and 103) is incorrect, any correction of the statutory basis for the rejection will not be considered a new ground of rejection if the prior art relied upon, and the rationale supporting the rejection, would be the same under either status.

5. The following is a quotation of the appropriate paragraphs of 35 U.S.C. 102 that form the basis for the rejections under this section made in this Office action:

> A person shall be entitled to a patent unless –(a)(1) the claimed invention was patented, described in a printed publication, or in public use, on sale or otherwise available to the public before the effective filing date of the claimed invention.

6. Claim(s) 1, 2, 5, 7, 8, and 12-20 is/are rejected under 35 U.S.C. 102(a)(1) as being anticipated by Subbotin et al (US 2008/0298794 A1).

As per claim 1, Subbotin discloses a photographic system (fig. 1 camera system 100), comprising:

Application/Control Number: 15/289,039 Page 6
Art Unit: 2664

a camera module, configured to sample a photographic scene according to exposure parameters (fig. 1 imaging device 150);

a strobe unit, configured to generate strobe illumination within the photographic scene according to strobe parameters (fig. 1 flash 155);

a processing unit in communication with the camera module (fig. 1 CPU 105, also see para 0009 related toward image processor) configured to:

receive a shutter release command (fig. 1 shutter release button 135);

cause the camera module to sample a first image of the photographic scene based on a first set of sampling parameters in response to the shutter release command (fig. 3a, capture baseline image 305, determine average luminance for each sector of baseline image 310);

store the first image within an image set (fig. 1 memory 125, also see para 0011);

cause the camera module to sample a second image of the photographic scene based on a second set of sampling parameters in response to the shutter release command (fig. 3a, capture test flash image 315, determine average luminance for each sector of test flash image 320);

store the second image within the image set (fig. 1 memory 125, also see para 0011);

specify a strobe intensity value based on a measured exposure for images in the image set (fig. 3a, determine flash affected zones based on average luminances of baseline and test flash image 325);

Application/Control Number: 15/289,039 Page 7
Art Unit: 2664

configure the strobe unit based on the strobe intensity value (figs. 3a and 3b, steps 330 and 340);

and in response to configuring the strobe unit, cause the camera module to sample a final image (fig. 3b, capture final image 350).

As per claim 2, Subbotin further discloses the photographic system of claim 1, wherein the first set of sampling parameters specifies a first set of exposure parameters and the second set of sampling parameters specifies a second set of exposure parameters (Subbotin discloses exposure parameters of first and second set is based on luminance values (i.e. brightness) of the two image frames, see para 0011).

As per claim 5, Subbotin further discloses the photographic system of claim 1, further configured to: recommend an image from the image set based on exposure quality metric values associated with images comprising the image set; and display the recommended image on a display unit (figs. 3a and 3b, steps 330-350 recommends that a final image should be captured based upon luminance of the pixel data captured from the previous captured images, step 340-350 are not performed every single time, therefore these steps are considered a type of recommendation, see associated written description).

Application/Control Number: 15/289,039 Page 8
Art Unit: 2664

As per claim 7, Subbotin further discloses the photographic system of claim 1, wherein a first strobe intensity and a second strobe intensity define an intensity range associated with a strobe intensity function (fig. 3a step 315 represents a first flash intensity, and fig. 3b steps 340-350 represents a second flash intensity, see associated written description).

As per claim 8, the photographic system of claim 7, wherein the second strobe intensity is adaptively determined based on at least one previously sampled image (fig. 3b steps 340-350 (second flash intensity) is based on baseline and test flash image).

As per claim 12, Subbotin further discloses the photographic system of claim 1, wherein the strobe intensity value is defined by a strobe intensity function (fig. 3b, flash intensity step 340).

As per claim 13, Subbotin further discloses the photographic system of claim 12, wherein the strobe intensity function adaptively generates the strobe intensity value based on at least one previously sampled image or a previously determined exposure (figs. 3a-3b, base line and test flash image are the basis for flash intensity step 340).

As per claim 14, Subbotin further discloses the photographic system of claim 1, wherein the strobe intensity value is for sequential images within the image set (figs. 3a-

Application/Control Number: 15/289,039 Page 9
Art Unit: 2664

3b, flash intensity step 340 is based on sequential images, baseline image and test flash image).

Claims 15-20 are the computer program claims corresponding to the photographic system of Claims 1, 5, 7, 8, 13 and 14 respectively, and are rejected based on the same reasoning/rationale.

Claim Rejections - 35 USC § 103

7. The following is a quotation of 35 U.S.C. 103 which forms the basis for all obviousness rejections set forth in this Office action:

> A patent for a claimed invention may not be obtained, notwithstanding that the claimed invention is not identically disclosed as set forth in section 102, if the differences between the claimed invention and the prior art are such that the claimed invention as a whole would have been obvious before the effective filing date of the claimed invention to a person having ordinary skill in the art to which the claimed invention pertains. Patentability shall not be negated by the manner in which the invention was made.

8. Claims 3 and 4 is/are rejected under 35 U.S.C. 103 as being unpatentable over Subbotin et al (US 2008/0298794 A1) in view of Cho et al (US 2015/0015740 A1).

As per claim 3, Subbotin further discloses the photographic system of claim 2, wherein the first set of exposure parameters specifies a first exposure time, and the second set of exposure parameters specifies a second exposure time.

Application/Control Number: 15/289,039 Page 10
Art Unit: 2664

Subbotin fails to teach the limitations as recited above in claim 3. However, Cho discloses an image processing method, in which two images are captured under two exposure times for adjusting the brightness (Cho, fig. 2 s210 and 220, also see para 0053).

Therefore, it would have been obvious to one of ordinary skill in the art, before the effective filing date of the claimed invention, to combine the teachings of Subbotin in view of Cho, as a whole, by incorporating the ability to adjust the exposure times as disclosed by Cho, into the imaging method as disclosed by Subbotin, because doing so would provide a more efficient way of adjusting the brightness of an image, thus enhancing overall image quality.

As per claim 4, the combined teachings of Subbotin in view of Cho, as a whole, further disclose the photographic system of claim 3, wherein the first exposure time is substantially equal to the second exposure time, and wherein the first exposure time is determined for the photographic scene with the strobe unit disabled (Cho, para 0053)

9. Claim 6 is/are rejected under 35 U.S.C. 103 as being unpatentable over Subbotin et al (US 2008/0298794 A1) in view of Feng et al (US 2014/0307117 A1).

Application/Control Number: 15/289,039 Page 11
Art Unit: 2664

As per claim 6, Subbotin further discloses the photographic system of claim 5, wherein each exposure quality metric value comprises a count of over-exposed pixels for a corresponding image

Subbotin fails to teach the limitations as recited above in claim 6. However, Feng discloses an exposure control method, in which sequential images are captured at different exposure settings and over-exposed pixel blocks are measured (Feng, fig. 7, para 0032).

Therefore, it would have been obvious to one of ordinary skill in the art, before the effective filing date of the claimed invention, to combine the teachings of Subbotin in view of Feng, as a whole, by incorporating the method of measuring pixel blocks of each individual pixels as disclosed by Feng, into the imaging method as disclosed by Subbotin, because doing so would provide a more efficient way of measuring over-exposed pixels, thus enhancing the flash/strobe lighting creating quality images.

10. Claim 9 is/are rejected under 35 U.S.C. 103 as being unpatentable over Subbotin et al (US 2008/0298794 A1) in view of Kasahara et al (US 2008/0019680 A1)

As per claim 9, The photographic system of claim 1, wherein causing the camera module to sample the first image is associated with a first time interval of less than two-

Application/Control Number: 15/289,039 Page 12
Art Unit: 2664

hundred milliseconds, and causing the camera module to sample the second image is associated with a second time interval of less than two-hundred milliseconds.

Subbotin fails to teach the limitations as recited above in claim 9. However, Kasahara discloses an imaging device with the ability to set the shutter speeds to any of eleven levels including a high level of 1/4000, which is an interval less than two-hundred milliseconds (Kasahara, para 0047).

Therefore, it would have been obvious to one of ordinary skill in the art, before the effective filing date of the claimed invention, to combine the teachings of Subbotin in view of Kasahara, as a whole, by incorporating the ability to adjust/set a shutter speed as disclosed by Kasahara, into the imaging method as disclosed by Subbotin, because doing so would provide a more efficient way of capturing images at various speeds, thus enhancing the customization of images being captured.

9. Claims 10 and 11 is/are rejected under 35 U.S.C. 103 as being unpatentable over Subbotin et al (US 2008/0298794 A1).

Claims 10 and 11 are related towards a generic structure of the strobe unit comprising either an LED or Xenon tube and how they light up. However, Examiner

Application/Control Number: 15/289,039 Page 13
Art Unit: 2664

takes Official Notice that it is well known in the art for strobes/flashes to be comprised of either LED or Xenon Tubes.

Therefore, it would have been obvious of one of ordinary skill in the art, at the time of the invention was made to make a flash comprising of either LED or Xenon Tube, because doing so provides a cheap and efficient way to integrate an outside light source for taking lighted images in dark areas, thus producing quality images.

Conclusion

Any inquiry concerning this communication or earlier communications from the examiner should be directed to JOHN H. MOREHEAD III whose telephone number is (571)270-3845. The examiner can normally be reached on Mon - Fri. 730-1700 est.

Examiner interviews are available via telephone, in-person, and video conferencing using a USPTO supplied web-based collaboration tool. To schedule an interview, applicant is encouraged to use the USPTO Automated Interview Request (AIR) at http://www.uspto.gov/interviewpractice.

If attempts to reach the examiner by telephone are unsuccessful, the examiner's supervisor, Lin Ye can be reached on (571) 272-7372. The fax phone number for the organization where this application or proceeding is assigned is 571-273-8300.

Application/Control Number: 15/289,039 Page 14
Art Unit: 2664

Information regarding the status of an application may be obtained from the Patent Application Information Retrieval (PAIR) system. Status information for published applications may be obtained from either Private PAIR or Public PAIR. Status information for unpublished applications is available through Private PAIR only. For more information about the PAIR system, see http://pair-direct.uspto.gov. Should you have questions on access to the Private PAIR system, contact the Electronic Business Center (EBC) at 866-217-9197 (toll-free). If you would like assistance from a USPTO Customer Service Representative or access to the automated information system, call 800-786-9199 (IN USA OR CANADA) or 571-272-1000.

JHM3

/DENNIS HOGUE/

Primary Examiner, Art Unit 2664

5/7/2017

LINCOLN LAW SCHOOL OF SAN JOSE
INTELLECTUAL PROPERTY SERIES

EXHIBIT: OFFICE ACTION RESPONSE

Applicant : Duelight Llc
Application No. : 15/289,039

Attorney's Docket No.: DUELP006A
Page : 2 of 14

Amendments to the Claims:

This listing of claims replaces all prior versions and listings of claims in the application:

1. (Currently Amended) A photographic system, comprising:

    a camera module, configured to sample a photographic scene according to exposure parameters comprising an exposure time and an exposure sensitivity;

    ~~a strobe unit, configured to generate strobe illumination within the photographic scene according to strobe parameters;~~

    one or more processors ~~a processing unit~~ in communication with the camera module, wherein the one or more processors execute instructions ~~configured~~ to:

    receive a shutter release command;

    cause the camera module to sample a first image of the photographic scene during a first time interval based on a first set of sampling parameters in response to the shutter release command, wherein the first set of sampling parameters specifies a first strobe intensity that is non-zero;

    store the first image within an image set;

    cause the camera module to sample a second image of the photographic scene during a second time interval based on a second set of sampling parameters in response to the shutter release command, wherein the second set of sampling parameters specifies a second strobe intensity that is non-zero and different than the first strobe intensity;

    store the second image within the image set,

    wherein strobe illumination is generated according to the first strobe intensity during the first time interval and the second strobe intensity during the second time interval,

    wherein the first strobe intensity and the second strobe intensity define an intensity range associated with a strobe intensity function;

    generate, using the strobe intensity function, a specified strobe intensity based on the first and second images;

Applicant : Duelight Llc
Application No. : 15/289,039

Attorney's Docket No.: DUELP006A
Page : 3 of 14

~~specify a strobe intensity value based on a measured exposure for images in the image set;~~

~~configure the strobe unit based on the strobe intensity value; and~~

~~in response to configuring the strobe unit,~~ cause the camera module to sample a ~~final~~ third image of the photographic scene during a third time interval based on a third set of sampling parameters in response to the shutter release command, wherein the third set of sampling parameters specifies a third strobe intensity that is non-zero and different than the second strobe intensity;

store the third image within the image set;

align at least a portion of the first image, the second image, and the third image within the image set;

generate a resulting aligned image by combining at least two of the images of the image set.

2. (Currently Amended) The photographic system of claim 1, wherein the first set of sampling parameters specifies a first ~~set of~~ exposure ~~parameters~~ sensitivity and the second set of sampling parameters specifies a second ~~set of~~ exposure ~~parameters~~ sensitivity.

3. (Currently Amended) The photographic system of claim 1[[2]], wherein the first set of ~~exposure~~ sampling parameters specifies a first exposure time, and the second set of ~~exposure~~ sampling parameters specifies a second exposure time.

4. (Currently Amended) The photographic system of claim 3, wherein the first exposure time is substantially equal to the second exposure time, and wherein the first exposure time is determined for the photographic scene with [[the]]a strobe unit disabled.

5. (Original) The photographic system of claim 1, further configured to:

recommend an image from the image set based on exposure quality metric values associated with images comprising the image set; and

Applicant : Duelight Llc
Application No. : 15/289,039

Attorney's Docket No.: DUELP006A
Page : 4 of 14

display the recommended image on a display unit.

6. (Original) The photographic system of claim 5, wherein each exposure quality metric value comprises a count of over-exposed pixels for a corresponding image.

7. (Cancelled)

8. (Currently Amended) The photographic system of claim [[7]]1, wherein the second strobe intensity is adaptively determined based on at least one previously sampled image.

9. (Currently Amended) The photographic system of claim 1, wherein ~~causing the camera module to sample the first image is associated with a~~the first time interval [[of]]is less than two-hundred milliseconds, and ~~causing the camera module to sample the second image is associated with a~~the second time interval [[of]]is less than two-hundred milliseconds.

10. (Currently Amended) The photographic system of claim 1, wherein ~~the strobe unit comprises a light-emitting diode (LED), and~~ strobe intensity is associated with average current driving the LED.

11. (Currently Amended) The photographic system of claim 1, wherein ~~the strobe unit comprises a Xenon tube, and~~ strobe intensity is associated with pulse duration for [[the]]a Xenon tube.

12. (Cancelled)

13. (Currently Amended) The photographic system of claim 1[[2]], wherein the strobe intensity function adaptively generates the specified strobe intensity ~~value~~ based on at least one previously sampled image or a previously determined exposure.

Applicant : Duelight Llc
Application No. : 15/289,039

Attorney's Docket No.: DUELP006A

14. (Currently Amended) The photographic system of claim 1, wherein the ~~strobe intensity value is for~~ first image, the second image, and the third image are sequential images within the image set.

15. (Currently Amended) A computer program product comprising computer executable instructions stored on a non-transitory computer readable medium that when executed by a processor instruct the processor to: ~~embodied in a non-transitory computer-readable medium that, when executed by a processor, causes the processor to generate an image set by performing a method comprising:~~

receive[[ing]] a shutter release command;

cause[[ing]] a camera module to sample a first image of a photographic scene during a first time interval based on a first set of sampling parameters in response to the shutter release command, wherein the first set of sampling parameters specifies a first strobe intensity that is non-zero;

store[[ing]] the first image within [[the]]an image set;

cause[[ing]] [[a]]the camera module to sample a second image of the photographic scene during a second time interval based on a second set of sampling parameters in response to the shutter release command, wherein the second set of sampling parameters specifies a second strobe intensity that is non-zero and different than the first strobe intensity;

store[[ing]] the second image within the image set,

wherein strobe illumination is generated according to the first strobe intensity during the first time interval and the second strobe intensity during the second time interval,

wherein the first strobe intensity and the second strobe intensity define an intensity range associated with a strobe intensity function;

generate, using the strobe intensity function, a specified strobe intensity based on the first and second images;

~~specifying a strobe intensity value based on a measured exposure for images in the image set;~~

Applicant : Duelight Llc
Application No. : 15/289,039
Attorney's Docket No.: DUELP006A
Page : 6 of 14

~~configuring a strobe unit based on the strobe intensity value; and~~

~~in response to configuring the strobe unit,~~ cause[[ing]] the camera module to sample a ~~final~~ third image of the photographic scene during a third time interval based on a third set of sampling parameters in response to the shutter release command, wherein the third set of sampling parameters specifies a third strobe intensity that is non-zero and different than the second strobe intensity;

store the third image within the image set;

align at least a portion of the first image, the second image, and the third image within the image set; and

generate a resulting aligned image by combining at least two of the images of the image set.

16. (Currently Amended) The computer program product of claim 15, ~~further comprising~~ wherein the processor is further instructed to:

recommend[[ing]] an image from the image set based on exposure quality metric values associated with images comprising the image set; and

display[[ing]] the recommended image on a display unit.

17. (Original) The computer program product of claim 15, wherein a first strobe intensity and a second strobe intensity define an intensity range associated with a strobe intensity function.

18. (Original) The computer program product of claim 17, wherein the second strobe intensity is adaptively determined based on at least one previously sampled image.

19. (Currently Amended) The computer program product of claim 17, wherein the strobe intensity function adaptively generates the specified strobe intensity ~~value~~ based on at least one previously sampled image or a previously determined exposure.

Applicant : Duelight Llc
Application No. : 15/289,039

Attorney's Docket No.: DUELP006A
Page : 7 of 14

20. (Currently Amended) The <u>computer program product</u> ~~photographic system~~ of claim 15, wherein the ~~strobe intensity value is for~~<u>first image, the second image, and the third image are sequential images within the image set.</u>

Applicant : Duelight Llc
Application No. : 15/289,039

Attorney's Docket No.: DUELP006A
Page : 8 of 14

Remarks:

Summary

Claims 1-20 were pending.

Claims 1–4, 8–11, 13–16, 19, and 20 have been amended, while claims 7 and 12 have been cancelled. Support for such amendments is found by way of example, inter alia, in Figures 4A-4H, as well as paragraphs [0063], and [0088]-[0106] of the present description. No new matter is introduced. Claims 1–6, 8–11, and 13–20 are now pending, including independent claims 1 and 15.

Rejections Under 35 U.S.C. 112(f)

The Examiner has interpreted Claims 1-20 under 35 U.S.C. 112(f) or 35 U.S.C. 112 (pre-AIA), sixth paragraph, as being indefinite for "because it uses/they use a generic placeholder "unit" coupled with functional language without reciting sufficient structure to achieve the function", as indicated by the Examiner. Such interpretation is deemed overcome by virtue of the amendments made hereinabove.

Interpretation Under 35 U.S.C. 102

The Examiner has rejected Claims 1, 2, 5, 7, 8, and 12-20 under 35 U.S.C. 102(a) as being anticipated by SUBBOTIN (U.S. Patent Pub. No. 2008/0298794). Applicant respectfully disagrees with such rejection, especially in view of the amendments made hereinabove to each of the independent claims.

Specifically, applicant has amended the independent claims, as follows:

> a camera module, configured to sample a photographic scene according to exposure parameters <u>comprising an exposure time and an exposure sensitivity</u>;
>
> <s>a strobe unit, configured to generate strobe illumination within the photographic scene according to strobe parameters;</s>
>
> <u>one or more precessors</u><s>a processing unit</s> in communication with the camera module, <u>wherein the one or more processors execute instructions</u> <s>configured</s> to:
>
> > receive a shutter release command;
> >
> > cause the camera module to sample a first image of the photographic scene <u>during a first time interval</u> based on a first set of sampling parameters in

Applicant : Duelight Llc
Application No. : 15/289,039

Attorney's Docket No.: DUELP006A
Page : 9 of 14

response to the shutter release command, wherein the first set of sampling parameters specifies a first strobe intensity that is non-zero;

store the first image within an image set;

cause the camera module to sample a second image of the photographic scene during a second time interval based on a second set of sampling parameters in response to the shutter release command, wherein the second set of sampling parameters specifies a second strobe intensity that is non-zero and different than the first strobe intensity;

store the second image within the image set,

wherein strobe illumination is generated according to the first strobe intensity during the first time interval and the second strobe intensity during the second time interval,

wherein the first strobe intensity and the second strobe intensity define an intensity range associated with a strobe intensity function;

generate, using the strobe intensity function, a specified strobe intensity based on the first and second images;

~~specify a strobe intensity value based on a measured exposure for images in the image set;~~

~~configure the strobe unit based on the strobe intensity value; and~~

~~in response to configuring the strobe unit,~~ cause the camera module to sample a ~~final~~ third image of the photographic scene during a third time interval based on a third set of sampling parameters in response to the shutter release command, wherein the third set of sampling parameters specifies a third strobe intensity that is non-zero and different than the second strobe intensity;

store the third image within the image set;

align at least a portion of the first image, the second image, and the third image within the image set;

generate a resulting aligned image by combining at least two of the images of the image set.

Applicant : Duelight Llc
Application No. : 15/289,039

Attorney's Docket No.: DUELP006A

(see this or similar, but not necessarily identical language in the independent claims, as amended).

With respect to the independent claims, applicant respectfully notes that the SUBBOTIN reference, as relied upon by the Examiner, discloses that:

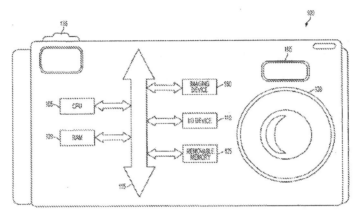

FIG. 1

SUBBOTIN. Figure 1.

Applicant : Duelight Llc
Application No. : 15/289,039

Attorney's Docket No.: DUELP006A

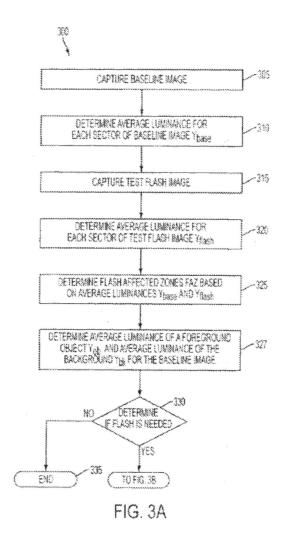

FIG. 3A

SUBBOTIN. Figure 3A.

(57) **ABSTRACT**

Methods and apparatuses for image exposure include capturing a first image under a first illumination condition, determining a luminance of the first image at a plurality of sectors, capturing a second image under a second illumination condition employing an artificial light source, determining a luminance of the second image at the plurality of sectors, and determining if the artificial light source should be used to capture a final image using the luminances of the first and second images at the plurality of sectors. If the artificial light source is to be used, an output level of the light source is determined.

SUBBOTIN. Abstract.

Applicant : Duelight Llc
Application No. : 15/289,039

Attorney's Docket No.: DUELP006A
Page : 12 of 14

However, disclosing a generic camera system (as in Figure 1), a method for determining if flash is needed (as in Figure 3), and/or "determining if the artificial light source should be used to capture a final image using the luminances of the first and second images", as in the SUBBOTIN excerpt(s) relied upon, does not teach or suggest, at a minimum "align at least a portion of the first image, the second image, and the third image within the image set," much less:

> receive a shutter release command;
>
> cause the camera module to sample a first image of the photographic scene <u>during a first time interval</u> based on a first set of sampling parameters in response to the shutter release command, wherein <u>the first set of sampling parameters specifies a first strobe intensity that is non-zero</u>;
>
> store the first image within an image set;
>
> cause the camera module to sample a second image of the photographic scene <u>during a second time interval</u> based on a second set of sampling parameters in response to the shutter release command, wherein <u>the second set of sampling parameters specifies a second strobe intensity that is non-zero and different than the first strobe intensity</u>;
>
> store the second image within the image set,
>
> > wherein <u>strobe illumination</u> is <u>generated</u> according to <u>the first strobe intensity during the first time interval and the second strobe intensity during the second time interval</u>,
> >
> > wherein the first strobe intensity and the second strobe intensity define an intensity range associated with <u>a strobe intensity function</u>;
> >
> > generate, using the strobe intensity function, <u>a specified strobe intensity based on the first and second images</u>;
> >
> > cause the camera module to sample a third image of the photographic scene during a third time interval <u>based on a third set of sampling parameters</u> in response to the shutter release command, <u>wherein the third set of sampling parameters specifies a third strobe intensity that is non-zero and different than the second strobe intensity</u>;

Applicant : Duelight Llc
Application No. : 15/289,039

Attorney's Docket No.: DUELP006A
Page : 13 of 14

>> store the third image within the image set;
>
> <u>align at least a portion of the first image, the second image, and the third image within the image set</u>;
>
> <u>generate a resulting aligned image by combining at least two of the images of the image set</u>.

(emphasis added), as claimed by applicant.

The Examiner is reminded that a claim is anticipated only if each and every element as set forth in the claim is found, either expressly or inherently described in a single prior art reference. Verdegaal Bros. v. Union Oil Co. Of California, 814 F.2d 628, 631, 2 USPQ2d 1051, 1053 (Fed. Cir. 1987). Moreover, the identical invention must be shown in as complete detail as contained in the claim. Richardson v. Suzuki Motor Co.868 F.2d 1226, 1236, 9USPQ2d 1913, 1920 (Fed. Cir. 1989). The elements must be arranged as required by the claim.

This criterion has simply not been met by the above reference excerpt(s), as noted above.

Rejections Under 35 U.S.C. 103

Claims 3, 4 stand rejected under 35 U.S.C. § 103(a) in view of U.S. Pat. Pub. No. 2010/0165178 (CHOU), U.S. Pat. Pub. No. 2008/0298794 (SUBBOTIN), and U.S. Pat. Pub. No. 2015/0015740 (CHO). Claims 4, 10, 11, 0053, stand rejected under 35 U.S.C. § 103(a) in view of U.S. Pat. Pub. No. 2010/0165178 (CHOU), U.S. Pat. Pub. No. 2015/0015740 (CHO), U.S. Pat. Pub. No. 2008/0298794 (SUBBOTIN), and U.S. Pat. Pub. No. 2014/0307117 (FENG). Claim 9 stands rejected under 35 U.S.C. § 103(a) in view of U.S. Pat. Pub. No. 2008/0298794 (SUBBOTIN) and U.S. Pat. Pub. No. 2008/0019680 (KASAHARA). Claims 10, 11 stand rejected under 35 U.S.C. § 103(a) in view of U.S. Pat. Pub. No. 2008/0298794 (SUBBOTIN). Applicant notes that such claims are allowable per the claim amendments herein and/or dependence on a now allowable independent claim.

Conclusion

It is believed that all of the pending issues have been addressed. Claims 1-20 are in condition for allowance per the claim amendments herein.

However, the absence of a reply to a specific rejection, issue, or comment does not signify agreement with or concession of that rejection, issue, or comment. In addition, because the arguments made above may not be exhaustive, there may be reasons for patentability of any or all pending claims (or other claims) that have not been expressed. Still yet, nothing in this reply

Applicant : Duelight Llc
Application No. : 15/289,039

Attorney's Docket No.: DUELP006A

should be construed as intention to concede any issue with regard to any claim, except as specifically stated in this reply. Finally, it should be noted that no claims are intended to be construed under 35 U.S.C. 112, paragraph 6.

In the event a telephone conversation would expedite the prosecution of this application, the Examiner may reach the undersigned at (408) 971-2573 or britten@zilkakotab.com. Applicant hereby requests an extension of time to respond and encloses the appropriate fee. Applicant does not believe that any additional fees are due. However, in the event that any other fees are due, the Director is hereby authorized to charge any required fees due (other than issue fees), and to credit any overpayment made, in connection with the filing of this paper to Deposit Account No. 50-1351 (Order No. DUELP006A).

Respectfully submitted,

Zilka-Kotab, PC.

/BRITTENSESSIONS/

Britten Sessions
Reg. No. 68,278

1155 N. 1st Street, Suite 105
San Jose, CA 95112-4925
408-971-2573

LINCOLN LAW SCHOOL OF SAN JOSE
INTELLECTUAL PROPERTY SERIES

EXHIBIT: OFFICE ACTION

EXHIBITS   511

UNITED STATES PATENT AND TRADEMARK OFFICE

UNITED STATES DEPARTMENT OF COMMERCE
United States Patent and Trademark Office
Address: COMMISSIONER FOR PATENTS
P.O. Box 1450
Alexandria, Virginia 22313-1450
www.uspto.gov

APPLICATION NO.	FILING DATE	FIRST NAMED INVENTOR	ATTORNEY DOCKET NO.	CONFIRMATION NO.
15/354,935	11/17/2016	Adam Barry Feder	DUELP022A/DL009	2154

135841   7590   02/08/2017
Zilka-Kotab, PC - DUEL
1155 N. 1st St.
Suite 105
SAN JOSE, CA 95112

EXAMINER
DAGNEW, MEKONNEN D

ART UNIT	PAPER NUMBER
2664	

NOTIFICATION DATE	DELIVERY MODE
02/08/2017	ELECTRONIC

Please find below and/or attached an Office communication concerning this application or proceeding.

The time period for reply, if any, is set in the attached communication.

Notice of the Office communication was sent electronically on above-indicated "Notification Date" to the following e-mail address(es):

zk-uspto@zilkakotab.com
eofficeaction@appcoll.com

PTOL-90A (Rev. 04/07)

PATENT PROSECUTION WORKBOOK

Office Action Summary	Application No. 15/354,935	Applicant(s) FEDER ET AL.
	Examiner MEKONNEN DAGNEW	Art Unit 2664 / AIA (First Inventor to File) Status: Yes

-- *The MAILING DATE of this communication appears on the cover sheet with the correspondence address* --

Period for Reply

A SHORTENED STATUTORY PERIOD FOR REPLY IS SET TO EXPIRE **3** MONTHS FROM THE MAILING DATE OF THIS COMMUNICATION.
- Extensions of time may be available under the provisions of 37 CFR 1.136(a). In no event, however, may a reply be timely filed after SIX (6) MONTHS from the mailing date of this communication.
- If NO period for reply is specified above, the maximum statutory period will apply and will expire SIX (6) MONTHS from the mailing date of this communication.
- Failure to reply within the set or extended period for reply will, by statute, cause the application to become ABANDONED (35 U.S.C. § 133). Any reply received by the Office later than three months after the mailing date of this communication, even if timely filed, may reduce any earned patent term adjustment. See 37 CFR 1.704(b).

Status

1) ☒ Responsive to communication(s) filed on *11/17/2016*.
   ☐ A declaration(s)/affidavit(s) under **37 CFR 1.130(b)** was/were filed on _____.
2a) ☐ This action is **FINAL**.   2b) ☒ This action is non-final.
3) ☐ An election was made by the applicant in response to a restriction requirement set forth during the interview on _____; the restriction requirement and election have been incorporated into this action.
4) ☐ Since this application is in condition for allowance except for formal matters, prosecution as to the merits is closed in accordance with the practice under *Ex parte Quayle*, 1935 C.D. 11, 453 O.G. 213.

Disposition of Claims*

5) ☒ Claim(s) *1-20* is/are pending in the application.
   5a) Of the above claim(s) _____ is/are withdrawn from consideration.
6) ☐ Claim(s) _____ is/are allowed.
7) ☒ Claim(s) *1-20* is/are rejected.
8) ☐ Claim(s) _____ is/are objected to.
9) ☐ Claim(s) _____ are subject to restriction and/or election requirement.

* If any claims have been determined <u>allowable</u>, you may be eligible to benefit from the **Patent Prosecution Highway** program at a participating intellectual property office for the corresponding application. For more information, please see http://www.uspto.gov/patents/init_events/pph/index.jsp or send an inquiry to PPHfeedback@uspto.gov.

Application Papers

10) ☐ The specification is objected to by the Examiner.
11) ☐ The drawing(s) filed on _____ is/are: a) ☐ accepted or b) ☐ objected to by the Examiner.
    Applicant may not request that any objection to the drawing(s) be held in abeyance. See 37 CFR 1.85(a).
    Replacement drawing sheet(s) including the correction is required if the drawing(s) is objected to. See 37 CFR 1.121(d).

Priority under 35 U.S.C. § 119

12) ☐ Acknowledgment is made of a claim for foreign priority under 35 U.S.C. § 119(a)-(d) or (f).
    Certified copies:
      a) ☐ All   b) ☐ Some**   c) ☐ None of the:
      1. ☐ Certified copies of the priority documents have been received.
      2. ☐ Certified copies of the priority documents have been received in Application No. _____.
      3. ☐ Copies of the certified copies of the priority documents have been received in this National Stage application from the International Bureau (PCT Rule 17.2(a)).
** See the attached detailed Office action for a list of the certified copies not received.

Attachment(s)
1) ☒ Notice of References Cited (PTO-892)
2) ☒ Information Disclosure Statement(s) (PTO/SB/08a and/or PTO/SB/08b) Paper No(s)/Mail Date _____.
3) ☐ Interview Summary (PTO-413) Paper No(s)/Mail Date _____.
4) ☐ Other: _____.

U.S. Patent and Trademark Office
PTOL-326 (Rev. 11-13) — Office Action Summary — Part of Paper No./Mail Date 20170202

Application/Control Number: 15/354,935 Page 2
Art Unit: 2664

DETAILED ACTION

1. The present application, filed on or after March 16, 2013, is being examined under the first inventor to file provisions of the AIA.

Claim Rejections - 35 USC § 112

2. The following is a quotation of 35 U.S.C. 112(f):

> (f) Element in Claim for a Combination. – An element in a claim for a combination may be expressed as a means or step for performing a specified function without the recital of structure, material, or acts in support thereof, and such claim shall be construed to cover the corresponding structure, material, or acts described in the specification and equivalents thereof.

The following is a quotation of pre-AIA 35 U.S.C. 112, sixth paragraph:

> An element in a claim for a combination may be expressed as a means or step for performing a specified function without the recital of structure, material, or acts in support thereof, and such claim shall be construed to cover the corresponding structure, material, or acts described in the specification and equivalents thereof.

Use of the word "means" (or "step for") in a claim with functional language creates a rebuttable presumption that the claim element is to be treated in accordance with 35 U.S.C. 112(f) (pre-AIA 35 U.S.C. 112, sixth paragraph). The presumption that 35 U.S.C. 112(f) (pre-AIA 35 U.S.C. 112, sixth paragraph) is invoked is rebutted when the function is recited with sufficient structure, material, or acts within the claim itself to entirely perform the recited function.

Absence of the word "means" (or "step for") in a claim creates a rebuttable presumption that the claim element **is not** to be treated in accordance with 35 U.S.C. 112(f) (pre-AIA 35 U.S.C. 112, sixth paragraph). The presumption that 35 U.S.C. 112(f) (pre-AIA 35

Application/Control Number: 15/354,935 Page 3
Art Unit: 2664

U.S.C. 112, sixth paragraph) is not invoked is rebutted when the claim element recites function but fails to recite sufficiently definite structure, material or acts to perform that function.

Claim elements in this application that use the word "means" (or "step for") are presumed to invoke 35 U.S.C. 112(f) except as otherwise indicated in an Office action. Similarly, claim elements that do not use the word "means" (or "step for") are presumed not to invoke 35 U.S.C. 112(f) except as otherwise indicated in an Office action.

Regarding claims 19, the following claim limitations has/have been interpreted under 35 U.S.C. 112(f) or pre-AIA 35 U.S.C. 112, sixth paragraph, because it uses/they use a generic placeholder coupled with functional language without reciting sufficient structure to achieve the function.

- a camera module, configured to sample a photographic scene
- a processing unit, coupled to the camera module, and configured to: configure one or more exposure parameters for the image stack

Furthermore, the generic placeholder is not preceded by a structural modifier. In each case, the modifier before "unit" merely refers to the recited function of the unit.

Since the claim limitation(s) invokes 35 U.S.C. 112(f) or pre-AIA 35 U.S.C. 112, sixth paragraph, claim(s) 19 has/have been interpreted to cover the corresponding structure described in the specification that achieves the claimed function, and equivalents thereof.

A review of the specification shows that the following appears to be the corresponding structure described in the specification for the 35 U.S.C. 112(f) or pre-AIA 35 U.S.C. 112, sixth paragraph limitation: each of the above recited units is a camera inside the mobile device and a CPU (see Fig. 3D element 370) respectively.

Application/Control Number: 15/354,935 Page 4
Art Unit: 2664

If applicant wishes to provide further explanation or dispute the examiner's interpretation of the corresponding structure, applicant must identify the corresponding structure with reference to the specification by page and line number, and to the drawing, if any, by reference characters in response to this Office action.

If applicant does not intend to have the claim limitation(s) treated under 35 U.S.C. 112(f) or pre-AIA 35 U.S.C. 112, sixth paragraph, applicant may amend the claim(s) so that it/they will clearly not invoke 35 U.S.C. 112(f) or pre-AIA 35 U.S.C. 112, sixth paragraph, or present a sufficient showing that the claim recites/recite sufficient structure, material, or acts for performing the claimed function to preclude application of 35 U.S.C. 112(f) or pre-AIA 35 U.S.C. 112, sixth paragraph.

For more information, see MPEP § 2173 *et seq.* and *Supplementary Examination Guidelines for Determining Compliance With 35 U.S.C. 112 and for Treatment of Related Issues in Patent Applications,* 76 FR 7162, 7167 (Feb. 9, 2011).

Claim Rejections - 35 USC § 103

3. In the event the determination of the status of the application as subject to AIA 35 U.S.C. 102 and 103 (or as subject to pre-AIA 35 U.S.C. 102 and 103) is incorrect, any correction of the statutory basis for the rejection will not be considered a new ground of rejection if the prior art relied upon, and the rationale supporting the rejection, would be the same under either status.

The following is a quotation of 35 U.S.C. 103 which forms the basis for all obviousness rejections set forth in this Office action:

A patent for a claimed invention may not be obtained, notwithstanding that the claimed invention is not identically disclosed as set forth in section 102, if the differences between the claimed invention and the prior art are such that the claimed invention as a whole would have been obvious before the effective

Application/Control Number: 15/354,935 Page 5
Art Unit: 2664

filing date of the claimed invention to a person having ordinary skill in the art to which the claimed invention pertains. Patentability shall not be negated by the manner in which the invention was made.

4. Claims 1-20 are rejected under 35 U.S.C. 103 as being unpatentable over McMahon et al. (US 2013/0147979 A1; hereinafter McMahon) in view of Terashima (US 2010/0194963).

Regarding Claim 1: McMahon teaches a camera module (¶0071), comprising: circuitry configured to (¶0075); initialize a pixel array within an image sensor of the camera module (¶0075,0093-0095,0097-0099); sample one or more ambient images within at least one corresponding analog storage plane (¶0106-0108,0111,0129,0135-0137).

McMahon does not explicitly teach "set one or more exposure parameters for an image stack; receive a capture command; determine whether a strobe unit is enabled; and if it is determined that the strobe unit is enabled, sample one or more strobe images within the at least one corresponding analog storage plane" as recited in present claimed invention.

However, the above-mentioned claimed features are well-known in the art as evidenced by **Terashima**. In particular, **Terashima** teaches set one or more exposure parameters for an image stack (any of the exposure value, the aperture value, the white balance, the focus, the ISO sensitivity, the shutter speed, the depth of field, and the presence or absence of flash, a combination thereof, and the like (¶ 0057)); receive a capture command; determine whether a strobe unit is enabled; and if it is determined that the strobe unit is enabled (for example with the flash disabled (See fig. 8: 651 which is captured without flash (¶ 0094))), sample one or more strobe images within the at least one corresponding analog storage plane ((¶ 0057, ¶ 0094, ¶ 0071, 0082) as recited in present claimed invention.

Application/Control Number: 15/354,935 Page 6
Art Unit: 2664

In view of the above, having the system of **McMahon** and given the well-established teaching of **Terashima**, Therefore, it would have been obvious to one of ordinary skill in the art at the time the invention was made (pre-AIA) or before the effective filing date of the claimed invention (AIA) to modify the system of **McMahon** as taught by **Terashima**, since **Terashima** state that such modification would to facilitate easy display of a user-preferred image for a plurality of images generated by bracketing capture (see (¶ 0009) of **Terashima**).

Regarding Claim 2: McMahon in view of Terashima further teaches the image stack comprises an ambient image and a strobe image (**Terashima** ¶0057 ¶ 0071, 00820094-0096).

Regarding Claim 3: McMahon in view of Terashima further teaches to set the one or more exposure parameters, the circuitry is configured to at least write one or more registers within the image sensor that specifies exposure time for each of at least one corresponding analog storage plane (**McMahon** teaches ¶0106-0108,0111,0129,0135-0137), or write one or more registers within the image sensor that specifies exposure sensitivity for each of the at least one corresponding analog storage plane, or write one or more registers within the image sensor that specifies exposure time and exposure sensitivity for at least one of the at least one corresponding analog storage plane (**McMahon** teaches ¶0106-0108,0111,0129,0135-0137).

Regarding Claim 4: McMahon in view of Terashima further teaches the camera module is implemented within at least one of a digital camera, or a mobile device (**McMahon** ¶0071,0075,0093-0095)

Application/Control Number: 15/354,935 Page 7
Art Unit: 2664

Regarding Claim 5: McMahon in view of Terashima further teaches to initialize the pixel array, the circuitry is configured to drive voltages on internal nodes of photo-sensitive cells within the at least one corresponding analog storage plane to a reference voltage (**McMahon** teaches ¶0106-0108,0111,0129,0135-0137).

Regarding Claim 6: McMahon in view of Terashima further teaches to determine whether the strobe unit is enabled, the circuitry is configured to directly enable the strobe unit (**Terashima** ¶0057 ¶ 0071, 00820094-0096).

Regarding Claim 7: McMahon in view of Terashima further teaches to determine whether the strobe unit is enabled, the circuitry is configured to detect that the strobe unit has been enabled (**Terashima** ¶0057 ¶ 0071, 00820094-0096).

Regarding Claim 8: McMahon in view of Terashima further teaches the camera module is configured to store both the one or more ambient images ambient images and the one or more strobe images concurrently within the at least one corresponding analog storage plane (**McMahon** teaches ¶0106-0108,0111,0129,0135-0137).

Regarding Claim 9: McMahon in view of Terashima further teaches the camera module is configured to offload at least of the one or more ambient images prior to sampling the one or more strobe images within the at least one corresponding analog storage plane (**McMahon** teaches ¶0106-0108,0111,0129,0135-0137).

Application/Control Number: 15/354,935　　　　　　　　　　　　　　　　　　　　Page 8
Art Unit: 2664

Regarding Claim 10: McMahon in view of Terashima further teaches the circuitry is further configured to enable simultaneous integration of a photographic scene for at least two corresponding analog storage planes (**McMahon** teaches ¶0106-0108,0111,0129,0135-0137).

Regarding Claim 11: McMahon in view of Terashima further teaches two or more analog sampling circuits within the at least two corresponding analog storage planes each integrate a respective image during a sampling interval (**McMahon** teaches ¶0106-0108, 0111, 0129, 0135-0137).

Regarding Claim 12: McMahon in view of Terashima further teaches the circuitry is further configured to: enable integration to proceed during a first sampling interval for at least two different analog storage planes (**Terashima** ¶ 0057 ¶ 0071, 00820094-0096. Note that when image is captured with a flash); disable integration for at least one analog storage plane of the at least two different analog storage planes; and enable integration to proceed during a second sampling interval for at least one analog storage plane of the at least two different analog storage planes (**Terashima** ¶0057 ¶ 0071, 00820094-0096.Note that when image is captured without a flash).

Regarding Claim 13: McMahon in view of Terashima further teaches the camera module is configured to transmit image data corresponding to each of the at least two different

Application/Control Number: 15/354,935 Page 9
Art Unit: 2664

analog storage planes to a processing unit (**McMahon** teaches ¶0106-0108,0111,0129,0135-0137).

Regarding Claim 14: McMahon in view of Terashima further teaches the processing unit is configured to generate exposure parameters (**Terashima** ¶0057 ¶ 0071, 00820094-0096).

Regarding Claim 15: McMahon in view of Terashima further teaches to sample the one or more ambient images and the one or more strobe images, the circuitry is configured to: assert an active low state to initialize cells of the pixel array, enable integration of a first signal from an associated photodiode on a first analog sampling circuit to generate an ambient sample comprising at least one ambient image of the one or more ambient images (**Terashima** ¶ 0057 ¶ 0071, 00820094-0096. Note that when image is captured with a flash); and determine whether the strobe unit is enabled; and if it is determined that the strobe unit is enabled, enable integration of a second signal from the associated photodiode on a second analog sampling circuit to generate a strobe sample comprising at least one strobe image of the one or more strobe images; wherein a strobe enable signal is asserted after the sampling the one or more ambient images is completed (**Terashima** ¶ 0057 ¶ 0071, 00820094-0096. Note that when image is captured with a flash).

Regarding Claim 16: McMahon in view of Terashima further teaches the circuitry is further configured to reset the photodiode after disabling integration of the signal on the first analog sampling circuit (**Terashima** ¶0057 ¶ 0071, 00820094-0096).

Application/Control Number: 15/354,935 Page 10
Art Unit: 2664

Regarding Claim 17: McMahon in view of Terashima further teaches to sample the one or more ambient images and the one or more strobe images, the circuitry is configured to: assert an active low state to initialize cells of the pixel array, enable integration of a first signal from an associated photodiode on a first analog sampling circuit; disable integration of the first signal on the first analog sampling circuit; enable integration of a second signal from the associated photodiode on a second analog sampling circuit **(Terashima ¶ 0057 ¶ 0071, 00820094-0096. Note that when image is captured without a flash)**; disable integration of the second signal on the second analog sampling circuit; and enable integration of the first signal on the first analog sampling circuit, wherein a strobe enable signal is asserted between two different sampling intervals for a same ambient image **(Terashima ¶ 0057 ¶ 0071, 00820094-0096. Note that when image is captured without a flash)**.

Regarding Claim 18: McMahon in view of Terashima further teaches to sample the one or more ambient images and the one or more strobe images, the circuitry is configured to: assert an active low state to initialize cells the pixel array, enable, during at least two separate time intervals, integration of at least one signal from an associated photodiode on at least two separate analog sampling circuits, disable, after the at least two separate time intervals, integration of the at least one signal on the at least two separate analog sampling circuits **(Terashima ¶ 0057 ¶ 0071, 00820094-0096. Note that when image is captured without a flash)**, determine whether the strobe unit is enabled after the at least two separate time intervals; and if it is determined that the strobe unit is enabled, enable integration of a third signal on a third analog sampling circuit, wherein the integrated at least first signal of the at least two separate analog sampling circuits comprises at least one respective ambient sample of at least one ambient image of the one or more ambient images, and the integrated third signal

Application/Control Number: 15/354,935 Page 11
Art Unit: 2664

of the third analog sampling circuit comprises a first strobe sample of a first strobe image of the one or more strobe images (**Terashima** ¶ 0057 ¶ 0071, 00820094-0096. Note that when image is captured with a flash).

Regarding Claim 19: **McMahon** teaches a system, comprising: a camera module (¶0071), configured to sample a photographic scene; a processing unit, coupled to the camera module, and configured to: configure one or more exposure parameters for the image stack; receive a capture command; initialize a pixel array within an image sensor of the camera module (**Terashima** ¶0075,0093-0095,0097-0099).

McMahon does not explicitly teach "sample one or more ambient images within at least one corresponding analog storage plane; determine whether a strobe unit is enabled; and if it is determined that the strobe unit is enabled, sample one or more strobe images within the at least one corresponding analog storage plane" as recited in present claimed invention.

However, the above-mentioned claimed features are well-known in the art as evidenced by **Terashima**. In particular, **Terashima** teaches sample one or more ambient images within at least one corresponding analog storage plane; determine whether a strobe unit is enabled (**Terashima** ¶ 0057 ¶ 0071, 00820094-0096. Note that when image is captured with a flash); and if it is determined that the strobe unit is enabled, sample one or more strobe images within the at least one corresponding analog storage plane (any of the exposure value, the aperture value, the white balance, the focus, the ISO sensitivity, the shutter speed, the depth of field, and the presence or absence of flash, a combination thereof, and the like (**Terashima** ¶ 0057; ¶ 0094 ¶ 0071, 0082) as recited in present claimed invention.

In view of the above, having the system of **McMahon** and given the well-established teaching of **Terashima**, Therefore, it would have been obvious to one of ordinary skill in the art

Application/Control Number: 15/354,935 Page 12
Art Unit: 2664

at the time the invention was made (pre-AIA) or before the effective filing date of the claimed invention (AIA) to modify the system of **McMahon** as taught by **Terashima**, since **Terashima** state that such modification would to facilitate easy display of a user-preferred image for a plurality of images generated by bracketing capture (see (¶ 0009) of **Terashima**).

Regarding Claim 20: **McMahon** teaches a method, comprising: receiving a capture command; initializing a pixel array within an image sensor of a camera module (¶0075).

McMahon does not explicitly teach "configuring one or more exposure parameters for an image stack ;sampling one or more ambient images within at least one corresponding analog storage plane; determining whether a strobe unit is enabled; and if it is determined that the strobe unit is enabled, sampling one or more strobe images within the at least one corresponding analog storage plane." as recited in present claimed invention.

However, the above-mentioned claimed features are well-known in the art as evidenced by **Terashima**. In particular, **Terashima** teaches configuring one or more exposure parameters for an image stack ;sampling one or more ambient images within at least one corresponding analog storage plane; determining whether a strobe unit is enabled; and if it is determined that the strobe unit is enabled, sampling one or more strobe images within the at least one corresponding analog storage plane (any of the exposure value, the aperture value, the white balance, the focus, the ISO sensitivity, the shutter speed, the depth of field, and the presence or absence of flash, a combination thereof, and the like **(Terashima** ¶ 0057, ¶ 0071, 0082) as recited in present claimed invention.

Application/Control Number: 15/354,935　　　　　　　　　　　　　　　　　　　　Page 13
Art Unit: 2664

In view of the above, having the system of **McMahon** and given the well-established teaching of **Terashima**, Therefore, it would have been obvious to one of ordinary skill in the art at the time the invention was made (pre-AIA) or before the effective filing date of the claimed invention (AIA) to modify the system of **McMahon** as taught by **Terashima**, since **Terashima** state that such modification would to facilitate easy display of a user-preferred image for a plurality of images generated by bracketing capture (see (¶ 0009) of **Terashima**).

Conclusion

5. Any inquiry concerning this communication or earlier communications from the examiner should be directed to MEKONNEN DAGNEW whose telephone number is (571)270-5092. The examiner can normally be reached on Monday-Thursday, 8AM-5PM EST.

Examiner interviews are available via telephone, in-person, and video conferencing using a USPTO supplied web-based collaboration tool. To schedule an interview, applicant is encouraged to use the USPTO Automated Interview Request (AIR) at http://www.uspto.gov/interviewpractice.

If attempts to reach the examiner by telephone are unsuccessful, the examiner's supervisor, Lin Ye can be reached on (571)272-7372. The fax phone number for the organization where this application or proceeding is assigned is 571-273-8300.

Application/Control Number: 15/354,935
Art Unit: 2664

Page 14

Information regarding the status of an application may be obtained from the Patent Application Information Retrieval (PAIR) system. Status information for published applications may be obtained from either Private PAIR or Public PAIR. Status information for unpublished applications is available through Private PAIR only. For more information about the PAIR system, see http://pair-direct.uspto.gov. Should you have questions on access to the Private PAIR system, contact the Electronic Business Center (EBC) at 866-217-9197 (toll-free). If you would like assistance from a USPTO Customer Service Representative or access to the automated information system, call 800-786-9199 (IN USA OR CANADA) or 571-272-1000.

/MEKONNEN DAGNEW/
Primary Examiner, Art Unit 2664

DETAILED ACTION

LINCOLN LAW SCHOOL OF SAN JOSE
INTELLECTUAL PROPERTY SERIES

EXHIBIT: OFFICE ACTION RESPONSE

Inventor: Adam Barry Feder
Application No.: 15/354,935

Attorney's Docket No.: DUELP022A
Page: 2 of 15

Amendments to the Claims:

This listing of claims replaces all prior versions and listings of claims in the application:

1. (Currently amended) A camera ~~module~~, comprising:

    circuitry configured to:

    set one or more exposure parameters for an image stack, including specifying exposure time for each of at least two corresponding analog storage planes, wherein each of the at least two corresponding analog storage planes comprises analog sampling circuits that form an image plane within an image sensor of the camera;

    receive a capture command;

    initialize a pixel array comprising the at least two corresponding analog storage planes within [[an]]the image sensor ~~of the camera module~~;

    sample one or more ambient images within the at least [[one]]two corresponding analog storage plane_s_;

    determine ~~whether~~ that a strobe circuit[[unit]] is enabled; and

    ~~if it is determined that the strobe unit is enabled,~~ sample one or more strobe images within the at least [[one]]two corresponding analog storage plane_s_.

2. (Currently amended) The camera ~~module~~ of claim 1, wherein the image stack comprises [[an]]one ambient image stored in a first analog storage plane of the at least two corresponding analog storage planes and [[a]]one strobe image stored in a second analog storage plane of the at least two corresponding analog storage planes.

3. (Currently amended) The camera ~~module~~ of claim 1, wherein to set the one or more exposure parameters, the circuitry is configured to at least write one or more registers within the image sensor that specifies the exposure time for each of at least [[one]]two corresponding analog storage plane_s_, or write one or more registers within the image sensor that specifies exposure sensitivity for each of the at least [[one]]two corresponding analog storage plane_s_, or write one or more registers within the image sensor that specifies the exposure time and the

Inventor : Adam Barry Feder
Application No. : 15/354,935

Attorney's Docket No.: DUELP022A
Page : 3 of 15

exposure sensitivity for <u>each of the</u> <s>at least one of the</s> at least [[one]]<u>two</u> corresponding analog storage plane<u>s</u>.

4. (Currently amended) The camera <s>module</s> of claim 1, wherein the camera <s>module</s> is <s>implemented within</s> at least one of a digital camera, or a mobile device.

5. (Currently amended) The camera <s>module</s> of claim 1, wherein to initialize the pixel array, the circuitry is configured to drive voltages on internal nodes of photo-sensitive cells within the at least [[one]]<u>two</u> corresponding analog storage plane<u>s</u> to a reference voltage.

6. (Currently amended) The camera <s>module</s> of claim 1, wherein to determine <u>that</u><s>whether</s> the strobe <u>circuit</u>[[unit]] is enabled, the circuitry is configured to directly enable the strobe <u>circuit</u>[[unit]].

7. (Currently amended) The camera <s>module</s> of claim 1, wherein to determine <u>that</u><s>whether</s> the strobe <u>circuit</u>[[unit]] is enabled, the circuitry is configured to detect that the strobe <u>circuit</u>[[unit]] has been enabled.

8. (Currently Amended) The camera <s>module</s> of claim 1, wherein the camera <s>module</s> is configured to store both the one or more ambient images <s>ambient images</s> and the one or more strobe images concurrently within the at least <u>two</u>[[one]] corresponding analog storage plane<u>s</u>.

9. (Currently Amended) The camera <s>module</s> of claim 1, wherein the camera <s>module</s> is configured to offload at least <u>one</u> of the one or more ambient images prior to sampling the one or more strobe images within the at least [[one]]<u>two</u> corresponding analog storage plane<u>s</u>.

10. (Currently amended) The camera <s>module</s> of claim 1, wherein the circuitry is further configured to enable simultaneous integration of a photographic scene for <u>the</u> at least two corresponding analog storage planes.

Inventor : Adam Barry Feder
Application No. : 15/354,935

Attorney's Docket No.: DUELP022A
Page : 4 of 15

11. (Currently amended) The camera ~~module~~ of claim 10, wherein two or more <u>of the</u> analog sampling circuits within the at least two corresponding analog storage planes each integrate a respective image during a sampling interval.

12. (Currently Amended) The camera ~~module~~ of claim 1, wherein the circuitry is further configured to:
    enable integration to proceed during a first sampling interval for at least two different analog storage planes<u> of the at least two corresponding analog storage planes</u>;
    disable integration for at least one <u>first</u> analog storage plane of the at least two different analog storage planes; and
    enable integration to proceed during a second sampling interval for at least one <u>second</u> analog storage plane of the at least two different analog storage planes.

13. (Currently amended) The camera ~~module~~ of claim 12, wherein the camera ~~module~~ is configured to transmit image data corresponding to each of the at least two different analog storage planes to a processing unit.

14. (Currently Amended) The camera ~~module~~ of claim 13, wherein the processing unit is configured to generate <u>the one or more</u> exposure parameters.

15. (Currently amended) The camera ~~module~~ of claim 1, wherein to sample the one or more ambient images ~~and the one or more strobe images~~, the circuitry is configured to:
    ~~assert an active low state to initialize cells of the pixel array;~~
    enable integration of a first signal from a~~n associated~~ photodiode <u>within</u>~~on~~ a first analog sampling circuit<u> of the analog sampling circuits</u> to generate an ambient sample <u>within a first analog storage plane of the at least two corresponding analog storage planes</u>~~comprising at least one ambient image of the one or more ambient images~~; and
    <u>disable integration of the first signal within the first analog sampling circuit</u>

Inventor : Adam Barry Feder
Application No. : 15/354,935

Attorney's Docket No.: DUELP022A
Page : 5 of 15

~~determine whether the strobe unit is enabled; and~~

~~if it is determined that the strobe unit is enabled,~~

~~enable integration of a second signal from the associated photodiode on a second analog sampling circuit to generate a strobe sample comprising at least one strobe image of the one or more strobe images;~~

~~wherein a strobe enable signal is asserted after the sampling the one or more ambient images is completed.~~

16. (Currently Amended) The camera ~~module~~ of claim 15, wherein the circuitry is further configured to reset the photodiode after disabling integration of the <u>first</u> signal on the first analog sampling circuit <u>of the analog sampling circuits</u>.

17. (Currently amended) The camera ~~module~~ of claim 1, wherein to sample the one or more ~~ambient images and the one or more~~ strobe images, the circuitry is configured to:

~~assert an active low state to initialize cells of the pixel array,~~

<u>store an ambient sample within a first analog storage plane of the at least two corresponding analog storage planes;</u>

enable integration of a first signal from a<u>n</u> ~~associated~~ photodiode <u>within</u>~~on~~ a first analog sampling circuit <u>of the analog sampling circuits, to generate a first strobe sample within a second analog storage plane of the at least two corresponding analog storage planes</u>[[;]]<u>,</u>

disable integration of the first signal on the first analog sampling circuit <u>of the analog sampling circuits</u>[[;]]<u>,</u>

<u>wherein the first analog storage plane comprises ambient samples forming a first ambient image and the second analog storage plane comprises strobe samples forming a first strobe image of the one or more strobe images</u>

~~enable integration of a second signal from the associated photodiode on a second analog sampling circuit;~~

~~disable integration of the second signal on the second analog sampling circuit; and~~

~~enable integration of the first signal on the first analog sampling circuit,~~

5

Inventor : Adam Barry Feder
Application No. : 15/354,935

Attorney's Docket No.: DUELP022A
Page : 6 of 15

~~wherein a strobe enable signal is asserted between two different sampling intervals for a same ambient image~~.

18. (Currently Amended) The camera ~~module~~ of claim 1, wherein to sample the one or more ambient images and the one or more strobe images, the circuitry is configured to:

~~assert an active low state to initialize cells the pixel array,~~

enable, during <u>a first time interval and a second time interval</u>~~at least two separate time intervals~~, integration of ~~at least one~~ <u>first</u> signal from a~~n associated~~ photodiode <u>within a first analog sampling circuit of the analog sampling circuits, to generate a first ambient sample of a first analog storage plan and a second analog sampling circuit of the analog sampling circuits to generate a second ambient sample of a second analog storage plane</u>~~on at least two separate analog sampling circuits~~,

<u>disable, after the first time interval, integration of the first signal from the photodiode within the first analog sampling circuit of the analog sampling circuits;</u>

disable, after the <u>second</u>~~at least two separate~~ time interval[[s]], integration of the ~~at least one~~ <u>first</u> signal <u>within the second analog sampling circuit of the analog sampling circuits;</u>~~on the at least two separate analog sampling circuits,~~

determine <u>that</u>~~whether~~ the strobe <u>circuit</u>[[unit]] is enabled after the <u>second time interval</u>~~at least two separate time intervals~~; and

~~if it is determined that the strobe unit is enabled,~~

enable integration of a <u>second</u>[[third]] signal on a third analog sampling circuit <u>of the analog sampling circuits, to generate a first strobe sample of a third analog storage plane</u>,

wherein the <u>first analog storage plane comprises ambient samples forming a first ambient image of the one or more ambient images, the second analog storage plane comprises ambient samples forming a second ambient image of the one or more ambient images, and the third analog storage plane comprises strobe samples forming a first strobe image of the one or more strobe images</u> ~~integrated at least first signal of the at least two separate analog sampling circuits comprises at least one respective ambient sample of at least one ambient image of the~~

Inventor : Adam Barry Feder
Application No. : 15/354,935

Attorney's Docket No.: DUELP022A
Page : 7 of 15

~~one or more ambient images, and the integrated third signal of the third analog sampling circuit comprises a first strobe sample of a first strobe image of the one or more strobe images~~.

19. (Currently amended) A system, comprising:

a camera ~~module~~, configured to sample a photographic scene;

a processing unit <u>in communication with</u>, ~~coupled to~~ the camera ~~module,~~ and configured to:

configure one or more exposure parameters for [[the]]<u>an</u> image stack<u>, including specifying exposure time for each of at least two corresponding analog storage planes, wherein each of the at least two corresponding analog storage planes comprises analog sampling circuits that form an image plane within an image sensor of the camera</u>;

receive a capture command;

initialize a pixel array <u>comprising the at least two corresponding analog storage planes</u> within [[an]]<u>the</u> image sensor ~~of the camera module~~;

<u>cause the camera to</u> sample one or more ambient images within <u>the</u> at least <u>two</u>[[one]] corresponding analog storage plane<u>s</u>;

determine <u>that</u>~~whether~~ a strobe <u>circuit</u>[[unit]] is enabled; and

~~if it is determined that the strobe unit is enabled,~~ <u>cause the camera to</u> sample one or more strobe images within the at least <u>two</u>[[one]] corresponding analog storage plane<u>s</u>.

20. (Currently amended) A method, comprising:

configuring one or more exposure parameters for an image stack<u>, including specifying exposure time for each of at least one corresponding analog storage plane, wherein each of the at least two corresponding analog storage planes comprises analog sampling circuits that form an image plane within an image sensor of a camera</u>;

receiving a capture command;

initializing a pixel array <u>comprising the at least two corresponding analog storage planes</u> within [[an]]<u>the</u> image sensor ~~of a camera module~~;

Inventor : Adam Barry Feder
Application No. : 15/354,935

Attorney's Docket No.: DUELP022A
Page : 8 of 15

sampling one or more ambient images within at least <u>two</u>[[one]] corresponding analog storage plane<u>s</u>;

determining <u>that</u><s>whether</s> a strobe <u>circuit</u>[[unit]] is enabled; and

<s>if it is determined that the strobe unit is enabled,</s> sampling one or more strobe images within the at least <u>two</u>[[one]] corresponding analog storage plane<u>s</u>.

Inventor : Adam Barry Feder
Application No. : 15/354,935

Attorney's Docket No.: DUELP022A
Page : 9 of 15

Remarks:

Summary

Claims 1-20 were pending.

Claims 1–20 are pending, with claims 1, 19, and 20 being independent. Claims 1–20 have been amended. Support for such amendments is found, inter alia, in paragraph [053] of the present application. No new subject matter has been added. Claims 1-20 are now pending, including independent claims 1, 19, and 20.

Rejections Under 35 U.S.C. 112(f)

The Examiner has rejected Claim 19 under 35 U.S.C. 112(c) or 35 U.S.C. 112 (pre-AIA), sixth paragraph, for allegedly reciting a single means. In particular, the Examiner has alleged that the term "camera module" and "a processing unit" have been interpreted to cover a corresponding structure. Applicant respectfully disagrees with such rejection, especially in view of the amendments made hereinabove to Claim 19.

Further, *assuming arguendo* that 35 U.S.C. 112(c) was still applicable, applicant respectfully notes that before the Examiner can assert that "camera module" and/or "a processing unit" is a single means, the Examiner must determine whether the claim limitation invokes the sixth paragraph of 35 U.S.C. § 112. MPEP § 2181(I) states that a claim feature will be presumed to invoke the sixth paragraph of 35 U.S.C. § 112 if the feature meets the following 3-prong analysis:

> (A) the claim limitations must use the phrase "means for" or "step for";
> (B) the "means for" or "step for" must be modified by functional language; and
> (C) the phrase "means for" or "step for" must not be modified by sufficient structure, material, or acts for achieving the specified function.

Further, MPEP § 2181(I) states that "a claim limitation that does not use the term "means" or "step" will trigger the rebuttable presumption that 35 U.S.C. 112(f) or pre-AIA 35 U.S.C. 112, sixth paragraph does not apply. See, e.g., Phillips v. AWH Corp., 415 F.3d 1303, 1310, 75 USPQ2d 1321, 1324 (Fed. Cir. 2005) (en banc); CCS Fitness, Inc. v. Brunswick Corp., 288 F.3d 1359, 1369, 62 USPQ2d 1658, 1664 (Fed. Cir. 2002); Personalized Media Commc'ns, LLC v. ITC, 161 F.3d 696, 703-04, 48 USPQ2d 1880, 1886–87 (Fed. Cir. 1998)."

In this case, Claim 19 does not include the recitation "means for" or "step for" and, therefore, cannot be considered to invoke the sixth paragraph of 35 U.S.C. § 112. In addition, the claim features are not written as a function to be performed, but instead recited as sufficient structure to preclude application of the sixth paragraph of 35 U.S.C. § 112. Because the term "camera module" and/or "a processing unit" cannot be interpreted to invoke the sixth

Inventor : Adam Barry Feder
Application No. : 15/354,935

Attorney's Docket No.: DUELP022A
Page : 10 of 15

paragraph of 35 U.S.C. § 112, Applicants respectfully submit that claim 19 does not recite a single means.

Accordingly, withdrawal of the rejection is respectfully requested.

Rejections Under 35 U.S.C. 103

Claims 1-20 stand rejected under 35 U.S.C. § 103(a) in view of U.S. Patent Application Pub. No. 2013/0147979 [MCMAHON] and U.S. Patent Application Pub. No. 2010/0194963 [TERASHIMA]. Applicant respectfully disagrees with such rejection, especially in view of the amendments made hereinabove to each of the independent claims.

Specifically, applicant has amended the independent claims, as follows:

> set one or more exposure parameters for an image stack, including specifying exposure time for each of at least two corresponding analog storage planes, wherein each of the at least two corresponding analog storage planes comprises analog sampling circuits that form an image plane within an image sensor of the camera;
> receive a capture command;
> initialize a pixel array comprising the at least two corresponding analog storage planes within [[an]]the image sensor of the camera module;
> sample one or more ambient images within the at least [[one]]two corresponding analog storage planes;
> determine whether that a strobe circuit[[unit]] is enabled; and
> if it is determined that the strobe unit is enabled, sample one or more strobe images within the at least [[one]]two corresponding analog storage planes

(see this or similar, but not necessarily identical language in the independent claims, as amended).

With respect to the independent claims, the Examiner has relied on paragraph [0057] from the TERASHIMA reference to make a prior art showing of applicant's claimed technique "set one or more exposure parameters for an image stack, including specifying exposure time for each of at least two corresponding analog storage planes, wherein each of the at least two corresponding analog storage planes comprises analog sampling circuits that form an image plane within an image sensor of the camera" (see this or similar, but not necessarily identical language in the independent claims).

Applicant respectfully notes that the TERASHIMA reference, as relied upon by the Examiner, discloses the following:

Inventor : Adam Barry Feder
Application No. : 15/354,935

Attorney's Docket No.: DUELP022A
Page : 11 of 15

> [0057] In addition, the processor 121 controls bracketing capture in accordance with a user's operation input from the operation unit 114. Here, bracketing capture is a captured image recording process of capturing a plurality of successive images of the subject for a short period of time while changing the image capturing conditions and recording the images. In a case where this bracketing capture is performed, the bracketing capture is performed using image capturing conditions for which each image capture parameter has been changed with regard to one or a plurality of image capturing condition objects. <u>Note that the image capturing condition objects include, for example, any of the exposure value, the aperture value, the white balance, the focus, the ISO sensitivity, the shutter speed, the depth of field, and the presence or absence of flash, a combination thereof, and the like.</u> In addition, in an embodiment of the present invention, at least one image capturing condition among a user-set bracketing capture condition and an auto-bracketing capture condition is used to perform bracketing capture. Here, the user-set bracketing capture condition is an image capturing condition that is set by a user's manual operation from the operation unit 114. In addition, the auto-bracketing capture condition is an image capturing condition that is set on the basis of the judgment information output from the image recognition unit 118.

See TERASHIMA, paragraph [0057] – emphasis added.

However, disclosing "image capturing condition objects" including "exposure value, the aperture value, the white balance, the focus, the ISO sensitivity, the shutter speed, the depth of field, and the presence or absence of flash," as in the TERASHIMA excerpt(s) relied upon, does not teach or suggest "set one or more exposure parameters for an image stack, including specifying <u>exposure time for **each** of at least two corresponding analog storage planes</u>, wherein <u>each</u> of the at least two corresponding <u>analog storage planes comprises analog sampling circuits </u>that form <u>an image plane</u> within an image sensor of the camera" (emphasis added), as claimed by applicant.

With respect to the independent claims, the Examiner has relied on paragraphs [0075], [0093]-[0095], and [0097]-[0099] from the MCMAHON reference to make a prior art showing of applicant's claimed technique "initialize a pixel array comprising the at least two corresponding analog storage planes within the image sensor" (see this or similar, but not necessarily identical language in the independent claims).

Applicant respectfully notes that the MCMAHON reference, as relied upon by the Examiner, discloses the following:

Inventor : Adam Barry Feder
Application No. : 15/354,935

Attorney's Docket No.: DUELP022A
Page : 12 of 15

4.3.3.1. Optimization of Conversion Gain

[0093] The performance of imagers within an imager array that are intended to capture specific sub-bands of the spectrum can be improved by utilizing pixels with different conversion gains tailored for each of the different capture bands. Conversion gain in a typical 4T CMOS pixel can be controlled by changing the size of the capacitance of the "sense node", typically a floating diffusion capacitor (FD). The charge to voltage conversion follows the equation $V=Q/C$ where Q is the charge, C is the capacitance and V is the voltage. Thus the smaller the capacitance, the higher the voltage resulting from a given charge hence the higher the

See MCMAHON, paragraph [0093] – emphasis added.

4.3.3.2. Optimization of Source Follower Gain

[0094] Additional performance gains can be achieved by changing the characteristics of the amplifiers in each pixel within a focal plane. The amplifier in a traditional 4T CMOS pixel is constructed from a Source Follower transistor. The Source Follower transistor amplifies the voltage across the FD so as to drive the pixel signal down the column line to the column circuit where the signal is subsequently sampled.

See MCMAHON, paragraph [0094] – emphasis added.

4.3.3.3. Optimization of Full Well Capacity

[0097] Another optimization that can be performed is through changing the full well capacity of the photodiodes. The full well capacity of the photodiode is the maximum number of electrons the photodiode can store in its maximally depleted state. The full well of the pixels can be controlled through the x-y size of the photodiode, the doping levels of the implants that form the diode structure and the voltage used to reset the pixel.

See MCMAHON, paragraph [0097] – emphasis added.

4.3.3.4. Three Parameter Optimization

[0098] As can be seen in the previous sections, there are three main characteristics that can be tuned in order to configure pixels within a focal plane that have the same capture band for improved imaging performance. The optimal solution for all three parameters is dependent on the targeted behavior of a particular focal plane. Each focal plane can be tailored to the spectral band it is configured to capture. While the design of the pixel can be optimized, in many embodiments the performance of the pixels is simply improved with

See MCMAHON, paragraph [0097] – emphasis added.

Inventor : Adam Barry Feder
Application No. : 15/354,935

Attorney's Docket No.: DUELP022A
Page : 13 of 15

However, disclosing various optimization techniques including optimization of conversion gain, of source follower gain, and of full well capacity, as well as three parameter optimization, in addition to generally disclosing an imager array, as in the MCMAHON excerpt(s) relied upon, does not teach or suggest "initialize <u>a pixel array</u> comprising the at least two <u>corresponding analog storage planes</u> within the image sensor" (emphasis added), as claimed by applicant.

To establish a prima facie case of obviousness, three basic criteria must be met. First, there must be some suggestion or motivation, either in the references themselves or in the knowledge generally available to one of ordinary skill in the art, to modify the reference or to combine reference teachings. Second, there must be a reasonable expectation of success. Finally, the prior art reference (or references when combined) must teach or suggest all the claim limitations. The teaching or suggestion to make the claimed combination and the reasonable expectation of success must both be found in the prior art and not based on applicant's disclosure. *In re Vaeck*, 947 F.2d 488, 20 USPQ2d 1438 (Fed.Cir.1991).

Applicant respectfully asserts that at least the third element of the prima facie case of obviousness has not been met, since the prior art excerpts, as relied upon by the Examiner, fail to teach or suggest all of the claim limitations, as noted above.

Dependent Claims

Applicant further notes that the prior art is also deficient with respect to the dependent claims. For example, with respect to Claim 2, the Examiner has relied on paragraphs [0057], [0071], [0082], and [0094]-[0096] from the TERASHIMA reference to make a prior art showing of applicant's claimed technique "wherein the image stack comprises one ambient image stored in a first analog storage plane of the at least two corresponding analog storage planes and one strobe image stored in a second analog storage plane of the at least two corresponding analog storage planes" (as amended).

Applicant respectfully notes that the TERASHIMA reference, as relied upon by the Examiner, discloses the following:

Inventor : Adam Barry Feder
Application No. : 15/354,935

Attorney's Docket No.: DUELP022A
Page : 14 of 15

> [0094] FIG. 8 is a diagram illustrating an example display on the occasion of the selection of a priority image from among bracketing-captured images being displayed on the display unit 208 in the embodiment of the present invention. In the example illustrated in FIG. 8, <u>image capturing conditions such as the shutter speed, the ISO sensitivity, the F-value, and with or without flash (flashlight)</u> are added and displayed in lower right portions of bracketing-captured images 651 to 653 being displayed on a priority image selection screen 650, by way of example. For example, in a case where it is difficult to find the difference between individual bracketing-captured images displayed on the display unit 208 on the screen, the image capturing conditions are displayed together with the individual bracketing-captured images, thereby allowing the user to easily select a priority image.

See TERASHIMA, paragraph [0094] – emphasis added.

However, generally disclosing "image capturing condition objects" as well as "image capturing conditions" including "with or without flash (flashlight)", as in TERASHIMA, does not teach or suggest applicant's claimed technique "wherein the <u>image stack</u> comprises one <u>ambient image stored</u> in a <u>first analog storage plane</u> of the at least two corresponding analog storage planes and one <u>strobe image stored</u> in a <u>second analog storage plane</u> of the at least two corresponding analog storage planes" (emphasis added), as claimed by applicant.

Again, as noted above, since at least the third element of the prima facie case of obviousness has not been met, a notice of allowance or specific prior art showing of each of the foregoing claim elements, in combination with the remaining claimed features, is respectfully requested.

Conclusion

It is believed that all of the pending issues have been addressed. Claims 1-20 are in condition for allowance per the claim amendments herein.

However, the absence of a reply to a specific rejection, issue, or comment does not signify agreement with or concession of that rejection, issue, or comment. In addition, because the arguments made above may not be exhaustive, there may be reasons for patentability of any or all pending claims (or other claims) that have not been expressed. Still yet, nothing in this reply should be construed as intention to concede any issue with regard to any claim, except as specifically stated in this reply. Finally, it should be noted that no claims are intended to be construed under 35 U.S.C. 112, paragraph 6.

Inventor : Adam Barry Feder
Application No. : 15/354,935

Attorney's Docket No.: DUELP022A

In the event a telephone conversation would expedite the prosecution of this application, the Examiner may reach the undersigned at (408) 971-2573 or britten@zilkakotab.com. Applicant does not believe that any additional fees are due. However, in the event that any other fees are due, the Director is hereby authorized to charge any required fees due (other than issue fees), and to credit any overpayment made, in connection with the filing of this paper to Deposit Account No. 50-1351 (Order No. DUELP022A).

Respectfully submitted,

Zilka-Kotab, PC.

/BRITTEN SESSIONS/

Britten Sessions
Reg. No. 68278

1155 N. 1st Street, Suite 105
San Jose, CA 95112-4925
408-971-2573

LINCOLN LAW SCHOOL OF SAN JOSE
INTELLECTUAL PROPERTY SERIES

EXHIBIT: EXAMINER AGENDA

IN THE UNITED STATES PATENT AND TRADEMARK OFFICE

In re Application of:	Title: SYSTEM, METHOD, AND COMPUTER PROGRAM PRODUCT FOR LOCATING LOST OR STOLEN ITEMS
Application No.: 14/718,083	
Applicant: Donald Arndt	
File Date: 2015-05-21	Examiner: YOUNG, PATRICIA
	Docket No.: ARND-P0001
	Confirmation No.: 8255

Proposed Amendment

Examiner:

Please review the following amendment(s) to be discussed in our upcoming interview.

Application No.: 14/718,083
Date: Jun 26, 2017
Patent Examiner Agenda

AMENDMENTS TO THE CLAIMS

Claim 1. (Currently amended) A <u>wearable device, comprising:</u>
<u>a non-transitory memory storing instructions; and</u>
<u>one or more processors in communication with the non-transitory memory,</u>
<u>wherein the one or more processors execute the instructions to</u><s>computing apparatus including a processor and a memory storing instructions that, when executed by the processor, configure the apparatus to perform a method comprising</s>:

determin<u>e</u>[[ing]] whether there are any RFID tags within a set range of a transceiver;

if at least one RFID tag is determined, query[[ing]] the at least one RFID tag;
identify[[ing]] each of the at least one RFID tag;
sav<u>e</u>[[ing]] the identification of the at least one RFID tag;
determin<u>e</u>[[ing]] that the RFID tag is no longer in a sensing zone;
<u>select a first video camera, among a plurality of cameras, on the wearable device, wherein the first video camera is selected based on at least one of an accelerometer, a gyroscope, one or more proximity sensors, and one or more photodetector;</u>
record[[ing]] a video, using <s>at least one</s> <u>the first</u> video camera <u>of the plurality of video cameras</u>, of surroundings associated with the at least one RFID tag;
record[[ing]] an audio, using at least one microphone, of the surroundings associated with the at least one RFID tag;
sav<u>e</u>[[ing]] the video recording and the audio recording; and
provid<u>e</u>[[ing]] access to view the saved identification, the saved video recording, and the saved audio recording.

Claim 2. (Currently amended) The <u>wearable device</u> <s>apparatus</s> of claim 1, further comprising two or more video cameras, and two or more microphones.

Application No.: 14/718,083
Date: Jun 26, 2017
Patent Examiner Agenda

Claim 3. (Currently amended) The <u>wearable device</u> ~~apparatus~~ of claim 2, wherein one video camera is selected among the two or more video cameras to record.

Claim 4. (Currently amended) The <u>wearable device</u> ~~apparatus~~ of claim 3, wherein the one video camera is selected based on at least one of an accelerometer, a gyroscope, one or more proximity sensors, and one or more photodetectors.

Claim 5. (Currently amended) The <u>wearable device</u> ~~apparatus~~ of claim 2, wherein two video cameras are selected to record.

Claim 6. (Currently amended) The <u>wearable device</u> ~~apparatus~~ of claim 1, further comprising recording, using at one audio input, sounds associated with an environment around the at least one RFID tag, saving the audio recording, and uploading the saved audio recording to a remote storage.

Claim 7. (Currently amended) The <u>wearable device</u> ~~apparatus~~ of claim 1, further comprising uploading the saved video recording or saved audio recording to a remote storage, wherein the remote storage includes storage located in the cloud.

Claim 8. (Currently amended) The <u>wearable device</u> ~~apparatus~~ of claim 7, wherein the uploading occurs automatically after the saved video recording or saved audio recording is completed.

Claim 9. (Currently amended) The <u>wearable device</u> ~~apparatus~~ of claim 7, wherein the uploading occurs in response to a user request after the saved video recording or saved audio recording is completed.

Claim 10. (Currently amended) The <u>wearable device</u> ~~apparatus~~ of claim 1, further comprising communicating with an external device, wherein the communicating includes receiving instruction from the external device to pair with the at least one RFID tag.

EXHIBITS 545

Application No.: 14/718,083
Date: Jun 26, 2017
Patent Examiner Agenda

Claim 11. (Currently amended) The wearable device apparatus of claim 10, wherein the communicating includes sending the saved identification or the saved video recording to the external device.

Claim 12. (Currently amended) The wearable device apparatus of claim 1, wherein the determining occurs at a set time intervals.

Claim 13. (Currently amended) The wearable device apparatus of claim 12, wherein the time interval is once every three minutes.

Claim 14. (Currently amended) The wearable device apparatus of claim 1, wherein the determining occurs based on GPS coordinates or cellular coordinates.

Claim 15. (Currently amended) A computer-implemented method, comprising:
determining, using a processor on a wearable device, whether there are any RFID tags within a set range of a transceiver;
if at least one RFID tag is determined, querying the at least one RFID tag;
identifying each of the at least one RFID tag;
saving the identification of the at least one RFID tag;
determining that the RFID tag is no longer in a sensing zone;
selecting a first video camera, among a plurality of cameras, on the wearable device, wherein the first video camera is selected based on at least one of an accelerometer, a gyroscope, one or more proximity sensors, and one or more photodetector;
recording a video, using at least one the first video camera of the plurality of video cameras, of surroundings associated with the at least one RFID tag;
recording an audio, using at least one microphone, of the surroundings associated with the at least one RFID tag;
saving the video recording and the audio recording; and

Application No.: 14/718,083
Date: Jun 26, 2017
Patent Examiner Agenda

providing access to view the saved identification, the saved video recording, and the saved audio recording.

Claim 16.   (Currently amended) A computer program product comprising computer executable instructions stored on a non-transitory computer readable medium that when executed by a processor instruct the processor to non-transitory computer-readable storage medium having stored thereon instructions including instructions that, when executed by a processor, configure the processor to perform a method comprising:

determin[[ing]]e, using a processor on a wearable device, whether there are any RFID tags within a set range of a transceiver;

if at least one RFID tag is determined, query[[ing]] the at least one RFID tag;

identify[[ing]] each of the at least one RFID tag;

save[[ing]] the identification of the at least one RFID tag;

determine[[ing]] that the RFID tag is no longer in a sensing zone;

select a first video camera, among a plurality of cameras, on the wearable device, wherein the first video camera is selected based on at least one of an accelerometer, a gyroscope, one or more proximity sensors, and one or more photodetector;

record[[ing]] a video, using at least one the first video camera of the plurality of video cameras, of surroundings associated with the at least one RFID tag;

record[[ing]] an audio, using at least one microphone, of the surroundings associated with the at least one RFID tag;

save[[ing]] the video recording and the audio recording; and

provide[[ing]] access to view the saved identification, the saved video recording, and the saved audio recording.

Claim 17.   (New)   The wearable device apparatus of claim 1, wherein the one or more processors further execute the instructions to simultaneously record a second video, using a second video camera of the plurality of video cameras.

Application No.: 14/718,083
Date: Jun 26, 2017
Patent Examiner Agenda

Claim 18. (New) The wearable device apparatus of claim 1, wherein the first video camera is given priority, in comparison to the plurality of cameras, based on having a view with least obstruction.

Claim 19. (New) The wearable device apparatus of claim 1, wherein the one or more processors further execute the instructions to, while recording the video, switching from the first video camera to a second video camera based on the second video camera having a view less obstructed than the first video camera.

Claim 20. (New) The wearable device apparatus of claim 1, wherein the determination that the RFID is no longer in a sensing zone triggers the recording of the video using the first video camera.

Application No.: 14/718,083
Date: Jun 26, 2017
Patent Examiner Agenda

REMARKS

LINCOLN LAW SCHOOL OF SAN JOSE
INTELLECTUAL PROPERTY SERIES

EXHIBIT: EXAMINER INTERVIEW SUMMARY

IN THE UNITED STATES PATENT AND TRADEMARK OFFICE

In re Application of:

Application No.: 14/718,083

Applicant: Donald Arndt

File Date: 2015-05-21

Title: SYSTEM, METHOD, AND COMPUTER PROGRAM PRODUCT FOR LOCATING LOST OR STOLEN ITEMS

Examiner: YOUNG, PATRICIA

Docket No.: ARND-P0001

Confirmation No.: 8255

Examiner Interview

Date of interview
Jun 27, 2017

Type of interview
Telephonic

Name of participant(s):   Examiner Young, Britten Sessions

Exhibit shown?
Appendix A

Claims discussed
Independent Claims and dependent claims 12, 17-20

Prior art discussed
N/a

Substance of interview
Reviewed proposed amendments with Examiner, asked Examiner if they had any suggestions to help proceed towards an allowance.

Agreement reached?
The amendments will merit a further search and consideration.

APPENDIX A

IN THE UNITED STATES PATENT AND TRADEMARK OFFICE

In re Application of:	Title: SYSTEM, METHOD, AND COMPUTER PROGRAM PRODUCT FOR LOCATING LOST OR STOLEN ITEMS
Application No.: 14/718,083	
Applicant: Donald Arndt	Examiner: YOUNG, PATRICIA
File Date: 2015-05-21	Docket No.: ARND-P0001
	Confirmation No.: 8255

Proposed Amendment

Examiner:

Please review the following amendment(s) to be discussed in our upcoming interview.

APPENDIX A

Application No.: 14/718,083
Date: Jun 26, 2017
Patent Examiner Agenda

AMENDMENTS TO THE CLAIMS

Claim 1. (Currently amended) A <u>wearable device, comprising:</u>
<u>a non-transitory memory storing instructions; and</u>
<u>one or more processors in communication with the non-transitory memory, wherein the one or more processors execute the instructions to</u><s>computing apparatus including a processor and a memory storing instructions that, when executed by the processor, configure the apparatus to perform a method comprising</s>:

determin<u>e</u>[[ing]] whether there are any RFID tags within a set range of a transceiver;

if at least one RFID tag is determined, query[[ing]] the at least one RFID tag;

identify[[ing]] each of the at least one RFID tag;

sav<u>e</u>[[ing]] the identification of the at least one RFID tag;

determin<u>e</u>[[ing]] that the RFID tag is no longer in a sensing zone;

<u>select a first video camera, among a plurality of cameras, on the wearable device, wherein the first video camera is selected based on at least one of an accelerometer, a gyroscope, one or more proximity sensors, and one or more photodetector;</u>

record[[ing]] a video, using <s>at least one</s> <u>the first</u> video camera <u>of the plurality of video cameras</u>, of surroundings associated with the at least one RFID tag;

record[[ing]] an audio, using at least one microphone, of the surroundings associated with the at least one RFID tag;

sav<u>e</u>[[ing]] the video recording and the audio recording; and

provid<u>e</u>[[ing]] access to view the saved identification, the saved video recording, and the saved audio recording.

Claim 2. (Currently amended) The <u>wearable device</u> <s>apparatus</s> of claim 1, further comprising two or more video cameras, and two or more microphones.

APPENDIX A

Application No.: 14/718,083
Date: Jun 26, 2017
Patent Examiner Agenda

Claim 3. (Currently amended) The <u>wearable device</u> ~~apparatus~~ of claim 2, wherein one video camera is selected among the two or more video cameras to record.

Claim 4. (Currently amended) The <u>wearable device</u> ~~apparatus~~ of claim 3, wherein the one video camera is selected based on at least one of an accelerometer, a gyroscope, one or more proximity sensors, and one or more photodetectors.

Claim 5. (Currently amended) The <u>wearable device</u> ~~apparatus~~ of claim 2, wherein two video cameras are selected to record.

Claim 6. (Currently amended) The <u>wearable device</u> ~~apparatus~~ of claim 1, further comprising recording, using at one audio input, sounds associated with an environment around the at least one RFID tag, saving the audio recording, and uploading the saved audio recording to a remote storage.

Claim 7. (Currently amended) The <u>wearable device</u> ~~apparatus~~ of claim 1, further comprising uploading the saved video recording or saved audio recording to a remote storage, wherein the remote storage includes storage located in the cloud.

Claim 8. (Currently amended) The <u>wearable device</u> ~~apparatus~~ of claim 7, wherein the uploading occurs automatically after the saved video recording or saved audio recording is completed.

Claim 9. (Currently amended) The <u>wearable device</u> ~~apparatus~~ of claim 7, wherein the uploading occurs in response to a user request after the saved video recording or saved audio recording is completed.

Claim 10. (Currently amended) The <u>wearable device</u> ~~apparatus~~ of claim 1, further comprising communicating with an external device, wherein the communicating includes receiving instruction from the external device to pair with the at least one RFID tag.

APPENDIX A

Application No.: 14/718,083
Date: Jun 26, 2017
Patent Examiner Agenda

Claim 11. (Currently amended) The wearable device apparatus of claim 10, wherein the communicating includes sending the saved identification or the saved video recording to the external device.

Claim 12. (Currently amended) The wearable device apparatus of claim 1, wherein the determining occurs at a set time intervals.

Claim 13. (Currently amended) The wearable device apparatus of claim 12, wherein the time interval is once every three minutes.

Claim 14. (Currently amended) The wearable device apparatus of claim 1, wherein the determining occurs based on GPS coordinates or cellular coordinates.

Claim 15. (Currently amended) A computer-implemented method, comprising:
    determining, using a processor on a wearable device, whether there are any RFID tags within a set range of a transceiver;
    if at least one RFID tag is determined, querying the at least one RFID tag;
    identifying each of the at least one RFID tag;
    saving the identification of the at least one RFID tag;
    determining that the RFID tag is no longer in a sensing zone;
    selecting a first video camera, among a plurality of cameras, on the wearable device, wherein the first video camera is selected based on at least one of an accelerometer, a gyroscope, one or more proximity sensors, and one or more photodetector;
    recording a video, using at least one the first video camera of the plurality of video cameras, of surroundings associated with the at least one RFID tag;
    recording an audio, using at least one microphone, of the surroundings associated with the at least one RFID tag;
    saving the video recording and the audio recording; and

EXHIBITS 555

APPENDIX A

Application No.: 14/718,083
Date: Jun 26, 2017
Patent Examiner Agenda

providing access to view the saved identification, the saved video recording, and the saved audio recording.

Claim 16. (Currently amended) A computer program product comprising computer executable instructions stored on a non-transitory computer readable medium that when executed by a processor instruct the processor to ~~non-transitory computer-readable storage medium having stored thereon instructions including instructions that, when executed by a processor, configure the processor to perform a method comprising~~:

determin[[ing]]e, using a processor on a wearable device, whether there are any RFID tags within a set range of a transceiver;

if at least one RFID tag is determined, query[[ing]] the at least one RFID tag;

identify[[ing]] each of the at least one RFID tag;

save[[ing]] the identification of the at least one RFID tag;

determine[[ing]] that the RFID tag is no longer in a sensing zone;

select a first video camera, among a plurality of cameras, on the wearable device, wherein the first video camera is selected based on at least one of an accelerometer, a gyroscope, one or more proximity sensors, and one or more photodetector;

record[[ing]] a video, using ~~at least one~~ the first video camera of the plurality of video cameras, of surroundings associated with the at least one RFID tag;

record[[ing]] an audio, using at least one microphone, of the surroundings associated with the at least one RFID tag;

save[[ing]] the video recording and the audio recording; and

provide[[ing]] access to view the saved identification, the saved video recording, and the saved audio recording.

Claim 17. (New) The wearable device apparatus of claim 1, wherein the one or more processors further execute the instructions to simultaneously record a second video, using a second video camera of the plurality of video cameras.

5

APPENDIX A

Application No.: 14/718,083
Date: Jun 26, 2017
Patent Examiner Agenda

Claim 18.   (New)   The wearable device apparatus of claim 1, wherein the first video camera is given priority, in comparison to the plurality of cameras, based on having a view with least obstruction.

Claim 19.   (New)   The wearable device apparatus of claim 1, wherein the one or more processors further execute the instructions to, while recording the video, switching from the first video camera to a second video camera based on the second video camera having a view less obstructed than the first video camera.

Claim 20.   (New)   The wearable device apparatus of claim 1, wherein the determination that the RFID is no longer in a sensing zone triggers the recording of the video using the first video camera.

EXHIBITS

APPENDIX A

Application No.: 14/718,083
Date: Jun 26, 2017
Patent Examiner Agenda

REMARKS

LINCOLN LAW SCHOOL OF SAN JOSE
INTELLECTUAL PROPERTY SERIES

EXHIBIT: NOTICE OF ALLOWANCE

EXHIBITS 559

UNITED STATES PATENT AND TRADEMARK OFFICE

UNITED STATES DEPARTMENT OF COMMERCE
United States Patent and Trademark Office
Address: COMMISSIONER FOR PATENTS
P.O. Box 1450
Alexandria, Virginia 22313-1450
www.uspto.gov

NOTICE OF ALLOWANCE AND FEE(S) DUE

| 127633 | 7590 | 07/25/2017 |

Intellectual Property Clinic
Lincoln Law School of San Jose
384 S Second Street
San Jose, CA 95113

EXAMINER
YOUNG, PATRICIA I

ART UNIT	PAPER NUMBER
2488	

DATE MAILED: 07/25/2017

APPLICATION NO.	FILING DATE	FIRST NAMED INVENTOR	ATTORNEY DOCKET NO.	CONFIRMATION NO.
14/718,083	05/21/2015	Donald J. Arndt	ARND-P0001	8255

TITLE OF INVENTION: SYSTEM, METHOD, AND COMPUTER PROGRAM PRODUCT FOR LOCATING LOST OR STOLEN ITEMS

APPLN. TYPE	ENTITY STATUS	ISSUE FEE DUE	PUBLICATION FEE DUE	PREV. PAID ISSUE FEE	TOTAL FEE(S) DUE	DATE DUE
nonprovisional	MICRO	$240	$0	$0	$240	10/25/2017

THE APPLICATION IDENTIFIED ABOVE HAS BEEN EXAMINED AND IS ALLOWED FOR ISSUANCE AS A PATENT. PROSECUTION ON THE MERITS IS CLOSED. THIS NOTICE OF ALLOWANCE IS NOT A GRANT OF PATENT RIGHTS. THIS APPLICATION IS SUBJECT TO WITHDRAWAL FROM ISSUE AT THE INITIATIVE OF THE OFFICE OR UPON PETITION BY THE APPLICANT. SEE 37 CFR 1.313 AND MPEP 1308.

THE ISSUE FEE AND PUBLICATION FEE (IF REQUIRED) MUST BE PAID WITHIN <u>THREE MONTHS</u> FROM THE MAILING DATE OF THIS NOTICE OR THIS APPLICATION SHALL BE REGARDED AS ABANDONED. <u>THIS STATUTORY PERIOD CANNOT BE EXTENDED.</u> SEE 35 U.S.C. 151. THE ISSUE FEE DUE INDICATED ABOVE DOES NOT REFLECT A CREDIT FOR ANY PREVIOUSLY PAID ISSUE FEE IN THIS APPLICATION. IF AN ISSUE FEE HAS PREVIOUSLY BEEN PAID IN THIS APPLICATION (AS SHOWN ABOVE), THE RETURN OF PART B OF THIS FORM WILL BE CONSIDERED A REQUEST TO REAPPLY THE PREVIOUSLY PAID ISSUE FEE TOWARD THE ISSUE FEE NOW DUE.

HOW TO REPLY TO THIS NOTICE:

I. Review the ENTITY STATUS shown above. If the ENTITY STATUS is shown as SMALL or MICRO, verify whether entitlement to that entity status still applies.

If the ENTITY STATUS is the same as shown above, pay the TOTAL FEE(S) DUE shown above.

If the ENTITY STATUS is changed from that shown above, on PART B - FEE(S) TRANSMITTAL, complete section number 5 titled "Change in Entity Status (from status indicated above)".

For purposes of this notice, small entity fees are 1/2 the amount of undiscounted fees, and micro entity fees are 1/2 the amount of small entity fees.

II. PART B - FEE(S) TRANSMITTAL, or its equivalent, must be completed and returned to the United States Patent and Trademark Office (USPTO) with your ISSUE FEE and PUBLICATION FEE (if required). If you are charging the fee(s) to your deposit account, section "4b" of Part B - Fee(s) Transmittal should be completed and an extra copy of the form should be submitted. If an equivalent of Part B is filed, a request to reapply a previously paid issue fee must be clearly made, and delays in processing may occur due to the difficulty in recognizing the paper as an equivalent of Part B.

III. All communications regarding this application must give the application number. Please direct all communications prior to issuance to Mail Stop ISSUE FEE unless advised to the contrary.

IMPORTANT REMINDER: Utility patents issuing on applications filed on or after Dec. 12, 1980 may require payment of maintenance fees. It is patentee's responsibility to ensure timely payment of maintenance fees when due.

PTOL-85 (Rev. 02/11)

560 PATENT PROSECUTION WORKBOOK

PART B - FEE(S) TRANSMITTAL

Complete and send this form, together with applicable fee(s), to: Mail   Mail Stop ISSUE FEE
Commissioner for Patents
P.O. Box 1450
Alexandria, Virginia 22313-1450
or Fax (571)-273-2885

INSTRUCTIONS: This form should be used for transmitting the ISSUE FEE and PUBLICATION FEE (if required). Blocks 1 through 5 should be completed where appropriate. All further correspondence including the Patent, advance orders and notification of maintenance fees will be mailed to the current correspondence address as indicated unless corrected below or directed otherwise in Block 1, by (a) specifying a new correspondence address; and/or (b) indicating a separate "FEE ADDRESS" for maintenance fee notifications.

CURRENT CORRESPONDENCE ADDRESS (Note: Use Block 1 for any change of address)

127633   7590   07/25/2017
Intellectual Property Clinic
Lincoln Law School of San Jose
384 S Second Street
San Jose, CA 95113

Note: A certificate of mailing can only be used for domestic mailings of the Fee(s) Transmittal. This certificate cannot be used for any other accompanying papers. Each additional paper, such as an assignment or formal drawing, must have its own certificate of mailing or transmission.

Certificate of Mailing or Transmission
I hereby certify that this Fee(s) Transmittal is being deposited with the United States Postal Service with sufficient postage for first class mail in an envelope addressed to the Mail Stop ISSUE FEE address above, or being facsimile transmitted to the USPTO (571) 273-2885, on the date indicated below.

_____ (Depositor's name)
_____ (Signature)
_____ (Date)

APPLICATION NO.	FILING DATE	FIRST NAMED INVENTOR	ATTORNEY DOCKET NO.	CONFIRMATION NO.
14/718,083	05/21/2015	Donald J. Arndt	ARND-P0001	8255

TITLE OF INVENTION: SYSTEM, METHOD, AND COMPUTER PROGRAM PRODUCT FOR LOCATING LOST OR STOLEN ITEMS

APPLN. TYPE	ENTITY STATUS	ISSUE FEE DUE	PUBLICATION FEE DUE	PREV. PAID ISSUE FEE	TOTAL FEE(S) DUE	DATE DUE
nonprovisional	MICRO	$240	$0	$0	$240	10/25/2017

EXAMINER	ART UNIT	CLASS-SUBCLASS
YOUNG, PATRICIA I	2488	348-143000

1. Change of correspondence address or indication of "Fee Address" (37 CFR 1.363).
   ❏ Change of correspondence address (or Change of Correspondence Address form PTO/SB/122) attached.
   ❏ "Fee Address" indication (or "Fee Address" Indication form PTO/SB/47; Rev 03-02 or more recent) attached. **Use of a Customer Number is required.**

2. For printing on the patent front page, list
   (1) The names of up to 3 registered patent attorneys or agents OR, alternatively,
   (2) The name of a single firm (having as a member a registered attorney or agent) and the names of up to 2 registered patent attorneys or agents. If no name is listed, no name will be printed.
   1 _____
   2 _____
   3 _____

3. ASSIGNEE NAME AND RESIDENCE DATA TO BE PRINTED ON THE PATENT (print or type)

PLEASE NOTE: Unless an assignee is identified below, no assignee data will appear on the patent. If an assignee is identified below, the document has been filed for recordation as set forth in 37 CFR 3.11. Completion of this form is NOT a substitute for filing an assignment.

(A) NAME OF ASSIGNEE   (B) RESIDENCE: (CITY and STATE OR COUNTRY)

Please check the appropriate assignee category or categories (will not be printed on the patent) :   ❏ Individual   ❏ Corporation or other private group entity   ❏ Government

4a. The following fee(s) are submitted:
❏ Issue Fee
❏ Publication Fee (No small entity discount permitted)
❏ Advance Order - # of Copies _____

4b. Payment of Fee(s): (**Please first reapply any previously paid issue fee shown above**)
❏ A check is enclosed.
❏ Payment by credit card. Form PTO-2038 is attached.
❏ The director is hereby authorized to charge the required fee(s), any deficiency, or credits any overpayment, to Deposit Account Number _____ (enclose an extra copy of this form).

5. **Change in Entity Status** (from status indicated above)
❏ Applicant certifying micro entity status. See 37 CFR 1.29
❏ Applicant asserting small entity status. See 37 CFR 1.27
❏ Applicant changing to regular undiscounted fee status.

NOTE: Absent a valid certification of Micro Entity Status (see forms PTO/SB/15A and 15B), issue fee payment in the micro entity amount will not be accepted at the risk of application abandonment.
NOTE: If the application was previously under micro entity status, checking this box will be taken to be a notification of loss of entitlement to micro entity status.
NOTE: Checking this box will be taken to be a notification of loss of entitlement to small or micro entity status, as applicable.

NOTE: This form must be signed in accordance with 37 CFR 1.31 and 1.33. See 37 CFR 1.4 for signature requirements and certifications.

Authorized Signature _____   Date _____

Typed or printed name _____   Registration No. _____

Page 2 of 3

PTOL-85 Part B (10-13) Approved for use through 10/31/2013.   OMB 0651-0033   U.S. Patent and Trademark Office; U.S. DEPARTMENT OF COMMERCE

EXHIBITS   561

UNITED STATES PATENT AND TRADEMARK OFFICE

UNITED STATES DEPARTMENT OF COMMERCE
United States Patent and Trademark Office
Address: COMMISSIONER FOR PATENTS
P.O. Box 1450
Alexandria, Virginia 22313-1450
www.uspto.gov

APPLICATION NO.	FILING DATE	FIRST NAMED INVENTOR	ATTORNEY DOCKET NO.	CONFIRMATION NO.
14/718,083	05/21/2015	Donald J. Arndt	ARND-P0001	8255

127633 7590 07/25/2017	EXAMINER
Intellectual Property Clinic Lincoln Law School of San Jose 384 S Second Street San Jose, CA 95113	YOUNG, PATRICIA I

ART UNIT	PAPER NUMBER
2488	

DATE MAILED: 07/25/2017

Determination of Patent Term Adjustment under 35 U.S.C. 154 (b)
(Applications filed on or after May 29, 2000)

The Office has discontinued providing a Patent Term Adjustment (PTA) calculation with the Notice of Allowance.

Section 1(h)(2) of the AIA Technical Corrections Act amended 35 U.S.C. 154(b)(3)(B)(i) to eliminate the requirement that the Office provide a patent term adjustment determination with the notice of allowance. See Revisions to Patent Term Adjustment, 78 Fed. Reg. 19416, 19417 (Apr. 1, 2013). Therefore, the Office is no longer providing an initial patent term adjustment determination with the notice of allowance. The Office will continue to provide a patent term adjustment determination with the Issue Notification Letter that is mailed to applicant approximately three weeks prior to the issue date of the patent, and will include the patent term adjustment on the patent. Any request for reconsideration of the patent term adjustment determination (or reinstatement of patent term adjustment) should follow the process outlined in 37 CFR 1.705.

Any questions regarding the Patent Term Extension or Adjustment determination should be directed to the Office of Patent Legal Administration at (571)-272-7702. Questions relating to issue and publication fee payments should be directed to the Customer Service Center of the Office of Patent Publication at 1-(888)-786-0101 or (571)-272-4200.

PTOL-85 (Rev. 02/11)

OMB Clearance and PRA Burden Statement for PTOL-85 Part B

The Paperwork Reduction Act (PRA) of 1995 requires Federal agencies to obtain Office of Management and Budget approval before requesting most types of information from the public. When OMB approves an agency request to collect information from the public, OMB (i) provides a valid OMB Control Number and expiration date for the agency to display on the instrument that will be used to collect the information and (ii) requires the agency to inform the public about the OMB Control Number's legal significance in accordance with 5 CFR 1320.5(b).

The information collected by PTOL-85 Part B is required by 37 CFR 1.311. The information is required to obtain or retain a benefit by the public which is to file (and by the USPTO to process) an application. Confidentiality is governed by 35 U.S.C. 122 and 37 CFR 1.14. This collection is estimated to take 12 minutes to complete, including gathering, preparing, and submitting the completed application form to the USPTO. Time will vary depending upon the individual case. Any comments on the amount of time you require to complete this form and/or suggestions for reducing this burden, should be sent to the Chief Information Officer, U.S. Patent and Trademark Office, U.S. Department of Commerce, P.O. Box 1450, Alexandria, Virginia 22313-1450. DO NOT SEND FEES OR COMPLETED FORMS TO THIS ADDRESS. SEND TO: Commissioner for Patents, P.O. Box 1450, Alexandria, Virginia 22313-1450. Under the Paperwork Reduction Act of 1995, no persons are required to respond to a collection of information unless it displays a valid OMB control number.

Privacy Act Statement

The Privacy Act of 1974 (P.L. 93-579) requires that you be given certain information in connection with your submission of the attached form related to a patent application or patent. Accordingly, pursuant to the requirements of the Act, please be advised that: (1) the general authority for the collection of this information is 35 U.S.C. 2(b)(2); (2) furnishing of the information solicited is voluntary; and (3) the principal purpose for which the information is used by the U.S. Patent and Trademark Office is to process and/or examine your submission related to a patent application or patent. If you do not furnish the requested information, the U.S. Patent and Trademark Office may not be able to process and/or examine your submission, which may result in termination of proceedings or abandonment of the application or expiration of the patent.

The information provided by you in this form will be subject to the following routine uses:
1. The information on this form will be treated confidentially to the extent allowed under the Freedom of Information Act (5 U.S.C. 552) and the Privacy Act (5 U.S.C 552a). Records from this system of records may be disclosed to the Department of Justice to determine whether disclosure of these records is required by the Freedom of Information Act.
2. A record from this system of records may be disclosed, as a routine use, in the course of presenting evidence to a court, magistrate, or administrative tribunal, including disclosures to opposing counsel in the course of settlement negotiations.
3. A record in this system of records may be disclosed, as a routine use, to a Member of Congress submitting a request involving an individual, to whom the record pertains, when the individual has requested assistance from the Member with respect to the subject matter of the record.
4. A record in this system of records may be disclosed, as a routine use, to a contractor of the Agency having need for the information in order to perform a contract. Recipients of information shall be required to comply with the requirements of the Privacy Act of 1974, as amended, pursuant to 5 U.S.C. 552a(m).
5. A record related to an International Application filed under the Patent Cooperation Treaty in this system of records may be disclosed, as a routine use, to the International Bureau of the World Intellectual Property Organization, pursuant to the Patent Cooperation Treaty.
6. A record in this system of records may be disclosed, as a routine use, to another federal agency for purposes of National Security review (35 U.S.C. 181) and for review pursuant to the Atomic Energy Act (42 U.S.C. 218(c)).
7. A record from this system of records may be disclosed, as a routine use, to the Administrator, General Services, or his/her designee, during an inspection of records conducted by GSA as part of that agency's responsibility to recommend improvements in records management practices and programs, under authority of 44 U.S.C. 2904 and 2906. Such disclosure shall be made in accordance with the GSA regulations governing inspection of records for this purpose, and any other relevant (i.e., GSA or Commerce) directive. Such disclosure shall not be used to make determinations about individuals.
8. A record from this system of records may be disclosed, as a routine use, to the public after either publication of the application pursuant to 35 U.S.C. 122(b) or issuance of a patent pursuant to 35 U.S.C. 151. Further, a record may be disclosed, subject to the limitations of 37 CFR 1.14, as a routine use, to the public if the record was filed in an application which became abandoned or in which the proceedings were terminated and which application is referenced by either a published application, an application open to public inspection or an issued patent.
9. A record from this system of records may be disclosed, as a routine use, to a Federal, State, or local law enforcement agency, if the USPTO becomes aware of a violation or potential violation of law or regulation.

EXHIBITS 563

	Application No. 14/718,083	Applicant(s) ARNDT ET AL.		
Notice of Allowability	Examiner PATTIE I. YOUNG	Art Unit 2488	AIA (First Inventor to File) Status Yes	

-- *The MAILING DATE of this communication appears on the cover sheet with the correspondence address--*

All claims being allowable, PROSECUTION ON THE MERITS IS (OR REMAINS) CLOSED in this application. If not included herewith (or previously mailed), a Notice of Allowance (PTOL-85) or other appropriate communication will be mailed in due course. **THIS NOTICE OF ALLOWABILITY IS NOT A GRANT OF PATENT RIGHTS.** This application is subject to withdrawal from issue at the initiative of the Office or upon petition by the applicant. See 37 CFR 1.313 and MPEP 1308.

1. ☒ This communication is responsive to <u>06/27/2017</u>.
   ☐ A declaration(s)/affidavit(s) under **37 CFR 1.130(b)** was/were filed on_____.

2. ☐ An election was made by the applicant in response to a restriction requirement set forth during the interview on _____; the restriction requirement and election have been incorporated into this action.

3. ☒ The allowed claim(s) is/are <u>1-21</u>. As a result of the allowed claim(s), you may be eligible to benefit from the **Patent Prosecution Highway** program at a participating intellectual property office for the corresponding application. For more information, please see http://www.uspto.gov/patents/init_events/pph/index.jsp or send an inquiry to PPHfeedback@uspto.gov.

4. ☐ Acknowledgment is made of a claim for foreign priority under 35 U.S.C. § 119(a)-(d) or (f).
   Certified copies:
   a) ☐ All   b) ☐ Some   *c) ☐ None of the:
   1. ☐ Certified copies of the priority documents have been received.
   2. ☐ Certified copies of the priority documents have been received in Application No. _____.
   3. ☐ Copies of the certified copies of the priority documents have been received in this national stage application from the International Bureau (PCT Rule 17.2(a)).
   * Certified copies not received: _____.

Applicant has THREE MONTHS FROM THE "MAILING DATE" of this communication to file a reply complying with the requirements noted below. Failure to timely comply will result in ABANDONMENT of this application.
THIS THREE-MONTH PERIOD IS NOT EXTENDABLE.

5. ☐ CORRECTED DRAWINGS (as "replacement sheets") must be submitted.
   ☐ including changes required by the attached Examiner's Amendment / Comment or in the Office action of Paper No./Mail Date _____.
   Identifying indicia such as the application number (see 37 CFR 1.84(c)) should be written on the drawings in the front (not the back) of each sheet. Replacement sheet(s) should be labeled as such in the header according to 37 CFR 1.121(d).

6. ☐ DEPOSIT OF and/or INFORMATION about the deposit of BIOLOGICAL MATERIAL must be submitted. Note the attached Examiner's comment regarding REQUIREMENT FOR THE DEPOSIT OF BIOLOGICAL MATERIAL.

Attachment(s)
1. ☐ Notice of References Cited (PTO-892)
2. ☐ Information Disclosure Statements (PTO/SB/08), Paper No./Mail Date _____
3. ☐ Examiner's Comment Regarding Requirement for Deposit of Biological Material
4. ☐ Interview Summary (PTO-413), Paper No./Mail Date _____ .
5. ☐ Examiner's Amendment/Comment
6. ☒ Examiner's Statement of Reasons for Allowance
7. ☐ Other _____.

/PATTIE I YOUNG/
Examiner, Art Unit 2488

/SATH V PERUNGAVOOR/
Supervisory Patent Examiner, Art Unit 2488

U.S. Patent and Trademark Office
PTOL-37 (Rev. 08-13)
20170714

Notice of Allowability   Part of Paper No./Mail Date

Application/Control Number: 14/718,083
Art Unit: 2488

Page 2

DETAILED ACTION

Notice of Pre-AIA or AIA Status

1. The present application is being examined under the pre-AIA first to invent provisions.

Reasons for Allowance

2. The following is a statement of reasons for the indication of allowable subject matter: Regarding **claims 1, 15, 16**, the closet prior art does not specifically teach or reasonably suggest RFID tag is no longer in a sensing zone, wherein the determination occurs at set time intervals; select a first video camera, among a plurality of cameras, on the wearable device, wherein the first video camera is selected based on at least one of an accelerometer, a gyroscope, one or more proximity sensors, and one or more photodetector; and the wearable device is intended to be worn on a wrist or a head. **Dependent claims 2-3, 5-11, 13-14, and 17-21** are allowed for the reasons concerning the independent claim.

3. Any comments considered necessary by applicant must be submitted no later than the payment of the issue fee and, to avoid processing delays, should preferably accompany the issue fee. Such submissions should be clearly labeled "Comments on Statement of Reasons for Allowance."

4. **Claims 1-3, 5-11, and 13-21** are allowed.

Application/Control Number: 14/718,083
Art Unit: 2488

Conclusion

Any inquiry concerning this communication or earlier communications from the examiner should be directed to PATTIE I. YOUNG whose telephone number is (571)270-1049 and fax phone number is (571)270-2049. The examiner can normally be reached on MON - THU 7:30AM TO 5PM.

If attempts to reach the examiner by telephone are unsuccessful, the examiner's supervisor, SATH PERUNGAVOOR can be reached on (571) 272-7455. The fax phone number for the organization where this application or proceeding is assigned is 571-273-8300.

Information regarding the status of an application may be obtained from the Patent Application Information Retrieval (PAIR) system. Status information for published applications may be obtained from either Private PAIR or Public PAIR. Status information for unpublished applications is available through Private PAIR only. For more information about the PAIR system, see http://pair-direct.uspto.gov. Should you have questions on access to the Private PAIR system, contact the Electronic Business Center (EBC) at 866-217-9197 (toll-free). If you would like assistance from a USPTO Customer Service Representative or access to the automated information system, call 800-786-9199 (IN USA OR CANADA) or 571-272-1000.

/PIY/
Examiner, Art Unit 2488
07/14/2017

/SATH V PERUNGAVOOR/
Supervisory Patent Examiner, Art Unit 2488

LINCOLN LAW SCHOOL OF SAN JOSE
INTELLECTUAL PROPERTY SERIES

EXHIBIT: NOTICE OF ALLOWANCE

EXHIBITS 567

UNITED STATES PATENT AND TRADEMARK OFFICE

UNITED STATES DEPARTMENT OF COMMERCE
United States Patent and Trademark Office
Address: COMMISSIONER FOR PATENTS
P.O. Box 1450
Alexandria, Virginia 22313-1450
www.uspto.gov

NOTICE OF ALLOWANCE AND FEE(S) DUE

127633	7590	05/10/2016

Intellectual Property Clinic
Lincoln Law School of San Jose
384 S Second Street
San Jose, CA 95113

EXAMINER
O'HERN, BRENT T

ART UNIT	PAPER NUMBER
1781	

DATE MAILED: 05/10/2016

APPLICATION NO.	FILING DATE	FIRST NAMED INVENTOR	ATTORNEY DOCKET NO.	CONFIRMATION NO.
14/742,430	06/17/2015	Monte Phillip Dauer	DAUM-P0001	1086

TITLE OF INVENTION: Dauer Board

APPLN. TYPE	ENTITY STATUS	ISSUE FEE DUE	PUBLICATION FEE DUE	PREV. PAID ISSUE FEE	TOTAL FEE(S) DUE	DATE DUE
nonprovisional	MICRO	$240	$0	$0	$240	08/10/2016

THE APPLICATION IDENTIFIED ABOVE HAS BEEN EXAMINED AND IS ALLOWED FOR ISSUANCE AS A PATENT. PROSECUTION ON THE MERITS IS CLOSED. THIS NOTICE OF ALLOWANCE IS NOT A GRANT OF PATENT RIGHTS. THIS APPLICATION IS SUBJECT TO WITHDRAWAL FROM ISSUE AT THE INITIATIVE OF THE OFFICE OR UPON PETITION BY THE APPLICANT. SEE 37 CFR 1.313 AND MPEP 1308.

THE ISSUE FEE AND PUBLICATION FEE (IF REQUIRED) MUST BE PAID WITHIN **THREE MONTHS** FROM THE MAILING DATE OF THIS NOTICE OR THIS APPLICATION SHALL BE REGARDED AS ABANDONED. **THIS STATUTORY PERIOD CANNOT BE EXTENDED.** SEE 35 U.S.C. 151. THE ISSUE FEE DUE INDICATED ABOVE DOES NOT REFLECT A CREDIT FOR ANY PREVIOUSLY PAID ISSUE FEE IN THIS APPLICATION. IF AN ISSUE FEE HAS PREVIOUSLY BEEN PAID IN THIS APPLICATION (AS SHOWN ABOVE), THE RETURN OF PART B OF THIS FORM WILL BE CONSIDERED A REQUEST TO REAPPLY THE PREVIOUSLY PAID ISSUE FEE TOWARD THE ISSUE FEE NOW DUE.

HOW TO REPLY TO THIS NOTICE:

I. Review the ENTITY STATUS shown above. If the ENTITY STATUS is shown as SMALL or MICRO, verify whether entitlement to that entity status still applies.

If the ENTITY STATUS is the same as shown above, pay the TOTAL FEE(S) DUE shown above.

If the ENTITY STATUS is changed from that shown above, on PART B - FEE(S) TRANSMITTAL, complete section number 5 titled "Change in Entity Status (from status indicated above)".

For purposes of this notice, small entity fees are 1/2 the amount of undiscounted fees, and micro entity fees are 1/2 the amount of small entity fees.

II. PART B - FEE(S) TRANSMITTAL, or its equivalent, must be completed and returned to the United States Patent and Trademark Office (USPTO) with your ISSUE FEE and PUBLICATION FEE (if required). If you are charging the fee(s) to your deposit account, section "4b" of Part B - Fee(s) Transmittal should be completed and an extra copy of the form should be submitted. If an equivalent of Part B is filed, a request to reapply a previously paid issue fee must be clearly made, and delays in processing may occur due to the difficulty in recognizing the paper as an equivalent of Part B.

III. All communications regarding this application must give the application number. Please direct all communications prior to issuance to Mail Stop ISSUE FEE unless advised to the contrary.

IMPORTANT REMINDER: Utility patents issuing on applications filed on or after Dec. 12, 1980 may require payment of maintenance fees. It is patentee's responsibility to ensure timely payment of maintenance fees when due.

PTOL-85 (Rev. 02/11)

PART B - FEE(S) TRANSMITTAL

Complete and send this form, together with applicable fee(s), to: **Mail** Mail Stop ISSUE FEE
Commissioner for Patents
P.O. Box 1450
Alexandria, Virginia 22313-1450
or Fax (571)-273-2885

INSTRUCTIONS: This form should be used for transmitting the ISSUE FEE and PUBLICATION FEE (if required). Blocks 1 through 5 should be completed where appropriate. All further correspondence including the Patent, advance orders and notification of maintenance fees will be mailed to the current correspondence address as indicated unless corrected below or directed otherwise in Block 1, by (a) specifying a new correspondence address; and/or (b) indicating a separate "FEE ADDRESS" for maintenance fee notifications.

CURRENT CORRESPONDENCE ADDRESS (Note: Use Block 1 for any change of address)

127633   7590   05/10/2016
Intellectual Property Clinic
Lincoln Law School of San Jose
384 S Second Street
San Jose, CA 95113

Note: A certificate of mailing can only be used for domestic mailings of the Fee(s) Transmittal. This certificate cannot be used for any other accompanying papers. Each additional paper, such as an assignment or formal drawing, must have its own certificate of mailing or transmission.

Certificate of Mailing or Transmission
I hereby certify that this Fee(s) Transmittal is being deposited with the United States Postal Service with sufficient postage for first class mail in an envelope addressed to the Mail Stop ISSUE FEE address above, or being facsimile transmitted to the USPTO (571) 273-2885, on the date indicated below.

_____ (Depositor's name)
_____ (Signature)
_____ (Date)

APPLICATION NO.	FILING DATE	FIRST NAMED INVENTOR	ATTORNEY DOCKET NO.	CONFIRMATION NO.
14/742,430	06/17/2015	Monte Phillip Dauer	DAUM-P0001	1086

TITLE OF INVENTION: Dauer Board

APPLN. TYPE	ENTITY STATUS	ISSUE FEE DUE	PUBLICATION FEE DUE	PREV. PAID ISSUE FEE	TOTAL FEE(S) DUE	DATE DUE
nonprovisional	MICRO	$240	$0	$0	$240	08/10/2016

EXAMINER	ART UNIT	CLASS-SUBCLASS
O'HERN, BRENT T	1781	428-106000

1. Change of correspondence address or indication of "Fee Address" (37 CFR 1.363).
   ☐ Change of correspondence address (or Change of Correspondence Address form PTO/SB/122) attached.
   ☐ "Fee Address" indication (or "Fee Address" Indication form PTO/SB/47; Rev 03-02 or more recent) attached. **Use of a Customer Number is required.**

2. For printing on the patent front page, list
   (1) The names of up to 3 registered patent attorneys or agents OR, alternatively,
   (2) The name of a single firm (having as a member a registered attorney or agent) and the names of up to 2 registered patent attorneys or agents. If no name is listed, no name will be printed.

   1 _____
   2 _____
   3 _____

3. ASSIGNEE NAME AND RESIDENCE DATA TO BE PRINTED ON THE PATENT (print or type)
PLEASE NOTE: Unless an assignee is identified below, no assignee data will appear on the patent. If an assignee is identified below, the document has been filed for recordation as set forth in 37 CFR 3.11. Completion of this form is NOT a substitute for filing an assignment.

(A) NAME OF ASSIGNEE   (B) RESIDENCE: (CITY and STATE OR COUNTRY)

Please check the appropriate assignee category or categories (will not be printed on the patent): ☐ Individual ☐ Corporation or other private group entity ☐ Government

4a. The following fee(s) are submitted:
☐ Issue Fee
☐ Publication Fee (No small entity discount permitted)
☐ Advance Order - # of Copies _____

4b. Payment of Fee(s): (**Please first reapply any previously paid issue fee shown above**)
☐ A check is enclosed.
☐ Payment by credit card. Form PTO-2038 is attached.
☐ The director is hereby authorized to charge the required fee(s), any deficiency, or credits any overpayment, to Deposit Account Number _____ (enclose an extra copy of this form).

5. **Change in Entity Status** (from status indicated above)
☐ Applicant certifying micro entity status. See 37 CFR 1.29
☐ Applicant asserting small entity status. See 37 CFR 1.27
☐ Applicant changing to regular undiscounted fee status.

NOTE: Absent a valid certification of Micro Entity Status (see forms PTO/SB/15A and 15B), issue fee payment in the micro entity amount will not be accepted at the risk of application abandonment.
NOTE: If the application was previously under micro entity status, checking this box will be taken to be a notification of loss of entitlement to micro entity status.
NOTE: Checking this box will be taken to be a notification of loss of entitlement to small or micro entity status, as applicable.

NOTE: This form must be signed in accordance with 37 CFR 1.31 and 1.33. See 37 CFR 1.4 for signature requirements and certifications.

Authorized Signature _____   Date _____

Typed or printed name _____   Registration No. _____

PTOL-85 Part B (10-13) Approved for use through 10/31/2013.   OMB 0651-0033   U.S. Patent and Trademark Office; U.S. DEPARTMENT OF COMMERCE

UNITED STATES PATENT AND TRADEMARK OFFICE

UNITED STATES DEPARTMENT OF COMMERCE
United States Patent and Trademark Office
Address: COMMISSIONER FOR PATENTS
P.O. Box 1450
Alexandria, Virginia 22313-1450
www.uspto.gov

APPLICATION NO.	FILING DATE	FIRST NAMED INVENTOR	ATTORNEY DOCKET NO.	CONFIRMATION NO.
14/742,430	06/17/2015	Monte Phillip Dauer	DAUM-P0001	1086

127633	7590	05/10/2016

Intellectual Property Clinic
Lincoln Law School of San Jose
384 S Second Street
San Jose, CA 95113

EXAMINER
O'HERN, BRENT T

ART UNIT	PAPER NUMBER
1781	

DATE MAILED: 05/10/2016

Determination of Patent Term Adjustment under 35 U.S.C. 154 (b)
(Applications filed on or after May 29, 2000)

The Office has discontinued providing a Patent Term Adjustment (PTA) calculation with the Notice of Allowance.

Section 1(h)(2) of the AIA Technical Corrections Act amended 35 U.S.C. 154(b)(3)(B)(i) to eliminate the requirement that the Office provide a patent term adjustment determination with the notice of allowance. See Revisions to Patent Term Adjustment, 78 Fed. Reg. 19416, 19417 (Apr. 1, 2013). Therefore, the Office is no longer providing an initial patent term adjustment determination with the notice of allowance. The Office will continue to provide a patent term adjustment determination with the Issue Notification Letter that is mailed to applicant approximately three weeks prior to the issue date of the patent, and will include the patent term adjustment on the patent. Any request for reconsideration of the patent term adjustment determination (or reinstatement of patent term adjustment) should follow the process outlined in 37 CFR 1.705.

Any questions regarding the Patent Term Extension or Adjustment determination should be directed to the Office of Patent Legal Administration at (571)-272-7702. Questions relating to issue and publication fee payments should be directed to the Customer Service Center of the Office of Patent Publication at 1-(888)-786-0101 or (571)-272-4200.

PTOL-85 (Rev. 02/11)

OMB Clearance and PRA Burden Statement for PTOL-85 Part B

The Paperwork Reduction Act (PRA) of 1995 requires Federal agencies to obtain Office of Management and Budget approval before requesting most types of information from the public. When OMB approves an agency request to collect information from the public, OMB (i) provides a valid OMB Control Number and expiration date for the agency to display on the instrument that will be used to collect the information and (ii) requires the agency to inform the public about the OMB Control Number's legal significance in accordance with 5 CFR 1320.5(b).

The information collected by PTOL-85 Part B is required by 37 CFR 1.311. The information is required to obtain or retain a benefit by the public which is to file (and by the USPTO to process) an application. Confidentiality is governed by 35 U.S.C. 122 and 37 CFR 1.14. This collection is estimated to take 12 minutes to complete, including gathering, preparing, and submitting the completed application form to the USPTO. Time will vary depending upon the individual case. Any comments on the amount of time you require to complete this form and/or suggestions for reducing this burden, should be sent to the Chief Information Officer, U.S. Patent and Trademark Office, U.S. Department of Commerce, P.O. Box 1450, Alexandria, Virginia 22313-1450. DO NOT SEND FEES OR COMPLETED FORMS TO THIS ADDRESS. SEND TO: Commissioner for Patents, P.O. Box 1450, Alexandria, Virginia 22313-1450. Under the Paperwork Reduction Act of 1995, no persons are required to respond to a collection of information unless it displays a valid OMB control number.

Privacy Act Statement

The Privacy Act of 1974 (P.L. 93-579) requires that you be given certain information in connection with your submission of the attached form related to a patent application or patent. Accordingly, pursuant to the requirements of the Act, please be advised that: (1) the general authority for the collection of this information is 35 U.S.C. 2(b)(2); (2) furnishing of the information solicited is voluntary; and (3) the principal purpose for which the information is used by the U.S. Patent and Trademark Office is to process and/or examine your submission related to a patent application or patent. If you do not furnish the requested information, the U.S. Patent and Trademark Office may not be able to process and/or examine your submission, which may result in termination of proceedings or abandonment of the application or expiration of the patent.

The information provided by you in this form will be subject to the following routine uses:
1. The information on this form will be treated confidentially to the extent allowed under the Freedom of Information Act (5 U.S.C. 552) and the Privacy Act (5 U.S.C 552a). Records from this system of records may be disclosed to the Department of Justice to determine whether disclosure of these records is required by the Freedom of Information Act.
2. A record from this system of records may be disclosed, as a routine use, in the course of presenting evidence to a court, magistrate, or administrative tribunal, including disclosures to opposing counsel in the course of settlement negotiations.
3. A record in this system of records may be disclosed, as a routine use, to a Member of Congress submitting a request involving an individual, to whom the record pertains, when the individual has requested assistance from the Member with respect to the subject matter of the record.
4. A record in this system of records may be disclosed, as a routine use, to a contractor of the Agency having need for the information in order to perform a contract. Recipients of information shall be required to comply with the requirements of the Privacy Act of 1974, as amended, pursuant to 5 U.S.C. 552a(m).
5. A record related to an International Application filed under the Patent Cooperation Treaty in this system of records may be disclosed, as a routine use, to the International Bureau of the World Intellectual Property Organization, pursuant to the Patent Cooperation Treaty.
6. A record in this system of records may be disclosed, as a routine use, to another federal agency for purposes of National Security review (35 U.S.C. 181) and for review pursuant to the Atomic Energy Act (42 U.S.C. 218(c)).
7. A record from this system of records may be disclosed, as a routine use, to the Administrator, General Services, or his/her designee, during an inspection of records conducted by GSA as part of that agency's responsibility to recommend improvements in records management practices and programs, under authority of 44 U.S.C. 2904 and 2906. Such disclosure shall be made in accordance with the GSA regulations governing inspection of records for this purpose, and any other relevant (i.e., GSA or Commerce) directive. Such disclosure shall not be used to make determinations about individuals.
8. A record from this system of records may be disclosed, as a routine use, to the public after either publication of the application pursuant to 35 U.S.C. 122(b) or issuance of a patent pursuant to 35 U.S.C. 151. Further, a record may be disclosed, subject to the limitations of 37 CFR 1.14, as a routine use, to the public if the record was filed in an application which became abandoned or in which the proceedings were terminated and which application is referenced by either a published application, an application open to public inspection or an issued patent.
9. A record from this system of records may be disclosed, as a routine use, to a Federal, State, or local law enforcement agency, if the USPTO becomes aware of a violation or potential violation of law or regulation.

EXHIBITS 571

	Application No.	Applicant(s)
Applicant-Initiated Interview Summary	14/742,430	DAUER, MONTE PHILLIP
	Examiner	Art Unit
	BRENT O'HERN	1781

All participants (applicant, applicant's representative, PTO personnel):

(1) <u>BRENT O'HERN</u>.   (3) _____.

(2) <u>Michelle Chen</u>.   (4) _____.

Date of Interview: <u>08 March 2016</u>.

Type: ☒ Telephonic ☐ Video Conference
      ☐ Personal [copy given to: ☐ applicant ☐ applicant's representative]

Exhibit shown or demonstration conducted: ☐ Yes ☒ No.
If Yes, brief description: _____.

Issues Discussed ☐101 ☐112 ☐102 ☐103 ☒Others
(For each of the checked box(es) above, please describe below the issue and detailed description of the discussion)

Claim(s) discussed: <u>1</u>.

Identification of prior art discussed: _____.

Substance of Interview
(For each issue discussed, provide a detailed description and indicate if agreement was reached. Some topics may include: identification or clarification of a reference or a portion thereof, claim interpretation, proposed amendments, arguments of any applied references etc...)

<u>Discussed possible amendments to overcome the rejections of record</u>.

Applicant recordation instructions: The formal written reply to the last Office action must include the substance of the interview. (See MPEP section 713.04). If a reply to the last Office action has already been filed, applicant is given a non-extendable period of the longer of one month or thirty days from this interview date, or the mailing date of this interview summary form, whichever is later, to file a statement of the substance of the interview

Examiner recordation instructions: Examiners must summarize the substance of any interview of record. A complete and proper recordation of the substance of an interview should include the items listed in MPEP 713.04 for complete and proper recordation including the identification of the general thrust of each argument or issue discussed, a general indication of any other pertinent matters discussed regarding patentability and the general results or outcome of the interview, to include an indication as to whether or not agreement was reached on the issues raised.

☐ Attachment

/BRENT O'HERN/
Primary Examiner, Art Unit 1781

U.S. Patent and Trademark Office
PTOL-413 (Rev. 8/11/2010)   Interview Summary   Paper No. 20160308

Summary of Record of Interview Requirements

Manual of Patent Examining Procedure (MPEP), Section 713.04, Substance of Interview Must be Made of Record
A complete written statement as to the substance of any face-to-face, video conference, or telephone interview with regard to an application must be made of record in the application whether or not an agreement with the examiner was reached at the interview.

Title 37 Code of Federal Regulations (CFR) § 1.133 Interviews
Paragraph (b)

In every instance where reconsideration is requested in view of an interview with an examiner, a complete written statement of the reasons presented at the interview as warranting favorable action must be filed by the applicant. An interview does not remove the necessity for reply to Office action as specified in §§ 1.111, 1.135. (35 U.S.C. 132)

37 CFR §1.2 Business to be transacted in writing.
All business with the Patent or Trademark Office should be transacted in writing. The personal attendance of applicants or their attorneys or agents at the Patent and Trademark Office is unnecessary. The action of the Patent and Trademark Office will be based exclusively on the written record in the Office. No attention will be paid to any alleged oral promise, stipulation, or understanding in relation to which there is disagreement or doubt.

The action of the Patent and Trademark Office cannot be based exclusively on the written record in the Office if that record is itself incomplete through the failure to record the substance of interviews.

It is the responsibility of the applicant or the attorney or agent to make the substance of an interview of record in the application file, unless the examiner indicates he or she will do so. It is the examiner's responsibility to see that such a record is made and to correct material inaccuracies which bear directly on the question of patentability.

Examiners must complete an Interview Summary Form for each interview held where a matter of substance has been discussed during the interview by checking the appropriate boxes and filling in the blanks. Discussions regarding only procedural matters, directed solely to restriction requirements for which interview recordation is otherwise provided for in Section 812.01 of the Manual of Patent Examining Procedure, or pointing out typographical errors or unreadable script in Office actions or the like, are excluded from the interview recordation procedures below. Where the substance of an interview is completely recorded in an Examiners Amendment, no separate Interview Summary Record is required.

The Interview Summary Form shall be given an appropriate Paper No., placed in the right hand portion of the file, and listed on the "Contents" section of the file wrapper. In a personal interview, a duplicate of the Form is given to the applicant (or attorney or agent) at the conclusion of the interview. In the case of a telephone or video-conference interview, the copy is mailed to the applicant's correspondence address either with or prior to the next official communication. If additional correspondence from the examiner is not likely before an allowance or if other circumstances dictate, the Form should be mailed promptly after the interview rather than with the next official communication.

The Form provides for recordation of the following information:
- Application Number (Series Code and Serial Number)
- Name of applicant
- Name of examiner
- Date of interview
- Type of interview (telephonic, video-conference, or personal)
- Name of participant(s) (applicant, attorney or agent, examiner, other PTO personnel, etc.)
- An indication whether or not an exhibit was shown or a demonstration conducted
- An identification of the specific prior art discussed
- An indication whether an agreement was reached and if so, a description of the general nature of the agreement (may be by attachment of a copy of amendments or claims agreed as being allowable). Note: Agreement as to allowability is tentative and does not restrict further action by the examiner to the contrary.
- The signature of the examiner who conducted the interview (if Form is not an attachment to a signed Office action)

It is desirable that the examiner orally remind the applicant of his or her obligation to record the substance of the interview of each case. It should be noted, however, that the Interview Summary Form will not normally be considered a complete and proper recordation of the interview unless it includes, or is supplemented by the applicant or the examiner to include, all of the applicable items required below concerning the substance of the interview.

A complete and proper recordation of the substance of any interview should include at least the following applicable items:
1) A brief description of the nature of any exhibit shown or any demonstration conducted,
2) an identification of the claims discussed,
3) an identification of the specific prior art discussed,
4) an identification of the principal proposed amendments of a substantive nature discussed, unless these are already described on the Interview Summary Form completed by the Examiner,
5) a brief identification of the general thrust of the principal arguments presented to the examiner,
   (The identification of arguments need not be lengthy or elaborate. A verbatim or highly detailed description of the arguments is not required. The identification of the arguments is sufficient if the general nature or thrust of the principal arguments made to the examiner can be understood in the context of the application file. Of course, the applicant may desire to emphasize and fully describe those arguments which he or she feels were or might be persuasive to the examiner.)
6) a general indication of any other pertinent matters discussed, and
7) if appropriate, the general results or outcome of the interview unless already described in the Interview Summary Form completed by the examiner.

Examiners are expected to carefully review the applicant's record of the substance of an interview. If the record is not complete and accurate, the examiner will give the applicant an extendable one month time period to correct the record.

Examiner to Check for Accuracy

If the claims are allowable for other reasons of record, the examiner should send a letter setting forth the examiner's version of the statement attributed to him or her. If the record is complete and accurate, the examiner should place the indication, "Interview Record OK" on the paper recording the substance of the interview along with the date and the examiner's initials.

EXHIBITS 573

	Application No.	Applicant(s)
Notice of Allowability	14/742,430	DAUER, MONTE PHILLIP
	Examiner	Art Unit	AIA (First Inventor to File) Status
	BRENT O'HERN	1781	Yes

-- *The MAILING DATE of this communication appears on the cover sheet with the correspondence address--*

All claims being allowable, PROSECUTION ON THE MERITS IS (OR REMAINS) CLOSED in this application. If not included herewith (or previously mailed), a Notice of Allowance (PTOL-85) or other appropriate communication will be mailed in due course. **THIS NOTICE OF ALLOWABILITY IS NOT A GRANT OF PATENT RIGHTS.** This application is subject to withdrawal from issue at the initiative of the Office or upon petition by the applicant. See 37 CFR 1.313 and MPEP 1308.

1. ☒ This communication is responsive to 4/15/2016.
    ☐ A declaration(s)/affidavit(s) under **37 CFR 1.130(b)** was/were filed on_____.

2. ☐ An election was made by the applicant in response to a restriction requirement set forth during the interview on _____; the restriction requirement and election have been incorporated into this action.

3. ☒ The allowed claim(s) is/are 1-3 and 5. As a result of the allowed claim(s), you may be eligible to benefit from the **Patent Prosecution Highway** program at a participating intellectual property office for the corresponding application. For more information, please see http://www.uspto.gov/patents/init_events/pph/index.jsp or send an inquiry to PPHfeedback@uspto.gov.

4. ☐ Acknowledgment is made of a claim for foreign priority under 35 U.S.C. § 119(a)-(d) or (f).
    Certified copies:
    a) ☐ All   b) ☐ Some   *c) ☐ None of the:
        1. ☐ Certified copies of the priority documents have been received.
        2. ☐ Certified copies of the priority documents have been received in Application No. _____.
        3. ☐ Copies of the certified copies of the priority documents have been received in this national stage application from the International Bureau (PCT Rule 17.2(a)).
    * Certified copies not received: _____.

Applicant has THREE MONTHS FROM THE "MAILING DATE" of this communication to file a reply complying with the requirements noted below. Failure to timely comply will result in ABANDONMENT of this application.
THIS THREE-MONTH PERIOD IS NOT EXTENDABLE.

5. ☐ CORRECTED DRAWINGS (as "replacement sheets") must be submitted.
    ☐ including changes required by the attached Examiner's Amendment / Comment or in the Office action of Paper No./Mail Date _____.
    Identifying indicia such as the application number (see 37 CFR 1.84(c)) should be written on the drawings in the front (not the back) of each sheet. Replacement sheet(s) should be labeled as such in the header according to 37 CFR 1.121(d).

6. ☐ DEPOSIT OF and/or INFORMATION about the deposit of BIOLOGICAL MATERIAL must be submitted. Note the attached Examiner's comment regarding REQUIREMENT FOR THE DEPOSIT OF BIOLOGICAL MATERIAL.

Attachment(s)
1. ☐ Notice of References Cited (PTO-892)
2. ☐ Information Disclosure Statements (PTO/SB/08), Paper No./Mail Date _____
3. ☐ Examiner's Comment Regarding Requirement for Deposit of Biological Material
4. ☒ Interview Summary (PTO-413), Paper No./Mail Date pn 20160308.
5. ☐ Examiner's Amendment/Comment
6. ☒ Examiner's Statement of Reasons for Allowance
7. ☐ Other _____.

/BRENT O'HERN/
Primary Examiner, Art Unit 1781

U.S. Patent and Trademark Office
PTOL-37 (Rev. 08-13)   Notice of Allowability   Part of Paper No./Mail Date 20160308

Application/Control Number: 14/742,430 Page 2
Art Unit: 1781

The present application, filed on or after March 16, 2013, is being examined under the first inventor to file provisions of the AIA.

REASONS FOR ALLOWANCE

1. The following is an examiner's statement of reasons for allowance:

A review of Applicant's arguments in the Papers filed 4/15/2016 and a review of the instant claims has convinced the examiner that the claims are allowable over the applied prior art of record.

2. Claims 1-3 and 5 are allowed.

3. Regarding independent claim 1 and the dependent claims, the prior art fails to teach or suggest a reinforced plywood panel comprising: a first sheet; a second sheet; a third sheet; a fourth sheet; a first mesh bonded with the first sheet and the second sheet using a first layer of glue; a second mesh bonded with the second sheet and the third sheet, wherein the material between the second sheet and the third sheet consists of the second mesh; and a third mesh bonded with the third sheet and the fourth sheet using a second layer of glue.

4. The closest prior art of Idestrup (US 2008/0152862) teaches a panel, however, fails to teach a reinforced plywood panel comprising: a first sheet; a second sheet; a third sheet; a fourth sheet; a first mesh bonded with the first sheet and the second sheet using a first layer of glue; a second mesh bonded with the second sheet and the third sheet, wherein the material between the second sheet and the third sheet consists of the second mesh; and a third mesh bonded with the third sheet and the fourth sheet

Application/Control Number: 14/742,430 Page 3
Art Unit: 1781

using a second layer of glue, especially where the material between the second and third sheet consists of mesh.

5. The other references of record do not teach or suggest the combined limitations not taught by Idestrup ('862).

6. Any comments considered necessary by applicant must be submitted no later than the payment of the issue fee and, to avoid processing delays, should preferably accompany the issue fee. Such submissions should be clearly labeled "Comments on Statement of Reasons for Allowance."

Conclusion

Any inquiry concerning this communication or earlier communications from the examiner should be directed to BRENT O'HERN whose telephone number is (571)272-6385. The examiner can normally be reached on Monday-Thursday, 9:00-6:00.

If attempts to reach the examiner by telephone are unsuccessful, the examiner's supervisor, Aaron Austin can be reached on (571) 272-8535. The fax phone number for the organization where this application or proceeding is assigned is 571-273-8300.

Application/Control Number: 14/742,430 Page 4
Art Unit: 1781

Information regarding the status of an application may be obtained from the Patent Application Information Retrieval (PAIR) system. Status information for published applications may be obtained from either Private PAIR or Public PAIR. Status information for unpublished applications is available through Private PAIR only. For more information about the PAIR system, see http://pair-direct.uspto.gov. Should you have questions on access to the Private PAIR system, contact the Electronic Business Center (EBC) at 866-217-9197 (toll-free). If you would like assistance from a USPTO Customer Service Representative or access to the automated information system, call 800-786-9199 (IN USA OR CANADA) or 571-272-1000.

/BRENT O'HERN/
Primary Examiner, Art Unit 1781
April 29, 2016

LINCOLN LAW SCHOOL OF SAN JOSE
INTELLECTUAL PROPERTY SERIES

EXHIBIT: COMMENTS ON STATEMENT OF REASONS FOR ALLOWANCE

IN THE UNITED STATES PATENT AND TRADEMARK OFFICE

In re Application of:	Confirmation No.: 7878
Brian J. Kindle	Examiner: Eueng Nan YEH
Application No.: 14/547,074	Art Unit: 2669
File Date: 2014-11-18	Docket No.: DUELP014/DL023
Title: SYSTEM AND METHOD FOR GENERATING AN IMAGE RESULT BASED ON AVAILABILITY OF A NETWORK RESOURCE	Date: Oct 19, 2016

COMMENTS ON STATEMENT OF REASONS FOR ALLOWANCE UNDER 37 C.F.R. § 1.104(e)

Commissioner for Patents
P.O. Box 1450
Alexandria VA 22313-1450

Examiner:

In response to the Notice of Allowance dated 08/19/2016, please enter the following remarks.

Application No.: 14/547,074
Date: Oct 19, 2016
Comments on Statement of Reasons for Allowance

Remarks:

Applicant has received the Examiner's Statement of Reasons for Allowance with the Notice of Allowance and Allowability regarding the above-identified application. Although Applicant agrees with the Examiner's conclusion that these claims are allowable, Applicant notes that the claims may be allowable for reasons other than those identified by the Examiner and does not concede that the Examiner's characterizations of the terms of the claims and the prior art are correct. Each of the claims stands on its own merits and is patentable because of the combination it recites and not because of the presence or absence of any one particular element.

In particular, on page 4 of the Notice of Allowance, the Examiner has indicated the reasons for allowance, as follows:

> However, none of the quoted and other searched prior art teaches the result derived from subset of one or more image operations requested is a preview of result using each of the one or more image operations. And therefore, arguments, see Remarks (filed on May 26, 2016) page 7, with the incorporations of allowable limitations of dependent claim 15 into independent claims 1, 19 and 20 have been fully considered and are persuasive and the previous art rejections are withdrawn.
>
> Thus, none of the prior art cited and searched alone or in combination provides the motivation to teach the following claimed features in combination with other recited limitations:
>
> - Receive a request for one or more image operations; identify the availability, whether communication with a network system via a digital radio is successful, of the network resource; when the network resource is available, receiving a second result using each of the one or more image operations; when the network resource is not available, receiving a first result using a subset of the one or more image operations, wherein if the network resource is not available the first result is a preview of the second result (independent claims 1, 19 and 20).

Application No.: 14/547,074
Date: Oct 19, 2016
Comments on Statement of Reasons for Allowance

In response, applicant respectfully points out the features of at least some of the independent claims (e.g. 1, 19, 20, etc.) are not necessarily the same as those the Examiner has highlighted above. For example, at a minimum, Claim 19 is directed to "communicating with a network resource, by a digital radio; receiving, by a processor complex coupled to the digital radio, a request for one or more image operations; identifying, by the processor complex, an availability of the network resource, wherein the availability is dependent on whether the communicating with a network service system via the digital radio is successful," in the context claimed. As such, at least some of the independent claims are not necessarily limited to the features that the Examiner has noted in the Examiner's Statement of Reasons for Allowance, as noted above (by way of example only). Instead, each of the claims should only be limited by the language existing therein.

The Examiner's Statement was not prepared by Applicant and only contains the Examiner's possible positions in one or more reasons for allowability. Thus, any interpretation with respect to the Examiner's Statement of Reasons for Allowance should not be imputed to the Applicant.

In the event a telephone conversation would expedite the prosecution of this application, the Examiner may reach the undersigned at (408) 971-2573 or Britten@zilkakotab.com. The Commissioner is authorized to charge any additional fees or credit any overpayment to Deposit Account No. 50-1351 (Order No. DUELP014).

Respectfully submitted,

Zilka-Kotab, PC.

___/BRITTEN SESSIONS/___

Britten Sessions
Reg. No. 68278

1155 N. 1st Street, Suite 105
San Jose, CA 95112-4925
408-971-2573

Made in the USA
Coppell, TX
19 November 2020